Effective Teaching
in
ELEMENTARY
SOCIAL STUDIES

Effective Teaching in ELEMENTARY SOCIAL STUDIES

TOM V. SAVAGE
Texas A&M University

DAVID G. ARMSTRONG
Texas A&M University

87-1173

MACMILLAN PUBLISHING COMPANY
New York

COLLIER MACMILLAN PUBLISHERS
London

Macmillan Publishing Company
866 Third Avenue, New York, New York 10022

Collier Macmillan Canada, Inc.

Library of Congress Cataloging-in-Publication Data

Savage, Tom V.
  Effective teaching in elementary social studies.

  Includes bibliographies and index.
  1. Social sciences—Study and teaching (Elementary)—
United States. I. Armstrong, David G.   II. Title.
LB1584.S34   1987   372.8′3044   86-16393
ISBN 0-02-406400-9

Printing: 2 3 4 5 6 7   Year: 7 8 9 0 1 2 3

ISBN 0-02-406400-9

Preface _____

Elementary social studies programs have three important aims. First, they develop youngsters' appreciation for the skills and understandings required of productive, contributing citizens. Young people need help in coming to terms with themselves and with the expectations of a society committed to democratic decision making.

Second, the social studies program assists pupils to think rationally about problems of all kinds. Adults are faced with many challenging problems, such as public-policy problems, family problems, and personal problems. Social studies educators believe that decisions based on evidence are to be greatly preferred over those based on whim or emotion.

Finally, the social studies program draws much of its content from history and the social sciences. Other content sources play a role as well. The insights from these major disciplines provide pupils with knowledge that has been organized systematically and verified according to the protocols of the individual academic disciplines. These academic subjects provide much of the raw material for problem solving. Content from the disciplines also contributes to the development of citizenship as pupils grow in their abilities to marshall well-documented evidence to support positions.

Today, teachers must have a sound background in the instructional process to defend what they are doing in the classroom. *Effective Teaching in Elementary Social Studies* has been written with a view to applying the principles associated with the instructional process to the social studies.

Specifically, the text lays out a systematic approach for organizing instruction in the social studies. This organizational scheme is designed to help teachers plan for instruction in different school settings. The text includes illustrations of ideas for implementing lessons.

Effective Teaching in Elementary Social Studies has been organized so that instructors can be flexible in terms of the order in which individual chapters are introduced. The first chapter introduces students to the general nature of the social studies. Chapters 2 and 3 focus on content sources that teachers use in planning units and lessons.

Chapters 4 and 5 describe the basic considerations when planning elementary social studies programs. Engaging pupils' active interests is a prerequisite for effective social studies instruction. Chapters 6, 7, and 8 focus on the different approaches that encourage this involvement. The special concerns about pupils' personal development and about their abilities to interact productively with others are highlighted in Chapter 9.

Chapters 10, 11, and 12 focus on the topics associated with social studies instruction. Work with maps and globes, an important part of the elementary program, is highlighted in Chapter 10. Chapter 11 provides practical information for helping pupils profit from instructional activities that require work with prose materials. Chapter 12 focuses on the important issue of evaluation; both formal and informal approaches to evaluation are included.

The final two chapters focus on the topics not encountered in most elementary social studies methods texts. Productive instruction requires a well-organized and well-managed classroom. Chapter 13 provides practical suggestions for dealing with management specifically in elementary social studies classrooms. Chapter 14 focuses on the special needs of youngsters in the primary grades. The authors have surveyed teachers of the primary grades, many of whom have expressed concern that many elementary social studies texts do not adequately address the special characteristics of younger children; Chapter 14 addresses this need.

This book could not have been completed without the assistance of many people. The authors would particularly like to thank Kathryn Atman of University of Pittsburgh, Leah Engelhardt of Mississippi State University, William Patton of Kent State University, Thomas Ryan of Western Michigan University, Helene Silverman of University of Tampa, Fred Tanner of North Texas State University, and Foster F. Wilkinson of Delta State University for lending their expertise in the review of the manuscript. We wish to acknowledge the excellent photographic work of Juliann Barbato. Pamela Romig was of inestimable assistance in preparing the drafts of the manuscript. Finally, we wish to thank our families for their devotion and tolerance during the time this book was being written.

T.V.S.
D.G.A.

Contents

7

Involving Pupils: The Individualized Approaches   153

8

Involving Pupils: Using Special Resources   173

9

Character Education   203

Effective Teaching
in
ELEMENTARY
SOCIAL STUDIES

Chapter 1

An Introduction to the Social Studies

(*Source:* © Juliann Barbato.)

This chapter provides information to help the reader:

1. State the ways social studies content relates to the lives of individuals.
2. Describe the importance of social studies instruction in the education of children.
3. Identify the major purposes of social studies instruction.
4. Point out the features of a comprehensive elementary social studies program.
5. Point out how the basic themes related to citizenship education, social science education, and problem-solving education are developed at each grade level.
6. Identify the most common curriculum-organization pattern of the elementary social studies program.
7. Suggest examples of the specific topics and focus questions used to guide instruction at each grade level of the elementary social studies program.

Overview

It is Saturday, at last! There is no school, no work. There are no outside activities. The wind blows, the rain pelts the side of the house. It is one of those days that you will want to spend by the fireplace, nursing a good cup of coffee.

You get out of bed, stretch, put the coffee on to perk, and slip out to retrieve the newspaper that has just landed with a thud on the front porch. Brewing coffee perfumes the kitchen as you open the paper. Your eyes move quickly across these headlines:

"Head of State Escapes Terrorist Attack"

"Wholesale Price Index Tumbles Again"

"Immigration Bill Stalled in House Debate"

"Big Three Automakers Brace for Strike"

"More Calls for Limiting Foreign Auto Imports"

"Declining Car Sales Reduce State Tax Revenues"

"Local Auto Supply Parts Plants Hurting"

"Superintendent Sees Eroding Local Tax Base"

What kinds of issues and problems do these headlines suggest? Are they problems engineers solve with books of tables and calculators? Are they problems research scientists ponder in their laboratories? Not quite. Certainly engineers and scientists produce knowledge useful for thinking about these issues, but these problems are not directly related to their fields.

The kinds of problems that *are* suggested by these headlines are *social problems*. These are problems that people face as they live together in communities, states, and nations. Solving these problems involves more than simple applications of information. It is true that subject matter from disciplines such as history, geography, economics, political science, sociology, anthropology, and oth-

2

ers is considered when people try to solve social problems, but these problems also involve choices people make based on their own values. The interplay between subject-matter content and personal values is at the heart of social problem solving. It is this interplay that is the concern of the exciting part of the elementary curriculum known as the social studies.

The People-Oriented Content of the Social Studies _____

Much of the fascination of the social studies program derives from its focus on people. Humans live in a variety of ways in a variety of places; they come in many sizes, shapes, nationalities, and loyalties. The differences among the world's peoples are remarkable, but perhaps even more striking are the similarities in the dilemmas all peoples have had to face (see Table 1–1).

History records, for example, that people everywhere have always tried to discover some meaning in their lives. Religions and philosophies developed throughout the world have sought to provide answers to this most fundamental human question. Furthermore, people have always found it necessary to live together. This drive to gather together has prompted a need for rules and regulations governing social life. Though governmental structures vary enormously across the earth, human beings everywhere have sensed a need for some mechanism to provide collective safety and order.

People everywhere have also had to come to terms with their physical environments. In the lush prairie lands of the American midwest you find people making productive use of their surroundings. In the remotest reaches of the Sahara other people have learned to live under conditions of perpetual water shortage and still make productive use of their environment. Responses to the need to adapt have been as diverse as the range of the earth's peoples and en-

TABLE 1–1   Common Human Dilemmas and Social Studies Focus Questions.

Dilemmas	Selected Focus Questions
Stability vs. change	How do we preserve what is "good" in society while adapting to meet changing conditions?
Reaction to differences	How can we live in harmony with people who are different? How can we avoid irrational prejudice?
Providing for wants	How can we organize ourselves for economic production? What should be produced? How should production be distributed?
Individual freedom vs. social control	How can we reconcile individual freedom with other needs (security, for example) that require collective action? What is the proper relationship between the individual and his or her government?
Population problems	What can be done to reduce the rates of population growth where they are too low? What places need fewer people? What accounts for the differences?
Environmental issues	How can we use the resources of the earth wisely? How do we assure that future generations will enjoy a quality of life at least equal to our own?
Technological changes	How do we prepare to deal with accelerating rates of change? What should the responses be to challenges resulting from innovations that bring people from very different cultural traditions into closer contact?

vironments. Technological developments, inventions, economic systems, and other human creations have reflected a truly incredible ingenuity. Few places on the earth have environmental conditions forbidding enough to frustrate the attempts of people to make adjustments necessary for the sustenance of their communities.

The social studies program centers on human beings as they have encountered and continue to encounter the challenges of life on earth. The elementary program investigates the infinite variety of humans and their ways of interacting with their environments. It celebrates people's successes and tries to learn from their failures. The study of social studies challenges each individual to find his or her own sense of identity and to understand the responsibilities and rights of a citizen. When viewed in this context, elementary social studies has to be considered one of the most basic and important school subjects.

The Motivation Problem

Despite the importance of social studies, many elementary youngsters do not rate their interest in the subject very high. Indeed, many surveys have found that the subject ranks close to the bottom of the list of subjects elementary pupils find interesting. Much of this reputation is a result not of the content of the subject, but rather of how the subject matter is approached (see Table 1–2).

Elementary youngsters are concerned about themselves and about other people. Consider how eager they are to share their personal and family experiences. Good elementary social studies programs build on this interest in people to extend youngsters' concerns beyond themselves and their families to other peoples and places. Instruction that helps pupils to make these connections places heavy demands on teachers. They cannot simply assign pages to be read in the textbook or engage in excessive lecture-oriented activity. Youngsters need opportunities to engage in social studies content directly. They must be able to *do* something with the content. They must see that it has a personal and immediate relevance. (Even older elementary pupils will not buy the argument that "You should read this now, because it will help you when you get to high school and college.")

TABLE 1–2 Motivation and the Elementary Social Studies Program.

Think About This

Try to recall your own elementary social studies classes. Then answer these questions:
1. What are your most vivid memories?
2. What topics did you study? How did you react to these topics? Why do you think you felt as you did about them?
3. What methods were used to teach social studies content? How did you react to these methods? Would you have preferred to do something else? If so, what and why?
4. How important for you personally did you find social studies content? If you did not much care for your social studies lessons, how could they have been improved?
5. What are some of your own ideas about how a social studies teacher might go about interesting children in the subject?

TABLE 1–3   Preparing to Teach: A Diagnostic Device.

At the beginning of your study it might be helpful for you to do a short self-evaluation to determine your knowledge and attitudes about the social studies. This kind of self-knowledge can contribute toward making your study a more profitable experience.

1. What are some specific memories that you have about social studies? Write down any specific lessons, units, or activities that you remember from your days as a pupil in the elementary school.
2. What is your attitude toward the social studies? Do you see the subject as one that is exciting and important or as one that is usually dry and boring?
3. How do you assess your knowledge of the social sciences? Is it poor, fair, or good? About which of the social sciences do you know the most? About which do you know the least?
4. Give a brief definition of the term _concept_ and the term _generalization_.
5. What kinds of things would you need to consider while planning a unit of instruction for an elementary social studies class?
6. What are the various components of the instructional act?
7. State what you know about the intellectual, social, and physical development of the children at the age level you would like to teach.
8. Define the role of the teacher in an inquiry or inductive learning experience.
9. Review the answers you have given to these questions. What do they suggest you might need to learn or do to prepare yourself to be a teacher of social studies in the elementary school? Where can you go to get the knowledge, skills, and attitudes that are necessary?

A number of ideas for helping pupils to become actively involved in the social studies are introduced in the subsequent sections of this book. These ideas can help generate the kinds of interest that the social studies program deserves. Successful social studies teaching, though, demands more than a teacher well versed in sound instructional techniques. The teacher himself or herself must be sincerely interested in the content of the program.

Elementary pupils are more perceptive than beginning teachers sometimes suppose they are. They are quick to spot a teacher who is simply "going through the motions" of teaching social studies, mathematics, science, or any other part of the curriculum. On the other hand, they can also identify a teacher who has a personal enthusiasm for the content he or she is teaching. This kind of enthusiasm can be contagious, and it can be a mighty force for generating pupils' interest.

Since this is true, you should apply yourselves diligently as you prepare to teach elementary social studies (see Table 1–3). If you develop a sincere interest in this vitally important part of the school program, you will find teaching the social studies to be one of the highlights of your career. You and your pupils will both be better informed and happier at the end of each school day.

The Purposes of the Social Studies _____

One of the reasons why social studies experiences are met with something less than enthusiasm by many teachers is that they are unsure about the purposes of the subject. Many do not understand what is supposed to be accomplished by social studies. As a result, some teachers often skip the social studies period altogether. Let us try to bring the purposes of the elementary social studies program into focus.

A report by the National Council for the Social Studies Task Force on Scope and Sequence (1984) makes the following statement concerning the social studies.

Social studies education has a specific mandate in regard to citizenship education. That mandate is to provide every school child and adolescent with the opportunity to learn the knowledge, the abilities and skills, and the beliefs and values that are needed for competent participation in social, political and economic life. Social studies has historically had a special responsibility for the attainment of such educational goals having to do with knowledge of the American heritage, the economic system, law and government, political processes, the history and geography of the world, world cultures, the Constitution and the Bill of Rights, and the principles and ideals of American democracy. (p. 250)

From this statement we can infer that one important objective of the social studies program is the promotion of *citizenship education*. Few individuals dispute the importance of citizenship education in the social studies program. However, this statement raises as many questions as it answers. For example, what is involved in educating a "good citizen?" Is a good citizen one who conforms to the status quo and dutifully obeys whatever the authorities decree? Is a good citizen one who is uncritically patriotic? Or is a good citizen one who is willing to stand up for his or her beliefs even to the point of facing a personal confrontation with others?

These questions are difficult to answer. In general, it is fair to say that there is broad support for the general idea of citizenship education, but people representing different philosophical positions do not agree on what should be taught and how it should be taught. Despite the difficulties involved, elementary social studies teachers must make some decisions about the citizenship content of their programs. A desirable beginning point for thought about this issue is consideration of what our country requires from a responsible citizen.

Our system is based on a set of values and ideals that include liberty, justice, informed decision making, responsibility, equality, and the freedom to dissent. These assumptions support the efforts to help youngsters grow to maturity as psychologically secure individuals who are willing to actively participate in our democratic decision-making process. Good citizenship seeks both to develop the individual and to stress the importance of active participation in public affairs.

The National Council for the Social Studies Task Force on Scope and Sequence defines the social studies in the following manner:

Social studies is a basic subject of the K–12 cirriculum that (1) derives its goals from the nature of citizenship in a democratic society that is closely linked to other nations and peoples of the world; (2) draws its content primarily from history, the social sciences, and, in some respects, from the humanities and science; and (3) is taught in ways that reflect an awareness of personal, social, and cultural experiences and developmental levels of learners. (p. 251)

This definition adds dimensions to the social studies that complement the purpose of citizenship education and makes reference to the content of the social studies. This emphasis on the social studies program might be termed *social science education*.

Citizenship demands active participation. Note the patriotic symbols and the demonstration placards.
(*Source:* © Juliann Barbato.)

The social sciences, history, and the other humanities have all developed some methods of investigation and understanding that are important for individuals who are able to live productive lives and exercise their responsibilities as good citizens. Citizenship requires information and knowledge.

Though we have chosen to call this dimension social science education, the content of this part of the social studies program is not limited to those subjects that are traditionally labeled as social science disciplines. Any component of any subject that deals with the social aspect of human behavior is appropriate content for the social studies program. This allows for the inclusion of content from a wide variety of subjects that may include some information even from engineering and the hard sciences.

For organizing information in the social science education component of the elementary social studies program, knowledge that can help young people understand their world is sought. Information about human beings and their interaction with others and with their environment that is derived from a variety of sources guides instructional planning. The important thing is not that the youngsters are studying a topic called history or geography, but that they are learning significant ideas about human beings.

Citizens of societies characterized by democratic decision making need effective thinking tools before they approach complex issues. Throughout their adult lives they will be called upon to make decisions that can influence their lives

This display helps pupils inquire about people in other lands.
(*Source:* © Juliann Barbato.)

and the lives of others in the community, state, and nation. Because of the centrality of decision making in life in democratic societies, *problem-solving education* plays an important role in the social studies program.

This important dimension of elementary social studies helps pupils develop techniques to address problems. Pupils are introduced to techniques for bringing issues into focus, gathering and organizing data, and formulating and testing hypotheses. There is also a heavy emphasis on teaching pupils how groups in our society work together to resolve complex issues.

The Components of Citizenship Education, Social Science Education, and Problem-Solving Education

For each broad social studies purpose there are three subareas that need to be identified. These are (1) knowledge, (2) skills, and (3) values (see Table 1–4).

The Components of Citizenship Education

Knowledge. Young people should be exposed to knowledge related to the American heritage; the Constitution; the Bill of Rights; the political processes followed at the local, state, and national levels; and other basic information an educated adult citizen is expected to know.

Skills. Elementary pupils need to be taught the processes associated with decision making in this country. They need to learn how to negotiate and compromise, to express views, and to work productively with others.

TABLE 1–4   A Social Studies Purposes Matrix.

The social studies purposes matrix illustrates the major components of a comprehensive elementary social studies program. Each cell of the matrix indicates an important emphasis. All of these components should be addressed somewhere during the total elementary social studies program. However, not necessarily all of them will be addressed during a given year. Also, conditions in individual places will result in various degrees of emphasis being accorded to each component in the matrix.

	Citizenship Education	Social Science Education	Problem-Solving Education
Knowledge			
Skills			
Values			

Values. Citizens do not make decisions based on information alone; they also consider social and personal values. Certainly pupils need to be exposed to the values associated with democratic decision making and with the values that undergird the operation of the local, state, and national government in the United States.

See Table 1–5 for an illustration of how citizenship education outcomes develop common themes from grade level to grade level.

TABLE 1–5   Some Examples of Citizenship Outcomes by Grade Level. (continued)

The social studies program attempts to build on basic themes in each grade level. Treatment becomes more sophisticated as pupils progress through school. Note these examples.

Citizenship Education: Knowledge

Basic Theme: Regulations and the Individual

Grade Levels:	K	1	2	3	4	5	6
State the classroom rules.	X						
Explain the need for community rules.		X					
Identify those who make rules in the local community.			X				
Identify an individual's responsibility to the community and state.				X			
Identify the basic functions of local state governments.					X		
Explain the basic rights and responsibilities of United States' citizens.						X	
Point out that both written and unwritten rules shape people's behavior in all world societies.							X

TABLE 1–5 Some Examples of Citizenship Outcomes by Grade Level. (concluded)

Citizenship Education: Skills

Basic Theme: Developing Group Membership Skills

	K	1	2	3	4	5	6
Grade Levels:							
Engage in fair play.	X						
Work cooperatively in a group.		X					
Cope with the group-individual conflict.			X				
Assist in establishing group goals.				X			
Decide how state citizens should work together to solve a problem.					X		
Simulate citizen actions to influence the decisions of the U.S. government.						X	
React as a group to problems that are worldwide in their scope.							X

Citizenship Education: Values

Basic Theme: Acceptance of the Roles of Group

	K	1	2	3	4	5	6
Grade Levels:							
Respect others.	X						
Accept the leadership of others.		X					
Volunteer for leadership roles.			X				
Accept the rights of others.				X			
Defend the importance of the rights of others.					X		
Accept the idea that people depend on one another to satisfy their needs.						X	
Commit to the idea that majorities rule, but that minorities have their rights, too.							X

The Components of Social Science

Knowledge. The academic disciplines, such as history and the social sciences, include many powerful insights that are related to human behavior. These need to be taught as part of the elementary social studies program.

Skills. Elementary social studies programs emphasize skills used by academic content specialists in gathering and assessing the importance of information. General information about how the scientific method can be used to verify and modify hypotheses is often included.

Values. There are certain values implicit in how academic content specialists gather and process information. For example, there is a predisposition to prize knowledge based on data more highly than knowledge based on simple intuition or feeling. Pupils in the elementary program need to be exposed to this value orientation.

See Table 1–6 for an illustration of how social science education outcomes develop common themes from grade level to grade level.

TABLE 1–6   Some Examples of Social Science Education Outcomes by Grade Level. (continued)

As is the case with citizenship education, the social studies program attempts to build on basic themes related to social science education at each grade level. Pupils deal with these themes in a more sophisticated manner at each successive grade level. Note these examples.

Social Science Education: Knowledge

Basic Theme: Economic Interdependence

Grade Levels:	K	1	2	3	4	5	6
Identify how different people help us to meet our needs.	X						
State how people with different jobs in the family contribute to helping the family as a whole.		X					
Describe how people in the community depend on one another to supply goods and services.			X				
Point out how the work of people in one community contributes to the well-being of people in other communities.				X			
Explain the economic ties between the pupil's state and the other parts of the United States.					X		
Describe the interdependence among the regions of the United States.						X	
Explain how the United States and other nations of the world are economically interdependent.							X

Social Science Education: Skills

Basic Theme: Finding Places on Maps and Globes

Grade Level:	K	1	2	3	4	5	6
Find things on a drawing of the classroom.	X						
Find things on a simple map of the school and the immediate neighborhood.		X					
Use a very simple coordinate system to find things on a simple map.			X				
Use a grid system to find things on a map of the community.				X			
Use latitude and longitude to locate places in the state on a globe.					X		
Use latitude and longitude to determine the locations of places in the United States.						X	
Use latitude and longitude to find places throughout the world using maps and globes.							X

Social Science Education: Values

Basic Theme: Tolerance of Diversity

Grade Level:	K	1	2	3	4	5	6
Allow others to express ideas.	X						
Listen attentively to the ideas of others.		X					
Demonstrate respect for the ideas of others.			X				

TABLE 1–6   Some Examples of Social Science Education Outcomes by Grade Level. (concluded)

Basic Theme: Tolerance of Diversity

	K	1	2	3	4	5	6
Grade Level:							
Support the view that the community profits from a diversity of opinions.				X			
Accept the idea that a diversity of opinions within the state makes the state a better place to live.					X		
Commit to the view that a diversity of views make the United States a good place to live.						X	
Respect the rights of people in other parts of the world to hold opinions that differ from those of most Americans.							X

The Components of Problem-Solving Education

Knowledge. Young people need to learn the basic information about how rational decisions are made. Steps in identifying problems and in applying relevant information are important concerns of this part of the social studies program. Additionally, pupils need to master the techniques associated with the organization and evaluation of data, and the formulation and testing of hypotheses.

Skills. The development of problem-solving abilities is promoted when pupils have opportunities to make decisions about real issues. In the lower elementary grades, problem-solving skills are developed as youngsters work with problems of personal and family importance. As pupils mature, they are provided with problem-solving experiences focusing on a broader range of social and civic problems.

Because many problems in a democratic society require collective decision making, part of the social studies skill development program in the area of problem solving involves helping pupils to work productively in groups. Pupils are provided with opportunities to engage in the kind of give-and-take discussion that characterizes group decision making.

Values. Instruction in this general area attempts to develop pupils' appreciation for problem-solving decisions that are based on rational thinking. It is hoped that they will come to prize decisions that rest on evidence and logic and to resist jumping to conclusions as a result of unexamined assumptions or restrictive biases. Development of a commitment to tolerance for diverse views is another purpose of this area of the social studies program.

See Table 1–7 for an illustration of how problem-solving education outcomes develop common themes from grade level to grade level.

The major purposes of citizenship education, social science education, problem-solving education, and the subcategories under each comprise the comprehensive elementary social studies program. Well-balanced programs should provide *some* experiences directed toward each of these components. However, it

TABLE 1–7   Some Examples of Problem-Solving Education Outcomes by Grade Level. (continued)

The elementary social studies program attempts to develop pupils' problem-solving skills as much as it seeks to promote citizenship education and social science education outcomes. Pupils learn to deal with common problem-solving themes in a more sophisticated manner at each successive grade level. Note these examples.

Problem-Solving Education: Knowledge

Basic Theme: Making Decisions

	Grade Level: K	1	2	3	4	5	6
Explain how a choice is made.	X						
State the specific steps used in solving a problem.		X					
Identify the problems faced by people in the neighborhood.			X				
Point out the problems that need to be solved by members of the community.				X			
Explain the kinds of information that people would need to solve a problem facing citizens of the state.					X		
Identify the criteria to be used in making a decision about a problem facing citizens of the United States.						X	
Describe how people in different parts of the world use different kinds of logic to arrive at conclusions.							X

Problem-Solving Education: Skills

Basic Theme: Applying the Decision-making Techiques

	Grade Level: K	1	2	3	4	5	6
Recognize that a problem exists.	X						
Propose a general plan of action for solving a problem.		X					
Suggest alternative solutions to a problem.			X				
Arrange data into categories that will be useful in solving a problem.				X			
Distinguish between fact and opinion when considering data to be used in solving a problem.					X		
State and test several hypotheses when seeking a solution to a problem.						X	
Compare and contrast viewpoints of several individuals who have proposed alternative solutions to a complex problem.							X

Problem-Solving Education: Values

Basic Theme: Commitment to Rational Decision-Making

	Grade Level: K	1	2	3	4	5	6
Accept the need to think about a personal problem before taking action.	X						
Commit to a pattern of socially acceptable dis-							

**TABLE 1–7   Some Examples of Problem-Solving Education Outcomes
by Grade Level. (concluded)**

Problem-Solving Education: Values

Basic Theme: Commitment to Rational Decision-Making

	Grade Level:	K	1	2	3	4	5	6
agreement when conflicts with others arise.			X					
Accept the need for compromise when working with others to solve problems.				X				
Demonstrate a willingness to follow through on a planned course of action once a decision has been made about how a problem should be solved.					X			
Commit to studying all the relevant aspects of a problem before making a decision.						X		
Accept as legitimate the questions about why a particular response to a problem has been selected.							X	
Commit to the view that decisions based on evidence are to be preferred over those based on unsupported opinion.								X

is unlikely that each of the areas will receive equal attention at each grade level. At a given grade level several areas might play primary roles while the others play less important parts. Some school districts will have priorities favoring the emphasis of certain program elements. Clearly, those designated as "high priority" areas will receive more attention than the others.

The Organization of the Elementary
Social Studies Curriculum _____

Understanding the importance of the social studies and the general purposes to be achieved is only the first step in the teaching process. The next step is understanding the content that is normally taught in the elementary grades. The sequence of topics generally studied follows the expanding horizons approach.

The Expanding Horizons Approach

The *expanding horizons approach* assumes that elementary children should begin with familiar and concrete experiences and gradually be introduced to more distant and abstract content. Content selected for study begins with the self and the family and gradually extends outward to include an "expanding horizon" as the child grows and experiences more of the world. Generally, the social studies curriculum is organized in this way:

Kindergarten: The Self and the School
First Grade: Families

Second Grade: Neighborhoods
Third Grade: Communities and Cities
Fourth Grade: State History or Geographic Regions
Fifth Grade: United States History
Sixth Grade: The Western Hemisphere or World Cultures

Some critics of this approach point out that it may fail to consider the world of present-day pupils. Today's child is familiar with many people beyond his or her own family circle. The universal availability of television and a trend for many families to move frequently have introduced even very young children to many different kinds of people. A narrow focus in the early elementary grades on the pupils' own families runs counter to their own experience. They already know that many other kinds of people live in the world.

Other critics have suggested that the traditional elementary curriculum tends to introduce stereotypes and an unrealistic view of the world. For example, some first-grade materials have featured a nuclear family of four people, including a father who goes to work each morning, a stay-at-home mother, and two children. Given the high incidence of one-parent families, the increase in the percentage of families where both parents are employed, and the inclusion of women in a wide range of occupations, such a stereotyped view of the world gives children a distorted image of today's American society. Children who live in families that

We've Got to Find Another Way to Solve These Arguments About the Purposes of the Social Studies Program.

(*Source:* Ford Button.)

do not conform to the "norm" presented in class may derive the false impression that they are "different" or "inferior."

Modifying the Expanding Horizons Approach

In response to the need for a social studies curriculum that takes the changing realities of life into account, elementary program specialists have directed their attention to some of the specific content addressed at each grade level of the expanding horizons approach. For example, first-grade programs no longer introduce stereotyped views of the American nuclear family; they emphasize that many kinds of families exist in this country.

Furthermore, recognizing that youngsters know something of the world beyond their neighborhood and local community, these programs include the study of families in other parts of the world. Social studies content at other grade levels has been similarly modified to draw on the broader experiences of today's young people and to allow them opportunities to compare and contrast different patterns of living. These youngsters still have a concrete base of experience from which to draw understanding, but now can also compare their experiences with those of youngsters in other parts of the world. The same thing is generally found when neighborhoods and communities are studied. New programs attempt to familiarize pupils with the ways of life in communities in other parts of the world, where the patterns of living vary from the patterns youngsters have observed in their home communities.

Relating the Program to the Basic Social Studies Purposes

In planning for instruction at a given grade level, it is easy to lose sight of the three basic purposes of the social studies program: (1) citizenship education, (2) social science education, and (3) problem-solving education. There is a need to plan for instruction on a given topic in light of how such instruction will be related to one of these major purposes.

For example, in a typical school district with a modified expanding horizons social studies program, the major focus of the first-grade program will be on families. In planning for first-grade instruction, the teacher asks, How can the study of the family be related to each major social studies purpose? The teacher might reflect on the nature of the focus topic itself, and on the prior experiences and developmental levels of the children.

Though some attention might be directed to each of the three purposes, the teacher could conclude that the developmental needs of the youngsters suggests a need for heavier emphases on citizenship education and problem-solving education than on social science education. Teachers at other grade levels need to go through a similar thinking process as they reflect on how their instruction will tie to the major social studies purposes.

Once a general decision is made regarding the relative emphases to be placed on citizenship education, social science education, and problem-solving education, it is useful for the teacher to identify some focus questions that will guide instruction. Cross-referencing questions to the major social studies purposes can assure that each purpose receives at least some attention in the instructional program.

An Example of Cross-Referenced Focus Questions by Grade Level

The focus questions introduced in Table 1–8 are not meant to be comprehensive. They are a few examples of what an individual teacher might develop to guide program planning.

TABLE 1–8 Focus Questions by Grade Level. (continued)

Kindergarten: The Self and the School

Focus Questions	Citizenship	Social Science	Problem Solving
What is our national flag like? our state flag?	X		
What are our classroom rules? our school rules?			
Why do we have rules?	X		
What are the names of our community, state, and nation?	X		
What are the basic directions (up, down, right, left)?		X	
What are the basic time concepts (minutes, hours, days)?		X	
What do the basic symbols and signs mean (road signs, and so on)?		X	
How do we make choices?			X
How do we know when a problem exists?			X
What kind of class rules do we need?			X

First Grade: Families

Focus Questions	Citizenship	Social Science	Problem Solving
Why do communities need rules?	X		
How can we work cooperatively in groups?	X		
What are some of our patriotic customs?	X		
How do different family members contribute to the family as a whole?		X	
How is the calendar divided into days, months, and years?		X	
How can a simple map of the classroom and school be made?		X	
What specific steps should be taken in solving a problem?			X
What kinds of problems do family members face?			X
How do family members work together to solve problems?			X

Second Grade: Neighborhoods

Focus Questions	Citizenship	Social Science	Problem Solving
How are rules made for people in the neighborhood?	X		
What happens when people break rules?	X		
What are fair rules like?	X		
How can time lines be used to depict a sequence?		X	

TABLE 1–8   Focus Questions by Grade Level. (continued)

Kindergarten: The Self and the School

Focus Questions	Citizenship	Social Science	Problem Solving
What important kinds of transportation and communication are there?		X	
How does the local environment change with the seasons?		X	
What kinds of problems do neighborhoods face?			X
How can groups work to solve problems?			X
What categories of information are needed to solve a problem?			X

Third Grade: Communities and Cities

Focus Questions	Citizenship	Social Science	Problem Solving
What is a person's responsibility to the community?	X		
What are the basic functions of local government?	X		
Who enforces laws in the community?	X		
How does the work of people in one community help people in other communities?		X	
What are the contributions of various ethnic and culture groups to the community?		X	
What kinds of maps display information about the community?		X	
What are some problems that the community must face?			X
What are some causes of the events in the community?			X
How can information best be arranged for problem solving?			X

Fourth Grade: State History or Geographic Regions

Focus Questions	Citizenship	Social Science	Problem Solving
What are the basic functions of state government?	X		
How do groups help governments to make decisions?	X		
How can a person develop group leadership skills?	X		
What economic ties are there between the state and other parts of the United States?		X	
How have people of the state used their environment in different ways at different times?		X	
How do landforms influence climate?		X	
What kinds of information do people need to arrive at solutions to problems facing the state?			X
How can a person tell the difference between statements of fact and of opinion?			X

TABLE 1–8 Focus Questions by Grade Level. (concluded)

Focus Questions	Citizenship	Social Science	Problem Solving
What might be the consequences of different approaches to solving a problem facing the state?			X

Fifth Grade: United States History

Focus Questions	Citizenship	Social Science	Problem Solving
What are the basic rights and responsibilities of citizens?	X		
What are the major political parties? What are their symbols?	X		
What qualities do people look for in national leaders?	X		
How are regions of the United States interdependent?		X	
What were the major historical events in the development of the United States?		X	
How do innovations change the economy of the United States?		X	
What criteria should United States' citizens apply as they attempt to solve problems facing the country?		X	
How can hypotheses about complex problems be developed and tested?			X
What role do personal values play in decisions people make?			X

Sixth Grade: The Western Hemisphere or World Cultures

Focus Questions	Citizenship	Social Science	Problem Solving
What unwritten rules shape citizens' behavior?	X		
What rights should minorities have in a democratic society?	X		
What are the expected relationships between the citizens of the United States and the citizens of other nations?	X		
How are the United States and other nations of the world interdependent?		X	
How are the climates in various parts of the world explained?		X	
What contrasts are there between the government of the United States and the governments of selected nondemocratic nations?		X	
What differences are there between the kinds of logic used by individuals in different parts of the world to solve problems?			X
How can cultural perspectives be recognized in a statement of position on a world problem?			X
Why do some problems have neither right nor wrong answers?			X

Dolls can stimulate interest in other cultures.
(*Source:* © Juliann Barbato.)

These questions are simply examples of those that might be developed. Note that Table 1–8 includes the same number of questions for each social studies purpose. In reality, planning probably will result in an unequal number of questions for each major purpose.

Program planning does not stop with the identification of focus questions. The questions need to be cross-referenced to the basic themes that are developed from grade level to grade level. (Refer back to Tables 1–5, 1–6, and 1–7 for examples of this kind of grade-to-grade development.) Additional planning tasks need to be addressed as well. Among these are the identification of major subtopics, key ideas, preferred teaching and learning strategies, instructional materials, and recommended assessment procedures. Some districts have social studies specialists to assist with this process. Cross-grade program planning always involves cooperative work among people with interests in different grade levels.

Think about the planning process as you do the activity in Table 1–9.

Key Ideas in Summary _____

The elementary social studies program focuses on human behavior. This can be one of the most fascinating and motivating parts of the pupil's day. However, it is a subject area that many pupils traditionally rate low. This often occurs be-

TABLE 1–9   Deciding About Your Own Social Studies Program.

Think About This

Choose one of the grade-level topics from those that are commonly taught in the social studies program. Do some brainstorming to think of content that might be taught at this grade level. Next, write down what you know about pupils at this grade level. Then, considering the major purpose areas of citizenship education, social science education, and problem-solving education, decide what you might include in your program at this grade level.

Grade Level Chosen:

Major Grade-level Focus:

Focus Questions Related to Citizenship Education:

Focus Questions Related to Social Science Education:

Focus Questions Related to Problem-Solving Education:

cause teachers do not understand what social studies is supposed to accomplish. To do well in his or her role, an elementary social studies teacher must have an understanding of the major purposes of this important part of the curriculum.

Among the major ideas the teacher needs to keep in mind are the following:

1. A major purpose of social studies is citizenship education. While most individuals agree with this purpose, the real problem occurs when citizenship is defined. Individuals have different perceptions of what is involved in citizenship education.
2. Social science education is the part of the social studies program that includes content drawn from history and the social sciences. This dimension supports citizenship by providing the knowledge about human behavior important for citizens.
3. Problem-solving education seeks to develop pupils' abilities to make rational decisions about personal, social, and civic issues. Learning outcomes in this area are important for young people who will come to maturity in a society that expects citizens to play active roles in the political decision-making process.
4. The subcomponents of citizenship education, social science education, and problem-solving education include (1) knowledge, (2) skills, and (3) values.
5. The sequence of topics that is normally taught in the elementary grades is organized around the expanding horizons approach. There have been some criticisms of this approach. Teachers need to make sure that throughout

the grades they include content samples that reflect the diversity of the world.

6. It is important to remember that the content or the topics are not in themselves the goal of the social studies. A study of a topic is only a means to help youngsters learn important ideas about themselves and the world around the. What is studied within each topic needs to be related back to the major purposes of the social studies.

Questions ——

Review Questions

1. What is the major focus of social studies education?
2. Why is it important for the teacher to have a positive attitude toward a subject?
3. What are the overarching purposes of social studies education?
4. What is included in social science education?
5. What is included in problem-solving education?
6. How does decision making relate to the three major thrusts of the social studies?
7. What has been the main organizing principle around which the curriculum sequence has been organized?
8. What must be done to assure that the social studies program takes in some of the realities of modern life?

Thought Questions

1. Why do you think social studies is so unpopular with many elementary pupils?
2. How can a social studies teacher plan a program when there are so many different views of citizenship?
3. What are some specific ways that the expanding horizons approach can be modified in order to provide the pupil with a broader perspective of the world?
4. Suppose someone asked you if you considered the social studies as one of the "basics." How would you respond, and what would be your reasons?
5. How can the social studies teacher meet the demands for more accountability without succumbing to the temptation to focus on the minor and unimportant aspects of the subject?

Extending Understanding and Skill ——————————————————————————

Activities

1. Choose a curriculum guide for the grade level of your choice. Evaluate the guide using the framework of goals outlined in this chapter (see Table 1–2). To what extent are citizenship education, social science education, problem-solving education, and decision making included in the guide?
2. Choose a topic taught at a grade level that interests you. Write at least one example of how each of the major purposes of the social studies might be included at that grade level.
3. Based on what you read in this chapter, develop a list of characteristics that you think would indicate a high-quality social studies program.

4. Prepare a complete list of focus questions to guide social studies instruction at a grade level of your choice.

Supplemental Reading

BARR, ROBERT D., BARTH, JAMES L., AND SHERMIS, S. SAMUEL. *Defining the Social Studies.* Bulletin 51. Washington, D.C.: National Council for the Social Studies, 1977.

HUNKINS, FRANCIS P., JETER, JAN, AND MAXEY, PHYLLIS F. *Social Studies in the Elementary School.* Columbus, OH: Charles E. Merrill Publishing Co., 1982.

JAROLIMEK, JOHN. *Social Studies in Elementary Education,* 7th ed. New York: Macmillan Publishing Co., Inc., 1985.

McFARLAND, MARY A. "Questions and Priorities for Improving Social Studies Instruction," *Social Education* (February 1984), pp. 117–120.

Reference _____

National Council for the Social Studies Task Force on Scope and Sequence. "In Search of a Scope and Sequence for Social Studies," *Social Education* (April 1984), pp. 249–262.

Chapter 2

Content Sources: History, Geography, and Economics

(*Source:* © Juliann Barbato.)

1. Point out the relationships among "facts," "concepts," and "generalizations" in the overall structure of knowledge.
2. Recognize that history, geography, and economics are disciplines from which much social studies content is drawn.
3. Describe the special perspectives of history, geography, and economics.
4. Point out the basic concepts of history, geography, and economics.
5. Cite examples of the generalizations associated with history, geography, and economics.
6. Describe the features of learning activities that draw upon history, geography, and economics.

Overview

Suppose that two experienced elementary teachers were asked to respond to this question: What content should we emphasize in the social studies? These are possible responses:

Teacher 1

These youngsters are going to leave us after a few years, and they need to be ready for the secondary school. In junior and senior high school, they'll study history, geography, economics and maybe some other specialized social science subjects. We need to prepare them for these courses. We should teach content related to these subjects so they will not be 'shocked' when they enter the secondary school program.

Teacher 2

Our kids are going to mature, and they'll have to take on the same sorts of responsibilities we carry now. I mean, they will be parents, taxpayers, voters . . . the same roles citizens of our country have always played. At the same time, we have to recognize that personal alienation has become one of the greatest tragedies of our time. Our social studies programs must place heavy emphasis on developing pupils' self-understanding. This and the development of general citizenship skills should be the primary purposes of the elementary social studies program.

The statements of these teachers reflect the basic positions that have been long debated by social studies professionals. Even today there are individuals who are so committed to one of these points of view that they organize the *entire* social studies program around the persepctive they favor. Most people, though, agree that the social studies should reflect some blend of the views presented in the comments of these two teachers.

It might be simpler if the social studies were directed at serving only a single purpose. But if the overall goal is to help youngsters better understand their world, any attempt to delimit the content of the social studies in a way that distorts the complex realities of life does pupils a disservice.

For example, a social studies program focusing on only history and the social sciences may suggest an artificial division of reality into tiny packages with such labels as "history," "geography," "economics," and so forth. Adults do not confront the world as fragments of reality from the academic disciplines. Rather, they see it as a whole, and they bring to bear the perspectives of the culture and their own personal values and attitudes. As Earl S. Johnson, a leading social studies educator, has noted: "The problems of mankind do not lend themselves to fruitful inquiry and resolution within the confines of separate disciplines" (Johnson, 1981, pp. 4–5). See Figure 2–1 for an illustration of the relationship of the academic disciplines to human beings.

This chapter focuses on history, geography, and economics. Though these and other disciplines are important sources of social studies content, they are not the *only* sources. Some content for the overall social studies program may be drawn from literature, art, music, science, mathematics, and other formal academic disciplines. Public issues and problems of all kinds represent a fruitful source of material for social studies lessons. The personal concerns of young people frequently provide the basis for excellent social studies learning experiences.

Though social studies programs draw content from many sources, they tend to focus heavily on information from history and the social sciences. This chapter introduces the special perspectives of history, geography, and economics. Chap-

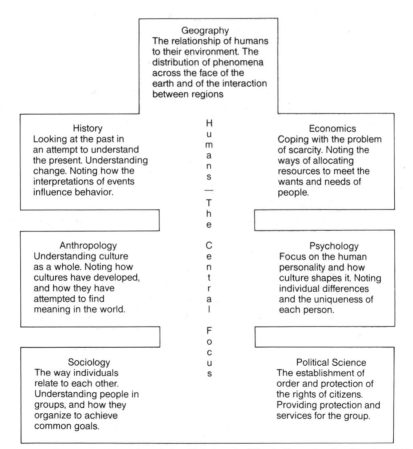

Figure 2–1   The Relationship of the Academic Disciplines to the Study of Human Behavior.

ter 3 reviews the perspectives of political science, sociology, anthropology, and psychology.

The Structure of Knowledge

Working with content from history, geography, and economics, teachers need a way to make sense out of the tremendous amount of information associated with each subject. Not all content from history, geography, economics, or any other source is equally important. The structure of knowledge approach, derived from the work of such figures as Bruner (1960) and Taba (1962), provides a way to scale content elements in terms of their importance.

The *structure of knowledge approach* presumes that a given element of content becomes more important as it increases its potential to provide information that applies to diverse situations. The more all-encompassing elements are assigned a higher priority than the elements that deal with very restricted bits of information.

There are three major content types in the structure of knowledge. From the narrowest (and least important) to the broadest (and most important) these are (1) facts, (2) concepts, and (3) generalizations. Figure 2–2 points out the relationships among these content types.

Facts

Facts have limited explanatory power. Facts refer to a specific set of circumstances and have little transfer value. Here are some examples of social studies facts:

- Lincoln was born in 1809.
- Mountains cover between 10 and 15 percent of New Mexico.
- Wyoming has fewer people than Colorado.
- Austin is the capital of Texas.
- Mexico City has a higher population than New York City.

Because there are so many facts related to every subject, it is never possible to teach all of them. A selection must be made. Facts that are specifically related to the next to content types in the structure of knowledge,—concepts and generalizations—should be selected. Facts can be used to broaden pupils' awareness of the meaning of concepts and to help them appreciate the accuracy of generalizations.

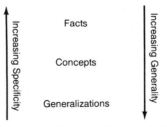

Figure 2–2   The Structure of Knowledge.

Concepts

Concepts are labels that help us make sense out of large quantities of information. For example, the concept "automobile" helps tie together ideas about makes and models, thoughts about production-line manufacturing, and other details as well. Concepts are very powerful organizers. Facts tend to be limited to specific situations while concepts are broad enough to apply to many different sets of conditions. Here are some examples of social studies concepts:

- Monsoon wind
- Latitude
- Folkway
- Inflation
- Self-determination

Concepts have assigned meanings. That is, their meanings depend on their definitions. The defining characteristics of a concept are called attributes. For example, the concept "triangle" is defined by these attributes: (1) it is a two-dimensional figure that is (2) enclosed by no more and no fewer than three straight lines.

One problem in the social studies is that few important concepts are as easily defined as "triangle." Concepts such as "democracy," "culture," "socialization," and so forth have many defining attributes. Often it is necessary to employ special teaching strategies to help pupils master these difficult concepts. Once mastered, however, these concepts provide youngsters with tools that can be used to grasp even more sophisticated content types known as generalizations.

Generalizations

Generalizations are statements of relationship among concepts. The "truth" of a generalization is determined by reference to evidence. Some generalizations that we accept today may have to be modified in the future in response to new evidence. Here are some examples of social studies generalizations:

Opinions that originate in an earlier period persist to be influential in a later period, both within a single lifetime and over generations.

. . .

The more demands a natural environment places on people for physical survival, the less attention people pay to supernatural phenomena.

. . .

As a society becomes increasingly educated and industrialized, its birthrate declines.

(Berelson and Steiner, 1967)

Note some of the concepts in the last generalization: "society," "educated society," "industrialized society," and "birthrate." Pupils need to understand the meanings of these labels before they can grasp the significance of the generalization. Because of the critical importance of concepts, social studies specialists have developed a number of special strategies for teaching them. Several of these are described in Chapter 6, "Involving Pupils: The Basic Approaches."

Each of the generalizations listed is supported by abundant research evidence. Generalizations concisely summarize a great deal of information. This feature makes them attractive to the planners of social studies programs. When pupils master generalizations, they take personal control of information that has broad explanatory power. Chapter 6 suggests some techniques for helping pupils grasp generalizations.

There are specialized concepts associated with history, geography, economics, and all other academic subjects. Furthermore, generalizations have been formulated that summarize the findings of researchers in these disciplines. In subsequent sections of this chapter, examples of concepts and generalizations associated with history, geography, and economics will be introduced.

History

Most elementary teachers have taken more courses in history than in any other social studies–related academic discipline. New teachers, as a result, often feel quite comfortable as they approach the task of planning lessons related to history. This planning takes into account the central questions, concepts, and generalizations associated with history. Some examples of these are provided in Table 2–1.

History is important in the elementary social studies program. Interpretations of historical events influence how people see themselves and others. People gen-

Understanding the lives of people helps pupils relate to history.
(*Source:* © Juliann Barbato.)

TABLE 2–1   Central Questions, Concepts, and Generalizations Associated with History.

The following are examples of central questions, concepts, and generalizations that are important to historians. They are useful to elementary social studies teachers when they make decisions about what to include in lessons related to history.

Central Questions (a selection)

What are the values and biases of the writer?
What parts of the account are fact? What parts are fiction?
What kind of language is used to describe an event or a person? How does this language influence the view of the reader?
Where did the writer get his or her information?
Where else might we get information about these events?
What do others say about what happened?

Concepts (a selection)

change, innovation, multiple causation, interpretation, movement, primary sources, secondary sources, era, period, epoch, century, A.D., B.C., season, year, calendar, medieval, ancient, modern, prehistoric, validity, time, chronology

Generalizations (a selection)

Continuous change is universal and inevitable.
The rate of change within a society varies with such factors as the values of the society, the amount of pluralism in the society, and the extent of the society's contacts with other cultures.
Events of the past influence events of the present.
The history of a society provides guidelines for understanding thought and action in a society's present-day affairs.
The history of a nation influences the culture, traditions, beliefs, attitudes, and patterns of living of its people.

eralize from their impressions of past events. Teachers have particular obligations to help pupils avoid misinterpreting isolated historical episodes and stereotyping groups of people as "lazy" or "unintelligent."

In its broadest sense, history encompasses everything that has happened in the past. No professional historian can hope to deal with more than a fraction of the total human experience. He or she is always confronted with the necessity of choosing what to include and what to exclude. These decisions reflect personal values. History as perceived and described by an individual who sees the class struggle as the dominant theme in human affairs will be quite different from history as perceived and described by someone who sees technological change as the dominant theme. The social studies program cannot be held accountable for teaching the total history of the human experience.

Because reported history reflects the perspectives of those who write it, the study of history demands more than the recall of provided information. Interpretations need to be challenged as pupils are taught to rethink historians' arguments, question interpretations of facts, and look for alternative explanations of events. Elementary social studies programs should promote active pupil involvement in the processes of historical inquiry. Lessons designed to familiarize pupils with these processes must be appropriate to the levels of sophistication. Some examples of these follow.

Sample History Activities

What the Visitor Wore. Make arrangements for the principal to come in briefly to ask you about something. When the principal leaves, ask youngsters to respond to questions such as these:

1. What was the principal wearing?
2. What side of the desk did the principal stand on?
3. Who spoke first (the principal or the teacher)?
4. About how long was the principal in the room?

A number of other questions might also be asked. These can lead into a productive discussion about how people who are physically present at an event do not always see it in the same way. With an older group of youngsters, the teacher can lead the discussion toward a consideration of the historian's use of eyewitness accounts of events. How reliable are these accounts? How might a historian decide whom to believe if eyewitness accounts vary?

Yesterday on the Playground. Ask class members to write a description of the recess period on the playground. This might be done individually or by pupils working together. When everyone has finished, the teacher reads the accounts to the class of posts them and invites youngsters to read them. When everyone in the class has become familiar with each account, the teacher leads a discussion.

As this discussion proceeds, it is useful for the teacher to keep a tally on the chalk board of the number of times a given event is mentioned. The teacher can ask the class why some events were mentioned by large numbers of people and others by only a few. In addition, references to the times of reported events can be compared from account to account. This helps build the concept of chronology. Another approach is to group events in terms of where on the playground they were reported to occur. This will highlight the geographic concept of location.

At the end of the discussion, the teacher uses an overhead transparency and works with pupils as they attempt to write an "official" history of what went on during the recess. This culminating activity will help pupils grasp the difficulties historians encounter in using primary evidence and will point out the need to consult multiple information sources to assure accuracy.

Conflicting Accounts of Events. To help youngsters grasp the differences in perspectives, teachers often find it useful to prepare short accounts of events written from the viewpoints of individuals who have widely different opinions. Consider the following example:

Event: The Burning of Washington in the War of 1812

Account 1

Victorious troops of the crown swarmed into Washington. With huzzahs all around, torches were passed. Officers led their men on a block by block campaign to torch the rebel capital. Officers of the general staff report this action may soon break the back of the American resistance. There is talk that before the year is out these rebel colonies will be rightfully returned to the crown. American resistance is said to be crumbling. Loyal subjects of the king are said to be waiting in Canada for the signal to return south and re-establish the colonial governments. (Report filed by a correspondent of the *London Gazette*.)

Account 2

The British barbarian showed his true colors today. Consistent with the pattern of 25 years ago when American rights were trampled into the ground, the undisciplined British troops took on Washington today with unprincipled savagery. With little regard for the safety even of women and children, they went on a rampage that resulted in the burning of most of the buildings in Washington. American troops are rallying. Spirits of the men have never been higher. All look forward to taking a revenge that will forever fling the British off this free continent. (Report filed by a correspondent of the *New York Review*.)

These accounts can be followed up with a debriefing discussion that might include questions such as these:

1. What are the similarities in the two accounts?
2. What are the differences in the two accounts?
3. How might you explain any differences?

Time and Chronology. History requires familiarity with many different kinds of time concepts, ranging from seconds, minutes, and hours to years, decades, centuries, and even longer periods. These time concepts are confusing for pupils, and many young children have very distorted notions. It is not uncommon for some of them to suppose that their parents rode dinosaurs to school.

Did You Like the Food They Served on the Mayflower, Dad?
(*Source:* Ford Button.)

Misunderstandings about the rate of technological change are often associated with confusion about basic time concepts. For example, this shaky understanding is frequently reflected in pupils' faulty assumption that all modern conveniences were invented in their own lifetimes. Large numbers of younger elementary pupils may answer "yes" to this question: Is it true that only fifteen years ago there were no electric street lights?

To help pupils gain more adequate understanding of time and change, use of a modified time line is helpful. A time-line chart references (1) the birthdates of members of the class, (2) the birthdates of their parents and grandparents, and (3) the times when selected items were invented. An example of a time-line chart of this type is provided in Table 2–2.

Note that youngsters are invited to comment on historical events occurring during the ten-year periods represented by each column. The time chart can help personalize historical events by putting them in a time context that takes on meaning because it includes the birthdates of relatives. Information on the chart may lead pupils to ask questions of relatives who were alive when certain events took place (World War II, for example). The time chart can be highly motivating for youngsters who see little relevance in historical information that is more traditionally presented in the pages of a textbook.

How Historians Judge the "Truth"

Even in the elementary grades it is not too soon to help youngsters understand that professional historians use special techniques to help them determine what is "true." Good history is *not* simply a matter of the personal opinion of the writer. It rests on the careful consideration of evidence.

As appropriate given their age, grade level, and general sophistication, youngsters should be introduced to the idea that historians consider (1) external validity and (2) internal validity when they attempt to establish whether something is true.

External validity concerns the issue of authenticity. Suppose that a historian was presented with a document that was alleged to have been written in the year 1610 in England. The historian might have chemical analyses run on the paper and the ink to establish whether that kind of paper and that kind of ink existed in 1610. The words used in the document might be compared with the words used in other documents known to be authentic 1610 (or thereabouts) materials. The historian would be interested in learning whether any vocabulary contained in the document was inconsistent with what might be expected in a document of this date. This kind of careful detective work is used to unmask forgeries.

The other major task for the historian would be to establish the *internal validity* of the document. It is possible that tests run on the document convinced the historian that it could have been produced in England in 1610, but he or she still must work hard to find out whether the information contained in the document is accurate. Was the person who allegedly wrote the document capable of doing so (did he or she have the proper education? and so forth)? Did this person have an interest in writing accurately, or did he or she have some personal motive to distort the truth? Are there "hidden messages" in the document?

Children in the elementary grades do not need to be exposed to the very sophisticated methodologies of the professional historian, but they should understand that a good historian is something of a sleuth. He or she looks for explanations that go beyond the obvious. This search is part of the excitement of the historian's craft.

History then is not just a matter of collecting and writing down information about the past. It is rather a question of disciplined thought about the past.

History can provide youngsters with a context for the present. As they are taught to think about the past, they learn to recognize key patterns in their own world. All people have an interest in their personal identity. This concern can be used to motivate children to learn how past events influenced people who are important to them. Lessons that include history's personal implications help elementary pupils develop an appreciation for the subject as they begin to develop a sense of their personal place in time.

Geography _____

Geography is the study of the patterns of spatial distribution and interactions across space. Patterns of all kinds of phenomena have been studied. One of the key tools of geographers is the map, which is used to highlight important patterns. Because patterns often are complex, geographers sometimes must study several types of maps before drawing their conclusions.

Major Subdivisions of Geography

The discipline of geography is subdivided into a number of major categories. Among these are (1) earth studies, (2) area studies, and (3) interactional studies.

Earth Studies. The subject matter in *earth studies* shares some common ground with geology. Earth studies lessons focus on topics such as climate, soils, water, and major terrain features. Geographers interested in earth studies seek to promote a better understanding of our planet's physical environment.

Area Studies. *Area studies* include the studies of regions. These may be political regions (China, for example), physical regions (a desert), or cultural regions (New England). Many other kinds of regions can be studied as well. Area studies emphasize the unique features of selected sections of the earth's surface. The features that give the focus area its special flavor are emphasized. Area studies lessons are very common in the elementary social studies program.

Interactional Studies. As the name suggests, *interactional studies* are concerned with the patterns of interaction of phenomena in the physical and social world. Some topics that interest geographers who specialize in interactional studies are (1) the patterns of locations of services in cities, (2) the changes in population in places, (3) the relationships between transportation systems and patterns of residence, and (4) the distribution of manufacturing facilities of various types. Interactional studies research highlights the point that many distributional patterns are relatively predictable in similar settings at different locations.

Geography lessons play an important part in the elementary program. Some

TABLE 2–2 Example of a Time Chart Showing Birthdates of Pupils, Pupils' Parents and Grandparents, and Dates of Selected Inventions*.

1905	1915	1925	1935	1945	1955	1965	1975	Birthdays of Class Members, Their Parents, and Their Grandparents
Grandfathers (father's side) Jones	*Grandfathers (father's side)* Adams, Cole, Finn, Barnes	*Grandfathers (father's side)* Daly, Estes, Howe, Isles		*Fathers* Adams, Cole, Daly, Finn, Howe	*Fathers* Barnes, Estes, Isles, Jones		*Our Class* Adams, Barnes, Cole, Daly, Estes, Finn, Howe, Isles, Jones, and so on	
	Grandfathers (mother's side) Adams, Cole, Jones	*Grandfathers (mother's side)* Daly, Estes, Finn, Howe, Isles		*Mothers* Adams, Daly, Howe	*Mothers* Barnes, Cole, Estes, Finn, Isles, Jones			
Grandmothers (father's side) Barnes	*Grandmothers (father's side)* Cole, Finn, Howe, Jones	*Grandmothers (father's side)* Adams, Barnes, Daly, Estes, Isles						
	Grandmothers (mother's side) Adams, Cole, Jones	*Grandmothers (mother's side)* Daly, Estes, Finn, Howe, Isles						

36

	1914	1924	1934	1944	1954	1964	1974	1984
Inventions	electric vacuum cleaner 1907	automatic toaster 1918	television 1927; electric razor, 1931	parking meter 1935	long-playing records 1948	laser 1958		
Kinds of Schools								
Games Children Played								
Wars								
Clothes People Wore								

Using the Time Chart: Each column represents ten years of time. Note, for example, the first column begins with the year 1905 and ends with the year 1914. Information in this column relates to events occurring during the time period 1905–1914. Labels on the right below the information about birthdays of children, parents, and grandparents will vary in terms of the content being emphasized. The idea here is to provide youngsters with a way to tie phenomena in the past to people with whom they can identify. For example, if a youngster notes that his or her grandmother was alive in the 1930s, she might be someone he or she could ask about what people wore then. Many teachers have found that use of this type of a time chart can provide youngsters with a good feel for historical sequence. The time chart is a very flexible teaching tool that the teacher can easily modify for use in a number of lessons drawing on content from history.

Current events help pupils develop a geographic perspective.
(*Source:* © Juliann Barbato.)

examples of these lessons are provided in the next section of the chapter. (See Table 2–3 for a parent's view of geography lessons.) In planning learning experiences, teachers need to consider the central questions, concepts and generalizations associated with geography. Some examples of these are provided in Table 2–4.

TABLE 2–3   Bring Back the Old Geography.

Recently a parent made these comments to a school board:

> I read an appalling piece of information in the paper last week. They surveyed one hundred adults and found that over half of them could not name more than six capitals of American states. This set me to thinking about the social studies program my own daughter is experiencing in the elementary schools here. In looking over her texts and the materials she brings home, I find very little emphasis on the kind of geography I had. I wonder whether our standards are eroding.
>
> I may be old fashioned, but I think no youngster should leave elementary school without being able to name all fifty states and their capitals. I think it would be a good idea, too, for them to know the counties in our state. This is where these folks are going to live. It stands to reason that they should at least be willing to put out effort to learn these names. Besides, it's good mental exercise for them.

Think About This

1. Why do you think this parent is concerned?
2. How do you think members of the school board would react to this statement?
3. If this parent confronted his or her child's teacher on this same issue, how do you think the teacher should respond?
4. How do you personally react to the parent's concern?

TABLE 2–4 Central Questions, Concepts, and Generalizations Associated with Geography.

The following are examples of central questions, concepts, and generalizations that geographers consider important. They provide guidance to elementary teachers as they plan lessons related to geography.

Central Questions (a selection)

Where are things located? Why are they there?
What patterns are reflected in the groupings of things?
How are these patterns explained?
How can things be arranged to create a "region?"
How do people influence the environment? How does the environment influence people?
What causes changes in the patterns of distribution over time?
How do these changes affect how people live?

Concepts (a selection)

environment, landform, climate, weather, latitude, longitude, latitude, elevation, spatial distribution, density, diffusion, interaction, spatial association, area differentiation, location, relative location, site, region, land use, urbanization, central place, accessibility, Equator, North Pole, South Pole, density, natural resource, settlement pattern, region, migration, rotation, revolution (of the earth)

Generalizations (a selection)

Human use of the environment is influenced by cultural values, economic wants, level of technology, and environmental perception.
Each culture views the physical environment in a special way, prizing particular aspects of it that may be different from those prized by other cultures.
Humans and the environment interact; the physical environment influences human activity, and humans influence the environment.
The character of a place is not constant; it reflects the place's past, present use, and future prospects.
Successive or continuing occupancy by groups of people and natural processes go together to give places their individual distinctiveness.
More change occurs near the boundaries of regions than in the interiors of regions.
The location of a place in relation to other places helps to explain its pattern of development.
The accessibility, the relative location, and the political character of a place influence the quantity and type of its interactions with other places.

Sample Geography Activities

Focusing on Location and Relative Location. A simple lesson focusing on the school can help youngsters bring concepts of *location* and *relative location* into focus.

1. Ask pupils where the busiest entrance to the school building is. Younger children will need some help from the teacher. Conduct a discussion designed to help pupils understand why this entrance is busier than the others.

2. Ask members of the class to explain where the office of the principal is. Then see if they know where the head custodian's office is. If they don't know, tell them.

3. Next, ask the class whether the principal's office or the custodian's office

is closer to the busiest entrance. (In the vast majority of buildings, the principal's office will be closer.)

4. Ask members of the class to suggest why the principal's office is closer than the custodian's to the busiest entrance. (Help them understand that the principal and his staff often have parents, central office administrators, and other people coming to see them. The custodian, on the other hand, usually has interactions with just a few people, often with only the principal. Thus, it is not important for the custodian's office to be as close as the principal's office to the busiest entrance.)

5. Point out that the basic pattern of the principal's office and custodian's office locations in their school is repeated in most other schools as well. Follow up with some other examples of the patterns of distribution of other goods and services, as appropriate.

Regions. The study of regions comprises an important part of the elementary social studies program. *Regions* share a certain characteristic or a common set of characteristics. The specific characteristic or set of characteristics used to define a region is chosen by the geographer.

Because one or more characteristics are used to define a region does not mean that other kinds of characteristics are not found in that region. This is a point of some confusion among young pupils. They may, for example, conclude that there are vast fields of corn in the "corn belt," but no cities. In teaching about regions it is important to point out that though certain distinctive features may make a given region different from other regions, in other respects these regions may share many common characteristics.

Regions do not need to be thought of as vast areas of territory on the earth's surface. A region can be quite limited in physical extent. For example, there are regions of activity even within a given room, building, or school playground. To help pupils grasp this idea, they might be encouraged to look at the school playground. With the help of the teacher, they can develop a simple map of the area. "Boundaries" might be drawn for regions such as those listed. (The categories can be altered to fit the playground characteristics at an individual school.)

1. The baseball-playing region
2. The soccer region
3. The upper-grades region
4. The lower-grades region
5. The swings region
6. The running-and-general-playing region
7. The no-running region
8. The lining-up-to-go-inside region

Follow-up questions can probe youngsters' reasons for establishing the boundaries of their regions. The teacher might ask whether these boundary lines are permanent. Under what conditions might they change? Comments here can lead into a more general discussion of the nature of regional boundaries. Some possibilities for additional consideration might include city boundaries, county boundaries, state boundaries, and national boundaries, as well as nonpolitical types of regional boundaries.

Migration and Diffusion. People, goods, and services move from place to place. An understanding of the nature of *migration* can help pupils grasp the nature of the linkages that tie places together. The following activity focuses on the issue of migration as a reflection of interactions among places.

1. Each youngster is given a homework assignment to identify the place of birth of his or her parents and grandparents. They should also try to find out all of the different places where each of these people have lived.
2. When youngsters have obtained this information, they are given opportunities to work with either United States or world maps. Their task is to identify and label the locations of the birthplaces and the places of residence. These maps can be posted on a bulletin board. Or a master map including all of the locations can be prepared.
3. A follow-up discussion can focus on questions such as these:
   (a) How many different states are represented?
   (b) How many different countries are identified?
   (c) Are there patterns of movement that we can talk about (east to west, north to south, rural to urban, and so forth)?
   (d) How can we explain these movements? (The teacher might help youngsters think about wars, economic opportunities, and so forth. Specifics will vary with the sophistication of the pupils.

A modification of this activity involves youngsters in interviewing parents and grandparents about their reasons for moving. Interviews can gather information about the places where these adults were born and have lived. The reasons for moving can form a basis for a discussion of migration.

Studies of *diffusion* focus on how tangible and intangible things are disseminated. Many geographers interested in this theme have considered the patterns of adoption of new inventions. Interestingly, new inventions do not sweep out in a smooth wave from the point the innovation was developed. Often the innovation "jumps" over huge expanses of territory before it is adopted in areas closer to the source of the invention. Consider the famous six-shooter. It was invented in New England, but it was first adopted in large numbers by people who lived on the far western frontier of the United States.

A popular exercise for teaching youngsters about the operation of diffusion is the "new joke" exercise.

1. The teacher finds a joke that is new to the youngsters in his or her class and tells it to five pupils. Each pupil is told to tell it to at least one friend. The next day the teacher checks to see that this has been done and reminds youngsters who have forgotten to pass along the joke.
2. Several days later, the teacher tells the joke to the entire class. Then members of the class are told to interview people from other classes on the playground. Other youngsters should be told the joke, asked whether they had heard it before and from whom, and asked whether it had been told in exactly the same way. Youngsters take short notes on their interviews and bring them to class where a discussion can bring out these questions:
   (a) How many had not heard the joke before?
   (b) From whom had those who had heard the joke heard it the first time?

       (c) When did those who had heard the joke before first hear it?

       (d) Was the joke told in a slightly different way to those who had heard it before?

  3. A final discussion might bring out these questions:

       (a) Did some kinds of people hear the joke before others (fourth graders before sixth graders, and so forth)?

       (b) Did people who regularly play in a certain part of the playground hear the joke before others?

       (c) Why might the joke have changed in some cases as it was told?

  4. A possible follow-up activity for older elementary youngsters might be a short paper on "A Short History of Our Joke."

Other possibilities are available for teachers wishing to help youngsters learn about the operation of diffusion. There might be discussions centering on people who were the first to buy home computers, videocassette players, or laser-disk players.

Environmental Perception. Geographers interested in *environmental perception* believe that human behavior is not adequately explained by the world "as it is." Rather, behavior is better explained by the world as people "think it to be."

There is a good deal of evidence suggesting that personal experiences contribute to people's view of the world. For example, surveys of people living in one part of the United States have found that they have quite different ideas than people living in another part of the country about the "best" place in the United States to live.

Misperceptions of distance are common among people who are not familiar with an area. Long-time residents of the northeastern United States often underestimate the distance between the far-off west coast cities of Los Angeles and San Francisco. West coast residents experience similar difficulty in sorting out distance relationships between pairs of cities such as Washington and New York or New York and Boston. Only Texans seem to appreciate that El Paso is closer to San Diego than to Houston.

There are many lessons that might be developed to help youngsters recognize that their personal experience influences their perceptions of the world. An exercise a number of teachers have used asks youngsters to imagine that they have been requested to design "the perfect park." The exercise begins with questions and concludes with a debriefing session.

  1. What kinds of things should be put in the park? (Teacher writes the responses on the chalkboard.)

  2. Where did your ideas come from? Did you see something before that you want in your park? If so, where?

  3. The teacher conducts a general, debriefing discussion to help pupils understand that their own past experiences have led to a good many of their selections. This discussion can be extended into other areas. (Why do some people prefer certain brands of cars and not others? Has past experience played a role in shaping their preferences? Why do some people like to take vacations in the city and others in the mountains?)

These activities are very brief samples of what might be done with content related to geography. Geography can provide the basis for lessons of a very involving, very personal nature. Certainly the discipline has much more to offer than rote memorization of the capitals of the states.

Economics ——————————————————————————————

Scarcity is the fundamental concern of economics. People's wants often exceed the resources available to satisfy them. Hence, decisions must be made regarding how limited resources are to be allocated and about which wants are

Developing an awareness of production costs helps pupils appreciate how a market economy works.

(*Source:* © Juliann Barbato.)

to be satisfied. *Economics* is the study of approaches to making decisions in response to the universal scarcity problem.

The Joint Council on Economic Education is an important information source for teachers interested in introducing economics-related content into their social studies programs. The Joint Council is an independent, nonprofit, nonpartisan organization dedicated to improving the teaching of economics in elementary and secondary schools. It provides many practical materials for elementary social studies classes. For information, write to:

Joint Council on Economic Education
1212 Avenue of the Americas
New York, NY 10036

Another source of economics information for elementary social studies teachers is the National Center for Economic Education for Children. The National Center publishes a quarterly journal called *The Elementary Economist*. Each issue provides teaching ideas for each elementary school grade. Information about the activities of the National Center can be obtained by writing to:

National Center for Economic Education for Children
Lesley College
35 Mellen Street
Cambridge, MA 02138

In addition to the Joint Council and the National Center, many economic education centers exist around the country. Most are affiliated with colleges and universities. Many of them produce materials designed for use in elementary and secondary classrooms.

Chambers of commerce, unions, private corporations, and other private and public organizations produce economics-related materials. Some of these materials reflect particular points of view, and teachers need to select with care to assure that pupils receive a balanced treatment of issues (see Table 2–5).

The Major Emphases of the Economics Program

Traditionally, many elementary economics lessons focused on consumer economics and personal economics. *Consumer economics* sought to teach youngsters how to become alert and careful buyers. *Personal economics* focused on skills such as personal budgeting, management of savings accounts, and (for older youngsters) balancing checkbooks.

The more comprehensive programs of today go beyond the treatment of consumer economics and personal economics. Increasingly, there is a feeling that youngsters should know something of the operation of the entire American economic system. Many programs today devote attention to teaching about the characteristics of economic systems in general and about the American system in particular.

Though there are variations, many programs begin by pointing out that all economic systems provide for these important social goals:

1. Economic growth
2. Economic efficiency

3. Security
4. Stability
5. Equity
6. Freedom

As economic systems attempt to respond to the general issue of scarcity, they must also attempt to provide for each of these important goals. The individual goals never receive equal emphasis in a given economic system. Economic lessons help pupils appreciate that different economic systems have established different priorities. Some, for example, place more emphasis on the goal of economic security than the goal of economic freedom.

As they are taught to think about how different economic systems respond to these basic goals, youngsters in the middle and upper grades are introduced to these three basic economic system types: (1) traditional economies, (2) command economies, and (3) market economies.

Traditional Economies. *Traditional economies* respond to the problem of scarcity by following long-standing patterns of custom. Such systems are found most frequently in technologically underdeveloped societies.

Command Economies. *Command economies* allocate scarce resources by following a master plan. The plan is devised and enforced by a strong central government. The Communist nations of the world tend to have command economies.

Market Economies. *Market economies* allocate resources in a decentralized way. There is no master plan. Governments play a relatively minor role. Re-

---

TABLE 2–5 Let's Keep Economics Out of the Elementary Schools.

Part of a recent citizens' elementary social studies curriculum study report contained these remarks:

> The Committee recognizes that the discipline of economics has a long and distinguished history. Economists have contributed greatly to our understanding of the world. Yet, the Committee reluctantly concludes that economic content should not be included in the elementary social studies curriculum.
>
> Unique among the social science disciplines, economics speaks to fundamental pocketbook issues. Because various interest groups in the national community have a vested financial stake in convincing future adults (our young people in the schools) of the "truth" of their particular economic positions, there has developed a truly regrettable proliferation of economics materials that reflect extremely narrow and rigid economic perspectives. The Committee sees no way to keep irresponsible bias out of the economics program in the elementary school. Hence, the Committee concludes that the only responsible course is to recommend deletion of economic content from this part of the school curriculum. Economic content can be more properly introduced at the secondary level when a more mature audience of young people will be less influenced by biases inherent in the instructional materials.

Think About This

1. How great *is* the problem of bias in economics materials? Why do you think so?
2. Does an elementary teacher have a responsibility for dealing with the issue of bias? If so, how should the issue be addressed?
3. How do you assess the general logic of the Committee's report?
4. If you were asked to make a response to the Committee's comments, what would you say?

sources are devoted to the production of those goods and services that individual consumers buy. The United States and many Western European nations have market economic systems.

Because the United States has a market economy, social studies programs often pay particular attention to helping pupils understand how such a system operates. Lessons may focus on the characteristics of a market system as identified by Allen and Armstrong (1978):

1. Private property
2. Economic freedom
3. Incentives
4. Decentralized decision making
5. Special and somewhat limited role for government

While planning economics-related lessons, teachers refer to central questions, concepts, and generalizations associated with the discipline. Some examples of these are introduced in Table 2–6.

TABLE 2–6 Central Questions, Concepts, and Generalizations Associated with Economics.

The following are examples of central questions, concepts, and generalizations associated with economics. They provide guidelines for elementary teachers interested in planning economics-related lessons.

Central Questions (a selection)

How have different societies coped with the problem of scarcity?
How can resources be allocated responsibly and fairly?
What is the proper role of government in regulating an economy?
Does the economic system provide an equality of opportunity?
Is the economic system stable, or is it characterized by uneven growth, high levels of unemployment, and high levels of inflation?
What is the overall quality of life provided by the economic system?

Concepts (a selection)

scarcity, resources, cost, opportunity cost, private property, land, labor, capital, public property, specialization, goods, market, traditional economy, command economy, market economy, services, interdependence, consumer, producer, price, competition, supply, demand, incentives, division of labor

Generalization (a selection)

The wants of people are unlimited whereas the resources to meet those wants are scarce; hence, individuals and societies must make decisions as to which wants will be met.
Allocating scarce resources can be done in a variety of ways.
Different nations have taken different approaches to solving the problem of economic scarcity.
Unequal distribution of resources and population makes trade a necessary ingredient of economic well-being.
Specialization and division of labor promote the efficiency of an economic system.
The economic development of a nation is related to the availability of resources and investment capital and the quality of the labor force.
The government plays an important role in the economic development of every society, but its role varies from place to place.

Sample Economics Activities

The following are examples of activities that can be used to help pupils master the ideas associated with economics.

Making Choices. The universality of scarcity requires all of us to make choices. This primary-level activity is designed to help younger elementary pupils develop an appreciation for the scarcity problem.

1. The teacher says, "Pretend I am Santa Claus. I want to know what to get you. I want to know five things you want. Draw me a picture of your five things."
2. The teacher collects the drawings. He or she uses several of them as a focus for the rest of the exercise. The teacher says, "All right, I have Sarah's list here. Now Sarah, pretend that I'm still Santa, but I've lost your list. To make up for it, I'm going to give you a nice crisp five-dollar bill for Christmas. Now you have some money to buy some of things on your list. But there's a catch. I am going to say that each item on your list costs two dollars. This means you'll be able to buy only two things. That will take four dollars. You'll still have a dollar for your piggy bank. Now, tell me what you'll buy."
3. The teacher concludes with a discussion focusing on questions such as:
   (a) Why couldn't Sarah buy everything she wanted?
   (b) How did you feel about choosing, Sarah?
   (c) What did you give up that you would most like to have had? Do you think other people sometimes have this problem? (This is a very brief introduction to "opportunity cost," an important idea in economics. When a decision to use a scarce resource in one way has been made, there is an "opportunity cost," in that this decision means the resource cannot be used in another way.)
   (d) Do people ever have enough money to buy everything they want? (This question should lead to the idea that human wants expand more rapidly than the resources necessary to satisfy them. The incomes of people grow more slowly than their wants.)

Economic Systems. Table 2–7 is an example of how one teacher approached teaching the basic features of traditional, command, and market economies.

Resource utilization. The term *resources* is very important to the understanding of economics. It is also a concept that elementary pupils find difficult to grasp. Part of the difficulty is that so many different kinds of things qualify as resources.

Economists identify three basic categories of resources. These are (1) natural resources, (2) capital resources, and (3) human resources.

Natural resources include phenomena occurring in nature that can be used to meet human needs. Good agricultural land, coal, petroleum, and forests are examples of natural resources. *Capital resources* are resources that are used to create additional production or wealth. Computers and machinery are examples of capital resources. *Human resources* refer to the talents of people. The pro-

TABLE 2–7 Simple Activities For a Lesson on Economic Systems.

Needed Materials

1. Three large cards captioned (1) traditional economy, (2) command economy, and (3) market economy, respectively.
2. A variety of small items (puzzles, marbles, and so forth) of interest to young children. There should be enough so that each child will have at least one small item.

Procedure

1. Whole Group Activity.
   (a) Ask pupils who are the eldest children in their families to stand. Tell others that these individuals will receive all of the wealth (all of the small items). The others will receive nothing. Hold up the large cards. Ask youngsters to guess which kind of economic system would be most likely to give all of the resources to the eldest children (traditional). Discuss children's feelings and the general features of a traditional economic system.
   (b) Announce that you are the "government." Arbitrarily identify two or three pupils who will get quite a few of the items of wealth. Select several others to get one or two items. Give youngsters no choice as to the specific item(s) they will receive. Select a final group who will get no items at all. Ask youngsters to identify the kind of economic system that might result in this kind of a distribution of wealth (command). Discuss children's feelings and the general features of a command economy.
   (c) This leaves the market system. Show the card with this label to the class. Ask youngsters to guess about the features of this system. Accept all ideas.
2. Interaction Activity.
   (a) Give each youngster one item. Then give members of the class an opportunity to trade with one another. Explain that they do not have to trade if they choose to keep what they have.
   (b) Ask members of the class to explain what happened as part of a debriefing discussion. Emphasize the characteristics of a market system. Point out that both the freedom to sell (or trade) and the freedom not to sell (or trade) are features of a market economy.

duction of wealth demands people who understand what must be done. For example, a firm specializing in highway surveys must have trained engineers; these engineers are among the firm's human resources.

To assist pupils in thinking about each of the three basic kinds of resources, teachers can provide them with a blank chart such as the following. Choose a business or economic activity the pupils know about. If there is a construction project nearby, that might provide a useful focus.

**Ace Construction Company
Resource Needs**

Natural Resources	Capital Resources	Human Resources
Petroleum	Cranes	Engineers
Water	Trucks	Steel workers
Wood products	Back hoes	Brick layers
Metal products	Tractors	Concrete finishers

It is useful to have pupils fill out similar charts on several different business operations. To make this easier, various firms might be assigned to each pupil or groups of pupils. Once the information is gathered, the teacher conducts a discussion focusing on such questions as these:

1. Where does the business get the resources it needs?
2. What types of skills do the human resources need to do their jobs?
3. Who decides how the resources will be used?

Economics-based lessons in the early grades, as is the case with lessons drawing content from other disciplines, should focus on the immediate experiences of pupils. Issues related to the economic specialization in the local community and the personal allocation of allowances and other scarce resources are examples. Applications to state, national, and international settings are appropriate for pupils as they progress through the middle- and upper-elementary grades.

Economic content has a good potential for being introduced in lessons that draw their primary information from other subject sources. For examples, in history lessons, the economic motivations of settlers can be included. Lessons focusing on the decisions of specific kinds of businesses to locate in particular places can combine information from economics and geography. Problems governments face in allocating tax revenues can draw on content from both political science and economics.

Key Ideas in Summary _____

History, geography, and economics are three academic disciplines from which much social studies content is drawn. Information from these disciplines is used by teachers as they prepare lessons designed to help their pupils learn more about human beings. History, geography, and economics are rich sources of information about the past, the distributional and interactional patterns, and the responses to the universal problem of scarcity.

1. In planning social studies lessons, teachers must make some sense out of the tremendous volume of information available in history, geography, economics, and other disciplines. A useful tool for doing this is the structure of knowledge. The structure of knowledge organizes information into the broad categories of (1) facts, (2) concepts, and (3) generalizations.
2. Facts are situation-specific. They tell us a great deal about a particular circumstance, but they cannot be used as generalizations for diverse situations. In practice, it is not possible for teachers to require pupils to master all of the facts connected with a given issue. Choices must be made. In general, the facts that are included are thought to be capable of illuminating concepts and generalizations.
3. Concepts are labels for broad categories of information. Mastery of a concept promotes efficient thinking. Concepts allow people to organize a great deal of information under a common label. For example, the concept "vegetable" brings to mind a great deal of related information.
4. Generalizations are statements of relationship among concepts. They summarize a tremendous amount of information in a very succinct way. Definitions derive their truth from research evidence. Hence, a generalization thought to be accurate today has the potential to be discounted in the light of information not presently available.

5. Lessons focusing on history help to give pupils a sense of their own place in time. These lessons seek to promote the idea that history is *thinking* about the past. Older elementary school pupils can be introduced to the methodologies of historians, especially as these methodologies relate to such issues as establishing the internal validity and the external validity of historical evidence.

6. Geography focuses on spatial patterns. Among the important subdivisions of the discipline are (1) earth studies, (2) area studies, and (3) interactional studies.

7. Economics lessons focus on scarcity and the human responses to this universal problem. Often pupils are introduced to the typical patterns of responses made by (1) traditional economies, (2) command economies, and (3) market economies.

8. While planning lessons based on history, geography, and economics, teachers find it useful to refer to the basic questions, concepts, and generalizations associated with each discipline.

9. Lessons drawing content from history, geography, and economics are not designed to create specialists in these disciplines. Rather, these academic subjects are used as sources of information that can be organized by the teacher to help pupils better understand themselves and other human beings.

Questions _____

Review Questions

1. What is the structure of knowledge used for?
2. What are the differences among facts, concepts, and generalizations?
3. What is the purpose of lessons drawing most of their content from history?
4. What are some of the major concerns of geographers?
5. What do economists study?

Thought Questions

1. How would you assess the relative importance in the elementary social studies program of content drawn from history, geography, and economics? Why do you make this judgment?
2. How would you go about personalizing lessons that draw content primarily from history, geography, or economics?
3. Would the elementary social studies program be stronger if content was drawn only from one academic discipline? Does the utilization of content from several disciplines dilute the quality of the overall program? Why, or why not?
4. How would you use the facts, concepts, and generalizations from history or geography or economics to begin planning social studies lessons?
5. In what ways is the study of content from history, geography, and economics in the elementary social studies program different from the study of these discipline at the high school level?

Extending Understanding and Skill _____

Activities

1. Review several elementary school textbooks. Select those written for a grade level you would like to teach. Determine the approximate percentage in each book of content that appears to have been drawn from (a) history, (b) geography, and (c) economics. Display the information on a chart, and present it to your instructor for review.
2. Identify a social studies topic you might like to teach. Describe the important social studies concepts from history, geography, and economics that you might wish to include. In a short paper, describe how content from these three disciplines might be integrated in your lesson.
3. Interview several elementary school teachers. Ask them how much formal course work they have had in history, geography, and economics. Ask them to comment on their relative comfort in presenting content derived from each of these three subjects. Present your findings to the class in the form of an oral report.
4. Design a learning activity focusing on one of the concepts included in Tables 2–1, 2–4, and 2–6. Share your activity with your instructor.
5. For a given concept from history, geography, and economics, prepare a file of resource materials that might prove useful in a future lesson you might teach. Share your file with your course instructor.

Supplemental Reading

ALLEN, JOHN W., AND ARMSTRONG, DAVID G. *Hallmark of a Free Enterprise System.* College Station, TX: Center for Education and Research in Free Enterprise, Texas A&M University, 1978.

BALDWIN, D. "The Thinking Strand in the Social Studies," *Educational Leadership* (September 1984), pp. 79–80.

FRITH, G. H. "A Major Objective of the Social Studies," *Clearing House* (May 1983), pp. 408–410.

GILL, CLARK C. "Interpretations of Indefinite Expressions of Time," *Social Education* (December 1962), pp. 454–456.

HATCHER, BARBARA, AND SUNAL, CYNTHIA. "Using Art to Study the Past," *The Social Studies* (May/June 1983), pp. 112–117.

PATTISON, WILLIAM D. "The Four Traditions of Geography," *Journal Geography* (May 1964), pp. 211–216.

References _____

ALLEN, JOHN W., AND ARMSTRONG, DAVID G. *Hallmark of a Free Enterprise System.* College Station, TX: Center for Education and Research in Free Enterprise, Texas A&M University, 1978.

BARR, ROBERT D., BARTH, JAMES L., AND, SHERMIS, S. SAMUEL. *Defining the Social Studies.* Bulletin 51. Washington, D.C.: National Council for the Social Studies, 1977.

BERELSON, BERNARD, AND STEINER, GARY. *Human Behavior: An Inventory of Scientific Findings.* New York: Harcourt Brace Jovanovich, 1967.

BRUNER, JEROME S. *The Process of Education.* Cambridge, MA: Harvard University Press, 1960.

Gross, Richard E., and Dynneson, Thomas L. "What Should We Be Teaching in the Social Studies?" *Phi Delta Kappa Fastbacks*, No. 199 (1983), pp. 7–53.

Johnson, Earl S. "Framework and Philosophy for an Integrated Curriculum," *The Social Studies* (January/ February 1981), pp. 4–7.

Taba, Hilda. *Curriculum Development: Theory and Practice*. New York: Harcourt, Brace & World, 1962.

Chapter 3

Content Sources:
Political Science,
Sociology, Anthropology,
and Psychology

(*Source:* © Juliann Barbato.)

1. Identify the relationships between the disciplines of political science, sociology, anthropology, and psychology and the elementary social studies program.
2. Describe the special perspectives of political science, anthropology, sociology, and psychology.
3. Point out the relationship between the social and behavioral sciences and the social studies.
4. Identify the selected basic concepts and generalizations from political science, anthropology, sociology, and psychology.
5. Develop elementary social studies lessons that draw content from political science, anthropology, sociology, and psychology.

Overview

All human beings, to some extent, are shaped by their social environment. All families have unique heritages. Groups with which individuals are associated predispose them to think and behave in certain ways. The kind of government people live under influences their attitudes toward leaders and political power. Other features of individuals' social worlds also contribute to the development of their basic convictions.

Social and behavioral scientists involved in the disciplines of political science, anthropology, sociology, and psychology study the earth's diverse human patterns. Each discipline provides a unique perspective that sheds some light on the complexity of the modern world. A balanced social studies program should incorporate some concepts and generalizations from each of these subjects.

Political Science

Elementary social studies programs have a long history of drawing content from political science. *Political science* focuses on the issue of power, particularly power as it is exercised by governments. The initial interest in the perspectives of political science developed in the nineteenth century when educators sought ways to "Americanize" the children of immigrants. The education for citizenship continues to be an important emphasis of the elementary social studies program.

Several basic themes can be developed through the study of content associated with political science. These themes are briefly described below.

Government and Governmental Processes. The theme of *government and governmental processes* emphasizes how decisions are made and how widely held values become formalized as laws. It also focuses on how leaders are selected and how authority is distributed.

Comparative Political Systems. The theme of *comparative political systems* emphasizes the ways people at various times and various places have organized

Content from political science can help pupils grasp the basic elements of our judicial system.
(*Source:* © Juliann Barbato.)

governments. Content emphasizes the ways of allocating power. It also focuses on how different governments strike a balance between providing for efficient decision making and, at the same time, responding to the concerns and rights of individual citizens.

Political Theory. *Political theory* deals with the issue of how people *ought* to be governed to preserve the rights of individuals and to assure the continuation of the society as a whole. Concepts such as "justice," "equality," and "freedom" are associated with this emphasis.

Sample Activities

Table 3–1 and the following activities illustrate how content from political science can enrich the elementary social studies program.

Rule Making. This rule-making activity is designed to help younger elementary school pupils (first or second graders) become familiar with making decisions about controversial issues. The selected focus issue must be interesting to these youngsters. Consider this example:

Teacher

Our student council has two ideas about our playground. We need to talk about these ideas. As you know, several people have been hurt on the swings.

The first idea is to allow only fourth, fifth, and sixth graders to use the swings, unless a teacher is present. If a teacher is there, then it would be all right for first, second, and third graders to swing.

**TABLE 3–1   Central Questions, Concepts, and Generalizations
Associated with Political Science.**

The following are examples of central questions, concepts, and generalizations that
are important to political scientists. They are useful to elementary social studies teachers when they make decisions about what to include in lessons related to political
science.

Central Questions (a selection)

Who decides the rules or laws?
Are the rules or laws accepted by the people that are governed?
What difference does it make who decides the rules or laws?
What values are reflected in the laws?
Who enforces the laws?
How much impact do the citizens have on the decisions made by the government?
What are the alternative ways that people have established for making political deci-
sions?
What is the decision-making process in different governmental systems?
How does the system change?
What happens if the system does not change in the direction that the people desire?

Concepts (a selection)

power, decision making, Constitution, law making, due process, justice, freedom, citizenship, state, nation, public services, equal protection, rights, responsibilities, civil liberty, separation of powers, conflict resolution, legal system, common law

Generalizations (a selection)

Every society establishes an authority structure that makes decisions and enforces
social regulations on members of the society.
A stable government facilitates the social and economic growth of a nation.
Some consent of the governed is required in all governments, and without it a government will eventually collapse.
The government acts to help resolve conflicts when individuals and groups have competing goals and values.
In order for a system of government to survive it must have the ability to change as
values and circumstances change.
A democratic society depends on the presence of educated and informed citizens who
have a willingness to compromise and a respect for the rights of minorities and the
loyal opposition.

The second idea is to require everybody who swings to attend a ten-minute lesson on swing safety. This would be taught on the playground by a teacher. No one
would *have* to take this lesson, but everybody who wanted to swing would have to
go. After each lesson, the teacher would give a button to those who attended.
People will have to wear these buttons before they can get on the swings. The
buttons will tell teachers on the playground that these people have had the swing
safety lesson.

Let's begin by thinking about the first idea:

(a) What do you like about this idea?
(b) What do you think the people who thought about this idea liked about it?
(c) Why do you think they want to restrict swing use to fourth, fifth, and sixth
    graders?
(d) What do you think the real purpose of this idea is?

(These are simply examples of the questions that might be asked. The idea is to help pupils recognize the specifics associated with a given position, the assumptions undergirding a given position [older pupils are less likely to get hurt than younger pupils], and the values underlying a position [health and safety are valued higher than the right of everybody to use the swings].)

Now let's think about the second idea:

(Follow here with the same kinds of questions introduced during the discussion of the first idea.)

Let's think about both ideas together:

(a) Which idea is the better one?
(b) Why do you think so?
(c) If the idea you like is adopted, what can you do to that see the new rule is carried out?
(d) What if the other idea is adopted? Will you have to obey it?
(e) Do other people have to accept things that they might not like but that have been favored by a majority?

(Similar questions follow.)

This discussion might conclude with the students deciding what they might do to influence the decision of the student council. Pupils can be helped to understand that group action can influence political decisions.

Conflict Resolution. One function of government is to resolve the conflicts among citizens. These conflicts often arise because individuals have different ideas about what is important. Government acts as a referee that brings conflicting ideas together, sets forth rules as to how to resolve these conflicts, and specifies how these resolutions should be enforced. Mock government exercises focusing, as appropriate, on a city council, a state legislature, the United States Congress, or the United Nations can help pupils become more familiar with the conflict-resolution function of government.

The following lesson is an example of how a mock government experience can be organized.

Introduction

The teacher summarizes for the class a newspaper report concerning a decision to build a new park. The newspaper account describes a City Council meeting at which several citizens protested a decision to build a new park near their homes. These citizens contended that the park would lower the value of their homes because of the increased noise and trash that would result.

Other park protesters contended that the proposed site was too expensive. They felt that the city would be better off selling the property to a firm wanting to build a new shopping center.

Another group of people supported the idea of building the park. They pointed out that the children of the community needed a place to play. They disputed the contention that the park would reduce the value of nearby homes. They also insisted that the new playground would be of more benefit than the money from the sale of the land to the city in the long run.

After the teacher discusses this basic information with the class, the lesson develops as follows:

STEP 1   *Defining the issue.* At this stage, the teacher leads a class discussion focusing on the issue at question. Special attention is paid to identifying the specific goals of the contending groups.

STEP 2   *Organizing the mock council.* Members of the class are divided into three groups. One group will represent the home owners opposed to the park because of a fear that their homes' values will drop. One group will represent the people who think that the city would benefit more from the money that could be had from selling the land. One group will represent the people who think that the park is needed to provide play space for the community's children.

STEP 3   *Establishing the council meeting rules.* Rules that will govern how council members will be called on, how long each will be permitted to speak, and how other matters will be handled need to be established. The teacher and the class can discuss these matters and make decisions together.

STEP 4   *Presenting positions.* The council meeting begins. The members of each group present their case.

STEP 5   *Identifying criteria and identifying alternatives.* At this stage of the exercise, the teacher leads a discussion designed to help pupils identify criteria that they will apply in deciding whether their decision is "good" and in identifying possible alternative decisions.

STEP 6   *Making the decision.* Members of the class, acting as a city council, make a decision about the location-of-the-park issue. The issue is decided by a majority vote.

STEP 7   *Debriefing.* The teacher leads a debriefing discussion, including a review of the entire decision-making process. The class examines the decision itself, decides why this particular decision was reached and the other possible alternatives were rejected; and explores other relevant matters.

See Table 3–2 for two views on teaching about communist governments.

Sociology

Sociology focuses on the collective behavior of human beings. In particular, sociologists are interested in how people act as members of groups because these groups prescribe certain roles for individuals. Sociologists are concerned with how people learn these roles.

Sociologists also study social institutions of all kinds. These institutions exercise some control over individuals, but, at the same time, they are modified by individuals' actions. The nature of the relationship between institutions and individuals is a keen interest of sociologists.

Patterns of social change represent another important interest. Sociologists

TABLE 3–2   Teaching About Communist Governments.

Two parents recently got into an argument. The following is part of the exchange that took place.

Parent 1	Parent 2
Communism is one of the great world menaces today. Our young people need to learn early that they'll spend much of their adult lives worrying about our national survival in a world that includes communist governments. There should be lessons about how the communist system works even in the lowest elementary grades. If youngsters don't know what communism is about, how can they be prepared for the threat it poses to our way of life?	Communism is dangerous, *too* dangerous for inclusion in the elementary school program. We are talking here about very young and unsophisticated children. They don't know anything about our own government. Why confuse them with information about a strange and dangerous system. It might be that poorly learned lessons could make some youngsters unduly sympathetic to the communists. I don't think the benefits are worth the risks.

Think About This

1. How logical are the claims of parent 1? Why do you think so?
2. How logical are the claims of parent 2? Why do you think so?
3. How would you respond to each of these parents?
4. What are your personal views on teaching elementary youngsters about communism?

are particularly intrigued by the social forces that tend to speed up or retard rates of change (see Table 3–3).

Sample Activities

The following are examples of elementary social studies activities that draw content from sociology.

Cooperation. Many teachers use lessons derived from sociology to build youngsters' skills in working in groups. Some teachers have found useful a simple exercise designed to help pupils see that collective, cooperative thought, rather than individual thought, on a problem often results in better, more comprehensive answers. Here is how the exercise works:

STEP 1   The teacher poses this problem to the members of the class:

You are a member of an army in the old days of knights and armor. Your general selects you to take a message back to headquarters. You leap on your horse and ride off.

After some hours, you see headquarters. But there is a big problem. Headquarters lies on the other side of a river that is too wide and too deep for the horse or for you to swim.

How will you get your message to headquarters? This is how I want you to let me know what you would do. I'm going to give you three minutes to write down every idea you have. Write as quickly as you can. Stop when I say "Stop."

STEP 2   The teacher asks each youngster to count the number of solutions he or she developed.

**TABLE 3–3 Central Questions, Concepts, and
Generalizations Associated with Sociology.**

The following are examples of central questions, concepts, and generalizations that
are important to sociologists. They are useful to elementary social studies teachers
when they make decisions about what to include in lessons related to sociology.

Central Questions (a selection)

How do individuals learn what is appropriate and what is inappropriate behavior in
society?
How are the roles and the values of society changing?
Who are the individuals that are ascribed high status in society?
How do the groups that we belong to influence our actions?
What are the people in society trying to achieve?
What are the basic social institutions of society?
How do individuals in society show their disapproval of unacceptable social behavior?
What are the forces that are facilitating change and what are the forces that are hind-
ering change in society?
What are the various levels of social class in society?

Concepts (a selection)

roles, values, sanctions, norms, customs, traditions, beliefs, social institutions, socialization, social stratification, social class, status, primary groups, secondary groups, minority groups, ethnic groups, social change, group interaction, conflict, cooperation,
assimilation, accommodation, competition

Generalizations (a selection)

The family is the basic social unit in most societies and the source of some of the most
fundamental learnings.
Social classes have existed in every society, although the basis of class distinction has
varied.
Every society develops a system of roles, norms, values, and sanctions that guides the
behavior of individuals within the society.
The norms and the values of society change over time; things that were considered
radical in one generation may be accepted in another.
People in groups may behave differently than individuals.
All societies develop institutions that condition people to accept core social values.
The satisfaction of social needs is a strong motivating force in individual behavior.
Status and prestige are relative to the values held by the social group. Behavior that is
rewarded in one group may be discouraged in another.

STEP 3   The teacher asks youngsters, one at a time, to identify each solution.
The teacher writes each solution on the chalkboard. When a solution
is mentioned by more than one pupil, a tally mark is made. At the
end of the exercise, the teacher counts up the total number of different solutions. ("I see we came up with 32 different ways to get
the message delivered. Good thinking!")

STEP 4   The teacher says:

Now I have a different problem for you. Listen carefully. You are fishing off
an ocean cliff. You are using an expensive new fishing rod and reel that your

father gave you for Christmas. The water you are fishing in is 30 feet deep. You do not know how to swim. There is no one with you. Suddenly, you drop your rod and reel. It falls to the bottom of the sea.

How many ways can you think of to get your rod and reel back? This is how I want you to think about this problem. When I say "Go," I want everybody in the class to start thinking about this problem. We won't write answers this time. Instead, I am going to call on you one at a time to give me your ideas. Listen carefully to what others say, then tell me what you think. Let's start with you, Bobby. I'll write your ideas on the chalkboard.

(The exercise proceeds. At the conclusion the teacher says, "That's everybody. Now let's see, we have 48 separate solutions. Very good.")

STEP 5   The teacher conducts a debriefing discussion.

(a) Why do you think we came up with more solutions to the second problem?
(b) How did you feel about working alone on the first problem?
(c) How did you feel about working as a group on the second problem?
(d) Do you think we can learn from others who are thinking about the same problems we are thinking about?

(Similar questions follow. This exercise is not foolproof, but in a surprisingly high number of cases, collective thinking will produce more solutions and more imaginative solutions than isolated thinking. This is consistent with findings of sociological research.)

Roles. All individuals in society learn roles. Often youngsters think that the roles they have learned for themselves are the natural roles for everyone. When they come into contact with individuals who have a different understanding of roles, conflict may result. The following activity is designed to help youngsters understand the variety of roles that men and women have in society.

STEP 1   As a homework assignment, have the class find as many pictures as they can of men and women performing different tasks.

STEP 2   When all the pictures have been gathered, have the class group the pictures of men and women into different groups, showing them doing a variety of tasks. Each picture should be labeled with a title that is appropriate for the task that is pictured. Each group can be made into a chart.

STEP 3   Divide the chalkboard into two sections, one section labeled Men and the other Women. Under each section list the variety of tasks that the class found the men and women performing.

STEP 4   Compare the two lists. Ask the class: "What similarities and differences did we find? How do you account for the similarities and differences? Where do people learn their ideas about appropriate tasks for men and women?" Are these ideas changing?

Norms and Sanctions. The following focus questions can be used to stimulate a discussion of norms and sanctions. The responses to the questions should be listed on the chalkboard so that they can be compared.

Monuments and other such symbols help pupils identify with their society.
(*Source:* © Juliann Barbato.)

1. What are some of the things that parents expect of you at home?
2. What are some of the things that are expected of people in your neighborhood?
3. What are some of things that are expected on the playground?
4. After listing and discussing the above, the teacher might tell the pupils that these expected behaviors are called *norms*. Students might discuss how norms vary from family to family and neighborhood to neighborhood. They might also discuss how norms in one place, at home, are different that norms at another, on the playground.
5. When you do not behave at home as your parents expect you to, what do they do to show you that they do not approve?
6. How do people in the neighborhood show that they do not approve of unexpected behavior?
7. How do people on the playground show that they do not approve?
8. A discussion can follow the responses in order to point out to the youngsters the variety of *sanctions* that are used by individuals in society and how those sanctions influence our behavior.

Sociologically based lessons, similar to lessons drawing content from other disciplines, should take advantage of youngsters' backgrounds and interests. This does not necessarily mean that all lessons must center on the school or the local community. Today's youngsters watch a great deal of television, see films, and have access to other information that tells them there is a world beyond the one they confront directly every day. Lessons derived from sociology and other similar sources often involve youngsters in comparing and contrasting the patterns of life near-to-home with those elsewhere. These lessons seek to help pupils better understand the nature of their membership in the total human community (see Table 3–4).

TABLE 3–4   Is Sociology Un-American?

A school board recently received a letter from a concerned citizen. Part of this letter is printed below.

> I take *strong* exception to the decision of the district to include content from sociology in the elementary social studies. For one thing, sociology is a weak, weak academic discipline. Some refer to it as 'pap'; others have referred to it in even less elegant terms. My concern, though, is that it is dangerous.
>
> Sociology places too much emphasis on the group. It downplays the actions of individuals. It ridicules free choice. Sociology claims that we are all helpless victims of our social environments. This is nonsense.
>
> Our country was built by strong leaders who refused to knuckle under to the values of the common person. This is the kind of person our world so desperately needs today. Sociology makes fun of such people. I regard the content as standing in direct contradition to our nation's values. Let's keep such un-American content out of our schools.

Think About This

1. How do you assess the logic of the letter writer?
2. How do you think the school board will respond?
3. What is your personal reaction to the position expressed in the letter?
4. Suppose that you decided to write a letter defending sociology as being consistent with core American values. What would you say?

Anthropology

Anthropology emphasizes the study of culture. It attempts to look at how people in a given culture interpret their world and discover its meaning. People within a given culture tend to be ethnocentric and believe that their way of living is the "natural" and "logical" way. Lessons based on anthropology help youngsters understand how common human problems have been addressed by different cultural groups. These lessons work best when they not only describe patterns in a given cultural setting but also encourage youngsters to compare and contrast these patterns with those of their own cultural group.

Topics in the curriculum, such as American Indians, Eskimos, African tribes, and early civilization, draw heavily on anthropological content. Anthropology also bridges the gap between social science and biological science, since anthropology is concerned with the biological characteristics of the human species, the change in the biological characteristics, and innate and learned behavior (see Table 3–5).

TABLE 3–5 Central Questions, Concepts, and Generalizations Associated with Anthropology.

The following are examples of central questions, concepts, and generalizations that are important to anthropologists. They are useful to elementary teachers when they make decisions about what to include in lessons related to anthropology.

Central Questions (a selection)

What is human about human beings, and how did they get those qualities?
What are the common characteristics of different cultures?
How do the religious beliefs of the culture influence the other parts of the culture?
How does the culture change to accommodate different ideas and beliefs?
What does the language tell us about the culture?
How does the language influence cultural and environmental perception?
How do individuals achieve adult status in the culture?
What is valued in the culture?
How are wealth and status measured in the culture?
How are information and tradition passed on from one generation to another?

Concepts (a selection)

culture, cultural change, cultural borrowing, cultural lag, adaptation, diffusion, religion, ritual, tradition, nuclear family, extended family, race, technology, artifact, innate behavior, learned behavior

Generalizations (a selection)

Every society has formed its own system of beliefs, knowledge, values, and traditions that may be called its culture.
Societies around the world have common needs, but they have created different cultural systems to meet these needs.
The art, music, architecture, food, clothing, and customs of a people produce a national identity and reveal the values of a culture.
Increased contact between the people from different cultures results in increased cultural change.

Sample Activities

There are many possibilities for building anthropologically oriented lessons. For example, the stamps and coins of various places often depict cultural features. Often these can be used as bases for good social studies discussions. Photographs from sources such as *National Geographic* and other magazines, and paintings also illustrate the responses of different peoples to common human problems.

Learning from an Artifact. The following exercise illustrates the point that cultural values are often reflected in very common objects.

Teacher

I want you to imagine that we live thousands of years in the future. We live on another planet. We have come to earth and have found nothing but ruins. We want to know how the people lived, and we begin digging in some promising place for clues. After a lot of hard work, somebody finds a jar. It is full of nickels. We don't

Museum models and artifacts promote interest in other cultures.
(*Source:* © Juliann Barbato.)

find anything else. It is our task to find out as much as we can about this culture by looking at the nickel. What might we be able to say?

(The teacher provides each youngster with a nickel to look at. Youngsters provide ideas. The teacher provides hints to keep youngsters thinking.)

Some possible ideas that might emerge include:

(a) These people must have been fairly technically advanced. They refined ores into metal; they were able to cut a perfect circle.

(b) They might have been bilingual. There are two languages on the coin, English and Latin.

(c) One of the Latin phrases, *E pluribus unum* ("one from many" in English) is confusing. Does it mean that this place had many parts, or does it mean this place was a part of something even larger?

(d) There is a male figure on the coin. He might have been a hero, a leader, or a representation of a god of some kind.

(e) These people prized liberty as a value.

(f) These people were also religious. The words "In God We Trust" are on the coin.

(g) There is a large number on each nickel. But this number is not the same on each coin. There are, for example, coins marked 1979, 1980, 1982, 1984, and 1987. This suggests a measure of time. What might have been the starting point for this counting?

(h) There is a building on the back. These people must have been skillful architects. It might have been an important building. It seems to have its own name, Monticello. This seems to be a word from a third language, Italian. What might it mean? (The teacher might take time to explain that Monticello was Thomas Jefferson's home and that the name means "little mountain." The house sits atop a small mountain in Virginia.)

(i) The words "five cents" indicate that this coin was worth five of some smaller denomination. The word "cents" means hundredths. This coin was worth five hundredths of something larger. What might that thing have been?

(j) The words "United States of America" might indicate a place name.

(k) The man on the front of the coin has his hair in a pigtail. Is this what was the style in the 1970s and 1980s?

This exercise can generate a surprising volume of information. It can also help youngsters understand that we often have incomplete information when we study other cultures, particularly cultures from the distant past. Hence, we cannot be absolutely sure that all guesses about what life was like are completely accurate.

Invention and Tool Making. The purpose of the following activity is to help the youngsters appreciate the importance of invention and how inventions and innovations might affect the culture.

STEP 1 Give the youngster several objects (ice cream sticks and string works well). The youngsters are then asked to invent a tool.

STEP 2 Compare and discuss some of the tools that were invented. Ask the class to identify what they had to think about as they underwent the process of invention.

The inventions of other cultures motivate pupils in lessons that draw content from anthropology.

(*Source:* © Juliann Barbato.)

STEP 3   Choose one or two of the inventions, and have the class predict the changes that might occur as a result of the invention. An alternative activity would be to provide the class with a hypothetical invention and have them predict the consequences. One activity that works well is to have the class predict the changes that would occur if a pill that took care of all of our food needs for a day at a time were invented.

STEP 4   Map an invention. Choose a common object and begin to map the prerequisites that led to the invention, and the consequences of the invention on society. For example, the clock is an invention that is familiar to the youngsters and can be mapped. To perform the mapping, the word "Clock" can be placed in a box near the center of a page. On the left-hand side of the page, the need that the invention met and other inventions that were needed before it could be created can be listed. On the right-hand side of the page, the changes that the invention brought about can be listed. If the level of the sophistication of the class allows, the items on both side of the paper can be connected, using lines to illustrate the relationships between the items on the lists.

Modern technologies draw the peoples of the world closer together. Today's youngsters will come into more direct contact than any previous generations with other peoples of the world. Lessons drawing content from anthropology can help them understand and work with individuals from widely differing cultural backgrounds (see Table 3–6).

TABLE 3–6   Is Content from Anthropology Too Confusing?

A parent recently made the following comments to a school principal.

> I want you to understand that I'm not complaining, but I do have some concerns about the social studies program I would like you to know about.
>
> When I was in school, I remember reading nice stories about early American settlers. It seems to me that some of the information the youngsters are getting now is focusing on some pretty strange groups. My daughter's class seems to be studying some Northwest Coast Indians. As I understand it, people in this group gained status by giving away as many of their possessions as possible. Apparently the idea was for them to become as poor as possible, as fast as possible.
>
> Personally, I find this very interesting. However, I question whether it's content that is appropriate for elementary school children. We parents work hard to get our children to take good care of their things and to value their personal property. I think the information they are getting about the attitudes of these Northwest Coast Indians may confuse our young people at the very time we are trying to get them to accept the way we do things here.

Think About This

1. Suppose you were the teacher of the class in which information about the Northwest Coast Indians had been introduced. If the principal asked you to explain the purpose of this content, how would you respond?
2. How do you feel about the parent's concern that school content should support the development of the values parents are trying to develop at home?
3. Do you personally see any danger in introducing children to the special perspectives of other world cultures?

Psychology _____

Commercial materials for elementary social studies programs focusing on content derived from psychology are less common than the materials oriented toward history and the other social science disciplines. Nevertheless, lessons based on psychology do have a place in elementary social studies lessons.

As a discipline, *psychology* has far-ranging concerns, but many of these concerns do not apply directly to the social studies program. Most lessons deriving content from psychology tend to be oriented toward fostering youngster's individual development. Many seek to build pupils' self-concepts and sense of self-acceptance. Some youngsters feel that there must be something wrong with them if they cannot succeed at everything. Social studies lessons that help youngsters understand that all people have strengths and weaknesses can help pupils overcome any lingering sense of personal inadequacy. The study of psychology can include the topics of individual differences, how individuals use their senses to learn, and the importance of human motives in understanding human behavior. The control of feelings and emotions as well as an empathetic understanding of others are important purposes to be achieved by including psychology in the social studies classroom.

Sample Activities

The issues youngsters must face as they mature during their elementary school years can provide a useful framework for planning psychology-oriented lessons. Some of these issues include the following:

1. How do I please my parents?
2. How can I get along with my brothers and sisters?
3. How do I deal with people who want me to do something wrong?
4. How do I handle verbal abuse from others?
5. What is my responsibility toward others who are being picked on?
6. How will I ever be able to do the complicated work I will be expected to do when I move to a new grade next year?
7. How come I can not hit the ball as well (print read as fast, or whatever) as some of the others?
8. How can I survive on the bus with all those big kids?

Understanding Perception. Individuals' values and previous experiences influence how they perceive reality. The following exercise combines art and social studies into a lesson designed to help pupils appreciate the importance of individual perception.

STEP 1   Pupils are given pieces of construction paper folded in the middle. They are asked to unfold the paper. A small drop of paint is dropped near the middle of each page along the fold line. Then pupils refold the paper and press it together. This will produce a symmetrical image as the paint spreads on both sides of the fold line.

I Started to Teach Them Psychology, But Then . . .
(*Source:* Ford Button.)

STEP 2   When the paint dries, post some of the prints. Ask individual members of the class to describe the objects they see in the "paintings." (Typically, different people will see different kinds of things.)

STEP 3   The teacher asks the class why everybody did not see the same things. The teacher might ask questions such as these:
(a) What did you see?
(b) Did something you have seen before help you to "see" something in the paintings?
(c) Do you think that what others might have seen before might have something to do with what they "saw" in the paintings?

STEP 4   The teacher extends the discussion to other events. He or she might ask such questions as these:
(a) What does this tell us about how different people might interpret something they see on the playground?
(b) Would it be helpful to know something about a person's past experience before we listened to what he or she had to say about something he or she had seen?

Observing Human Behavior. Psychologists observe individuals and study their reactions to different situations. Elementary social studies lessons can help to sharpen pupils' own observational behaviors. The following activity illustrates how this might be done.

STEP 1   *Gathering data.* Have the class divide into teams to collect data by observing individuals in different settings. For example, one team might be asked to observe pupils on the playground. Another team might observe the younger children, and another the older children.

Other observation areas might include the school cafeteria and the principal's office. The teams should be provided with a form they can use as they observe and record the data.

The following is an example of a form a teacher might provide for this activity.

An Observation Record

_____

Place of Observation:

Time of Observation:

People Who Are Observed:

Observation Sequence:

Time   **Behavior Observed**

_____

_____

STEP 2   *Interpreting data.* After the information has been entered on the form, have the members of each observation team look for patterns. They should try to answer such questions as these:
(a) Who were the individuals who were together?
(b) How many people were alone?
(c) How was the behavior of the people in groups different from that of the people who were alone?
(d) How and why were the behaviors of people observed different from one another?
(e) What special features of the place you observed contributed to what the people did there?

STEP 3   *Class discussion.* The teacher leads a discussion that focuses on all the information that has been gathered. Focus questions might include these:
(a) Were people of different ages observed doing different things?
(b) Did people in similar groups do similar kinds of things? If so, how do groups influence what people do?
(c) What motivated people to behave as they did?
(d) How do people learn what kind of behavior is appropriate for a given place?

Psychologists know that human beings tend to follow certain patterns of development as they mature. Younger children have not yet developed these patterns, and many of them do not realize that such patterns exist. For example, many pupils think that no other young people experience the kinds of problems they face. Lessons that help elementary pupils realize that "they are not alone" can go a long way toward smoothing their maturational development. Psychology offers a fertile source of content material for instructional activities of this kind (see Table 3–7).

TABLE 3–7   Central Questions, Concepts, and
Generalizations Associated with Psychology.

The following are examples of central questions, concepts, and generalizations that
are important to psychologists. They are useful to elementary teachers when they make
decisions about what to include in lessons related to psychology.

Central Questions (a selection)

In what ways are all people alike, and in what ways are they different?
Why do people who observe the same event have different explanations of the event?
Why do people behave as they do?
Why do some people feel capable and others feel inadequate?
How do we use our different senses to learn?
What influences the way people develop and grow?
What are the basic needs of all people?
How do different people meet these basic needs in different ways?
How can people help each other meet their needs?

Concepts (a selection)

learning, self-concept, individual differences, personal needs, personality, acceptance,
security, leadership, aggression, fear, achievement, habits, motives, perception,
uniqueness

Generalizations (a selection)

All individuals share some common needs, yet have individual differences.
Heredity and environment both play a part in shaping the unique personality of individ-
uals.
Human behavior is influenced much more than the behavior of other species by learned
patterns.
Individual perception of events is influenced by a variety of factors, including values,
motives, and expectations.
All individuals have the needs to achieve, to belong, to be accepted, and to achieve
freedom from fear.
Humans are social beings who seek to establish positive relationships with others.

Content Sources and Interdisciplinary Topics _____

In elementary social studies classes, information drawn from several academic
disciplines is often used when pupils study specific social issues. These issues are
brought into better focus when content from several academic subjects is included in unit and lesson plans.

Many interdisciplinary topics have been introduced in elementary studies
programs in recent years. A sampling of these includes issues such as sex equity,
multiethnic education, international education, environmental education, career
education, death education, peace education, and drug-abuse prevention. In the
subsections that follow, specific references are made to the kinds of content from
history and the social sciences that can be used to develop learning experiences
related to (1) sex equity, (2) multiethnic education, (3) international education,
(4) environmental education, and (5) career education.

Sex *Equity*

Sex-role stereotyping has occurred and continues to occur in many cultures. In our own society, there is an interest in developing each individual to his or her own potential. This implies a need to assure both male and female pupils that virtually all life roles are open to them. Neither boys nor girls should feel that their sex is a bar to pursuing a career or other important life interest. Social studies lessons with a focus on the principle of *sex equity* often draw content from several disciplines. Focus questions such as those that follow illustrate the potential contributions from history and the social sciences.

History
- How have the roles of men and women changed over time?
- What have been the contributions of women to our history?

Geography
- What is the distribution of women in different regions of the nation?
- Do opportunities for women vary by region?

Economics
- Is there a division of labor according to sex in the workplace?
- How do the salaries and wages of women compare to those of men?
- What changes in the workplace might be expected as more jobs become open to both men and women?

Political Science
- What specific political objectives are sought by people interested in sex equity?
- What impact do women have in the political process?
- What political issues seem to be of special concern to women?

Sociology
- What are some examples of sex-role stereotyping?
- How has the status accorded to women changed in recent years?
- How have norms and sanctions limited the contributions of women to society?
- What is the impact of changing sex roles for men and women on the family?

Anthropology
- How do the roles of men and women vary in different cultures?
- How do the specialized roles of men and women influence the development of a culture?

Psychology
- Where do people learn sex-role stereotyping?
- What is the impact of sexism on the behavior of individuals?
- What are the feelings of the women who are among the first to break the sex-role barriers?

Multiethnic Education

Many ethnic groups populate our world. Surprisingly large numbers are found within our own borders. In the past, educators tended to de-emphasize the ethnic differences within the United States in favor of a focus on the more general "American" characteristics. Today, social studies educators recognize that the development of a national identity does not require a person to downplay his or her own unique ethnic heritage.

Multiethnic education themes are introduced in elementary social studies programs for two basic purposes: the first is a desire for pupils to understand their

Ethnic foods help children to appreciate the contributions of other groups.
(*Source:* © Juliann Barbato.)

own cultural and ethnic heritage, and the second is a desire for pupils to appreciate and respect the cultural and ethnic heritages of others. Units and lessons that attempt to promote a multiethnic perspective draw content from many disciplines. The following focus questions illustrate the kinds of content for multiethnic education that can be drawn from history and the social sciences.

History
- What are the important events in the histories of selected ethnic groups?
- What contributions have members of different ethnic groups made to our nation?

Geography
- What are the geographical roots of various ethnic groups?
- Why are the members of some ethnic groups primarily located in cities while the members of other groups tend to live in both rural and urban areas?

Political Science
- What policy goals are sought by groups that are organized along ethnic lines?
- How do groups organized along ethnic lines seek to influence political decisions?

Sociology
- Why have some ethnic groups become more assimilated than others into the majority group culture?
- What status differences have there been from time to time among ethnic groups, and what accounts for them?

Anthropology
- What are the basic beliefs of selected ethnic groups?
- How have the members of various ethnic groups coped with cultural change?

Psychology
- Which personal traits are prized by members of different ethnic groups?
- What kinds of personal conflicts arise when the expectations of a person's ethnic group differ from the expectations of the larger society?

International Education

Technology is drawing the parts of the world closer together. One result of this is an increase in the interdependence among nations. This interdependence makes it imperative for *international education* to help pupils develop a global perspective. Events in distant places have implications for how people feel, think, and act in our own country.

The elementary social studies program can help pupils develop a sense for their future roles not only as citizens of the United States but also as citizens of the world. The following focus questions suggest the kinds of content from history and the social sciences that can be used to prepare units and lessons focusing on international education.

History
- What are the historical origins of cooperation and conflict among nations?
- How does an individual nation's history help explain its position on today's controversial issues?

Geography
- What are the patterns of resource distribution across the face of the earth?
- How do unequal distributions of population and resources influence international relations?

Economics
- How are nations of the world tied together economically?
- How do the economic problems of one nation influence nations in other parts of the world?

Political Science
- What patterns of government exist in the different nations of the world?
- How are the disputes between and among nations resolved?

Sociology
- How do people in different parts of the world define "the good life."
- How has technology changed the norms of behavior in different parts of the world?

Anthropology
- What common values are shared by people in all parts of the world?
- How have world cultures sought to retain their individual identities in the face of accelerating change?

Psychology
- How are the personal and social needs of people met in different parts of the world?
- What are the differences in perceptions of "normal" behavior of people in varying parts of the world?

Environmental Education

To survive, cultures must consider the impact of human activities on the physical environment. Cultural attitudes and values play a role in the decisions that weigh the potential benefits of technological advances and the potential dangers these advances pose for the environment. Content from history and the social sciences is integrated in many elementary social studies programs that include *environmental education* topics. The focus questions that follow suggest the kinds of environmental education information that might be selected from the individual disciplines.

History
- How have different societies changed their use of the environment over time?
- What have been the consequences of past abuses of the physical environment?

Geography
- What relationships exist between the locations of environmental problems and the patterns of population distribution?
- How can changes in land use influence the physical environment?

Economics
- What costs are associated with conservation and environmental protection?
- What trade-offs must be made in order to protect the environment?

Political Science
- What groups come into conflict over environmental issues?
- What are the approaches to resolving international environmental problems?

Sociology
- What is the relationship between how a society sees "the good life" and environmental issues?
- How have groups cooperated to protect the environment?

Anthropology
- How do different cultures view their relationships with the environment?
- What American cultural values influence how we view the environment?

Psychology
- Why do some individuals resist changes and continue actions that damage the environment even when confronted with evidence that their actions are harmful?
- What sorts of events make people truly appreciate the potential dangers to the environment?

Career Education

Career options and the world of work are themes often pursued in elementary social studies classes. Units and lessons related to career education focus on such issues as the importance of work in one's life, the interdependence of workers of all kinds, and the contributions to the general welfare made by people in a variety of occupations. *Career education* instruction draws content from a number of disciplines. Questions such as the following suggest the kinds of content that can be incorporated from history and the social sciences.

History
- What kinds of new careers have become available during the past fifty years?
- How has the world of work changed since the time of our parents and grandparents?

Geography
- How has career specialization led to increased interdependence among regions?
- What patterns characterize the spread of new careers across the world?

Economics
- How has job specialization led to increased efficiency?
- Why are different wages and salaries paid to people in different occupational groups?

Political Science
- What is the role of government in protecting the rights and health of workers?
- What roles do governments in different parts of the world play in deciding what occupations individual citizens are obligated to follow?

Sociology
- Why do some careers have a higher status than others?
- What is the relationship between work and leisure in our society?

Anthropology
- What values do other cultures place on work?
- How have cultural values been challenged by changes in the world of work?

Psychology
- Why do individuals feel the way they do about the world of work?
- What are the long-term consequences of a person doing a job he or she does not like?

Key Ideas in Summary _____

Political science, sociology, anthropology, and psychology offer perspectives that help us understand ourselves and our social world. Content from each plays an important part in the elementary social studies program. Some key ideas related to these content sources include the following:

1. Political science focuses on power, especially power as it is exercised by government. Lessons drawing content from political science often familiarize youngsters with the principles of democratic decision making. Older youngsters learn the rudimentary governmental organizational patterns and functions.

2. Sociology is concerned with the behavior of individuals in groups. Lessons based on sociology familiarize youngsters with group processes of various kinds, especially with the kinds of roles that they can play in groups.
3. Lessons derived from anthropology shed light on the concept of culture. These lessons are often used to give youngsters insights about different cultures and to point out that different cultural groups respond to common human problems in different ways.
4. Learning experiences based on psychology often focus on issues related to personal development. Many of these experiences seek to build youngster's self-concepts and self-images. Other lessons that are directed toward pupils' individual development may draw content from sources other than academic psychology.
5. There are numerous interdisciplinary concerns that need to be addressed through the social studies curriculum. One way of dealing with these topics is to approach them from the perspectives of history and the social sciences.

Questions _____

Review Questions

1. What are some of the academic disciplines that are often used as content sources for elementary social studies programs?
2. What are some of the major subdivisions of political science?
3. What kinds of topics do sociologists study?
4. What kinds of topics do anthropologists study?
5. What social science discipline is an important content source for lessons focusing on pupils' individual development?
6. Describe a major purpose of instruction focusing on the theme of sex equity.
7. Why should multiethnic education be a part of the elementary social studies program?
8. What kinds of issues might be investigated in elementary social studies programs focusing on environmental education?
9. For what purposes might career education be included in the elementary social studies program?

Thought Questions

1. Suppose that you were asked to defend the idea of including content derived from sociology and anthropology in the elementary social studies program. What would you say?
2. How would you respond to individuals who argue that lessons based on political science should be restricted only to American government? Suppose that these individuals contend that any mention of communism is unpatriotic. How would you reply to them?
3. How can social studies teachers strike a balance between the need to help pupils master their society's expected patterns of behavior and the need to help pupils develop as individuals?
4. Some people claim that including lessons related to sex equity teaches pupils about roles that may be contradictory to family values and beliefs. Can sex-equity studies be taught in such a way so that conflict with family values and religious values is avoided?

5. Many interdisciplinary topics that can be included in the social studies problems involve the study of controversial issues. How should the elementary social studies teacher approach teaching these issues?

Extending Understanding and Skill

Activities

1. Conduct several interviews with experienced teachers of the grade level you would like to teach. Ask them to describe kinds of self-concept problems youngsters in this grade tend to have. Ask them to comment on some instructional responses to the need to develop pupils' sense of self-worth. Share the comments of these teachers with the class.
2. Do some reading in the general area of citizenship. Prepare a short paper for your instructor in which you attempt to define as specifically as possible what citizenship competencies youngsters ought to acquire as a consequence of their exposure to social studies instruction.
3. Review several social studies textbooks written for the grade level you would like to teach. Approximately what percentages of the text are devoted to content derived from (a) political science, (b) sociology, (c) anthropology, (d) psychology, and (e) other content sources? Prepare a chart summarizing your findings, and present it to your instructor for review.
4. Choose one of the special content areas that you would like to teach. Write a series of short paragraphs indicating how the topic might be approached using content drawn respectively from (a) history, (b) geography, (c) economics, (d) political science, (e) sociology, (f) anthropology, and (g) psychology. Write one paragraph about each of these disciplines.
5. Put together a resource file of photographs, drawings, art work, journal articles, and newspaper articles that might be used as part of a lesson in elementary social studies focusing on an interdisciplinary topic. Describe how each item in your file will contribute to pupils' understandings.

Supplemental Reading

ABRAHAM, K. G. "Political Thinking in the Elementary Years: An Empirical Study," _Elementary School Journal_ (November 1983), pp. 221–231.

BALDWIN, D. "The Thinking Strand in Social Studies," _Educational Leadership_ (September 1984), pp. 79–80.

FRITH, G. H. "A Major Objective of Social Studies," _Clearing House_ (May 1983), pp. 408–410.

MILLER, S. D., and BRAND, M. "Music of Other Cultures in the Classroom," _The Social Studies_ (March/April 1983), pp. 62–64.

References

BARR, ROBERT D., BARTH, JAMES L., and, SHERMIS, S. SAMUEL. _Defining the Social Studies._ Bulletin 51. Washington, D.C.: National Council for the Social Studies, 1977.

CONTE, ANTHONY E., and MCAULAY, JOHN D. "The Need for Individually Guided Social Studies." _The Social Studies_ (March/April 1978), pp. 52–55.

DYNNESON, THOMAS L. "An Anthropological Approach to Learning and Teaching: Eleven Propositions," *Social Education* (September/October 1984), pp. 410; 412; 416–418.

GROSS, RICHARD E., and DYNNESON, THOMAS L. *What Should We be Teaching in the Social Studies?* Bloomington, IN: Phi Delta Kappa Fastback Series, No. 199, 1983.

JAROLIMEK, JOHN. "Curriculum Trends: Social Studies," *Educational Leadership* (November 1983), p. 78.

JOHNSON, EARL S. "Framework and Philosophy for an Integrated Curriculum," *The Social Studies* (January/February 1981), pp. 4–7.

Chapter 4 _____

The Instructional Act

(*Source:* © Juliann Barbato.)

1. Plan objectives that vary in type and sophistication.
2. Do a task analysis, and develop an appropriate teaching sequence.
3. Point out the uses of intrinsic and extrinsic motivation in teaching social studies.
4. Describe the importance of modeling as a teaching tool.
5. Explain the purposes of follow-up activities and the ways of implementing these activities.
6. Describe the importance of closure in the learning process.

Overview

Classroom instruction is the most exciting and most important task of the teacher. Exceptional classroom instruction does not occur by accident; it is a result of careful planning and attention to the basic principles of instruction. The act of teaching is essentially a decision-making task. The learning principles outlined in this chapter are intended to provide the teacher with a framework for making these decisions.

Teachers work in a variety of settings with an enormous variety of pupils. No single set of prescriptions as to "what ought to be done" can be broad enough to take these variables into account. Successful teaching requires disciplined thinking on the part of the teacher. This thinking should take into account (1) planning based on the objectives; (2) analyzing the task; (3) motivating pupils; (4) presenting new information; (5) helping pupils apply, extend, and transfer new learning; and (6) planning for closure.

Instructional Objectives

Instructional objectives give the teacher a clear focus on what his or her pupils should be able to do as a consequence of instruction. Furthermore, the objectives specify criteria that are necessary to determine whether a given pupil has performed at a satisfactory level. This feature of instructional objectives makes them very valuable as sources of evidence for legislatures and other groups interested in the degree to which young people are learning mandated content. Here are several examples of instructional objectives:

- Each pupil will correctly locate at least eight of ten given places on a map quiz when given the coordinates of latitude and longitude.
- Each first-grade pupil will correctly name the months of the year and the days of the week when asked to do so by the teacher.
- Each member of Laura's group will explain the differences in climate between Juneau, Alaska, and Philadelphia, Pennsylvania, by writing about two pages in response to an essay question. Each response must make spe-

cific references to the continental location of each place, the prevailing wind direction in each place, and the impact of water on temperature in each place.

A number of formats for writing good instructional objectives are available. One that is widely used is introduced in the next section.

The A, B, C, D Approach

According to the _A, B, C, D approach,_ a complete instructional objective must have four components. These are (1) the _A_ component, or _Audience;_ (2) the _B_ component, or _Behavior;_ (3) the _C_ component, or _Condition;_ and (4) the _D_ component, or _Degree._

A, or Audience. The _A_ component of the objective identifies the person or persons to whom the instruction is directed. This might be the entire class, a small group, or an individual. The focus on the audience draws attention to the pupils and prompts teachers to inquire whether or not the students have the necessary prerequisites to accomplish the objective. In addition, specifying the audience can communicate exactly who is going to be expected to master the objective. Typical examples of the _A_ component might be:

- All fifth-grade pupils completing the westward-movement unit will . . .
- Zelda Zike will . . .
- All individuals choosing the learning center activities on the Lewis and Clark expedition will . . .

B, or Behavior. The _B_ component of the objective defines the behavior that the pupil will be expected to demonstrate. Note that the emphasis is on the pupil's behavior and not on the teacher's behavior. Sometimes beginners make the mistake of listing the intended behavior of the teacher in the instructional objective.

It is essential that the behaviors be described using verbs indicating clearly observable actions. Verbs such as "know," "appreciate," or "understand," though perfectly acceptable for general-purposes statements, are not precise enough for use in instructional objectives. The teacher needs to decide what a pupil must do to indicate what he or she "knows," "appreciates," or "understands." Verbs indicating these more precise behaviors need to be chosen.

The following are some examples of the _B_ component.

- . . . trace the route of the Lewis and Clark expedition . . .
- . . . describe the sequence of events leading to the adoption of the Bill of Rights . . .
- . . . state a probable consequence if the United States had decided not to make the Louisiana Purchase . . .
- . . . list the steps in passing a bill into a law . . .
- . . . draw a picture of a covered wagon . . .

C, or Conditions. The *C* component of the objective describes the conditions under which the pupil will be expected to demonstrate the behavior. The conditions component might specify whether pupils will be able to use other resources, such as books or notes; whether they will need to demonstrate the behavior individually or in a group; or whether there will be a time limit for performing the task. The conditions component might specify whether or not the behavior will be measured on a test or in some other form.

The following are some examples of the *C* component.

- . . . on a multiple-choice test . . .
- . . . using notes gathered from several sources . . .
- . . . while working with a group of pupils . . .
- . . . working independently from memory . . .

D, or Degree. The *D* component of the objective relates to the issue of how well the pupil must perform to demonstrate the behavior to the teacher's satisfaction. One criterion teachers often apply is that of repeated successful performance.

Consider a pupil who does something correctly one time. Is this a valid indicator that the objective has been learned? In most cases the answer is "probably not." One success might be a result of mere chance. The teacher needs to consider what would be the minimum response necessary in order for him or her to have confidence that the pupil has learned. The teacher's decision on the degree of response might specify the number of correct answers needed on test items pertaining to the objective, the number of things to be included in a learning project, or the number of inferences the pupil should make when confronted with an unresolved situation.

The following are some examples of the *D* component.

- . . . will respond correctly to 8 out of 10 test items that relate to the journey of Lewis and Clark.
- . . . will make three inferences about a place from a climatic map.
- . . . will state at least one probable consequence of the choice.
- . . . will identify at least one value held by the individual making the choice.

Putting It All Together. When preparing an instructional objective, the specific order of the *A*, *C*, and *D* components is not important. The components are typically arranged in an order that gives the statement of objective its clearest logical flow. Though the order of their occurrence is not important, it is critical that each of the four elements be included.

The following are two examples of complete instructional objectives. Note that the *A*, *B*, *C*, and *D* components have been indicated in italics and by letters in parentheses.

1. *Each pupil in the first grade (A)* will *cite the names of the days of the week and the months of the year (B) with no errors (D) orally as requested by the teacher (C).*
2. *Each fifth grader (A)* will *identify proper examples of countries, counties,*

and continents (B) by responding correctly on a true/false test (C) to at least 15 of 20 items (D).

Instructional Objectives and the Kinds of Learning

The intended kind of learning must be considered when instructional objectives are written. There are three of these categories or domains: (1) the cognitive domain, (2) the affective domain, and (3) the psychomotor domain.

The Cognitive Domain. The *cognitive domain* refers to learning of an intellectual nature. Requiring primary pupils to learn the days of the week and the months of the year is an example of a cognitive domain activity.

In the 1950s, Benjamin Bloom and several other scholars set out to develop a scheme to identify the subordinate categories of the cognitive domain. A classic educational document resulted from their work—*Taxonomy of Educational Objectives: Handbook I: The Cognitive Domain* (Bloom, 1956).

This document, generally referred to as *Bloom's Taxonomy*, describes six levels of cognitive thinking. These levels range from relatively simple mental tasks to extraordinarily difficult and sophisticated thought processes. These categories, as described in *Bloom's Taxonomy*, are presented in Table 4–1.

As the expected levels of learning grow more complex (that is, as they proceed along the taxonomy from knowledge toward evaluation), more time is required to prepare youngsters to demonstrate the more complex expected outcomes. It takes longer to teach evaluation-level thinking than application-level thinking. Similarly, application-level thinking requires more instructional development time than knowledge-level thinking.

These different time requirements make it essential for a teacher to think seriously about the cognitive-level issue as he or she develops instructional objectives. Some teachers find it useful to lay out this information in a *table of specifications* like the one depicted in Table 4–2.

The table of specifications allows for a quick visual inspection of the cognitive level of each instructional objective. The focus topics of the objectives that require high-level pupil thinking will need more instructional time. Teachers can use this information as they organize lessons focusing on these learning outcomes.

The Affective Domain. The *affective domain* refers to values and attitudes. Social studies teachers are often interested in raising pupils' interest in topics associated with history and the social sciences. One broad concern is encouraging elementary youngsters to commit to widely held American values such as respect for the individual and the tolerance of diversity.

Instructional objectives in the affective domain concern pupils' attitudes and values. Krathwohl and others (Krathwohl et al., 1956) developed a hierarchy of affective domain thinking. Raths, Harmin, and Simon (1966) did useful additional work on the nature of values. Collectively, the work of these specialist in values' education suggests that value formation is initiated when people open themselves to receiving and interpreting new ideas. Values become truly established only when people develop commitments so deeply that they are willing to act publicly on them.

**TABLE 4–1   The Levels of the Cognitive Domain and
Examples of the Objectives Written at Each Level.**

Knowledge

This lowest level of the taxonomy refers to the recall of specific elements of previously learned information. A pupil at this level will be asked to do little beyond naming or describing something. Note the sample objective.

> Each pupil will correctly name the five days of the week orally when asked to do so by the teacher.

Comprehension

This level implies an ability to simultaneously recall several pieces of previously learned information. The pupil should also be able to arrange the elements in a proper order or sequence. He or she should also be capable of changing the form of the original information. Note the sample objective.

> Each fifth grader will recognize the steps a bill goes through to become a law and what happens at each step by responding correctly to 12 out of 15 true/false questions related to these issues.

Application

Application-level thinking requires that information learned in one context be used in a different and unfamiliar setting. Pupils are called upon to "do something" with the content they have learned previously. Note the sample objective.

> Each pupil will use the scale on the globe as a basis for determining the correct point-to-point distances between at least four of five given pairs of cities.

Analysis

Analysis calls on pupils to describe the characteristics of something by comparing and contrasting its individual parts. Analysis requires them to look at the separate but related fragments of a whole and describe the general characteristics of the whole. Note the sample objective.

> Each sixth grader will describe the characteristics of an assigned nation in Asia. Assessment will take the form of an essay. Each essay must make specific references to this nation's (1) religious practices, (2) form of government, (3) industrial and agricultural development, and (4) people and their racial and ethnic make-up.

Synthesis

Synthesis-level thinking calls on pupils to look at isolated pieces of information and to create brand new information (at least information that is new to them) from these pieces. Often, creative thinking is involved in synthesis thinking. Note the sample objective.

> On an essay, each pupil will predict the probable climatic consequences for California if all the mountains in the state suddenly disappeared. Each response must include specific references to the (1) rainfall patterns, (2) wind patterns, and (3) temperature patterns.

Evaluation

Thinking at the level of evaluation requires pupils to make judgments in light of specified criteria. The "specified criteria" provision is important. Without these criteria, attempts to elicit evaluation-level thinking may produce little more than exchanges of unsupported personal opinion. Note the sample objective.

> Each sixth grader, on an oral examination, will critique one of the proposals for a new federal 'flat tax.' Specific references must be made to (1) fairness, (2) satisfactory ability to raise needed money, and (3) ease of administration. Furthermore, each pupil must explain clearly what he or she means by "fairness," "satisfactory ability to raise money," and "ease of administration."

**TABLE 4–2 A Table of Specifications for a
Cognitive Domain Instructional Objective.**

| | | Cognitive Level | | | | | |
		Knowledge	Comprehension	Application	Analysis	Synthesis	Evaluation
	1	X	X	X			
Instructional Objective Number	2	X					
	3	X	X	X	X		
	4	X					
	5	X	X				

The *X* farthest to the right indicates the cognitive level of each instructional objective. Note that the first objective is at the level of application, the second objective is at the level of knowledge, and so forth. The *X*'s to the left of the terminal *X* (the one farthest to the right) imply that pupils are expected to be able to function at all of these levels when they finish the unit of instruction. For the first objective, pupils need to be able to function at the knowledge, comprehension, and application levels; for the second objective, pupils need to be able to function at only the knowledge level; and so forth.

Think About This

1. Which of these objectives would probably require the most instructional time? Why do you think so?
2. Which of these objectives would probably require the least instructional time? Why do you think so?
3. Which objectives would probably require you to gather together the largest number of instructional resources? Why do you think so?
4. Would it be prudent to start instruction directed toward some of these objectives at the beginning of a new unit of instruction? Why do you think so?

A number of schemes have been developed to describe the different levels of the affective domain. These categories and a sample instructional objective for each one are provided in Table 4–3.

As in the cognitive domain, more time is required for pupils to achieve the high-level affective-domain objectives than is required for them to master the low-level objectives. Not every objective can be at the level of sharing because there simply is not enough time for youngsters to progress to this level. Think about the issue of establishing priorities among the affective-domain objectives as you look at Table 4–4 and answer the associated questions.

The whole area of effective learning poses dilemmas for social studies educators. Teachers do not want to intrude on personal and family values, yet they are reluctant to abandon all consideration of values and attitudes. Carried to its logical conclusion, this position could lead to an acceptance of the actions of a mass murderer on the grounds that this individual was simply following the dictates of his or her personal conscience. There *are* limits on the actions of individuals. The broad social norms that limit these actions need to be taught to pupils in the elementary school.

**TABLE 4–3 Affective Categories and
Examples of the Objectives Written at Each Level.**

Receiving

Behavior at the level of receiving is characterized by a pupil's willingness to be exposed to new content with an open mind. The intent is to remove any "blockages" that might be there because of misconceptions or general hostility to the content. Note the sample objective.

> Each pupil will demonstrate a willingness to consider the study of new topics by not raising serious objections to more than 5 percent of the topics introduced during any one grading period.

Approaching

The level of receiving is concerned with a pupil's general willingness to take in new content. Approaching goes a step further. It refers to his or her predisposition to look at the individual aspects of content, one at a time. There should be no rejection of information before it has been seriously considered on its merits. Approaching involves a willingness to suspend judgment until evidence has been carefully weighed. Note the sample objective.

> Each pupil will consider the individual issues on their merits and will not make statements to the teacher indicating that hasty prejudgments have been made on more than 5 percent of issues associated with any assigned topic of study.

Deciding

Deciding-level thinking is characterized by pupils' arriving at personal decisions that have been made without prejudgment and after consideration of the individual merits of issues. Note the sample objective.

> Each pupil will orally inform the teacher of choices he or she has made after prejudice-free consideration of issues on at least 90 percent of those occasions when such judgments are possible.

Sharing

At the sharing level, pupils demonstrate a willingness to share their personal decisions with others. Sharing is characterized by commitments that run so deeply that pupils do not hesitate to state them publicly. Note the sample objective.

> Each pupil will freely and without coercion make a public statement of his or her position regarding at least three social studies–related issues introduced during one grading period.

On the other hand, we need to be careful about taking hardline value positions on issues that remain open to much public debate. A teacher who tries to mandate "right" positions on issues such as mercy killing, abortion, and capital punishment is sure to draw fire from the partisans of competing views.

In addition to building youngsters' commitment to widely accepted social norms (for example, sanctions against murder and other crimes), it is legitimate for social studies teachers to help youngsters develop rational processes of thinking. Efforts to motivate pupils' interests in other school subjects can also be defended. Few patrons of the schools will object to nurturing the development of these kinds of attitudes and values in elementary children.

The Psychomotor Domain. The _psychomotor domain_ refers to learning that depends on fine-muscle coordination. Activities such as jumping a rope or hitting

**TABLE 4–4   A Table of Specifications for an
Affective Domain Instructional Objective.**

		Affective Domain Level			
		Receiving	**Approaching**	**Deciding**	**Sharing**
	1	X	X	X	
	2	X	X	X	X
Instructional Objective Number	3	X	X		
	4	X	X	X	
	5	X	X	X	X

The X farthest to the right indicates the affective level of each instructional objective. Note that the first objective is at the level of deciding, the second objective is at the level of sharing, and so forth. The X's to the left of the terminal X imply that pupils are expected to be able to function at all of these levels when they finish the unit of instruction. For the first objective, pupils need to be able to function at the receiving, approaching, and deciding levels; for the second objective, pupils need to be able to function at all the levels; and so forth.

Think About This

1. For a grade level you would like to teach, identify some affective instructional objectives. For each objective, identify the intended outcome level. Arrange the objectives in an affective table of specifications. What does this table tell us about your priorities?
2. What kinds of social studies content do you believe best lend themselves to affective instructional objectives? Why do you think so?
3. Can you envision some topics for which you would include no affective instructional objectives? How could you justify not including affective learning outcomes in your planning?

a baseball depend on this kind of coordination. Psychomotor requirements are also closely associated with the academic subjects in school.

For example, social studies activities that require young pupils to measure distances with rulers require more than just an intellectual understanding of the task. Pupils must have sufficient control of their fine muscles to properly hold the pencil and to make marks where they intend to make them.

A number of schemes have been developed to illustrate the various levels within the psychomotor domain. These levels and a sample instructional objective for each one are illustrated in Table 4–5 (Armstrong and Savage, 1983).

As with cognitive and affective instructional objectives, the higher the level of the psychomotor objective, the longer the time required to teach it. Free practice assumes a level of proficiency so high that pupils can perform tasks with no teacher supervision. This expertise requires much more learning time than the simple familiarization kind of learning associated with the awareness level of the psychomotor domain. Think about the issue of establishing priorities among the psychomotor domain objectives as you answer the questions associated with the table of specifications illustrated in Table 4–6.

TABLE 4–5   The Levels of the Psychomotor Domain and Examples of the Objectives Written at Each Level.

Awareness

At this level, a pupil must be able to correctly describe what he or she must do to perform a given psychomotor task properly. This psychomotor level is closely related to the cognitive-domain levels of knowledge and comprehension. Note the sample objective.

> Each pupil will tell the teacher, with no errors, how the tape measure will be held and the individual units of scale marked off when determining point-to-point distances of a map.

Individual Components

Psychomotor learning at this level requires pupils to demonstrate the individual parts of a complex activity one at a time. The pupil should be able to do each step called for with no errors. Note the sample objective.

> Each pupil will demonstrate, with no errors, his or her ability to do each of the following on request: (1) align the tape on the map properly, (2) point to the lines indicating centimeters and millimeters, (3) mark the number of centimeters and millimeters representing 100 kilometers on the work map, and (4) count the number of 100-kilometer intervals between two locations on the work map.

Integration

At this level, pupils should be able to perform an entire sequence of psychomotor activities under the guidance of the teacher. The teacher should be available to provide help, if needed. Note the sample objective.

> Each pupil will be able to measure the appropriate point-to-point distance (within five kilometers) of the actual distance between two given locations. This will be done using a work map with a centimeter and millimeter scale and a tape measure with a centimeter and millimeter scale.

Free Practice

At this level, pupils are expected to demonstrate a mastered sequence of psychomotor behavior in diverse settings, with no direct teacher assistance or supervision. Note the sample objective.

> Each pupil, on request, will be able to measure point-to-point distances on a work map with a centimeter and millimeter scale, using a tape measure with a centimeter and millimeter scale. In no case will the estimated distance be less than or greater than 100 kilometers of the actual point-to-point distance.

Interrelationships Among the Cognitive, Affective, and Psychomotor Domains of Learning

Though we sometimes isolate thinking about cognitive, affective, and psychomotor learning when planning for instruction, the three domains, in reality, are interconnected. Every instructional objective contains some element of learning from *each* of the three domains. Think about this as you read the following account of a playground episode.

> At 9:45, Joey, a second grader, was building his own snow fort on the playground. Robert, unseen by Joey, crept up quietly behind him. Robert quickly scooped up a handful of fresh snow. In a flash, he pushed it down Joey's back. Joey jumped

TABLE 4–6 A Table of Specifications for a Psychomotor Domain Instructional Objective.

		Psychomotor Domain Level		
	Awareness	Individual Components	Integration	Free Practice
1	X			
2	X	X	X	
Instructional Objective Number 3	X			
4	X	X	X	X
5	X	X	X	X

The *X* farthest to the right indicates the psychomotor level of each instructional objective. Note that the first objective is at the level of awareness, the second objective is at the level of integration, and so forth. The *X*'s to the left of the terminal *X* imply that pupils are expected to be able to function at all of these levels when they finish the unit of instruction. For the first objective, pupils need to be able to function at only the awareness level; for the second objective, pupils need to be able to function at the awareness, individual components, and integration levels; and so forth.

Think About This

1. Which of the instructional objectives listed in the table of specifications above would take the longest to teach? Why do you think so.?
2. Why might a teacher ever have an interest in teaching pupils only to the level of awareness.
3. For a grade level and topic that interest you, develop three or four instructional objectives in the psychomotor domain. Arrange them in a table of specifications. Why have you established the priorities reflected in your table?

up, whirled around, and let forth an anguished howl. He desperately tried to unzip his jacket and pull his shirt tail loose so that he could shake out the cold snow.

What did Joey learn? First, he already knew that snow is cold. He knew that cold things do not feel good against warm skin. He had two cognitive understandings that helped him react.

Second, the experience triggered an emotional, or affective, response. Joey was not happy about what happened. We know this from his cry of surprise and rage. We suspect, too, that if Joey were not angry at Robert, he might at least harbor some desire for revenge.

Third, Joey had a psychomotor reaction. The nerve endings flashed a message to his brain that something was amiss. From past experience, he used his hands to unzip his jacket and begin pulling his shirt tail out of his pants, and he initiated a shaking action to free the snow. These maneuvers required him to use his psychomotor abilities.

As with this playground incident, classroom learning represents an interplay of cognitive, affective, and psychomotor learning. What instructional planners mean when they refer to cognitive objectives, affective objectives, or psycho-motor objectives is that one or another of these domains tends to be more heav-ily represented than the others. The others, though, are always present to some degree.

For example, suppose pupils were asked to read some pages in a book about Thomas Jefferson. On the surface, this exercise would appear to be almost exclu-sively directed at cognitive learning, which probably does play the most impor-tant role. However, depending on how the teacher made the assignment, an individual youngster's reading proficiency, the quality of the prose, the lure of competing activities, and other variables, the assignment will also have an affec-tive dimension. Psychomotor skills (eye coordination, for example) are involved in this task as well.

Task Analysis

Task analysis begins once the instructional objectives have been identified. It requires the teacher to identify all the tasks a pupil must accomplish if he or she is to achieve the objective. There are two basic parts to task analysis: the iden-tification of the specific information pupils will need and the determination of the logical entry points for instruction.

Identifying the Specific Information Pupils Will Need

Task analysis begins with this question: Given this objective, what would a pupil need to know or be able to do to master it? A listing of all the needed prerequisites that come to the teacher's mind can follow.

Suppose a teacher had decided on the following objective:

Each pupil will draw a neighborhood map that will include the school grounds and the correct labeling of the four surrounding streets.

Looking at this objective, the teacher identifies the knowledge and skills pu-pils must have to accomplish the task. After considering this objective, a teacher might identify the following cognitive and psychomotor knowledge:

Needed Cognitive Knowledge
- The names of the four streets
- The locations of the four streets relative to each other
- The general characteristics of a map
- How to properly lay out directions on a map
- The simple ideas about scale on a map

Needed Psychomotor Knowledge
- The experience in successfully completing simple line drawings

This focus objective is not complex. Even so, pupils must become familiar with a great deal of information before they can be expected to successfully com-plete it.

Determining the Logical Entry Points for Instruction

Once the needed information has been identified, it is necessary to decide upon an appropriate sequence. Ordinarily, the sequence follows a pattern of easy to difficult. Next, some determination must be made regarding the content that pupils already know.

For example, in the case of the objective focusing on the neighborhood-map project, the teacher might know that earlier lessons had taught youngsters the basic mechanics of drawing a simple map. If the teacher were confident that these skills had been well learned, they would not need to be retaught. On the other hand, if this material had not been introduced earlier, or if pupils had failed to master the material when it was first presented, then these skills would need to be taught as part of the neighborhood-map exercise.

The issue of the appropriate place to begin instruction (the *entry point*) requires the teacher to do a good deal of thinking about what the members of the class can and cannot do. The idea is to find an entry point that takes advantage of past learning and begins new instruction at the place where content begins to deviate from what has been previously taught.

Motivation _____

Motivation is a highly important component of the instructional act. Today, some educators claim that pupils are harder to motivate than they were in the past. Because many pupils report that social studies is one of the subjects they enjoy least, the role of motivation is even more important for elementary teachers when they are dealing with this part of the school program.

Even experienced teachers are often not satisfied with their abilities to motivate the pupils in their classes. But, with attention to some of the basic principles, there are things that can be done to increase the number of days when motivational activities really do work to enhance youngsters' interest.

There are two basic types of motivation: intrinsic motivation and extrinsic motivation. Intrinsic motivation is the most powerful type, and it comes from within the individual.

Intrinsic Motivation

Intrinsic motivation is useful in social studies instruction. One of the most important of the intrinsic motivators is the sense of curiosity that we all possess. Youngsters come to school with a strong sense of inquisitiveness. They wonder why things happen, how things work, what makes things happen, and why people behave the way they do. Unfortunately, the schools have not done enough to capitalize on this sense.

What is the major focus of this curiosity? The answer is simple . . . *people.* Since people are the major subjects of study in the social studies, there is a built-in interest that clever teachers can turn to their advantage.

This concern for human beings has abundant possibilities for establishing ties to youngsters' own lives and interests. Effective social studies teachers bring a sense of wonder to the classroom as they encourage youngsters to ask questions about patterns of human life that may, at first, appear very commonplace. Part of the fascination of social studies lies in its ability to help youngsters understand the patterns and adaptations all people apply to the physical landscapes they call home. A teacher can use an example like the following to help youngsters' think about these patterns.

> I'm sure that many of you have noticed the new store being built down the road from the school. Why do you think someone chose that location to build a store?

A second intrinsic motivator is the *identification motive*. Individuals seek to be like others who seem to command desirable resources. These resources might include prestige, fame, money, and power. This identification tendency is evident in many young people who pattern their dress habits and styles after rock stars or movie stars. Elementary social studies teachers can use this element of motivation as they seek to emphasize the personal dimension of a subject. People in the social studies should be introduced not just as names to be learned but as fascinating human beings. As pupils identify "heroes" in their study of people, their interest in the subject tends to increase.

Youngsters have interests in different things. It is difficult to determine exactly how these personal enthusiasms develop. Teachers do not need to be concerned with how this development occurs, but they do need to learn what interests the members of their classes. These interests can be used to build support for the social studies program. Note how a teacher can use the following example to capitalize on some of the enthusiasms of youngsters in the class:

> I noticed when I asked about things that interest you that many of you mentioned that you were interested in "Star Wars" and space travel. What do you think it would be like to take off for an unknown place where you did not know anybody? Suppose you had no idea what the creatures or the place would be like. How would you feel about that? (Pupils respond.) Today we are going to learn about two men, Lewis and Clark, who set out into lands unknown and frightening.

In addition, the teacher can develop pupils' interests by making what is studied meaningful. ("These men were not sure about what they would find. They probably were a little scared. Have you ever felt that way? Would you have kept going as they did?") When an aspect of a subject connects to the personal experience of a pupil, it begins to take on meaning. He or she is then drawn to learn more about this subject. If the meaning is obscure or abstract, pupils may perceive the focus of the lesson as unimportant. Such lessons are often more endured than enjoyed.

Interest can also be stimulated by adding novelty or vividness to an activity. Something original or different captures our attention for at least a short time. This means that every lesson and every day should not be like all the others. Some teachers have capitalized on the novelty principle by dressing up in period costumes, starting the lesson with a unusual problem, or using a cartoon or a picture that contains some surprising elements. The vividness of the learning experience can be enhanced by involving the pupils at the beginning of the lesson. Notice how a teacher can use the following to motivate pupils by using the unusual or novel.

TABLE 4–7   Motivating Pupils in the Classroom.

Motivating pupils challenges experienced as well as beginning teachers. Teachers have an interest in this issue because motivated pupils apply more of the intellectual resources to academic tasks than do nonmotivated pupils. Motivated pupils also retain more of what they have learned. Finally, motivated youngsters are less likely than unmotivated youngsters to be discipline problems.

Think About This

Think about an elementary grade level you would like to teach. Identify a social studies topic you would introduce to the members of your class. Consider what you might do to motivate youngsters as you respond to these questions.
1. What pupil interests might be used to increase enthusiasm for this topic?
2. What specific things might you do to appeal to pupils' curiosity and sense of wonder?
3. How might you take advantage of the principle of achievement motivation?
4. What kinds of behavior would you reinforce as pupils studied the new material? What kinds of reinforcers would you use?

In this picture we see the ruins of some buildings that were constructed by a group of people known as the Mayans. They were an advanced group of people with a calendar and a number system. They built many impressive buildings. However, they deserted their cities. They walked away leaving unfinished buildings with tools scattered around and dishes on the table. It is almost as if they all decided to take a hike in the jungle and never returned. What do you think could explain why they deserted their cities?

Success is another powerful motivator. Students are attracted to activities in which they have experienced previous successes. The need for achievement is a strong force. What this implies for the teacher is that social studies lessons should offer an opportunity for success to all youngsters. For example, success should not depend on the mastery of a specific skill, such as reading for comprehension. Though this kind of reading is important, techniques for presenting content information should be sufficiently diverse so that they do not penalize youngsters with particular learning deficiencies.

Everyone has certain needs and desires. These range from basic needs—such as attaining food, clothing, and shelter—to needs for achievement, attention, and affection. The teacher might first ask if there is any useful purpose for the lesson. How does it relate to the needs of the pupils? One consideration that can be especially useful to social studies teachers is that individuals are interested in understanding the world around them. This is really what the social studies ought to be about.

Extrinsic Motivation

Extrinsic motivation also offers many opportunities for the teacher. Although not as powerful or as enduring as intrinsic motivation, it is related to the environment and therefore under more teacher control. One principle of extrinsic motivation is that the clearer the purpose is, the better the motivation will be. Good lesson objectives should be established. Individuals want to know what they are to do, why they are to do it, and how they will know if they have succeeded.

Another aspect of extrinsic motivation relates to establishing a frame of reference or a learning set for the material that follows. Individuals tend to see or hear what they think they are going to see or hear. Some teachers use this principle when they refer to the key points that will be covered or to the critical questions that will be answered; others use it to give pupils a study guide or a partial outline to their inquiry. Notice how a teacher can use the following to establish a learning set.

> In our last unit we learned how the colonists were influenced by their background in establishing their new colony. Today we are going to study another colony. Let's see if we can see ways in which their background influenced their way of life in the new colony.

Reinforcement is another extremely useful tool of the teacher. A basic principle of reinforcement is that activities that are followed by desirable consequences are likely to be repeated. If engaging in social studies lessons helps the student achieve desirable consequences, it is likely that the student will engage in additional social studies activities. The teacher needs to ask, What do I want pupils to do during the lesson, and what will I do for reinforcement?

Attention and praise are often good reinforcers. If these are unsuccessful, the teacher might need to consider more concrete reinforcers, such as tokens that can be exchanged for things the pupils desire. Activity reinforcers are another option that the teacher might consider. Activities that are of high interest to pupils can be used to motivate them in low-interest areas. For example, a child who enjoys reading can be reinforced to engage in a low-interest activity by allowing him or her to engage in reading after the other activity has been successfully completed. A teacher can use the following as an activity reinforcer to promote motivation for additional social studies lessons.

> I know that the class enjoys sharing riddles with each other. Today you did such a good job during social studies that I'm going to give the class five minutes to share riddles. Who would like to be first?

In summary, teachers who succeed in motivating their pupils adhere to certain basic principles. Knowledge of the characteristics of pupils as well as the motivational opportunities that are inherent in the social studies can go far toward successful motivation. Giving youngsters a reason for learning and attempting to relate what is studied to their interests are two important considerations.

The learning climate surrounding the social studies needs to be a pleasant, achievement-oriented one. Providing for success, and making sure that pupils are reinforced frequently will help the teacher capture the attention of the students and get them started on the right track.

The Presentation of the Material

Once pupils are motivated and their attention is focused on a task, the material needs to presented in a manner that will promote learning and retention. This is the heart of good instruction. The manner in which the information is

First, You Have to Get Their Attention.
(*Source:* Martha Campbell.)

presented relates directly to what is learned, retained, and transferred to new situations. In this section, several principles that can help the teacher to make sound decisions about how to present information will be outlined.

Teachers' Verbal Behavior

Despite the efforts to minimize the amount of teacher talk in the classroom, teaching is still largely a verbal activity. Teacher talk plays a central role in presenting new information; clear verbal communication is an essential ingredient of good teaching.

Teachers' verbal communication must be logically organized. Points to be covered in the lesson should be systematically connected, and the point-to-point transitions must be smooth. Young children often have difficulty organizing ideas and distinguishing between relevant and irrelevant details. Therefore, the teacher needs to eliminate unnecessary digressions when speaking to youngsters about content.

Clarity is an important teacher-presentation skill.
(*Source:* © Juliann Barbato.)

Logically organized teacher talk is only the first step. Youngsters may still not grasp the important ideas, so these ideas must be emphasized. If teachers do not do this, youngsters may focus on minor, unimportant details.

One way the teacher can help students is by using marker expressions. *Marker expressions* highlight important points, the things that the teacher wants the pupils to remember. Teachers often use marker expressions such as "Now remember this" or "This is important" to alert the youngsters. In written work, underlining or using different colors of print can highlight the important points.

TABLE 4–8 Providing Clear Directions.

The following directions were recently given by a sixth-grade teacher at the beginning of a social studies lesson:

> You remember that inferencing session we did yesterday? You know the one where we came up with lots of ideas? Well, get out your outline maps again, just like we did yesterday. Now, to begin with, we're not going to be doing anything like we did yesterday. Today, I want you to ask some entirely different kinds of questions. Joe, do you want to go first?

Think About This

1. What is it exactly that these pupils are supposed to do?
2. In what specific ways is today's lesson to be different from that the pupils' experienced yesterday?
3. What is your overall assessment of this teacher's clarity?
4. How could you repair these directions to assure better pupil understanding?

Planned redundancy, or *repetition,* is another way to help youngsters grasp the important ideas. Mentioning an item once will not insure that pupils will remember it. At various points in the lesson important ideas must be reviewed. Repeating an item several times in succession is not an effective approach to repetition; it is better to repeat an item three or more times at spaced intervals. Slightly altering the language or providing new examples can help youngsters retain the key ideas.

Vague and ambiguous terms must be eliminated from teachers' speech because when they are used, massive pupil confusion and frustration can result. Unclear references to "a bunch of these" or "about this much" often suggest a lack of teacher preparation. These expressions fail to convey precise meanings. They may also undermine the credibility of the teacher as a person who knows or cares about the content.

Even experienced teachers sometimes fall into the trap of assuming that pupils understand concepts that have not been defined as part of the instructional plan. To avoid misunderstandings, teachers need to take time to find out whether their assumptions about what youngsters know are accurate. This might be done by asking questions at key points during the lessons, summarizing at the appropriate points, or asking youngsters to define the terms in their own words. These practices help the teacher to monitor understanding and serve to keep pupils alert and accountable.

The Need for Variety

When presenting new information, the teacher should keep in mind that young children have limited attention spans. To maintain attention, it is useful to alter the presentation modes. Pupils should not be expected to listen for extended periods of time or to sit quietly reading lengthy passages of text. Learning aids such as pictures, maps, charts, and overhead transparencies can introduce variety into a lesson.

Rotating the input of information with the output of information also introduces variety. After youngsters have been introduced to material, they should be given opportunities to do something with it. Activities based on new content can keep a class highly involved with a lesson.

Teacher demonstrations and modeling can also add variety. *Modeling* is an effective teaching technique. It is especially important in new situations, or where the expected performance of the pupil is unclear; for example, at the beginning of the school year or when introducing an unfamiliar unit of work.

Teaching Problem-Solving Skills

Pupils do not automatically know how to approach and solve problems. One way to teach them to do this is to have the teacher think out loud as a problem or topic is approached. The whole idea is to make the teacher's thought processes "visible". The teacher can describe what he or she is doing or thinking as a solution to a problem is attempted.

Many of us have had the frustrating experience of trying to learn a new job. Often the person doing the training will say, "Just watch what I do." However, if the demonstration is given without any verbal explanation of what is being done, an attempt to duplicate the task often results in failure. A demonstration accompanied by a verbal explanation is more effective. Consider this example:

> Today we are going to be thinking about why people move from one community to another. I have here a picture of something called a "ghost town." Who can tell me what a ghost town it? (Students respond with definitions.) Once people lived in this place but now they are all gone. I'm interested in finding out why they left. The first thing I might want to do is to look for any clues in the picture. Are there any signs of fire or accidents that might help explain this situation? Do any of you see clues that might be helpful? (Class responds.) Next, I would want to gather some information. Where is this place? When did the people leave? What did they do when they lived here? What other events might be related to the life of this place?

In this example the teacher is thinking out loud and helping the pupils see how to approach a problem. Teachers can approach curiosity in the same way. They can question the ordinary by asking questions about common occurrences: Why did that store close? What would happen if everyone stopped littering? How did those vegetables get to our supermarket?

Helping youngsters relate new information to what they already know facilitates learning. Familiar contexts are a real aid to understanding and success. When youngsters succeed, they derive important personal satisfaction from the learning process.

Follow-up Activities _____

People need opportunities to use the new material that they have learned. This is where follow-up activities come in. These activities serve two basic purposes. First, they allow the teacher to determine whether pupils have mastered the material. Second, they ensure that the learning will have some degree of permanence.

The type of follow-up activity designed depends on the objective of the lesson. One type of activity could be the practice of a new skill, another the application of a concept or generalization, and a third the extension of the learning by looking for new meanings or applications. Note how a teacher can use the following example to tie the follow-up activity to the lesson objective.

> Our objective for today was to learn some map symbols. All of you have just been given a map that contains some map symbols. Now we are going to practice our skill. At the bottom of the map you see a list of different things. Find the symbol that represents that thing and place the number and letter of the map location of that thing next to the name. Now let's try one together.

In this example, the teacher provides practice on a new skill, which is an important function of follow-up activities. A certain amount of practice helps make new learning permanent. For practice to be effective, it must have real meaning. The teacher must build a bridge between what the pupils are going to do and what their needs or experiences are.

There are two types of practice that can be used, guided practice and independent practice. *Guided practice* is a short, intense practice period that is closely

This class is concluding a study of different cultures by preparing foods from other countries.
(*Source:* © Juliann Barbato.)

monitored by the teacher. *Independent practice* is practice that a pupil undertakes with a minimum of guidance. A good example of independent practice is homework (see Table 4–9). Guided practice should precede independent practice.

Several principles should be considered when planning and implementing a guided-practice session. First, the teacher should check to make sure that all pupils know how to do the required task. This means that the teacher needs to monitor performance and provide corrective feedback if the task is being performed incorrectly. Pupils should not independently practice something until they have been provided with this feedback. Continued practice of incorrect responses or behavior will interfere with learning, not enhance it. A common culprit here is homework. The recent emphasis on providing more homework sometimes has resulted in pupils being asked to do school tasks at home when they have not yet attained an adequate proficiency level. In this situation, the homework is a hindrance to the learning process.

A second consideration in planning for practice should be to keep the practice sessions relatively short and intense. Spacing the practice over short practice sessions is far more efficient than using one long session. The shorter sessions keep the pupils focused on the task, and spacing the practice time over several periods provides for some reinforcement of the learning.

Another purpose that can be met during the follow-up activity period is for pupils to apply the new learning. This can be done in several ways. In some

TABLE 4–9 Should Homework Be Banned?

Recently, a parent raised the following issues with an elementary school teacher.

> The "idea" of homework sounds great. But, let's see how it *really* works. The youngster coming from a well-to-do family takes the assignment home and has sets of encyclopedias and other aids available. If he or she has college-educated parents, then they, too, can be called on to help.
>
> But what about the youngster from a poorer family. This boy or girl isn't likely to find shelves of resource books in their homes. It is a hassle for parents to take these children to libraries. Parents, themselves, may not have sufficient personal knowledge to help their youngsters.
>
> The result of all this is that homework gives an unfair advantage to certain pupils. This is not right. All assignments should be done during the school day when the teacher is available and when youngsters have access to library resources.

Think About This

1. What evidence supports the claims of this parent?
2. What evidence refutes the claims of this parent?
3. How would you personally respond to this parent?
4. Should elementary schools have specific policies governing the kind of and extent of homework that can be assigned? If so, what should these policies be?
5. What kinds of homework assignments might be made to overcome some of the problems cited by this parent?

instances they may be asked to find some new examples of the material that has been learned. For example, youngsters may be asked to identify some examples in their community or in their experience. In another case they might be asked to apply the new learning by drawing or constructing an example of what has been learned. Such an application activity might extend over more than one day, and would probably occur near the end of a learning sequence. Using the new learning in application contexts facilitates the transfer of learning, an important educational aim. In the following example, the teacher is seeking to help youngsters transfer information learned in a previous unit to a new situation.

> We have just learned why the First Amendment to the Constitution was written. Now I'm going to give you a situation that was recently described in the newspaper. I want you to state whether you think this person's First Amendment rights were violated.

Another type of activity that might be included in the follow-up activity section is one that seeks to help pupils extend their learning. Since individual pupils have different rates of learning, some will master an idea or concept faster than others. The teacher needs to provide opportunities for these faster pupils to enrich their learning by going into more depth or by looking for additional applications. If this sort of enrichment activity is not provided, brighter youngsters may become bored, and boredom can breed discipline problems. Enrichment can provide divergent and creative thinking opportunities for these brighter pupils. Notice how this is done in the following example.

> We have learned how the climate of a place is influenced by the nearness of bodies of water and the direction of wind currents. What do you think would happen to our climate if the wind currents were to change and blow in the opposite direction?

In summary, the follow-up activities component of the instructional act is important. It can be used to provide practice for new learning, to provide an opportunity for pupils to practice new learning, and to extend the learning into new areas. These activities involve pupils and provide opportunities for them to receive feedback about their progress.

Closure

The term *closure* is applied to those activities that bring a lesson to its conclusion. Closure is important because the end of a lesson is a strategic point for helping pupils to retain the new content.

During closure, the teacher reviews and highlights the important material covered in the lesson. Closure also gives the teacher an opportunity to assess whether the class has accomplished the established objectives. This information can be used to determine whether the lesson needs to be retaught in some altered form. If the class has been successful in mastering the objectives, then the teacher can reinforce the lesson by helping pupils understand how their new knowledge will help them in the next lesson.

Activities related to closure should be kept brief and tightly focused on the content that has been taught. The teacher may re-emphasize the objectives and the main points pupils should remember, or the pupils may make a final demonstration of a new task or skill. It is particularly desirable to involve pupils directly in this review process.

Key Ideas in Summary

Teaching is complex. Successful teaching requires attention to a number of important components of the instructional act. When teachers make wise decisions regarding each of these components, chances that pupils will learn are enhanced. The information introduced in this chapter includes the following:

1. Good instruction flows toward some purposes. These purposes are reflected in a teacher's instructional objectives. Objectives built around the A, B, C, D framework can be used for learning in the cognitive domain, affective domain, and psychomotor domain.
2. The table of specifications is a tool that can be used to help teachers determine how much instructional time will be required to prepare pupils to master each instructional objective. The more complex and sophisticated instructional objectives require more teaching time than do the less complex and simpler instructional objectives.
3. The task analysis procedure is used to clearly identify specific requisite knowledge and skills youngsters must master en route to mastering content referenced in the instructional objectives. Task analysis can help teachers to identity the appropriate places to begin a sequence of instruction on a new topic with a group of pupils.

4. A most important component of the teaching act is motivating pupils. Both intrinsic and extrinsic motivation can be used. Intrinsic motivation focuses on factors that are internal to the pupil. Extrinsic motivation focuses on factors that are external to the pupil. There are many opportunities for intrinsic motivation in the social studies. This is true because the main focus of the social studies is people, a topic in which many youngsters have a built-in interest.

5. The principle of reinforcement or reinforcing the pupils when they do what is expected is a powerful means of implementing extrinsic motivation and enhancing pupil willingness to be involved in later social studies lessons. In short, the social studies should be a successful experience.

6. There are several principles to be followed when presenting material to an elementary social studies classroom. One important aspect of a classroom presentation is the clarity of the communication. The presentation should be logically organized and at the appropriate vocabulary and concept understanding level of the pupils. Furthermore, it should be free from vague and ambiguous use of terms and phrases.

7. The key ideas in a presentation need to be highlighted. This can be done using marker expressions to cue pupils to pay close attention to critical elements of content. These key ideas should be repeated at several points during the lesson to enhance retention.

8. Modeling is an effective teaching tool. It is especially important when presenting unfamiliar content or procedures. The teacher needs to make sure that the pupils are confronted with the correct model so that they will observe what is expected of them. The teacher needs to provide a model of enthusiasm and curiosity as well as a model of problem solving.

9. The follow-up activities included in a lesson should relate back to the objectives of the lesson. They should not be just an exercise in busy-work. Follow-up activities provide an opportunity for the pupils to practice what they have learned. The two basic types of practice are guided practice and independent practice. A pupil should not be assigned independent practice until after feedback has been given so that he or she will not practice inappropriate responses.

10. The final element of the instructional act is that of closure. During closure, the key ideas and important parts of the lesson should be summarized. Closure helps pupils review and retain new content.

Questions _____

Review Questions

1. What are the three major domains of learning?
2. How does the *A, B, C, D* approach to writing instructional objectives work?
3. What is the purpose of a table of specifications?
4. How do intrinsic motivation and extrinsic motivation differ?
5. What is the use of task analysis?
6. How are marker expressions used in the presentation of material?

7. Why should guided practice precede independent practice?
8. What should be included in the closure portion of a lesson?

Thought Questions

1. A table of specifications can help a teacher identify those objectives that will require a large quantity of instructional time and those that will require a small quantity of instructional time. What should a teacher consider in selecting objectives that will require a large quantity of scarce instructional time?
2. Homework is often cited as an important component in the learning process. What should be considered when assigning homework, and under what conditions might homework interfere with learning?
3. Why is it important that teachers understand the use of modeling as a teaching tool? How might unplanned teacher modeling have an unintended negative influence on pupil learning?
4. How might a teacher go about avoiding vague terminology when introducing new content? Specifically, how could a teacher plan in advance to avoid use of these unclear words and terms?
5. Do you agree that pupils are less motivated to learn school tasks than in the past? If so, what could explain this problem, and how would you respond to it?

Extending Understanding and Skill _____

Activities

1. Choose a grade level that interests you. Identify the social studies content normally taught at that grade level. Write at least three objectives that could be used by a teacher.
2. Do a task analysis for one objective that you wrote. Be as specific as possible in spelling out what a pupil would have to know to achieve the objective.
3. Motivation should not occur only at the beginning of a lesson but should be included at various points. Develop a motivational plan for a lesson. State how motivation might be used at the beginning of the lesson, during the lesson, and at the conclusion of the lesson.
4. Teach a group of peers a social studies lesson of a few minutes' duration. Have them critique you on logical organization, clarity of presentation, use of marker expressions, use of vague terms, and use of modeling.
5. Interview a group of pupils at the grade level you would like to teach. Conduct an interest survey to discover the types of things that might be used to motivate them.

Supplemental Reading

EGGEN, PAUL D., KAUCHAK, DONALD P., and HARDER, ROBERT J. _Strategies for Teachers: Information Processing Models in the Classroom._ Englewood Cliffs, NJ: Prentice-Hall, Inc., 1979.

GOOD, THOMAS L., and BROPHY, JERE E. _Looking in Classrooms,_ 3d ed. New York: Harper & Row, 1984.

LEMLECH, JOHANNA KASIN. _Curriculum and Instructional Methods for the Elementary School._ New York: Macmillan Publishing Co., 1984.

SEILER, WILLIAM J., SCHUELKE, L. DAVID, and LIEB-BRILHART, BARBARA. *Communication for the Contemporary Classroom.* New York: Macmillan Publishing Co., 1984.

References ——

ARMSTRONG, DAVID G., and SAVAGE, TOM V. *Secondary Education: An Introduction.* New York: Macmillan Publishing Co., Inc., 1983.

BIEHLER, ROBERT F. *Psychology Applied to Teaching,* 2d ed. Boston: Houghton Mifflin Co., 1974.

BLOOM, BENJAMIN S. (ed.), et al. *Taxonomy of Educational Objectives: Handbook I: The Cognitive Domain.* New York: David McKay Co., Inc., 1956.

DICK, WALTER, and CAREY, LOU. *The Systematic Design Instruction.* Glenview, IL: Scott Foresman & Co., 1978.

GALLAGHER, JACK R. *Changing Behavior: How and Why.* Morristown, NJ: Silver Burdett Co., 1980.

HUNTER, MADELINE. *Improved Instruction.* El Segundo, CA: T.I.P. Publications, 1976.

KRATHWOHL, DAVID, BLOOM, BENJAMIN S., and MASIA, BERTRAM B. *Taxonomy of Educational Objectives: Handbook II: Affective Domain.* New York: David McKay Co., Inc., 1956.

LAND, MICHAEL, and SMITH, LYLE. "Effect of a Teacher Clarity Variable on Student Achievement," *Journal of Educational Research,* Vol. 72 (1979), pp. 196–198.

RATHS, LOUIS, HARMIN, MERRILL, and SIMON, SIDNEY. *Values and Teaching.* Columbus, OH: Charles E. Merrill Publishing Co., 1966.

SMITH, L. P., and COTTEN, M. L. "Effect of Lesson Vagueness and Discontinuity on Student Achievement and Attitudes," *Journal of Educational Psychology,* Vol. 72 (1980), pp. 670–675.

Chapter 5

Planning for Instruction

(*Source:* © Juliann Barbato.)

This chapter provides information to help the reader:

1. Identify the elements that are to be included in planning a unit.
2. Develop a format to be used in writing a unit.
3. State the criteria to be used when evaluating a unit.
4. List the purposes of daily lesson planning.
5. Identify the elements to be considered when constructing daily lesson plans.
6. State how the special needs of pupils may be accommodated in daily lessons.

Overview

An observer watching a skilled professional teacher working with a group of youngsters might be forgiven for commenting: "Teaching is easy. Everything flows so smoothly." Instruction delivered by a competent, unflappable teacher may *appear* to indicate a line of work that poses few real challenges to its practitioners. This appearance fails to mirror the reality.

Teachers, similar to good professionals in any field, spend a great deal of time planning and preparing for their work day. When an observer sees a smoothly functioning classroom, this performance is almost always a result of careful teacher planning.

The development of competent planning skills is a high-priority task for prospective teachers. Success in the classroom depends to a large degree on a teacher's expertise in this important area of professional practice.

Teaching is a decision-making process. During a given day a teacher will make a great number of decisions, which vary from the simple to the very complex. At different times, the teacher may be called upon to make a range of decisions, from whether to allow the use of a pencil sharpener to more serious issues such as how to respond to a discipline problem or whether to reteach a lesson.

Many of these decisions cannot be anticipated or predicted. No amount of planning will eliminate the unexpected events that develop during a typical day. The secret to handling these events is making certain that time is available to respond to them. This time is more available to teachers who take care to plan for those parts of the instructional day that *do* follow more or less predictable patterns.

Planning for instruction assumes that learning is enhanced when certain principles are followed. Good planning considers the nature of pupils in the class, the basic principles of learning psychology, and the particular learning objectives being pursued. Though planning attempts to meet the special needs of every pupil, two categories of youngsters merit special attention.

The Special Needs of Handicapped and Gifted and Talented Pupils

During planning, the needs of exceptional learners must be considered. Public Law 94-142, "The Education for All Handicapped Children Act," requires that youngsters with handicapping conditions be placed in regular classrooms to

108

the greatest extent possible. The term used to describe such placement is *mainstreaming*.

Mainstreamed children add an important dimension to the elementary social studies program. Their presence in the classroom provides an opportunity for teachers to help all pupils in the class to be accepting of and sensitive to the needs of people who may differ from themselves.

Not all special pupils have handicapping conditions. Gifted and talented youngsters, for example, also constitute a special population of pupils. Their needs, too, deserve attention when instruction is being planned.

Handicapped Pupils

Numerous physical handicaps may interfere with pupils' abilities to succeed in elementary social studies classes. These impediments include hearing impairment, sight impairment, physical handicaps, and certain emotional disorders. Obviously, the nature of the handicapping conditions present in a given classroom must be considered by teachers when they plan lessons.

For example, a film might be a very poor choice as a means of transmitting information to a hearing-impaired youngster. If the film will work well for the majority of pupils, the least the teacher can do is to provide hearing-impaired pupils with either an outline of content presented in the film or a general summary of the information introduced.

Sight-impaired pupils need to be seated near the front so that they can clearly see the chalkboard. Those with severe visual handicaps may need material in Braille, or they may require cassette recordings containing information that is visually presented to the other pupils. Pupils with certain other handicaps must be provided with open spaces for crutches or wheelchairs. Arrangements have to be made to allow such pupils more time to move from one place to another.

Other special requirements face teachers as they work with handicapped youngsters. Good responses to special needs require teachers to stretch their personal creative talents as they try to organize instruction that maximizes the learning potentials of mainstreamed youngsters. Teachers who plan well find that most mainstreamed youngsters fit well into the classroom.

Gifted and Talented Pupils

Gifted and talented youngsters also present special challenges to the classroom teacher. They often quickly complete their work. As a result, they may get bored and seek excitement in undesirable ways. A common mistake of many teachers is to assign more work to gifted and talented pupils who finish early. It does not take bright pupils long to spot this pattern. When they do, some try to hide their talents by working much more slowly than necessary, so as to avoid the extra work. This is not a desirable behavior pattern because it encourages these youngsters to underuse their abilities.

It makes more sense for the teacher to provide enrichment activities that challenge these pupils to go deeper, or that encourage them to apply the concepts they have learned in new and interesting ways. Giftedness needs to be utilized, not penalized. Teachers who design good enrichment activities find that gifted and talented youngsters get very excited about what they are doing and take a great deal away from their experiences in school.

Planning seeks to meet other individual differences as well. A subsequent section of this chapter and Table 5–1 touch on this issue. A more detailed treatment of special approaches for individualizing instruction in the elementary social studies classroom is found in Chapter 7.

All planning divides into two broad categories. These are long-range planning and daily lesson planning.

TABLE 5–1 Does Planning Stifle Creativity?

A beginning teacher was overheard making the following comments to some colleagues in the faculty lounge of an elementary school.

> I think we plan too much. It really can get in the way of good teaching. I mean, my youngsters sometimes will get off on a really exciting topic or issue that I haven't planned for at all. I feel it's my obligation to take advantage of these kinds of opportunities.
>
> Lesson plans, it seems to me, can turn us all into just so many robots who mechanically plod on through what the lesson plan says, regardless of how our kids are reacting. I think we would all do a better job if we simply "went with the flow" of the class and made the most of opportunities as they develop.

Think About This

1. What logic does this teacher use to defend the position taken in the comments above?
2. Suppose you were a teacher who had listened to these observations. What would your reactions be?
3. How do you think a district supervisor in social studies or a principal might react to these comments?
4. What potential legal dangers might await a teacher who refused to plan?

Long-Range Planning _____

A brief overview of social studies programs quickly reveals that a great deal of content can be included. One of the common frustrations of teachers is that they do not have enough time in the year to cover all the content. In times when teacher accountability is a major issue, it is imperative that the limited time available be used as effectively as possible.

The long-range *planning* process begins with a careful study of any content that has been mandated by the state or local authorities. This content must be assigned a high priority. Not every teacher will agree that these specific elements of content are important; however, the decision to emphasize this material has been made elsewhere. It has the force of lawful authority behind it. Such content must be included.

Many other content elements are left to the discretion of the individual classroom teacher. These can be selected to reflect a teachers' own background and priorities.

Planning should begin with the "must-be-included" kinds of content. This will assure that these legally mandated elements will be included in the teacher's program and that the teacher will not be open to a charge of failing to teach what has been prescribed.

Several questions are useful as teachers initiate the planning process. The answers help focus this important professional activity.

Preplanning Questions

1. What is the content normally taught at this grade level? Teachers are usually expected to teach the subject matter that is prescribed for their particular grade level by the state or local school district. The school district does have the right to require that certain topics be taught. Academic freedom does not allow teachers to teach just any content that might happen to interest them at a particular time. However, the guidelines regarding what *must* be taught are often broad. Teachers typically enjoy a good deal of latitude in deciding what specific elements of the topic will be included in their instructional programs.

As the teacher reviews the subject matter to be included for the year, attention might be directed to identifying the content elements of potential interest to pupils, the natural subdivisions in the content, and the materials that might be helpful when teaching the content. These activities represent a responsible beginning to the planning process.

2. What are the important social studies goals that can be accomplished within the context of the subject? The next step of the planning process involves a review of the major goals and purposes of the social studies. This step is often overlooked as teachers attempt to merely cover the content. This is an important step because it helps the teacher make decisions regarding what will be emphasized and what may be omitted during the course of study. The major elements discussed in Chapter 1 need to be reviewed. What citizenship elements can be included? Which social science understandings relate to this topic? How can the topic be used to develop the personal goals? What knowledge, skills, and values need to be included in each of the three purposes?

An early consideration of these issues will make sure that the broad categories of social studies goals and purposes are included. When this is not done, the teacher may fall into the trap of teaching facts without establishing their relevance or meaning for pupils. Some teachers find it useful to make a large chart with the major goals that should be included jotted down opposite each major component of the year's study. This can be modified as the year unfolds, if the need arises. Such a chart can provide a much-needed sense of direction during the early phases of planning.

3. What are the major subdivisions of the topic? This step involves breaking the year-long study into major units of instruction. At times, the subdivisions may appear to be natural or obvious. Teachers often simply follow the subdivisions of the textbook, even though this might not be the most appropriate way of dividing the content for teaching purposes. The text is merely one of several resources that might be used in teaching. It need not prescribe the entire curriculum. The teacher might decide upon a more motivating or efficient way of dividing the content into units. Once this task has been accomplished, it is time to begin the actual process of unit development.

The Basic Elements of the Unit

Units represent a practical approach to organizing instruction that focuses on large blocks of content. They allow teachers opportunities to exercise their own

TABLE 5–2 Mandated Content and Preplanning Questions.

Identify an elementary grade level. Gather information from people such as elementary social studies supervisors, classroom teachers, and your instructor as you respond to the following questions. You might also wish to consult your library.

Think About This

1. Are there some state requirements regarding what must be taught at this grade level? If so, what are they?
2. Are there additional local requirements? If so, what are they?
3. What major topic(s) is (are) ordinarily taught at this grade level?
4. How is (are) this topic (these topics) subdivided?
4. What important social studies goals might be accomplished at this grade level?

creativity. They assuage teachers' anxiety by providing a clear sense of direction for the entire instructional process.

Kaltsounis, a prominent elementary social studies specialist, gives an excellent overview of the advantages of unit planning. The unit, he states, ". . . localizes the teaching-learning situation, puts the teacher in control of the learning process, and makes schooling relevant to the children's experiences" (Kaltsounis, 1979; p. 146). Well-planned units are capable of accomplishing all of these things.

Individual units are never "done." Superior teachers always change units that they have prepared previously to make them better, using experiences with pupils as a basis for making these changes. They recognize, too, that pupils change from year to year. Something that appealed to the interests of last year's class may only draw yawns from this year's youngsters.

Unit development is a systematic process. Nine general steps are involved.

1. Identifying the basic theme of the units. This step may be quite simple. The content that is to be taught might suggest an appropriate theme for the unit. However, the outstanding teacher will consider a theme that youngsters will find appealing. What youngsters find interesting will vary from group to group and from age level to age level.

For example, a fifth-grade teacher might have a unit dealing with the discovery and exploration of the new world. An unimaginative teacher might be satisfied with a theme title such as Explorers of the New World. This lacks emotive power. A better choice for a group of adventure-loving fifth graders might be Facing the Unknown. This title not only has the potential to attract youngsters' interest, but it also suggests some general approaches that might be taken to introduce the elements of content. A good theme title *is* important. It can establish a frame of reference for both teachers and pupils that can make learning experiences associated with the unit much more meaningful.

2. Identifying the basic generalization, concepts, knowledge, skills, and values to be developed. The theme of the unit and the content to be covered will suggest the general nature of the generalizations that need to be developed. Ordinarily, one or two are sufficient to guide the development of a unit.

Selecting these generalizations demands some knowledge of the basic social sciences and the generalizations that have been developed to explain human behavior. This selection is very important. Generalizations summarize the broad learnings the teacher hopes pupils will have by the end of the unit. The focus on these broad generalizations provides a context for the study of related concepts and facts.

Suppose a teacher has decided to use this generalization as one of those that would provide a unit focus:

> As a country becomes more industrialized, more and more people live in large cities than in small towns and on farms.

This generalization suggests a need to familiarize pupils with concepts such as "country," "industrialization," "city," "town," and "farm." Examples, or facts, need to be gathered about several highly industrialized and several less-industrialized countries. These facts will illustrate the truth of the generalization.

When selecting generalizations, it is necessary to consider carefully exactly which knowledge, skills, and values are to be emphasized in the unit. Most generalizations are derived from the social sciences, but the teacher should also consider how content elements related to citizenship education and personal education might be reflected in the selected generalization(s).

3. *Performing a task analysis.* The next step is simply that of asking, What will the students need to know or be able to do in order to formulate these generalizations and values and to perform these skills? At this point, the teacher might want to prepare a list of all the knowledge, skills, and values that pupils will need to achieve success. Once these have been identified, the question of sequence must be addressed. The teacher must decided which things to teach first, second, third, and so forth. This decision requires careful consideration of the relationships among the individual content elements. For example, which elements of content are the prerequisites of other elements of content? A task analysis helps the teacher to decide the order in which the elements of content will be taught, and suggests how much time should be devoted to each. The more complex and important content elements require more instructional time than the less complex and less important ones.

4. *Determining the pupil entry level.* There are several things that must be considered if the teacher is to expect lesson success. First, the teacher needs to consider whether pupils have the necessary prerequisites to even begin the unit. If they do not, then the necessary prerequisite content will have to taught. If this is not done, pupils will become frustrated. Frustrated pupils are unhappy pupils, and unhappy pupils cause classroom management problems for the teacher.

Next, the teacher needs to determine what pupils already know about the subject. If pupils have already mastered most of the content, they will certainly be bored when instruction on the new topic begins. If pupils know a few things, but not all of what is to be taught, then the teacher needs to identify a good beginning point for instruction.

Every effort should be made to match the difficulty of the content and of the learning materials to the characteristics of each individual. The idea is to design a unit so that a large majority of the youngsters will succeed. Success is motivating. It encourages pupils to learn more. On the other hand, failure depresses pupils' enthusiasm. Unless at least 80 percent of the pupils succeed, the teacher may face some severe motivational and behavioral problems.

5. *Writing the specific instructional objectives.* Once the appropriate entry levels have been determined, specific instructional objectives should be developed. These focus on what students will be able to do or demonstrate at the conclusion of the unit of instruction. There should be enough instructional objectives to cover each of the content elements identified during the task-analysis phase of unit planning.

6. *Developing a tentative time line.* The important task here is to determine how many days will be spent teaching each of the specific objectives that have been developed. Some lessons will be able to accomplish several objectives, while other lessons will require several days' instruction time to accomplish their objectives.

A time line can help the teacher determine where time adjustments can be made if a given section takes longer to teach than was originally anticipated. Time management is essential. Without attention to this planning detail, some important aspects of content will not receive the instructional attention they deserve. Many inexperienced teachers find themselves spending too much time on the early units or on the early parts of a given unit, only to discover that they have run out of time and are forced to eliminate some important application activities. When this occurs, students may fail to achieve an adequate grasp of the guiding generalizations.

7. *Locating the relevant resources and materials.* At this step the teacher needs to begin locating learning resources that can be used in teaching the unit. Some resources that might be considered are films, filmstrips, picture sets, books, objects, maps, worksheets and people in the school and community. Teachers often find certain "gaps" in the resources that are available to them. They may have to prepare materials of their own to cover some of the content in a unit. Since it takes time to develop good resource materials, units should be planned well in advance of the time they are to be taught.

Even some resources that are available may not be free for use at all times. Films, for example, often must be ordered days and even weeks in advance.

Many commercial resources are available for elementary social studies teachers.
(*Source:* © Juliann Barbato.)

Unit planners who wish to use films must identify the dates when the films will be needed and place orders far in advance.

8. *Deciding on a tentative teaching approach for each objective.* Once the instructional objectives have been prepared, and relevant learning resources have been identified, the teacher must decide how content related to each objective is to be taught. At this point the details of the specific lessons do not need to be identified.

The first decision a teacher must make relates to *initiating activities.* These are activities that will launch instruction focusing on the new unit. Initiating activities must be motivating. They must be capable of helping youngsters master the basic content they will need to know.

Next, a variety of instructional approaches must be identified. These approaches must be capable of serving several purposes, including presenting new information, allowing for the practice of new skills, providing opportunities for pupils to use and supply new knowledge, and allowing for the creative expression of pupils' ideas. Additional details about instructional approaches will be introduced in Chapters 6, 7, and 8.

Furthermore, the teacher needs to think about how he or she will deal with youngsters who complete their work early. These students need to be provided with opportunities for extending and enriching their learning, but this must be done without making them feel somehow punished for finishing early and doing well.

Some youngsters in the class will be mainstreamed. The teacher needs to consider how youngsters with various kinds of handicapping conditions can be introduced to unit content in such a way that their potentials for success will be maximized.

At this time, teachers often give consideration to the issue of grouping. Some kinds of content lend themselves to large group activities of various kinds. Other kinds are better suited to small group activities. There may also be certain kinds of content that some pupils might profitably study as individuals. A great deal of teacher creativity can go into the single issue of group-size design as the unit planning effort goes forward.

9. *Developing a plan for evaluating pupil learning and the effectiveness of the unit.* College and university students sometimes find themselves frustrated by tests that seem to bear little relationship to content that has been presented in a given course. Elementary youngsters share this kind of frustration, and teachers must take care to assure that testing programs do bear some real relationship to the subject matter that has been covered. Competent teachers work hard to establish a tie between the objectives and their evaluation procedures. Since the learning activities are also tied to the objectives, the results of this approach are tests that focus on content featured during a given block of instruction.

Because of the close relationship between the objectives and the evaluation procedures, some preliminary consideration must be given to evaluation when the objectives that will guide instruction throughout the unit are developed. An explanation of the procedures used in formulating objectives that make specific reference to proposed evaluation techniques was provided in Chapter 4. Information regarding the techniques used in formatting individual kinds of evaluation is provided in Chapter 12.

See Table 5–3 for a recapitulation of the unit planning steps.

TABLE 5–3   A Checklist for the Unit-Planning Steps.

There are nine basic steps in planning an instructional unit. These have been listed below. As each is accomplished, a checkmark can be placed in the appropriate space.

_____ 1. Identifying the basic theme of the unit.

_____ 2. Identifying the basic generalizations, concepts, knowledge, skills, and values to be developed.

_____ 3. Performing a task analysis.

_____ 4. Determining the pupil entry level.

_____ 5. Writing the specific instructional objectives.

_____ 6. Developing a tentative time line.

_____ 7. Locating the relevant resources and materials.

_____ 8. Deciding on a tentative teaching approach for each objective.

_____ 9. Developing a plan for evaluating pupil learning and the effectiveness of the unit.

Unit Format

Many acceptable unit formats exist. Deciding exactly how a unit should be formatted is a matter of a teacher's personal preference. The design selection should be one that displays relevant information in a way that allows for the quick and easy retrieval of individual items. It should also be capable of showing clear relationships among the instructional objectives, the teaching approaches selected, the needed learning materials, and the evaluation procedures.

Many successful elementary social studies teachers begin the unit-planning process by preparing a general unit-planning document. Because units often are used by several teachers, these teachers will frequently work together to complete this document. The general unit-planning document should include the basic information related to several key points.

1. Identifying the grade level. It is helpful to identify the grade level for which the unit is intended. This information will be helpful to other teachers who might have an interest in using the unit and who will wish to know the specific grade level for which it was initially designed (see Table 5–4).

2. Identifying the unit theme. The theme will suggest how the topic to be studied will be approached. The theme statement can set the general tone of the unit.

3. Noting the intended learning outcomes. This is one of the most important components of the unit, and it must be given careful thought. Several categories of intended outcomes may need to be noted. These categories relate back to the broad goals of the social studies curriculum.

   (*a*) What will be citizenship outcomes? The knowledges, skills, values, and decision-making opportunities related to citizenship should be listed.

   (*b*) What will be the history and/or the social science outcomes? Comments here may refer to the generalizations, skills, values, attitudes, and decision-making opportunities associated with history and/or the social sciences.

TABLE 5–4   Do We Need to Plan Different Units for Each Grade Level?

Two teachers recently had the following discussion while waiting for a meeting to begin after school.

Teacher A	Teacher B
We spend too much time planning. I think we *do* need to prepare units, but not separate ones for every topic at every grade level. I think units should be open-ended enough so any teacher can adapt them to any grade level or any group. I mean, teachers should have enough professional know-how to do this without having to depend on a written document.	I can't agree with you. Topics are so different from grade level to grade level and youngsters vary so much from class to class that I just don't see how we can avoid planning units for every topic and class. I just don't think a unit that we would all use would be very helpful. It just wouldn't have enough specific information.

Think About This

1. What do you see as the major strengths of Teacher A's argument? The major weaknesses?
2. What do you see as the major strengths of Teacher B's argument? The major weaknesses?
3. What basic position would you take on this issue? Why?
4. What might you surmise about Teacher A's and Teacher B's previous experience with the unit-planning process? What led you to your conclusions?

(c) How can problem-solving be included? This area is often overlooked. When it is included, instruction can take on more personal meaning for pupils.

4. *Identifying the necessary prerequisite knowledge.* Any prerequisite understandings or skills that pupils absolutely need *before* instruction in the unit begins must be identified. If these important prerequisites are not identified and youngsters' proficiency levels are not checked before the instruction on the new unit begins, some pupils will have trouble mastering the material. A teacher should not begin a unit and then discover that the pupils are unable to succeed.

5. *Organizing the body of the unit.* The next step is to organize the body of the unit itself in a way that makes clear the interrelationships among its parts. Initially, this information does not have to be excessively specific. Additional details can be added when the daily lessons are prepared. The following form is one that teachers have found useful to organize information in a manner that allows for quick visual reference.

Social Science Generalization(s): _____

_____

_____

Specific Objectives	Teaching Approach	Materials

6. *Identifying the evaluation information.* The general unit-planning document process should conclude with some specific information regarding how pupils' levels of performance are to be measured. Sample checklists, observation instruments, sample test items, or descriptions of projects pupils will turn in should be included. These evaluation suggestions may change when individual lessons are planned, but many teachers will find them very helpful when assessing youngsters once the actual instruction has begun.

7. *Completing a final review of the new unit.* A number of criteria can be applied to assess the general quality of a new unit. Many teachers have found the following list helpful.

(a) Is the whole range of social studies outcomes included?
(b) Is the unit sequenced in a logical manner so that early learnings build a basis for later learning? Is it organized so that the generalizations and the main ideas as well as facts can be learned?
(c) Are specific pupil objectives identified?
(d) Is there a variety of teaching approaches? Are the teaching approaches consistent with the intent of the objective? Do the approaches include opportunities for the presentation of new information, practice, application, and creative expression?

An example of a completed unit plan is provided for review in Table 5–5.

When the unit plans have been developed and the actual units have been constructed, the next concern is that of developing the daily lesson plans. Lesson plans translate the more general guidelines provided in the instructional unit into concrete terms.

Daily Lesson Planning

The final step in the process is *daily lesson planning.* Lesson plans are usually developed for each day of the unit. Lessons should not be prepared too far in advance of the time when they will be taught, however, because pupils sometimes surprise their teachers by requiring either more time or less time to grasp certain content than had originally been anticipated.

Lesson plans provide several special benefits for teachers. First, they help pinpoint the potential problem areas before actual instruction. When these areas are identified, teachers can think of ways to respond to them, so that pupils' learning of the content will be advanced. The probability that the instructional sequence will flow more smoothly and with fewer problems is ample compensation for the time that must be spent laying out the individual lessons.

One of the authors recalls a specific episode that underscores the importance of lesson planning to avoid potential problems. An individual who had a very successful student-teaching experience returned to work as a substitute teacher in the same class to which she had been assigned as a student teacher. While she had had few problems with these youngsters as a student teacher, her day as a substitute was a disaster. She ended the experience with her confidence very much shaken.

TABLE 5–5 A Sample Unit Plan. (continued)

Grade Level: Fifth
Unit Theme: Why Do People Move?

Intended Learning Outcomes

Social Science Understandings

1. The promise of increased economic opportunity, religious freedom, political freedom, adventure, or values associated with a given lifestyle motivates people to move.
2. Conflict often occurs when one group of people moves into an area where people of a different culture already live.
3. The advances and changes in technology change the opportunities that people see in certain places.

Citizenship Understandings

1. A variety of groups of people have contributed to the development of our nation.
2. The rights of minorities need to be respected by those who have power.
3. Whenever people live together in a group they must establish rules to govern their behavior.

Personal Understandings

1. The need for adventure and novelty is something that all individuals experience.
2. What might be the correct choice for one person may not be the correct choice for another.
3. The values that people hold shape their decisions.
4. The dignity of all human beings needs to be respected and preserved.
5. Change is a constant feature of life that everyone needs to understand.

Prerequisite Knowledge

1. Pupils need to be able to read maps and identify the significant features of the United States.
2. Pupils need to know how to work together in groups.
3. The basic concepts of time and chronology—such as year, decade, and century—need to be understood.
4. Pupils need to have an understanding of scale and distance.
5. Pupils need to understand direction and location.
6. Pupils need a basic understanding of the events preceding the westward movement.

Unit Outline

Focus Generalization(s)

A variety of motives cause people to move to new places. When two groups or cultures come into contact, conflict often results.

Specific Objective	Teaching Approach	Materials
Unit Initiation and Development		
The class will demonstrate an interest in the topic by seeking books or materials or by asking questions about the topic.	Pose a problem situation: How would you feel if your parents said you were going to move? Relate to the feelings of the pioneers.	Bulletin board with pictures of wagon trains, etc. Play tape of an interview with a pioneer woman.
Individuals can identify significant events and people who helped open the West to settlement.	Read from text; view filmstrips.	Text, supplementary books. Filmstrips: "Lewis and Clark," "Mormon Trek," "California!"

TABLE 5–5   A Sample Unit Plan. (continued)

Specific Objective	Teaching Approach	Materials
Individuals can identify at least three reasons why people moved west.	Large group discussion to share and relate material. Use music as a source of data by listening to songs of the West.	Records, record player. Large sheet of paper to record data.
Individuals can identify the different groups of people who already lived in the West, and their locations.	Read in text. Map exercise for homework.	Text. Outline maps of U.S.
Pupils can identify the values and lifestyle characteristics of those already living in the West.	Small groups view filmstrips; read resource material.	Filmstrips: "Indians of the Plains," "The Spanish in the West," "Old Fort Vancouver."
Pupils can identify how the values and lifestyle elements of those already in the West may have conflicted with the values and lifestyle elements of those moving West.	View film. Use chart to make inferences and generalizations.	Film: "Westward Ho!"
Individuals can provide at least two examples of conflicts that arose between those already in the West and those moving to the West.	Read text. Review in large group.	Text. Large sheet of paper to record data.
Pupils can cite at least two reasons that encouraged people moving to the West to cross the Great Plains before settling down.	Use inquiry to pose problem: Why did the pioneers seek to move farther west? Follow by reading in text to test hypotheses.	Text. Outline maps.
Pupils can identify the impact of an innovation on the settling of the Great Plains.	View film. Do homework on an invention.	Film: "The Iron Horse." Assignment sheet for homework.
Individuals can identify present problems resulting from the contact between cultures during settlement of the West and can suggest how new innovations affected settlement patterns.	Engaging in generalizing and inferring after charting data in small groups.	Newspapers and news magazines.
Pupils will state feelings and choices they might have made if confronted with the prospect of a move West.	Large group discussion.	
Pupils will identify criteria they used in deciding to move or not to move West.	Simulation activity.	Handouts, maps of imaginary land.

Culminating Activity

Pupils will work in groups of 2–3 or individually to create a project that illustrates some aspect of moving West.	Group work on projects.	Art supplies, models.

Evaluation Procedures

1. Multiple-choice quiz on significant events, people, and innovations.
2. Checklist on work habits to evaluate each individual while he or she works with a group.
3. Checklist for evaluating the final product. The checklist should include knowledge of geography, knowledge of settlers, knowledge of values, knowledge of problems, etc.
4. Grade homework assignments for accuracy and completeness.

What contributed to the difference between her "success" as a student teacher and "failure" as a substitute? The key element was a presence of anticipatory planning during the student teaching and a total absence of it during the substitute teaching. The person took this hard lesson to heart and went on to become a very successful elementary school teacher.

In addition to helping teachers plan the responses to potentially difficult situations, lesson planning also acts to give the teacher a sense of confidence and security. Pupils are quick to pick up signals that indicate an insecure teacher.

Lesson planning is one of the most important tasks of the elementary social studies teacher.

(_Source:_ © Juliann Barbato.)

They tend to respond much less positively to teachers who reflect insecurity than to those who reflect a secure sense of themselves as professionals.

In summary, lesson plans provide important benefits to teachers, particularly to beginners. Some of the elements introduced in the subsequent section should be included in every lesson plan. When all these components are present, the likelihood of youngsters' mastering the focus content increases.

The Elements of the Daily Lesson Plan

1. Focusing on pupil objectives. Lesson planning begins with a consideration of the specific pupil objectives identified in the unit plan. For every specific objective there should be one or more lesson plans. The specific objective gives the lesson a focus and identifies what the pupils should be able to do as a result of the lesson.

2. Considering the components of the instructional act. Once the objectives for the lesson have been identified, the individual preparing the plan needs to consider the components of the instructional act. (For specific information about these components, review the material in Chapter 4.)

One of the first tasks is to decide how the lesson will be started and what will be done to motivate the pupils. The initial activities need to help youngsters understand the general objective of the lesson. Successful motivation often occurs when the teacher can relate something that is to be learned to the personal experience of the pupils. This kind of relationship is easier to establish for some kinds of content than for others.

3. Presenting the material. New material can be introduced in many ways. Each potential approach has its particular strengths and weaknesses. Each, too, presents specific challenges to the teacher. For example, if pupils are to obtain information through reading, provisions must be made for those who have reading difficulties. If the material is to be presented by the teacher, he or she needs to make sure that the presentation features the use of clear and precise terms that are appropriate for youngsters' comprehension levels.

The teacher must devise ways to keep pupils involved in the lesson. For example, the teacher needs to decide how he or she will check for understanding once the lesson is in progress. Plans must be made, too, for monitoring pupils and keeping them focused on the task.

4. Practicing. The next step in the lesson-planning process is a consideration of the issue of practice. Do the pupils need opportunities to apply what they have learned? If so, planning must provide the opportunities for guided practice before pupils are allowed to pursue activities of a more independent.

5. Planning closure. Finally, the teacher needs to plan how to bring a lesson to conclusion, or closure. Closure is the final part of the lesson that draws together all of the material that has been introduced. Closure reinforces new learning and promotes the retention of content.

Beginning teachers sometimes fail to direct adequate attention to closure as they plan their lessons. Learning psychologists tell us that the end of a lesson is a particularly good time for learning to take place. Hence, it makes sense for teachers to pay particular attention to planning for closure.

6. Managing the materials. In addition to the components of instruction, there are a few other factors that must be considered when lessons are being

I Know You're Great on Motivation, But Can You Plan?
(*Source:* Ford Button.)

planned. For example, the materials needed must be identified. These might include items such as books, paper, pencils, and handouts. The planner needs to determine that these items will really be available at the time the lesson will be taught. If there is an availability problem, even the best planned lesson may turn into a classroom disaster.

7. *Managing the classroom.* Several classroom management issues need to be considered when planning the lesson. Transition times between parts of the lesson sometimes pose problems. What specific instructions will be provided to pupils to make transitions smoother? How will this information be introduced? If lessons call upon pupils to move from place to place, procedures to make such movement smooth and purposeful need to be planned. What routes will pupils take? What "rules" must be observed (no talking, no shoving, and so forth) when moving to another place in the classroom. General administrative matters such as taking attendance and the lunch count must be planned so the teacher's attention is not long diverted from working directly with pupils.

Note the sample lesson-plan format shown in Table 5–6.

TABLE 5–6   A Sample Lesson-Plan Format.

Unit Theme: _____   Lesson Plan Number: _____

Learner Objective: _____

_____

Needed Prerequisites: _____

_____

New Vocabulary or Concepts: _____

Lesson Sequence	Materials
Learning set/motivation	
Presentation of new content	
Practice/extension/application	
Closure/evaluation of learning	

Teacher Evaluation of Lesson Effectiveness: _____

_____

_____

Key Ideas in Summary _____

Attention to planning is a hallmark of the successful teacher. Planning helps the teacher anticipate events and think through appropriate responses. Planning gives teachers self-confidence. This self-confidence is communicated to pupils and helps make teachers' jobs easier. Some key ideas related to planning include the following:

1. Long-range planning should integrate the content taught at a particular grade level with the important purposes of the social studies. If this step is ignored, the teacher may be tempted to simply "cover" the material. This kind of instruction can miss the central purposes of the social studies.
2. Developing units of instruction around the major subdivisions of the topic covered in a grade level puts teachers in control of the learning environment and enables them to make the learning relevant to the interests of a given group of pupils.
3. These are the basic components of the unit: (1) identifying the theme; (2) identifying the significant generalizations, concepts, knowledge, skills, and values; (3) completing a task analysis; (4) determining the pupil entry levels; (5) specifying the instructional objectives; (6) developing a time line; (7) compiling a list of resources and materials; (8) developing teaching approaches for each objective; and (9) preparing evaluation techniques for determining pupil mastery.
4. Daily lesson plans should include: (1) focusing on a specific objective, (2) describing the components of instruction, (3) presenting the specifics about the nature and management of needed materials, (4) practicing, (5) planning closure, (6) managing the materials, and (7) managing the classroom.
5. When planning for daily lessons, the teacher should also consider how to meet the specific learning needs of specific pupils in the classroom. Special planning must be provided for handicapped pupils, gifted and talented pupils, and other special groups.

Questions _____

Review Questions

1. What is the importance of selecting a basic theme for a unit?
2. How does task analysis relate to the development of objectives and individual lessons?
3. Why is it important to consider the evaluation of learning when a new unit is being planned?
4. What are the basic elements of the lesson plan?
5. Why has planning for special pupil needs frequently improved teachers' overall level of instructional expertise?

Thought Questions

1. Where would you begin your planning process if you were hired to teach in a school district that has no curriculum guides?
2. What do you consider to be the most challenging aspects of planning units and lessons?
3. How detailed should planning be in unit plans? in lesson plans?
4. Individual youngsters in classrooms have many special needs. To which kinds of special needs do you feel least prepared to respond? Why?

5. Lengths of units should be different for different groups of pupils. Why is this so?
6. Think about the issue of transitions within lessons. What are some specific things you might do to make transitions smoother?

Extending Understanding and Skill _____

Activities

1. Think about a grade level you would like to teach. For this grade level, identify a social studies topic you would like to teach. Identify a theme, and plan a unit centering on that topic for a group of pupils.
2. For the unit you have developed, write at least two lesson plans that could be used to teach two different objectives.
3. Invite a teacher to the class and share several examples of lesson plans he or she has prepared.
4. Think about some special materials you might need to develop an important unit. Prepare a list of sources of materials you might use to supplement information pupils would find in their texts or in other social studies materials owned by the school.
5. For each of the handicapping conditions listed, prepare a list of ways that lessons might be adapted in order to accommodate those special needs. The handicapping conditions are: learning disability, hearing impairment, sight impairment, physical handicap, and emotional disorder.

Supplemental Reading

DICK, WALTER, and CAREY, LOU. *The Systematic Design of Instruction*. New York: Nichols Publications, 1984.

DUNN, RITA, and DUNN, KENNETH J. "Learning Styles/Teaching Styles: Should They . . . Can They . . . Be Matched?" *Educational Leadership* (January 1979), pp. 238–244.

GUENTHER, JOHN, and HANSEN, PATRICIA. "Social Studies Activity Centers," *The Social Studies* (March 1977), pp. 65–69.

MERKLE, D. R. "Thematic Units for the Classroom," *New England Reading Association Journal* (Winter 1984), pp. 12–17.

OCHOA, ANNA, and SHUSTER, SUSAN K. *Social Studies in Mainstreamed Classrooms*. Boulder, CO: ERIC Clearinghouse for Social Studies/Social Science Education, 1980.

PERRY, P. J., and HOBACK, J. R. "Grid Planning: A Tool in Programming for Talented and Gifted Students," *Roeper Review* (February 1984), pp. 139–142.

References _____

HUNTER, MADELINE. "Diagnostic Teaching," *The Elementary School Journal* (September 1979), pp. 8–18.

JAROLIMEK, JOHN. *Social Studies in Elementary Education*, 6th ed. New York: Macmillan Publishing Co., Inc., 1982.

KALTSOUNIS, THEODORE. *Teaching Social Studies in the Elementary School: The Basics for Citizenship*. Englewood Cliffs, NJ: Prentice-Hall, 1979.

McCUTCHEON, G. "How Do Elementary School Teachers Plan? The Nature of Planning and Influences on It," *The Elementary School Journal* (September 1980), pp. 4–23.

MARSH, C. T. "Teachers' Knowledge of and Use of Social Studies Curriculum Materials in Public Elementary Schools," *Journal of Educational Research* (March/April 1984), pp. 237–243.

MARTORELLA, PETER H. *Elementary Social Studies*. Boston: Little, Brown and Co., 1985.

ROMISZOWSKI, A. J. *Producing Instructional Systems*. New York: Nichols Publications, 1984.

SHAVELSON, R. J. "Review of Research on Teachers' Pedagogical Judgments, Plans, and Decisions," *Elementary School Journal* (March 1983), pp. 392–413.

Chapter 6

Involving Pupils: The Basic Approaches

(*Source:* © Juliann Barbato.)

This chapter provides information to help the reader:

1. State the factors that need to be considered when selecting an instructional approach.
2. Define the main elements of direct instruction.
3. List the steps and define the teacher's role in brainstorming.
4. Compare and contrast two different approaches to teaching concepts.
5. Describe the organization of data and the steps involved in teaching generalizations.
6. Define the roles of teachers and pupils in the inquiry approach.

Overview

A great deal of debate in education centers on the issue of the "best" method of teaching. Throughout the history of education, various approaches have captured educators' attention and enjoyed a brief reign as *the* method. After an initial period of excitement, enthusiasm for the method faded, to be replaced by the glowing claims for another.

Much of the discussion concerning the best method is misplaced. Social studies involves a wide variety of objectives that are taught by different kinds of teachers in an incredible number of settings. Not surprisingly, this diversity assures that *no single method* is the best for all the social studies objectives, for all the pupils, and for all the settings.

In this chapter, several methods of teaching social studies content are introduced. Each relates to the components of the instructional act that were presented for the first time in Chapter 4. These methods represent a sample of the wide variety of methods from which teachers can select, based on the analyses of their own particular sets of circumstances.

The Criteria to be Used in Choosing a Method

Recall that Chapter 1 introduced the major goals of the elementary social studies program. The nature of the goal being pursued at a particular time affects the method selection. Obviously, you do not teach independent decision making in the same way you teach the recall of basic information.

The first step in selecting an instructional approach is to review the established objectives. What is it that pupils are going to be expected to know or to do? What does that imply in terms of how they should be taught? For example, if the intent is to convey some specific pieces of information, then a direct approach (in which information is presented to pupils and their mastery is later assessed) makes sense. However, if the intent is to help pupils apply their skills, then pupils need instruction that allows them to confront new situations.

A second consideration in choosing the instructional method is the nature of the pupils themselves. Their skills, interests, and previous learning need to be considered. Some methods demand that pupils have some previous knowledge or skills. For example, a discussion will not prove to be worthwhile if pupils have not had prior experience with the approach; it is unwise to select discussion as an instructional approach until pupils have been taught how to profit from the method.

Teachers need to remember that pupils in their classrooms change dramatically from year to year. An approach that worked last year may not work this year. A method that worked with one group of third graders may prove to be of little value with another group of third graders.

A third element that needs to be considered when designing an instructional approach is the availability of needed resources. All methods must be supported by materials of some kind, but the support demands of some approaches are heavier than the demands of others. If the necessary materials are not available, then the use of a particular approach should be postponed. This does not mean that all the materials must be available at the time instruction is planned. The teacher may have to see administrators and take other actions to acquire the resources needed to support a given approach once it has been planned and before it is implemented.

Finally, the skills and abilities of the teacher need to be considered. Some teachers may not possess the attitudes, philosophies, knowledge, or skills needed to succeed with a particular instructional approach. For example, a teacher who believes his or her role is only to present information and conclusions or who does not know how to ask good questions may experience great difficulty in using an inquiry approach that depends heavily on pupil-provided information and on the ability to frame good questions. The successful teacher considers his or her strengths and weaknesses and seeks to acquire an appropriate set of attitudes and a broad array of skills. These characteristics allow him or her to experience success when using a variety of instructional techniques (see Table 6–1).

TABLE 6–1   Teacher Beliefs.

Teacher beliefs and skills play an important role in the selection and use of various teaching approaches. Teachers can use a self-assessment as they attempt to widen the range in their selection of teaching methods.

Think About This

1. Which of the following goals do you think are the most important in elementary social studies: learning basic skills, learning concepts and generalizations, developing creativity, or learning how to learn?
2. What do you see as the primary role of the elementary teacher: dispensing information, arranging the environment so that learning can occur, or serving as a facilitator or guide?
3. Do you feel most comfortable working with individuals or presenting to a large group?
4. Are you bothered if the right answers are not presented at the conclusion of a lesson?
5. Are you concerned that pupils do not have the motivation to learn on their own, and, therefore, that allowing them the freedom to pursue information on their own will result in wasted time and an uncontrolled classroom?
6. Do you feel most comfortable with quiet and highly structured classrooms, or do you prefer some movement and informality?

A Sampler of Instructional Methods

Numerous approaches are available for teaching social studies. These methods combine the components of the instructional act in different ways. Each method uniquely incorporates the elements of motivation, presentation of content, practice, application, and closure. Furthermore, the roles of teachers and pupils vary, depending on the technique selected.

Brainstorming

Brainstorming is an approach that utilizes pupil knowledge and ideas. It can help pupils break loose from the more obvious solutions to problems and explore creative alternatives. The basic design of a brainstorming session is presenting an open situation and creating an environment where pupils feel free to contribute their ideas without fear of ridicule or failure. The following rules of brainstorming are quite simple.

1. Pupils are presented with a problem or situation.
2. Pupils are invited to share as many ideas as they can generate. They are encouraged to suggest as many ideas as possible.
3. Pupils are told that they are not to comment on the ideas or remarks of others. All the ideas are to be accepted.

Active pupil participation is an important part of all of the instructional methods.
(*Source:* © Juliann Barbato.)

4. The teacher or a designated pupil is asked to record all the ideas.
5. The exercise is stopped when the flow of ideas begins to drop off noticeably and pupil interest begins to diminish.
6. In order to bring closure, the teacher and the pupils review and discuss the ideas that were shared. The ideas might be organized and grouped for the purpose of future investigation.

Brainstorming can be used for several purposes: It can help pupils recognize new and unfamiliar solutions to problems, it can stimulate their creativity and problem-solving abilities, and it can prompt the participation of a high percentage of pupils in a given class.

Brainstorming is sometimes used at the beginning of a unit of study. When this happens, the teacher presents a stimulus relevant to the unit that is to be studied. This might be a story, a film, a series of pictures, or anything else that captures pupils' interest. After the stimulus is presented, the teacher prompts the members of the class to ask as many questions as possible about the topic.

To implement such a procedure for a unit focusing on history, a teacher might begin by posting art prints reflecting the period to be studied. For example, if the unit were on the age of exploration, pictures of explorers, sailing ships, old maps, and other items from this period of history might be included in the display.

The teacher could start by asking pupils to look at the pictures and make mental notes of anything that seems unusual, puzzling, or interesting. This could be followed by the teacher asking youngsters to share what they have observed with the class. One pupil might be asked to neatly print these observations on an overhead-projector transparency.

To begin the brainstorming exercise, the projector is turned on so pupils can see all of the information that has been generated. Then the teacher asks youngsters to think about what they see and about what questions this information raises. The teacher might simply ask, "What are some questions you now have about explorers and exploration?"

Students are encouraged to call out questions as quickly as they occur. The teacher writes these on the chalkboard. After a number of questions have been asked (perhaps ten to twenty), the teacher stops the activity. Similar questions may be grouped together at this point.

The questions that pupils have developed provide a focus for the study of the new unit. One or more questions may be selected to guide each day's lesson. At the beginning of each lesson, the selected question(s) is (are) written on the chalkboard. The teacher reads what he or she has written and says, "Today, let us try to find an answer to this question (these questions)." At the end of the lesson, the teacher focuses again on the question(s), and tries to elicit responses from the members of the class.

Brainstorming and the Components of the Instructional Act. Brainstorming utilizes the principles of motivation in several ways. Often, something novel or of high interest to the students forms the stimulus for the activity. Pupils experience a high degree of success because all the responses are accepted.

Brainstorming does not present new information. Although pupils may learn something from what the other members of the class say, that is not the purpose.

The intent is to create interest and stimulate creativity. Therefore, this approach is not a good choice if the intended outcome is the learning of new information. The components of practice and application are not emphasized; during this approach, pupils learn how to ask questions and generate ideas. These are important outcomes, and it is hoped that the pupils will apply these skills when they confront situations in the world outside the classroom (see Table 6–2). Closure is provided by conducting a review and organizing items for further study.

TABLE 6–2 Applying Brainstorming.

Brainstorming is a technique often used to prompt youngsters to think creatively about problems. It is characterized by the rapid-paced sharing of ideas. This technique can help pupils combine a large number of approaches to a common focus problem.

Think About This

1. Would you feel comfortable using the brainstorming approach? If not, what are the things about the method that concern you?
2. Survey the content of a grade level that interests you. Identify two or three questions or problems that might be used as the focus for brainstorming lessons.
3. Do you think brainstorming is an appropriate approach for all grade levels? Why or why not?
4. What would you do if you considered the responses generated by the pupils to be inappropriate or insignificant?

Direct Instruction

Direct instruction has been strongly supported by research findings on how the instructional processes affect pupil achievement. It has been found to increase pupil achievement on tests of the basic skills (Good and Brophy, 1984). These findings have prompted a high interest in the approach.

Direct instruction, as the name implies, is a teacher-directed and teacher-centered approach. The teacher controls both the pace of classroom activity and the pattern of classroom interaction. Large-group instruction is used, as opposed to small-group or individualized instruction. There is an emphasis on keeping pupils busy on academic activities and on increasing their total "time on task" (time spent on activities directly related to academic content).

Classroom time is highly structured by the teacher. Time spent on any non-academic tasks is kept to a bare minimum. The class is run in a businesslike manner. Teacher presentation of new information is followed by a highly controlled period when pupils do individual or group work. Free time or independent-work time is eliminated.

The kinds of teacher questions advocated by proponents of direct instruction call upon pupils to recall very specific information. Typically, the following question/answer pattern is observed. First, the teacher asks a question. Then a pupil responds. This is followed by appropriate feedback to the pupil. Then the sequence begins again with another teacher question. During these question periods, there is little deviance from this pattern and almost no interaction among pupils.

Feedback, as mentioned in the questioning sequence and in other contexts, is an important component of direct instruction. Corrective feedback and praise feedback are routinely provided by the teacher, as appropriate. *Corrective feedback* is provided immediately when pupils make an error. *Praise feedback* is given when pupils respond properly. Praise is to be moderate rather than lavish, and is to be delivered sincerely. The following short segment from a direct-instruction lesson illustrates the use of corrective feedback and praise feedback.

TEACHER: John, which Amendment to the Constitution concerns freedom of religion?

JOHN: The First Amendment.

TEACHER: That's right, John. Mary, which one of the Amendments provides for a trial by jury?

MARY: The Fourth Amendment.

TEACHER: No, Mary. The correct answer is the Seventh Amendment. Each of you has a worksheet on the top of your desk. I want you to write the Amendment relevant to each of the cases described on the paper, I will be circulating around the room, helping those who have problems. Bill, please review the directions for our worksheet for the class.

Direct instruction follows a pattern that is quite different from the patterns of the less-formal approaches favored by many educators. It is an appropriate approach for helping some pupils achieve some objectives. Direct instruction, for example, has been found to be effective for teaching low-achieving pupils the basic skills' content. On the other hand, this approach has not been found to work well when attempting to enhance pupils' problem-solving or creative-thinking abilities. Furthermore, it has been discovered that high-achieving, task-oriented pupils who feel they have a great deal to do with their own successes or failures do not profit from the direct-instruction approaches (Peterson, 1979).

In summary, direct instruction helps some pupils master the basic skills or recall the objectives. However, it has generally not been found to be effective for teaching objectives that call upon learners to perform at the higher cognitive levels.

Direct Instruction and the Components of the Instructional Act. Motivating pupils challenges teachers who wish to use direct instruction because there is little novelty inherent within the approach. Teachers must make conscious efforts to create pupil interest. The direct and quick feedback feature of the technique can enhance the motivation of those youngsters who know the correct answer. The predetermined questioning sequence motivates all pupils to pay attention because each child recognizes that he or she may be called upon to respond during the lesson.

Direct instruction allows teachers to present information in a systematic manner. Learning tasks are broken into small steps that are sequenced and introduced to the members of the class. Direct instruction also provides opportunities for guided and independent practice of new learning. Monitoring and feedback are included as part of the teacher's effort to provide guided-practice opportunities.

Closure can be provided in direct instruction by including a review session at the conclusion of the lesson. At this time, the lesson objective can be re-emphasized, and the key points can be highlighted.

Some people have accused direct instruction of being a cold and boring approach to learning. This does not need to be the case. A teacher can be warm and supportive while using this technique. With adequate preparation, a teacher can even make direct instruction exciting. When used for appropriate purposes with appropriate pupils, direct instruction can be a satisfying experience for both teachers and their pupils (see Table 6–3).

TABLE 6–3 The Characteristics of Direct Instruction.

1. *There is high percentage of academic learning time.* Pupils spend a high percentage of class time working on academic tasks on which they experience success.
2. *The classroom is organized in a businesslike yet warm manner.* The teacher engages the class on the task promptly and keeps youngsters on the task until it is completed.
3. *The teacher is actively involved with the class for the entire class period.* The teacher is active explaining, demonstrating, monitoring, and providing feedback. The teacher does not perform other duties, such as record keeping, during the class time.
4. *The pacing of the total program and of the individual lessons is brisk.* The instructional program is organized so that it moves forward relatively quickly. This is done to avoid pupil boredom. Furthermore, lessons are also designed so the instruction moves forward at an efficient rate. However, pacing never becomes so brisk that the possibility for pupils to achieve success is jeopardized.
5. *The interactions among pupils are minimized.* Pupils are kept focused on the task by the teacher. Socialization among pupils is discouraged in favor of high levels of teacher monitoring and control.
6. *Mastery learning is emphasized.* Pupils are provided with many opportunities to practice what they have learned. Remedial teaching is provided when necessary.
7. *Ordered turns are used in soliciting pupil responses to questions.* To insure that all pupils remain alert, a predetermined sequence of questions is used to assure that all youngsters will have to respond.
8. *Praise is used in moderation.* Praise is not overused. When it is used, it should be tied to an appropriate pupil answer or response. Teachers are careful to provide corrective feedback when pupils make mistakes.

Teaching Concepts and Generalizations

Many social studies lessons require pupils to learn concepts and generalizations, which can be taught through the use of a variety of techniques. Even direct instruction can be used. But this method is not appropriate when the teacher's intent is for youngsters to do more than memorize the concept definitions or the generalization statements. More frequently, teachers are interested in teaching their pupils to develop concepts or generalizations of their own or to appreciate the rather sophisticated implications of selected concepts and generalizations.

As a preface to thinking about teaching concepts, a review of the meaning of the term *concept* may prove helpful. Concepts are common labels applied to phenomena that are grouped according to their common characteristics. For example, personal vehicles with four wheels, a gasoline or diesel engine (also, but rarely, an electric engine), and a steering wheel are given the common label "automobile." This broad label helps us group the many different kinds of personal vehicles into a common reference category: automobile. The concept, then, is a kind of shorthand used to prompt the recall of many kinds of related items through the use of single common label.

Sometimes, teachers are more interested in teaching the *process* of concept formation rather than the meaning of a specific concept. Some feel that youngsters profit from the experience of placing phenomena in categories and thinking about possible concept labels. A procedure some teachers use to teach pupils the process of concept formation is concept formation/diagnosis.

In the subsections that follow, the concept attainment and concept formation/diagnosis approaches will be contrasted.

Concept Attainment. *Concept attainment* focuses on teaching pupils the concepts that the teacher has selected for study. This approach is easily applied to a wide range of concept-centered lessons. The basic steps are as follows:

1. The teacher introduces the concept by name.
2. The teacher presents examples of the concept.
3. The teacher introduces nonexamples of the concept.
4. A mixture of examples and nonexamples is presented. Pupils are asked to identify the correct examples of the concept.
5. Next, pupils are asked to attempt to define the concept.
6. Pupils finally try to apply their understanding by finding additional examples of the concept.

This process can be used to teach a variety of concepts. If a fairly simple concept such as "desert" were the focus, the teacher might begin by presenting pictures of desert regions. Next pictures of nondesert regions might be introduced. Then a display including pictures of both desert regions and nondesert regions would be made available. Pupils would be asked to select the pictures of desert regions. Then the teacher would ask them to attempt to define "desert." Finally, pupils would be asked to find pictures of deserts in sources such as a classroom supply of *National Geographic* magazines.

This basic approach can also be used to teach complex concepts such as "justice" and "democracy." When very sophisticated concepts are selected, the process may require several days instruction time. Though the time required greatly exceeds that required for less-sophisticated concepts, the basic procedure remains the same.

Concept Attainment and the Components of the Instructional Act. The concept-attainment procedure includes most of the elements of the instructional act. As with direct instruction, motivating pupils is a concern for teachers who use concept attainment. Pupils must be made to understand how they will personally benefit from learning the focus concept the teacher has selected.

In concept attainment, the presentation of information is accomplished by introducing examples and nonexamples of the focus concept. Pupils bear much responsibility for their own learning as they make and compare observations, and formulate concept definitions. If they are unable to articulate a good definition, the teacher may need to provide more guidance and to review the examples and nonexamples of the concept.

Guided and independent practice can be provided as pupils seek other examples of the concept they have learned. This activity requires pupils to apply new learning. During this phase, they receive feedback from the teacher about how appropriate their decisions are. Closure can be provided in a final review session.

Concept Formation/Diagnosis. The *concept formation/diagnosis approach* is chosen when the interest is teaching pupils the process of concept development rather than the meanings of particular concepts that the teacher feels they must know. This procedure, based on the work of the late Hilda Taba (1967), helps develop youngsters' thinking skills. It also helps the teacher to diagnose any serious misunderstandings youngsters in the class might have. The process follows these three basic steps:

1. In response to a stimulus provided by the teacher, often a question, pupils provide a number of responses. The teacher writes these where pupils can see them.
2. Pupils organize the responses into categories.
3. Pupils develop concept labels that define the common characteristics of the responses in each group created in step 2.

To get such an exercise started, a teacher might ask questions such as these: What are the types of jobs the people have today? What kinds of buildings are there in our town? What would you tell a friend who was going to move to our state? What do you think you would find if you visited Brazil?

Pupils' responses to the questions are listed on the chalkboard, butcher paper, a chart, an overhead transparency, or some other appropriate writing surface. The teacher should restate the contributions of each pupil as their questions are added to the list. No effort should be made to correct misinformation. The misinformation is important. It can tell the teacher about a pupil's misconceptions, and can be used as a basis for planning future lessons. Because of the potential diagnostic value of pupils' comments, all ideas are freely accepted without judgment.

Once the list is prepared, the teacher initiates the next step of the exercise by asking this question: Which things on our list go together in groups? As youngsters suggest groups, the teacher asks them about their reasons for suggesting these arrangements. As this part of the exercise proceeds, the teacher should remind pupils that it is perfectly acceptable for some items to belong to more than one group.

The next phase is also initiated by a question. The teacher might say, What could we call each group? As pupils respond, the teacher needs to prompt them to develop labels that are neither too broad nor too narrow. Labels that are too broad often encompass all of the items in several groups; labels that are too narrow cannot accommodate all of the items within even one group.

Concept Formation/Diagnosis and the Components of the Instructional Act. In the concept formation/diagnosis process, motivation is accomplished through the use of a question designed to stimulate pupil interest. Therefore, the phrasing of the question used to begin the exercise is critically important. Sometimes it is wise to preface the question with a short introduction that stresses the importance of the content the question will introduce.

Since this technique uses and builds on the responses of pupils, some intrinsic

TABLE 6–4   Suggested Questions for Concept Formation/Diagnosis.

This strategy requires the teacher to plan some questions to prompt responses from the members of the class. Questions will vary with the particular topic the youngsters will be studying. The questions that follow are examples of those that function well when this strategy is being used.

1. What things can be bought at the store?
2. What jobs do people have?
3. Draw a picture of something we do in school.
4. Draw a picture of things for which families spend money.
5. What buildings do we find in our community or town?
6. If you were to tell friends about our state, what would you say?
7. What would you expect to see on a visit to _____?
8. What are some of the ways people earn money?
9. If you were a pioneer moving west, what would you take along?
10. What comes to mind when you hear the word "democracy"?
11. What do you think of when you think of summer?
12. What did you see on our field trip?

motivation often accompanies the process. Since there are no wrong answers, the fear of failure diminishes. The technique does not depend on pupils' reading abilities or on previous knowledge. In short, it is hard for an individual youngster to feel that he or she will "lose" because of some personal shortcoming. When pupils understand this, they often eagerly participate in the activity.

Relatively little new information is presented when this activity is used. The information that is presented centers on telling youngsters what they must do at each stage of the process. Furthermore, there is neither guided nor independent practice during the lesson. Closure, though, plays an important part. At the conclusion of the lesson, the teacher reviews what has been done and why it has been done. This helps pupils appreciate the process they have experienced.

Inducing Generalizations. Elementary social studies programs place heavy emphases on helping pupils master generalizations about the social and physical world. Generalizations are statements of the relationships among concepts. They are succinct statements reflecting what the best available evidence has found to be "true" about the world.

Consider this generalization: The global location of a nation or a region contributes to its importance in international affairs. This brief statement sums up volumes of scholarship on this issue. It references important concepts such as "global location," "nation," "region," and "international affairs."

Several approaches are available to teachers interested in passing on important social studies generalizations to their pupils. One of these involves inducing a generalization.

The *inducing-a-generalization technique* is designed to help students arrive at a well-established generalization by considering the evidence and following the logic of their own thought processes. The teacher begins the activity by selecting a powerful focus generalization. The idea is for the teacher to provide students with evidence supporting the "truth" of the generalization so that they can infer the generalization on their own.

To be successful, the teacher must first take action to ensure that youngsters understand the meanings of the major concepts associated with the generaliza-

Involving pupils in plays can reinforce their understanding of generalizations.
(*Source:* © Juliann Barbato.)

tion. For example, given the generalization noted above, youngsters who are ignorant of the concepts "global location," "nation," "region," and "international affairs" would find it impossible to infer the generalization.

Second, the teacher must make sure that enough examples of the generalization's "truth" are available, so that pupils will have a reasonably good chance of inferring the generalization. If such information is not available, pupils are sure to become frustrated.

These are the steps followed in the inducing-a-generalization activity (also see Table 6–5):

1. Gather and organize evidence related to the focus generalization selected by the teacher.
2. Compare and contrast the data. Note the relationships.
3. Make a statement that explains these relationships that can be applied to other situations.

In the first step, the teacher introduces specific information that supports the "truth" of the focus generalization that has been selected. The pupils, with teacher help as needed, may wish to organize the information into categories. If categories are identified, the teacher may ask youngsters to find additional information related to each category on their own. In some situations, the teacher may provide additional information. Revise as indicated.

TABLE 6–5   Organizing an Inducing-a-Generalization Lesson.

The following chart is a visual illustration of how the data for such a lesson might be displayed. This generalization might be selected by the teacher as a focus for this lesson: The types and varieties of services change as the size of a community changes. One axis of the chart displays communities of different types. The other axis indicates different types of businesses and services. Below the chart are the questions that the teacher might use in guiding the class session.

Size of Community	Types of Services Available		
	Government Services	Types of Industries	Types of Stores
Small Rural Community			
Moderate-sized Suburban Community			
Large City			

Step 1: What do you notice about the types of government services in the different communities?
What do you notice about the types of businesses?
What do you notice about the types of stores?
Step 2: What are the similarities and differences you notice among these communities?
Step 3: Why do you think there are differences among these communities?
What statements can we make that might help us explain what we might find in other communities?

The second step involves pupils in considering all the information that has been gathered. To do this, it is essential that this information be displayed so that all youngsters can see it. Some teachers find that writing it on the chalkboard works well. The teacher uses questions to prompt pupils to think about this information. These are examples of questions that might be asked: What do you notice about the types of jobs in our community and the types in other communities? What do you notice about the differences in climate between place A and place B? How were the conditions in this colony different from the conditions in that colony?

The third step requires pupils to develop a general statement that explains the relationships mentioned in the second step. This part of the exercise is something many pupils initially find difficult. They are asked to make inferences exceeding the literal limits of the data. Some learners may be hesitant to participate in this "risky" process. The teacher must do all he or she can to help them overcome the fear of making an inappropriate response. It is particularly important that youngsters feel confident that their ideas will not be ridiculed.

This step begins with questions from the teacher such as these: Why do you think different types of jobs are available in different types of communities? Why do places change at different rates? How can you explain all of these things? Pupils are encouraged to suggest all the relationships they see. The teacher probes gently so that youngsters justify their generalizations in terms of the information with which the class is working. All pupil-developed generalizations are written down by the teacher and saved for future reference. These generalizations can be tested against the additional content to which pupils will be exposed. Some generalizations will be supported. Others will need to be revised as the new information suggests needed modifications.

The following episode indicates how an inducing-a-generalization activity might proceed.

STEP 1 *Teacher:* Each of your groups has studied communities of different sizes. We now have all of this information on this large sheet of butcher paper. Let's look at it together. What do you notice about the population of each community? What jobs are available in each community? What services are available in each community?

(Pupils respond to each question.)

STEP 2 *Teacher:* What do you notice about the different types of jobs in each community? What do you notice about the types of services available in each of the communities? In what ways are these communities alike? In what ways are these communities different?

(Pupils respond to each question.)

STEP 3 *Teacher:* You have identified the important differences in jobs and services available in these communities. What explains these differences? Why do you think some services exist in all of the communities we studied? Why do some communities have so many different kinds of jobs available? Why do some have more services available? What statements can you make that might help us understand other communities we might study?

(Pupils respond to each question.)

Inducing Generalizations and the Components of the Instructional Act. Motivating pupils can be difficult when the inducing-generalizations approach is used. This is particularly true when pupils first encounter the process. For newcomers to the activity, teachers must provide a good deal of encouragement, especially during the phase of the process that requires youngsters to go beyond the limits of the data to form explanatory generalizations. When youngsters have experienced success with the activity and found themselves capable of developing generalizations that can help them explain and understand the elements of their world, they can more eagerly embrace the subsequent uses of the procedure.

Data can be presented in several ways by teachers interested in having their pupils induce generalizations. The information might be introduced orally. Pupils may gather the information themselves through a variety of individual or group activities involving direct observation, reading, or other data-gathering skills. If the teacher decides youngsters will gather the basic information themselves, he or she must monitor the learning closely and provide continuous feedback to assure that the gathered information is appropriate. Inaccurate basic information will result in the development of faulty generalizations.

The inducing-generalizations activity allows youngsters to practice many important skills. They can sharpen their note-taking skills during the basic data-gathering process, be involved in sorting relevant from irrelevant information, and practice organizing data. Finally, they can make inferences that require them to think beyond the limits of the given information.

Once the generalizations have been suggested, pupils have opportunities to apply them. Immediately, the teacher asks them to defend their generalization's explanatory power in terms of the basic information they have used to induce it. ("That is an interesting generalization, Robert. Now tell me, does it explain *all* of the information we have here?") Subsequently, pupils encounter new information. When this happens, they are asked to test the accuracy of their generalizations against these new data. In some cases, the "truth" of their generalizations will be confirmed. In others, they will find it necessary to revise their generalizations.

It's Part of his Roman History Inquiry Lesson. He's Plotting the Best Route Across the Rubicon.

(*Source:* Ford Button.)

Closure plays an important role in the inducing-generalizations process. Teachers promote closure by reviewing and suggesting the implications of each generalization suggested by pupils. Next, they review the whole process that led to inducing the generalizations, and conclude by helping youngsters understand that they are capable of forming generalizations that can contribute to their understanding of the world.

The inducing-generalizations approach can be used at all grade levels. Teachers of very young elementary children can present information in simple pictorial forms. Older youngsters can deal with more-sophisticated data sources. The language youngsters use in their generalizations will vary with age levels and grade levels, but even pupils in the primary grades are capable of making statements describing large categories of information, and they should be encouraged to do so.

Inquiry Methods

Over the past twenty years, a number of approaches have been developed that collectively have come to be labeled _inquiry_. To simplify matters, we are going to define inquiry in this way: Inquiry is the application of the scientific methods to teaching.

The scientific method involves (1) an awareness of a problem, (2) a development of a hypothesis, (3) a testing of a hypothesis, and (4) a decision to accept, modify, or reject a hypothesis. These basic features can be used to organize inquiry lessons (see Table 6–6).

Inquiry has some features that clearly differentiate it from the other instructional approaches. One of these features has to do with what the teacher does. In an inquiry lesson, for example, responsibility for gathering data shifts from the teacher to the students. Pupils must decide what information they need. They are encouraged to ask the teacher questions to get this information. This represents a reversal of the more typical pattern, in which the teacher interrogates the pupils.

Pupils are taught to formulate and evaluate hypotheses, and identify relevant data in light of this information. These may appear to be very sophisticated skills, but they can be applied in limited ways by even very young elementary children. This inquiry activity is primarily directed toward teaching pupils a process of thinking about puzzling problems. The primary objective is not to teach specific information. The rationale for the activity is that people are confronted with difficult situations that demand decisions throughout their lives. Hence, it makes sense to provide pupils with instruction on how these problems can be systematically attacked. This is what inquiry instruction attempts to do.

The following steps clarify how an inquiry lesson might proceed in an elementary classroom:

STEP 1   _Establishing a focus for inquiry._ The teacher bears the responsibility for establishing the inquiry focus. This is done by presenting a problem or a puzzling situation to the class. It is important that the focus be something that captures the interest of the members of the class.

The presentation of the problem can take a variety of forms. It might be an unfinished story, an unfinished film, a photograph, a

TABLE 6–6   The Skills to Accompany Questions in Inquiry Lessons.

Teachers have obligations in inquiry lessons that go beyond asking good questions. They must appropriately structure the situation and listen and respond properly to what pupils say. Some of the following skills are among the most essential.

Focus setting and refocusing. The inquiry problem needs to be explained clearly. If pupils do not understand the problem or issue, they cannot formulate hypotheses. Once the discussion is in progress, the teacher needs to watch for digressions and to be prepared to refocus attention on the focus problem.

Structuring the inquiry. The teacher may need to help the class to pose hypotheses and phrase questions so that the information they will need will be forthcoming. However, the teacher must be cautious not to force the students to proceed in a predetermined direction.

Clarifying. Clarifying the intent of the questions presented is vital. The teacher must work to assure that all pupils understand what is being asked of them.

Responding to questions. This is one of the most difficult skills. The teacher needs to analyze the question and decide whether a pupil question is a probe for data or a request for a confirmation of a hypothesis. If it is a request for data the teacher then needs to decide whether or not a simple Yes or No is sufficient or whether additional data might be needed. If the question is a request for confirmation of a hypothesis, the teacher needs to ask youngsters what information might be useful to them in deciding if the hypothesis is verified.

Tolerating silence. This is another difficult skill for teachers, but it is one that must be mastered. Pupils need adequate time to work on the problem. Thinking takes time. At least seven seconds should pass before a teacher even thinks about rephrasing the question, answering it, or calling on another pupil.

Bringing closure. With many open-minded types of inquiry, teachers have a difficult time knowing when to terminate a lesson. If the class arrives at a conclusion that satisfies the group, then a decision to terminate the lesson is in order. The teacher may restate what the class has concluded and review the process that was used. However, the lesson might also be terminated if there is a high amount of frustration or if the investigation seems to be bogged down. If interest lags, a decision to bring closure might be a good choice.

---

painting, or something else. The problem must be clearly stated by the teacher and clearly understood by each pupil. To check on the clarity of communication, some teachers like to ask youngsters to restate the problem in their own words. This helps the teacher diagnose any difficulties in understanding.

STEP 2   *Formulate possible solutions.* The teacher initiates the process by asking the class, What could explain this situation? Several solutions or explanations need to be elicited from the members of the class. It is a good idea to record these ideas, perhaps on the chalkboard. They can guide pupil work during the data-gathering phase of the activity. When pupils suggest the solutions or explanations, the teacher should be as nonjudgmental as possible. He or she might need to work on the language of pupils' ideas to be sure that communication is clear.

STEP 3   *Data gathering.* If the teacher believes the data gathering will require several days, the class can be organized into groups. Groups will be assigned to gather information to test the accuracy of the suggested solutions. If the problem can be gathered within a given day, the teacher may decide to act as the "data source." In this case, youngsters will be encouraged to ask the teacher questions relevant to the problem. Some forms of inquiry require youngsters to ask only questions that can be answered by only Yes or No. This is not recommended for pupils who are being introduced to inquiry for the first time. They find the constraint on the kinds of questions they can ask to be very frustrating.

As the data-gathering phase goes forward, the teacher needs to refocus attention on the specific problem being addressed and the solutions that were suggested in step 2. The teacher should ask pupils to consider the kinds of information they would need to test the accuracy of the proposed solutions.

STEP 4   *Evaluating proposed solutions.* During this phase, the data gathered in step 3 is used to determine the accuracy of the solutions suggested in step 2. It is a good idea for the teacher to write the relevant data that have been gathered under the specific solution to which the information applies. When all the data have been gathered, then the class can begin evaluating the worth of each of the solutions proposed during step 2.

STEP 5   *Formulating a conclusion.* After all the data have been displayed, then youngsters try to formulate a solution that is most consistent with all of the information that has been gathered. This might mean the acceptance of one of the original solutions. It might mean the modification of one of the original solutions. Or it might mean the development of a solution that was not suggested in step 2.

The following example illustrates how an inquiry lesson might develop in an elementary classroom. This example was one of a series of lessons focusing on how communities and cities change.

TEACHER: Can anyone in the class tell me what a ghost town is?

PUPIL A: That's a town where all the people have moved away.

TEACHER: Yes, that's right. Do you think our town could become a ghost town?

PUPIL B: No, our town is too large. It could never become deserted.

TEACHER: Well, let's look at a town that is now a ghost town. (A slide is projected on the screen. It depicts several deserted buildings.) This town once had about 23,000 people. Now just a few people live here to show tourists around. How large is our town today?

PUPIL C: I think about 40,000 people live here.

TEACHER: Yes, that's about right. So this town once was more than half the size of our town. Now that's quite a few people. Why do you think the people might have left?

PUPIL D: Maybe the people just didn't like the place. Maybe they moved to a city where things were cleaner.

TEACHER: All right, that's a possibility. Let's write our possible reasons on the board. Who has another one?

(Additional pupils respond. The teacher writes their reasons on the chalkboard).

PUPIL E: How old is that town?

TEACHER: Good question. There are lots of things you might want to know about this ghost town to help you decide which of these reasons is the best explanation for why people left. Let's do this. You ask me any question you want about this town, and I'll give you the information. But this is my rule: I won't answer questions that ask me *why* something happened. You need to get other information from me that *you* can use to decide why people left this place. Now, the first question was, How old is that town? Why would that be important to know?

PUPIL C: Well, if it were a thousand years old it just might have been so out of date that people couldn't live there anymore. Maybe they just didn't have electricity or something.

TEACHER: All right. Let me give you an answer. The first people settled this town in 1859. What else do you need to know?

PUPIL F: Were there any big factories there where they built things?

TEACHER: No, there were no large factories. How does that information help us?

PUPIL A: Well, I thought maybe the factory closed so that people didn't have jobs anymore and moved away. That happened to my uncle who worked in a steel plant.

TEACHER: That was a good question. Even though the answer was No, we still got some useful information.

PUPIL H: Is there a highway that goes by there?

TEACHER: Well, there is one road that goes to the town and ends, but there is no highway.

This basic pattern continues until the class discovers a fairly large quantity of information and arrives at an explanation that seems to fit the data. At the conclusion of the exercise, the teacher may choose to suggest that the pupils' answer conforms to the conclusions generally found by others who have investigated the issue. However, it is by no means essential for the teacher to provide the "right" answer. If the class is dissatisfied when the teacher refuses to provide this information, the teacher should point out that many things have happened for which no certain explanations have ever been found. Furthermore, youngsters should be encouraged to develop confidence in their own abilities to arrive at conclusions based on data. In their adult lives, no one will be available to tell them whether they have made the correct responses to difficult problems. Even elementary children need to begin making decisions based on careful examinations of evidence without expecting a confirmation from another person that the proper response has been made.

Inquiry and the Components of the Instructional Act. One of the claimed strengths of inquiry is its ability to motivate. Pupils are motivated by the novel and the puzzling. Hence, when teachers carefully select focus problems that *are* novel and puzzling, pupils do tend to begin the exercise with genuine enthusiasm.

In the brief example of inquiry featuring the deserted town, the teacher set the stage with some questions to introduce the puzzling situation. Motivation was further heightened by asking youngsters to relate this town to their own place of residence.

Sustaining motivation requires more than careful problem selection and introduction. Youngsters also need to feel something meaningful was accomplished as they reflect on their experience once the exercise is over. If they feel that inquiry amounts to a directionless activity that produces no conclusions, they will lose interest in the approach very quickly.

Though inquiry can be motivating, this approach should not be overused. If it is, the novelty wears off, and its motivational value is greatly diminished. Inquiry needs to be intermingled with the other instructional approaches to maximize its effectiveness (see Table 6–7).

Modeling can be especially valuable in inquiry lessons presented to students who have not encountered the approach before. Teachers can show youngsters how to proceed by suggesting the kinds of information that they might need to arrive at conclusions about the focus problem. The best modeling occurs when teachers demonstrate an inquiring attitude throughout the school day. When pupils see teachers using the inquiry processes to seek solutions to problems, they attach a great deal more credibility to inquiry than when the teacher only "talks" about the importance of systematic decision making.

The presentation of information in the inquiry process differs from what youngsters encounter when other teaching techniques are used. The presentation of new information is not a major purpose of inquiry instruction. The new information that is presented represents only a means to an end. The real objec-

---

TABLE 6–7   How Appropriate is Inquiry for the Elementary Classroom?

A. Claimed Advantages of Inquiry

1. It helps individuals learn how to learn.
2. Individuals need to learn how to gather data on their own with a minimum of guidance.
3. It allows for divergent thinking to take place.
4. It involves the pupil in the learning process and allows him or her to make more choices.
5. It facilitates the transfer of learning to new situations.
6. It is more motivating than the other methods.

B. Potential Problems with Inquiry

1. It is too abstract and complex for young children.
2. It is too time consuming for the potential benefits.
3. There is no evidence that it does help the pupil to learn or to transfer learning to new situations.
4. It works only for highly motivated, older children.
5. The process is frustrating for many youngsters because they need the confirmation of getting the right answer—something they do not get in inquiry lessons.
6. There are more efficient ways to teach the pupils how to think and solve problems.

Think About This

1. Which of the above arguments do you think are the most important?
2. What information might you need to verify the validity of the arguments?
3. Do you have some concerns about inquiry that are not stated?
4. How often do you think inquiry should be included in a social studies unit?

tive is to teach the processes of inquiry. Since this is the purpose, many traditional ways of introducing information (for example, the teacher telling something to the pupils) are not appropriate. In inquiry lessons, youngsters get information only when they actively ask for it or seek it out in other ways.

The entire inquiry lesson is a form of practice. What is practiced is the scientific method as applied to a social studies problem. Pupils have opportunities to ask questions, and gather and evaluate data. Learning is active, not passive, throughout the entire inquiry exercise.

Inquiry teaches pupils a process that can be applied to many different kinds of problems. It stimulates an inquiring attitude, and requires pupils to actively use higher-level thinking skills.

Achieving closure presents a problem for teachers when they use inquiry approaches. Sometimes it is difficult to know when to stop an inquiry process. There are times when the class arrives at a good conclusion to a problem in a very short time; but there are other times when youngsters may work for a long time, perhaps several class periods, and still never arrive at a satisfactory conclusion. Ultimately, the teacher must decide when to bring an inquiry lesson to closure.

Closure in an inquiry lesson should involve a review of the inquiry process. The teacher should ask pupils about how they went about solving the problem and why they took the approaches they did. This kind of a review helps them to grasp more completely the steps of the inquiry process and to think about how the process might be applied to other issues.

Closure does not mean that the inquiry process, as applied to the focus problem, must necessarily stop. Sometimes pupils will continue gathering data on their own if they want to come up with a more satisfactory explanation than the one available at the time the formal lesson ended. One of the authors once received a letter about an inquiry lesson problem from an individual who had been in his class two years earlier!

Key Ideas in Summary _____

There are many approaches to teaching that might be used in planning an instructional program. Teacher decision making involves choosing the appropriate method for the objectives and the pupils. An effective teacher will develop a wide repertoire of methods and will use and adapt each method as the situation demands. Some ideas about the issues introduced in this chapter include the following:

1. There is no best approach to instruction. An effective teacher utilizes a variety of approaches, matching the selected approach to the objectives, the characteristics of the pupils, and the availability of the resources.
2. Brainstorming is an approach that maximizes pupils' involvement by encouraging them to contribute their ideas without the fear of failure. It is useful for stimulating creativity and problem solving.
3. Direct instruction is a very structured, teacher-centered approach. The

teacher controls the pace of the classroom activity and the pattern of the classroom interaction. Direct instruction has been found to be effective for teaching basic skills and knowledge.

4. The concept attainment approach is effective in teaching youngsters the concepts that have been deemed important for all of them to learn. It focuses on the teaching of the defining features (called critical attributes) of the concepts selected for study.

5. The major focus of concept formation/diagnosis is teaching youngsters how to develop concepts of their own. It emphasizes the *process* of concept development. Teachers also use the approach to diagnose what pupils already know about a topic.

6. Inducing generalizations is an instructional approach designed to help youngsters formulate generalizations of their own and appreciate the explanatory power of generalizations. It involves the steps of (1) gathering and organizing evidence, (2) comparing and contrasting data and noting the relationships, and (3) making general statements that explain the perceived relationships.

7. Inquiry approaches are based on an application of the scientific method to teaching. The roles of the teacher and pupil are quite different in this approach than in the other instructional methods. Specifically, a great deal of responsibility is placed on pupils. The teacher acts as an information source rather than in information dispenser. Youngsters' questioning skills are sharpened. The emphasis of the approach is on teaching youngsters a systematic decision-making process, not on teaching them the specific elements of history or social science content.

Questions _____

Review Questions

1. What are the basic steps in a brainstorming activity?
2. What is the role of the teacher in the direct instruction approach?
3. What goals are best achieved using the direct instruction approach?
4. What purposes are served by the concept attainment approach?
5. What are the three major steps in the concept formation/diagnosis approach?
6. How should information be organized in order to facilitate the development of generalizations?
7. What is the teacher's role in the inquiry approach?

Thought Questions

1. How would you respond to the following statement? Inquiry methods are inappropriate because they are time consuming and do not have the redeeming virtue of teaching the class much information.
2. Some people promote direct instruction as the best method to use in the classroom. How do you react to this claim?
3. What obstacles might teachers face in attempting to use a formulating-generalizations approach in the classroom?

4. Learning *how* to learn is every bit as important as mastering the subject-matter content. Which of the approaches described in this chapter focuses most directly on teaching an important learning process? Why did you make this choice?
5. Do you think that all of the approaches described in this chapter could be used at all grade levels? Explain your answer.

Extending Understanding and Skill _____

Activities

1. Review a social studies unit for a grade level of your choice. Identify the places in the unit where brainstorming, concept formation, concept attainment/diagnosis, direct instruction, inquiry, and inducing generalizations might be best used.
2. Select a grade level you might like to teach. For the grade level, identify a number of key social studies concepts that would need to be taught. Develop two lesson plans that describe in detail how you would use a direct-instruction approach to teach them. Share the lesson plans with your instructor.
3. Review a social studies textbook. Identify some of the central social studies concepts from one chapter. Develop at least one concept attainment lesson for one of the concepts.
4. Identify a set of puzzling situations or questions that could be used as a focus for inquiry lessons. Exchange your materials with others in the class so that all students will have a large resource file of these materials.
5. Identify a generalization that might be used as a focus for a lesson. Develop a chart to illustrate how the data might be displayed. Prepare a series of questions to help pupils move beyond the data to develop their own generalizations.

Supplemental Reading

GOOD, THOMAS L., and BROPHY, JERE E. *Looking in Classrooms*, 3d ed. New York: Harper & Row, 1984. Chapter 10.

KALTSOUNIS, THEODORE. *Teaching Social Studies in the Elementary School: The Basics for Citizenship.* Englewood Cliffs, NJ: Prentice-Hall, 1979. Chapter 4.

MASSIALAS, BYRON G., and ZEVIN, JACK. *Creative Encounters in the Classroom: Teaching and Learning Through Discovery.* New York: John Wiley & Sons, Inc., 1967. Chapters 1 and 3.

SEEFELDT, CAROL. *Social Studies for the Pre-School Primary Child,* 2nd ed. Columbus, OH: Charles E. Merrill Publishing Co., 1984. Chapter 4.

TANCK, MARLIN L. "Teaching Concepts, Generalizations, and Constructs," in Dorothy McClure Fraser (ed.), *Social Studies Curriculum Development: Problems and Prospects.* 39th Yearbook of the National Council for the Social Studies, 1969. Washington, D.C.: National Council for the Social Studies, 1968, pp. 99–138.

References _____

ARMSTRONG, DAVID G. *Social Studies in Secondary Education.* New York: Macmillan Publishing Co., Inc., 1980.

GOOD, THOMAS L., and BROPHY, JERE E. *Looking in Classrooms,* 3rd ed. New York: Harper & Row, 1984.

JAROLIMEK, JOHN. *Social Studies in Elementary Education*, 6th ed. New York: Macmillan Publishing Co., Inc., 1982.

PETERSON, PENELOPE. "Direct Instruction Reconsidered," in Peterson and Walberg (eds.), *Research in Teaching: Concepts, Findings and Implications*. Berkeley, CA: McCutchan, 1979.

TABA, HILDA. *Teacher's Handbook for Elementary Social Studies*. Reading, MA: Addison-Wesley, 1967.

TRAVERS, R. M. W. *Essentials of Learning*. New York: Macmillan Publishing Co., Inc., 1982.

Chapter 7

Involving Pupils: The Individualized Approaches

(*Source:* © Juliann Barbato.)

1. Identify the approaches to accommodating pupils' individual differences.
2. State the variables that may be altered when individualizing instruction.
3. Design a social studies' learning activity center.
4. Describe the uses of learning contracts.
5. Point out how grades are assigned when the Student-Teams Achievement Divisions approach is used.
6. Describe how the Jigsaw Method might be implemented in the classroom.

Overview

Accommodating pupils' individual differences has been a long-standing priority for teachers. Pupils in the elementary classrooms are tremendously diverse. They represent a cross-section of the abilities and attitudes of the entire population of young people. Teachers, unlike some other professionals, cannot screen their "clients." They must work with all of the children from the community.

Because pupils in the elementary classroom represent such wide-ranging abilities, interests, and attitudes, no single instructional approach will satisfy the needs of all of them. The approaches to instructional planning that seek to serve the needs of the hypothetical "average pupil" will not serve the needs of pupils who deviate from this image. For example, bright youngsters may become bored, while youngsters who cannot maintain the pace of the "average pupil" may become frustrated.

Planning that truly serves the interests of all students in the classroom must differentiate some learning experiences to accommodate their special interests and needs. Individualized-instruction planning places obligations on teachers to design a variety of instructional experiences. These are selected according to the individual interests and ability levels. The sections that follow suggest some approaches to individualization that are appropriate for the elementary social studies classroom.

Altering the Variables to Accommodate the Differences

What does the term individualized instruction mean? For some people, the term means an independent study situation where each student works alone, with no contact with others. Other people have interpreted independent study to mean that the student should have free rein to choose what and when he or she wishes to study.

Both of these conceptions of individualized instruction represent limited understandings of the term. We favor a view of individualized instruction that is broader in scope: *Individualized instruction* represents systematic alternation of

While We All Believe that Each Child has His or Her Own Best Learning Style, Ms. Perkins, Nevertheless . . .
(*Source:* Ford Button.)

one or more instructional variables to better assist as given pupil to master an instructional task. These variables are changed, as needed, to personalize instruction to fit the special needs of each individual.

Given this view, it is clear that individualized instruction by no means implies that a pupil must always work alone. Working alone might be a very poor choice based on the nature of the instructional task and the specific characteristics of the pupil. Individual needs are often best accomplished in small- (and sometimes even in large-) group settings. Furthermore, individualization for some pupils may involve giving them considerable latitude to select from among several learning options; for others, this latitude may not be desirable. The needs of the individual child are the key to determining the exact nature of the individualized program.

There are a number of specific instructional variables that can be manipulated in planning for individualized instruction. These variables include (1) the rate of learning, (2) the content of learning, (3) the method of learning, and (4) the goals of learning.

Altering the Rate of Learning

The rate of learning refers to the pacing of instruction. In a classroom where only one instructional experience is planned for all pupils, it is assumed that all of them will be capable of mastering the material at approximately the same rate. In reality, some pupils will grasp the material quickly, and others will not be able to learn it in the time allotted.

Individualized planning that varies the pacing of instruction in response to pupil differences seeks to provide experiences that challenge the brighter youngsters and give the less-able pupils a chance to succeed. When the learning-rate variable is manipulated in an effort to individualize, the content and the basic requirements are not changed. What *is* altered is the time allowed for the completion of tasks. Pupils are allowed to complete the tasks at their own rate. Altering the learning rate makes sense when the purposes of instruction are very clear and the progress toward the attainment of these purposes can be easily measured.

When planning an individualized program based on altered rates of learning, the teacher must first break the learning sequence into small, measurable steps. This can be done by using the task analysis approach. Next, a test for each learning step is developed. A pupil is permitted to go on to a new step as soon as he or she passes the previous step's test. If the pupil fails the test, he or she is asked to work through the material again. This is called recycling. When the recycling process has been completed, the pupil is given an opportunity to take the step test again.

An example of this kind of individualized instruction is *programmed instruction*. When this approach is used, pupils typically work alone rather than in groups. This is true because, at a given time, each youngster is likely to be at a different place in the instructional program.

Altering the Content of Learning

In individualized programs that have altered the content-of-learning variable, different people in the classroom study different content at the same time. There may be a common set of objectives guiding the instruction, but the specific information that individual youngsters are studying may vary.

When this approach to individualizing instruction is used, pupils are often given the freedom to select objectives-related content from among a variety of options. Some activities in British Open Education involve individualizing the content-of-learning variable. For example, students may be guided by an overall objective related to the mastery of research and writing skills, and may be given a selection of research topics about which to write.

One scheme that has been widely used to provide some structure for this kind of individualized approach is the learning activity package. (A complete description of a learning activity package is provided in a subsequent section of this chapter.) A learning activity package is a document that describes the important goals and objectives and provides an array of learning experiences that youngsters may use to achieve them. Pupils choose the learning experiences that are of the most personal interest.

When the content-of-learning variable is manipulated to individualize instruction, some pupils may work alone and others may work in small groups. Small group work is likely to occur when several youngsters select the same learning activity.

Successful individualized programs focused on providing alternative contents include the use of a rich variety of learning resources and materials. A great deal of teacher planning and organization is required. When such programs are properly implemented, youngsters' individual needs are met.

Altering the Method of Learning

Individualized instructional programs that focus on varying the method of learning attempt to respond to differing learning styles of youngsters in the classroom. The objectives and the content are the same for all. The individualization is defined by how a given learner chooses to master the content. Typically, the teacher provides some options from which learners choose. For example, youngsters may be offered choices such as using the textbook, viewing filmstrips, building a project, or drawing a picture.

Alternative methods are sometimes offered in learning activity packages, and learning centers often provide pupils several optional learning methods. (A complete description of learning centers is provided in a subsequent section of this chapter.)

Altering the Goals of Learning

Individualized instructional programs that alter the goals of learning are not common. Such programs allow pupils to make the major decisions about what they want to learn. Furthermore, pupils are encouraged to develop their own approaches to mastering content. The teacher's role is that of a facilitator who listens to pupils and helps them clarify their interests. This kind of individualized instruction presumes that each pupil is the best judge of his or her long-term needs.

A few individualized programs of this type were established in the late 1960s and early 1970s, when some critics attacked the schools for imposing too much formal structure. In more-recent years, the efforts to hold teachers and students accountable for attaining the prescribed content have caused diminished interest in programs of this type.

The specific decisions about which variable or variables should be the focus of an individualized instructional program reflect teachers' own values and priorities, the expectations of the school and the community, and the nature of the subject matter (see Table 7–1). Some of the methods of "packaging" individualized instruction that have been briefly mentioned in this section are explained more completely in the pages that follow.

TABLE 7–1 Altering the Variables for Individualized Instruction.

Variable	Pupil Role	Teacher Role
Learning rate	Works at own pace; seeks assistance when needed.	Makes assignments; monitors work; provides assistance; checks for mastery.
Content	Chooses topics to be studied in working toward goals; works at own pace; finds materials.	Sets learning goals; provides alternative topics for study; monitors work; evaluates products.
Methods	Decides how to study a topic; arranges environment for study; works at own pace.	Establishes goals; identifies content to be studied; evaluates learning; provides learning alternatives; monitors pupils.
Goals	Chooses goals to be accomplished; helps establish criteria for evaluation; submits final product when satisfied.	Challenges pupils to consider what is important for them to learn; negotiates goals evaluation and timeline with pupils; provides assistance; evaluates product according to criteria jointly established with pupil.

Developing Learning Centers _____

Learning centers are frequent features of individualized social studies programs. Learning centers are designated areas of the classroom that feature materials for pupils and directions telling them what to do.

There often is an attractive visual display designed to motivate interest in the focus topic at the learning center. Typically, centers include learning materials such as books, pictures, filmstrips, tape recorders, worksheets, assignment sheets, and study guides.

Fold-down learning centers with cardboard sides, which include general instructions and information, are popular. These can be set up on tables when they are needed, and can be folded for easy storage once youngsters have completed the work on the focus topic. Figure 7–1 illustrates a learning center that focuses on map and globe skills.

In the learning center displayed in Figure 7–1, a projector with a filmstrip and an accompanying audio tape recorder with a cassette containing explanatory information are set up. Earphones allow individual pupils to listen to the information without disturbing the others in the class. Pupils are asked to use the center one at a time. Each is free to go to the center when no other pupils are using it.

Study guides are typically included at a learning center. Table 7–2 illustrates a study guide that is designed for use in the center illustrated in Figure 7–1.

The learning center approach can accommodate the different rates of learning. Some youngsters may take a long time to accomplish all of the tasks, and others may be able to do them quickly. Some learning centers provide alternative learning

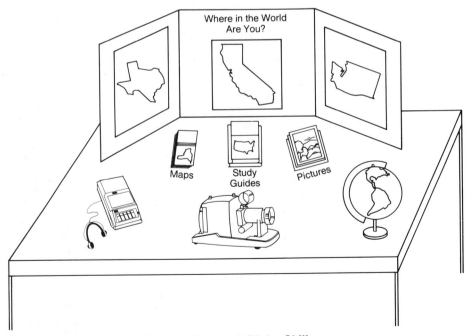

Figure 7–1   A Learning Center: Map and Globe Skills.

TABLE 7–2   A Learning Center Study Guide.

Where in the World are You?

Objective

When you complete this learning center, you should be able to identify the type of map that is needed to solve a given problem.

Sequence of Activities

1. Take a minute to look at all the material in the learning center. What do you think this center's purpose is? What do you already know about this topic? Think about this.
2. Pick up the worksheet that goes with the filmstrip. Look at the filmstrip and listen to the tape. When you have completed the worksheet, give it to your teacher. If you do not understand some part of the filmstrip, look at it again until you do. If you still have trouble, raise your hand and the teacher will come to help you.
3. Use the maps in the center as you answer these questions.
   (a) Which maps would be the best for identifying the populations of cities?
   (b) Which maps would be helpful if you wanted to know the elevation of a place?
   (c) Which maps would be helpful if you wanted to say something about the kinds of things grown in different places?
4. *Application activity.* Construct a map of our own community. In your map, show something that is not usually included on a street map. (Examples: the types of trees, the locations of apartment houses, the kinds of stores, and so forth.)

options. For example, the directions may allow a pupil the alternative to get information from a cassette tape, a reading selection, or a video tape. Though the rate of learning the sources of information may vary, all pupils at a learning center pursue the same basic objectives.

Sometimes several learning centers are set up in the classroom at the same time. Pupils are allowed to begin work at any vacant center and to work through the rest of them at their own rate. It may be necessary for teachers to set some broad time limits. For example, pupils may be told that "All the centers must be completed by Friday." Pupils who finish early can be provided with enrichment activities. Sometimes they are permitted to tutor others in the class who may be experiencing difficulty with the work at one or more of the centers.

Learning Activity Packages _____

The learning activity package (LAP) is often used to organize individualized instructional programs. Sometimes LAPs are included as parts of learning centers. Sometimes various LAPs are given to different youngsters to complete on their own. Occasionally, all students will be assigned to work on the same LAP.

All LAPs share certain common features. They usually include a pretest, a list of the activities to be completed, an explanation of the resources to be used, and a posttest or other evaluation procedure. Sometimes the pretest is set up so that pupils with high scores are allowed to skip some of the listed learning activities.

LAPs must be designed so that pupils have the prerequisite skills and knowledge to accomplish the assigned tasks. Otherwise, the experience will be frustrating, and pupils will place very heavy demands on the teacher.

All of the information a pupil may need to complete the activities is not necessarily included in the LAP itself. The instructions in the LAP may direct pupils to other learning resources. For example, a given LAP might direct a pupil to read part of a textbook, to read a book in the school library, and to view a film or filmstrip. Sometimes LAPs ask pupils to use out-of-class resources. For example, a pupil might be asked to see an evening news program or to report on an account in a local newspaper of a speech given by the President.

The LAP is basically a management tool. It allows the teacher to gather the instructions for pupils in a convenient way and can be designed to individualize learning experiences. The LAP places on pupils heavy responsibilities for completing the assigned tasks. See Table 7–3 for an example of a LAP.

LAPs are especially useful tools for guiding pupils as they work on research projects. LAPs help pupils to know exactly what they are to do. Pupils who are working on LAPs need to be monitored carefully by the teacher. Without this kind of teacher attention, some youngsters may procrastinate and fail to complete tasks. Furthermore, the teacher can help youngsters overcome any special difficulties that they may encounter with the assigned activities.

As do learning centers, LAPs present the same content and learning objec-

TABLE 7–3   A Learning Activity Package.

Primary Sources

I. Pretest

This learning activity package is about primary sources. If you think you know what a primary source is, answer the following questions and take them to the teacher. If you do not know, proceed directly to the introduction.
1. What is a primary source?
2. Is our social studies textbook a primary source?
3. Why are primary sources important?

II. Introduction

When you read our social studies textbook, do you ever wonder how the writers found out about the events they describe? For some recent events, they may have observed or participated in the event. However, for events they did not participate in or see, they had to rely on the descriptions provided by others.

When you read an account of an event, it is important to know whether the writer personally observed the event or learned about it by reading a report written by someone else. Information tends to get confused as it is passed from person to person. You may recall that this has happened to you when you have heard something a friend heard from someone else. When this happened, the information your friend shared may have been quite different from what actually took place.

III. Objectives

When you complete this LAP, you should be able to:
1. Define a primary source.
2. Define a secondary source.
3. Identify examples of primary sources.
4. Identify primary sources, and use them in reporting about an historic event.

IV. Activities

Definition. A primary source is a person or a record written by a person who was either a participant or an observer of an event. For example, an eyewitness to an accident would be considered a primary source. Other records, such as the repair bill and pictures of the damaged car would be considered primary sources. However, the reports of others about the accident, such as a newspaper account, would be secondary source. If a friend saw the accident and told you about it, he would be a primary source. If you tell someone else about it, you are a secondary source.

1. Which of the following are most likely to be primary resources in learning about the Civil War?
   (a) A diary of a soldier who was in the war.
   (b) Our textbook.
   (c) The miniseries "North and South."
   (d) The letters of one General to another General.
2. Read the story of the "Shot Heard Around the World" in our social studies textbook. Next, read the diary account of a British soldier. In the space below, state the ways the two accounts differ, and explain why you think they differ.
3. What do these differences tell you about the uses of primary sources when trying to determine what happened?
4. If you were to write an account of how our school has changed in the past ten years, what would be some of the primary sources that you could use?

V. Evaluation Activity

Choose an event from the recent history of our nation or community. Identify a person or some records that could be considered a primary source. Prepare an account of the event. If you use a person, you may ask them to describe the event to you on a cassette tape. Before you do this you will need to develop some questions to ask the person. The teacher can help you with this. When you finish, give your teacher the account or the tape.

---

tives for all pupils. Some allowances are provided for pupils requiring different amounts of time to complete the assigned tasks.

Activity Cards _____

Activity cards provide pupils with choices regarding how they go about learning some of the assigned content. Each card indicates several tasks to be completed. Typically, a set of activity cards will relate to a single objective. Pupils are not given any options in terms of the objectives to be pursued.

Youngsters are given the choice of selecting one (or sometimes several) activity card. Teachers allow children to work individually, in pairs, or in small groups when doing the activities listed on a single activity card. When the work on the card(s) has been completed, then the pupil is credited with having finished the work associated with the objective.

Activity cards are easy to organize and store. A large number of them can be kept in a small file or a shoe box. The tasks listed on activity cards often represent extensions of the instruction, provided in other ways. Sometimes the tasks listed on activity cards are used for extra-credit assignments. Table 7–4 illustrates the kinds of information included on three separate activity cards that

TABLE 7–4 Three Examples of Activity Cards.

Activity Card 1

Topic: The Division of Labor
Grade Level: Primary
Purpose: The pupil will state examples of the division of labor.

Activities

1. Look through the magazines in the learning center.
2. Cut out five pictures of jobs that people are doing.
3. For each job, write one sentence describing how this job helps other people.
4. Draw a picture of a job that you have at home.
5. Write a sentence telling how your job helps your family.

Activity Card 2

Topic: Goods and Services
Grade Level: Upper Elementary
Purpose: The pupil will identify businesses that provide goods and those that provide services.

Activities

1. Look through the Yellow Pages. Make a chart like the one below. In the "Goods" column, place at least ten businesses that provide goods. In the "Services" column, place at least ten businesses that provide services. Identify at least three businesses that provide both goods and services.

Goods	Services	Both

2. Interview a relative or friend. Find out whether or not the job he or she has provides a good or a service. Identify what he or she must know to provide this good or service.

Activity Card 3

Topic: Local History
Grade Level: Middle Elementary
Purpose: The pupil will research an event in local history.

Activities

1. Are there any historical markers or important historical sites in our community? If there is a marker, visit this site. Write down what the marker says. Talk with other people in the community to find out what they might know about the event described on the historical marker.
2. Once you have gathered information about the event, do one of the following:
    (a) Prepare an oral report about the event.
    (b) Draw a picture of the event.
    (c) Write a play about the event, and act it out for the class.

were developed for use in elementary social studies classes. Sets of activity cards are often developed by teachers as they plan individual units. In time, this results in a set of activity cards to accompany each social studies unit that will be taught during the year.

Learning Contracts _____

A learning contract is an agreement between a teacher and a pupil. It describes in very specific terms what the pupil agrees to do to satisfy certain learning requirements. There are two basic types of learning contracts: open and closed.

Open learning contracts are those that give the student a great deal of discretion in deciding what the objectives of the contract, the specific assignments, the kinds of learning activities, and the evaluation procedures will be. Open learning contracts are suitable for use with only motivated, mature, and very independent students.

Closed learning contracts are much more common. The teacher plays a large role in determining the objectives, assignments, learning activities, and assessment procedures. The individual needs of pupils are considered as the teacher plans these requirements.

Learning contracts are written in very specific language. They almost always explain what a pupil is to do, the resources that are to be used, the nature of any "product" that the pupil is to prepare, the nature of the evaluation that is to be used, and a date that indicates when all the work must be completed. An example of a learning contract is provided in Table 7–5.

TABLE 7–5 An Example of a Learning Contract.

Contract

Topic:

I _____ , agree to do the following:

1.

2.

3.

4.

The following criteria will be used in evaluating the activities and products of the contract.

1.

2.

3.

I agree that the activities will be completed by _____ .

_____   _____   _____

Student's Signature   Teacher's Signature   Date

Cooperative Learning _____

Cooperative learning is an approach to individualizing that emphasizes working together. Pupils enjoy working together. For this reason, cooperative learning tends to be popular. This procedure is especially appropriate for social studies lessons, because it attaches great importance to how people work and live together in groups as social beings.

In recent years, a number of guidelines have been developed for implementing cooperative learning in a productive way (Slavin, 1982; p. 2). The essence of this approach is having a group work toward a common objective. Each member of the group is given a specific task to accomplish. The evaluation of each group member depends on the overall quality of the group's work, and can be approached in several ways.

For example, if a test will be used to assess the quality of the work, the group's average can be used to evaluate the group's effort. Since the group members understand that the individual grades will be determined by the quality of the work of the group as a whole, there is an incentive for pupils to help one another to improve the overall test performance.

Sometimes the teacher assesses a group paper or group project to evaluate the performance. Each pupil is assessed in terms of the teacher's appraisal, the paper, or the project. Because students understand they will be evaluated in this way, they tend to work productively with one another to assure that the final paper or project will be of high quality.

This chart shows the scoring of teams organized for a cooperative-learning activity.

(*Source:* © Juliann Barbato.)

The purpose of cooperative learning is not simply arranging for youngsters to work together. Incentives that will encourage pupils to work closely with one another to accomplish the assigned tasks should be included in this approach.

Research that has been conducted on cooperative learning suggests that this results in higher levels of mastery and better retention and transfer of concepts than the approaches in which pupils compete against one another as individuals. Pupils tend to be better motivated, and their attitudes toward school tend to be more positive. As a result, their self-esteem tends to be higher. (Roy, 1982; pp. 5–6).

Several approaches to cooperative learning are introduced in the subsections that follow.

Student-Teams Achievement Divisions

According to Slavin (1978), the *Student-Teams Achievement Divisions* approach begins with the teacher dividing the class into four- or five-member teams. Each team should include a sprinkling of high achievers, low achievers, boys, girls, and youngsters from various ethnic backgrounds. After the class as a whole has been introduced to new content through traditional large-group instruction, each team is given a set of study worksheets. The worksheets describe the tasks to be accomplished and the problems to be solved. These tasks and problems relate to the content that has been introduced to the class as a whole.

Each team begins to work. The members may quiz each other, tutor each other, or take other actions that they deem necessary to accomplish the assigned tasks. Once the group has finished its work, the team members take a test about the material. They may not help one another on the test. The scores of the individual team members are combined to yield a team score, which is determined by how much the score of each individual exceeded his or her previous average score on tests. The individual pupils are graded based on the level of their team score.

Some teachers do not rely on past tests. Instead, they set a predetermined expected standard of performance for each pupil. If a given pupil scores higher than his or her expected standard or base score, then points are contributed toward the team total. In general, one point is assigned toward the team score for every point a pupil makes above his or her base score. Usually there is a maximum number of points (often ten points) that any one pupil can contribute to the team total. This would mean, for example, that a youngster with a base score of 32, who scored 80 on a test, would still only contribute the ten-point maximum to the team. An example of a group score for an achievement team is provided in Table 7–6.

Note in Table 7–6 that Calvin, though he had the lowest score on the test, still contributed ten points to his team's total. This occurred because his test score was much higher than his base score. As a result of his or her effort, each member of this team was awarded 32 points.

This approach has merit as a means of encouraging the efforts of slower pupils. They have an incentive to do as well as they can. Even though their individual scores may not be high, they have an opportunity to make an important contribution to the overall scores of the teams to which they are assigned. The

TABLE 7–6 Group Score for an Achievement Team.

Student	Base Score	Quiz Score	Team Points
Alan	49	56	7
Bertha	50	48	0
Calvin	20	35	10
Dinah	85	90	5
Carlos	75	100	10
Total Team Points			32

scoring system also encourages the brighter youngsters to help the members of their team who are not as quick to grasp new content. All the participants come to understand that they have a role to play in helping all the members of the team to learn.

The Jigsaw Method

The *Jigsaw Method* is a group-learning procedure that requires each member of the group to complete a portion of a larger assignment (Aronson, 1978). The entire assignment cannot be completed until all the parts of the "jigsaw" are fitted together.

In preparation for the Jigsaw Method, the teacher divides the class into teams of five or six pupils each. Each group has the same number of members (to the extent that is possible). Care is taken to provide a mixture of ability levels in each group.

The teacher breaks down the assigned activity into as many parts as there are members of the individual groups. If groups have five members, then there are five major tasks. In each group, one pupil is assigned to do each task. Since the tasks may vary in difficulty, the teacher usually plays some role in assigning them to individual pupils.

There are two major steps in the Jigsaw Method. Suppose a teacher has devised five major tasks. Each group has one pupil assigned to task A, one to task B, one to task C, one to task D, and one to task E. After an initial meeting as a team, the members of each group disperse and form new groups. All of the pupils working on task A form a group. New groups consisting of pupils working on tasks B, C, D, and E also form.

In these new groups (sometimes called task-alike, or expert, groups) pupils—with teacher guidance—discuss how they will go about completing their task. Then, working either alone or with others, pupils in these expert groups start working on their tasks. When this work has been completed, pupils reassemble in their original groups.

In the reassembled group, the pupil responsible for task A shares his or her information with the others. Pupils responsible for the other tasks share their information as well. Once all the information has been shared, the group members begin assembling the information to complete the overall assignment, which is then given to the teacher for evaluation.

The Jigsaw Method promotes productive contributions in groups. Pupils learn to listen attentively to others because they will need their information to complete the assignments. Gathering individuals who are working on similar tasks helps develop cooperative and supportive attitudes among students.

The Learning Together Method

Johnson and Johnson (1975) have developed a cooperative learning approach that is characterized by a somewhat less-formal organizational structure than the Jigsaw Method. In the _Learning Together Method_, the teacher organizes pupils into groups. The members are selected so that each group reflects a variety of interests and abilities.

Once the groups are formed, the teacher gives each group an assignment that requires the attention and involvement of all the group members. The assignment usually requires pupils to develop a "product" of some kind. This might be a set of written responses to a set of questions, a research report, a play to be presented to the class, or a group oral report. The members of the group are graded on the basis of the quality of the group's final product.

The successful implementation of the Learning Together Method requires the teacher to monitor each group carefully. Pupils will have problems that need to be resolved. The teacher needs to be available so that misunderstandings do not interfere with the completion of assigned tasks.

All the cooperative learning approaches involve much more than simply assigning pupils to work in groups. Pupils need to be taught how to work and interact in group settings. They need help in developing ways to organize their group's work and their own work within the groups. Since so much decision making in our country occurs in committees, skills in group learning can provide life-long benefits.

Table 7–7 is an example of the steps that might be followed when planning for a cooperative learning exercise in the classroom.

In summary, the cooperative learning experience requires the following teacher decisions:

1. Selecting a topic that lends itself to group work.
2. Making decisions about group size and composition.
3. Providing appropriate materials.
4. Identifying the parts of the lesson and sequencing the lesson.
5. Monitoring the work of pupils in groups.
6. Intervening when necessary, to solve problems.
7. Evaluating outcomes.

Not every social studies objective lends itself to a cooperative learning activity. Some basic information is better introduced by the teacher to the class as a whole. Occasionally, it may be desirable for students to work independently on tasks. However, the "social" nature of the social studies suggests that cooperative learning activities do merit an important place in the elementary program.

TABLE 7–7 Planning a Cooperative Learning Exercise.

Subject Focus: Procedures and Consumers

Procedures

1. *The instructional objective.* Each pupil will identify pictures of people who are producers and people who are consumers.

2. *Group size.* Depending on the ages of pupils and the nature of the task, there should be at least three but no more than five pupils in a group. Groups should contain members of a variety of ability levels.

3. *Classroom arrangement.* At the beginning of the lesson, all pupils are grouped for review and instruction. Each small group is dismissed one at a time to move to a table where it will work. Each table will need at least five magazines, five pairs of scissors, paste, and a large piece of poster paper.

4. *Large-group phase.* In the large group, the teacher will ask the pupils to review what they have learned about producers and consumers. Some examples will be given and the total class will be asked to identify whether the examples given were "producers" or "consumers."

   Small-group phase. The teacher gives pupils instructions about what they are to do. Each group will be required to find four pictures of producers and four pictures of consumers. Pupils are to cut the pictures out of the provided magazines and paste them on the poster board under either the label "producer" or "consumer." The teacher explains that the assignment will be complete when the pictures have been identified, when all the group members have agreed as to the classification of each picture, and when the poster has been completed. Each member of the group must write his or her name at the bottom of the poster. This lets everyone know that each member of the group helped and that the group as a whole agrees on the classification of people as "producers or "consumers."

5. *Identify the expected behaviors and ground rules.* The teacher says: "When you have found a picture in your magazines, you must say to each member of your group, 'I think this is a picture of a producer. Do you agree?' You must look each member in the eye and if every person says, 'Yes, I agree,' you may cut out the picture and paste it on your chart. If they do not agree, then you may say, 'I think it is a producer because . . . ' If you cannot convince the others, then look for another picture."

6. *Monitoring during small-group work.* The teacher circulates around the room and looks for the following:
   (a) Comprehension of the directions.
   (b) Understanding of producers and consumers.
   (c) Participation by all group members.
   (d) Pupils skill in solving disagreements.
   (e) Groups having trouble cooperating. (When this happens, the teacher needs to work with the group to resolve the problem.)
   (f) Ideas about how to group pupils in the future.

7. *Evaluation criteria.* Each group that has at least four pictures correctly grouped will be checked as having successfully completed the assignment. Those that do not will be recycled through the assignment.

Key Ideas in Summary _____

Individual differences can be accommodated in a variety of ways in elementary social studies classes. Individualizing instruction does not mean that every student must work independently. Some of the newer cooperative learning approaches use individual differences as a vehicle for building social skills through group interaction. Some of the ideas about these issues that were introduced in this chapter include the following: ·

1. Individual differences in a classroom can be used to enhance the teaching of social studies. While the management concerns must be addressed, the individual strengths and learning styles can be used to maximize social learning.

2. A number of variables can be manipulated to individualize instruction. Among these are variables associated with (1) the rate of learning, (2) the content of learning, (3) the method of learning, and (4) the goals of learning.

3. Learning centers are frequently used in individualized social studies programs. The learning center is a place where a variety of materials are kept for pupils to use when studying a given topic. Most learning centers provide a study guide that instructs pupils about how they are to proceed.

4. Learning activities packages are self-contained programs that direct pupils to the materials and prescribe the activities that must be completed. They allow pupils some choice in the activities and have some provisions for pupils with different learning rates.

5. Activity cards prescribe activities for pupils to complete. Typically, pupils are allowed to select from among a number of activity cards. Activity cards are often used to supplement other instruction related to social studies units.

6. A learning contract is an agreement between a teacher and a pupil. It typically specifies what the pupil will study, how the material will be studied, and how learning will be evaluated.

7. Cooperative learning involves placing youngsters in groups and giving them a group task to perform. Group performance on the task is used to assign the individual grades. Cooperative learning accommodates individual differences by allowing the group members to decide how they will accomplish the group task.

8. Student-Teams Achievement Divisions represents another approach to cooperative learning. In this method, each member of the group is given a base score that is determined by his or her past performance. The group score is determined by how much each member exceeds this base score. It provides an incentive for peer motivation and tutoring. It is probably best used when a clear task such as a test is used as the criterion measure.

9. The Jigsaw Method requires the teacher to break a major assignment into a limited number of tasks. If five tasks are selected, the teacher divides the class into groups of five. One person in each group is responsible for accomplishing one of the tasks. After these initial groups have met, then the class organizes itself into new groups that include all of the people working on a given task. These people decide how to approach their responsibility. Then they go to work. When everyone has completed his or her work, the original groups meet again. Each pupil presents the information he or she has gathered to everyone in his or her group. The overall performance of the group on a test is used as a basis for assigning grades to the group members.

10. In the Learning Together Method, the members of groups decide how each member will contribute. The final "product" of learning is a group product rather than an individual product. The teacher works closely with the group members as they pursue their individual responsibilities.

Questions _____

Review Questions

1. In what situations might it be appropriate to individualize by altering the rate of learning?
2. What is one way of altering the content of learning?
3. How might a teacher provide for different learning styles by altering the methods of learning?
4. What is the role of the teacher when altering the goals of learning?
5. What are the items that need to be included in a learning center?
6. What elements are included in a learning activity package?
7. How is cooperative learning defined?
8. How are grades assigned to individuals in the Student-Team Achievement Division approach?
9. What is the function of the expert groups in the Jigsaw Method?
10. Is the Learning Together Method different from the Student-Team Achievement Divisions approach and the Jigsaw Method?

Thought Questions

1. What are the barriers to individualizing instruction?
2. What are the conditions that need to exist before a teacher can feel free to alter the goals of learning?
3. How does the role of the teacher change when individualizing instruction?
4. How would you respond to someone who told you that elementary school children lack sufficient maturity to profit from individualized instruction?
5. What are the strengths and weaknesses of the several cooperative learning approaches?
6. What is your reaction to assigning individual grades based on a group score as in the Student-Teams Achievement Divisions approach?

Extending Understanding and Skill _____

Activities

1. Review a social studies unit. Identify the places in the unit where learning centers, learning activity packages, and activity cards might be used.
2. Choose a unit of instruction for the grade level of your choice. Design a learning center for that unit. In your design, include the pictures that you will use for the learning center display, the types of learning activities that you will include, a learning guide for the center, and the criteria that you will use for evaluation.
3. Develop a set of at least five activity cards to go with a given topic of instruction. The activity cards should include a variety of activities and levels of sophistication in order to accommodate the different pupil interests and abilities.
4. Identify social studies content that might be taught using the Student-Team Achievement Divisions approach. Describe how the teams might be arranged and how the group scores would be determined.
5. Develop a group approach using the Jigsaw Method. Identify the different roles or expert groups that will be needed and the materials that each group would need.
6. Develop a checklist of things that you would look for if you were to observe the process of a cooperative learning group.

Supplemental Reading

CORNETT, C. E. *What You Should Know About Teaching and Learning Styles.* Bloomington, IN.: Phi Delta Kappa, 1983.

JAROLIMEK, J. *Social Studies in Elementary Education.* New York: Macmillan Publishing Co., Inc., 1982, 6th ed., Chapter 10.

LARKIN, J. M., and WHITE, J. J., "The Learning Center in the Social Studies Classroom," in W. W. Joyce and F. L. Ryan (eds.), *Social Studies and the Elementary Teacher: Promises and Practices* (Bulletin 53). Washington D.C.: National Council for the Social Studies, 1977.

SLAVIN, R. E. *Cooperative Learning: Student Teams.* Washington, D.C.: National Education Association, 1982.

References _____

ARONSON, E. *The Jigsaw Classroom.* Beverly Hill, CA: Sage Publications, 1978.

FENSTERMACHER, G. D., and GOODLAD, J. I. (eds.), *Individual Differences and the Common Curriculum, 82nd Yearbook.* Chicago: National Society for the Study of Education, 1983.

JOHNSON, D. W., and JOHNSON, R. T. *Learning Together and Alone.* Englewood Cliffs, NJ: Prentice-Hall, Inc., 1975.

ROY, P. A. (ed.), *Structuring Cooperative Learning Experiences in the Classroom, The 1982 Handbook.* Minneapolis, MN: A Cooperative Network Publication, 1982.

SLAVIN, R. E. "Student Teams and Achievement Divisions," *Journal of Research and Development in Education* (Fall 1978), pp. 39–49.

Chapter 8

Involving Pupils: Using Special Resources

(*Source:* © Juliann Barbato.)

This chapter provides information to help the reader:

1. Point out the contributions that might be made by microcomputers in elementary social studies programs.
2. Identify several specific software needs of elementary school social studies programs that utilize microcomputers.
3. Describe the criteria to be used in evaluating the quality of software in the social studies.
4. Describe the characteristics of programs focusing on the local community.
5. Explain several ways in which newspapers can be used to promote social learning in the elementary grades.

Overview

Learning resources suitable for use in elementary social studies classes are really limited only by the imagination of the teacher. Textbooks have often been used extensively. Perhaps this is natural, given their ready availability. But other information sources may prove to be more effective, at least in some circumstances. Even the best textbooks are not capable of providing the kind of active, hands-on learning experiences that sometimes can be provided in lessons drawing on other information sources and presentation techniques.

Computer programs, newspapers, and the aspects of the local community are examples of the nontextbook learning resources used by elementary social studies teachers. The sections that follow suggest how each resource might be used.

Computers and School Programs

The use of computers in the schools has increased dramatically over the past ten years. Today, computers are being used for a wide variety of purposes. However, the nature of computer use is by no means uniform in all schools.

The first computers found their way into the schools at the secondary level, often in the mathematics or business-education departments. At this level, there was a very heavy emphasis on teaching programming skills to students. Even today, computers are used more for teaching programming than for any other purpose.

Programming, of course, was an educational purpose of very little interest to elementary educators. Almost from the beginning, computers were used to supplement the elementary instructional program. The idea was to teach pupils some basic computer-literacy skills (how to load and use simple programs without fear) and, perhaps, to work on some simple academic content at the same time.

In the elementary school, there was an emphasis on programs that provided for drill and practice. Several simple games that focused on simple tasks, often of a repetitive nature, were devised. Many programs represented little more than a rebirth of the old-fashioned pupil workbook in the form of a floppy disk.

I Wonder if There is Life in Other Modules?
(*Source:* Ford Button.)

Instead of filling in the blanks with a pencil on a paper, youngsters filled in the blanks on a screen by moving a keyboard cursor and striking the appropriate keys. Some critics contend that this kind of computer-based instruction represents a misuse of the technology and provides nothing that the older technologies could not provide as well, and at a lower cost. Despite these criticisms, drill-and-practice programs are still very heavily used in the schools.

Though the situation is improving, relatively few computer programs in the schools involve youngsters in production tasks. These are tasks that ask them to do something with the provided information that will result in some kind of a new "product." Though the potential is great, simulations, word processing, and problem-solving activities are underutilized in today's school computer activities.

This underutilization is not caused by educators who fail to appreciate the desirability of providing youngsters with production-task–oriented computer activities. The problem is a result of a lack of software that has been designed to provide youngsters with these kinds of experiences in a school setting.

Today, this situation is changing very rapidly. The number and quality of educational computer programs for schools is increasing. Groups such as the International Council for Computers in Education have been working hard to encourage this kind of software development and to suggest ways for disseminating the software to the schools at a modest cost. In the future, there should be more and better software available. As this software becomes available, more intelligent use of the computer's technological features will become feasible (see Table 8–1).

The Status of Computer Use in the Social Studies

Elementary teachers who have used computers have not generally made extensive use of them in the social studies. The social studies program has not been one of the curriculum areas that people have thought about when the issue of computer use has come up. For example, inservice programs in the area of the social studies have rarely addressed the issue of computer use (Glenn and Rawitsch, 1984).

The general issue of software mentioned in the discussion of computers in the school has special relevance for the social studies. Here, until quite recently, the

TABLE 8-1 Should We Wait for Better Software?

Read the responses of these two speakers.

Speaker A	Speaker B
Social studies software is just so *poor!* These kids are really doing nothing they couldn't have done before we got our computers. Yet, we're paying $60 to $150 for *each* of these programs. I think we ought to call a halt on software purchases until something really *good* comes out. I mean, something that will make the kids think.	I don't like much of the software, either. But if we avoid using what we can get, the people who write this stuff will give up on social studies entirely. I mean, if they can't sell their stuff, they'll turn their talents elsewhere. Then where will we be? I think we should continue to use what we can get now. But we should let everybody know that it's *not* good enough.

Think About This

1. Why *is* so much software not much different from exercise-book or workbook material?
2. How do you explain the shortage of elementary social studies software that really makes youngsters think?
3. How do you respond to the ideas of Speaker A? Why?
4. How do you respond to the ideas of Speaker B? Why?
5. If you were to join this argument, what would your position be? On what is your position based?

pool of available software was especially poor. This situation has begun to improve, but the software in the elementary social studies area continues to lag woefully behind the software now available in subject areas such as mathematics or science.

Because relatively few elementary teachers have made use of computers in their social studies programs, the commercial developers of software have been reluctant to commit large sums of money to this area. They have been concerned that the market for such products might be too small to warrant the heavy investment. As more and more teachers begin to use software in the social studies, this situation may change. Indeed, there have been noticeable improvements in the quality of social studies software over the past several years.

Elementary teachers are especially interested in social studies software that will help develop youngsters' problem-solving skills. They want programs that will require youngsters to take basic information, engage in analytical thinking, and arrive at and test the quality of decisions.

In addition to programs that will stretch youngsters' thinking abilities, software that has been designed with an appreciation for the overall social studies curriculum is needed. Teachers increasingly want to know how a given program or series of programs will fit into the entire social studies program. Software developers are being asked to suggest what long-term curriculum objectives are served by a given program and exactly how the program will contribute to youngsters' grasp of these objectives.

Finally, social studies teachers are asking software developers to pay closer attention to the issue of reading. Many computer programs require youngsters to read information off the screen, yet few programs recognize the differences in reading proficiency among youngsters at a given grade level. Because of the teachers' concerns, we may expect to see future programs that are formatted in several versions so that they can be used successfully by youngsters of widely differing reading abilities.

The Kinds of Computer-Supported Instruction in Elementary Social Studies

Two professionals who have thoroughly investigated the computer use in social studies programs are Allen Glenn and Don Rawitsch. They suggest a number of roles that can be played by computers in the social studies (Glenn and Rawitsch, 1984; pp. 8–14). Among these are the following:

1. Delivering content.
2. Retrieving and analyzing information.
3. Developing thinking skills.
4. Studying computers as a technological phenomenon.
5. Managing classroom tasks.

Delivering Content. Content can be delivered in various ways and for various kinds of learning outcomes. For example, many computer programs are designed to enable students to practice the information that they have learned previously. These *drill programs* focus on content such as the recall of names, places, dates and on applications of simple processes; for example, finding locations on maps given the measures of longitude and latitude.

Tutorial programs impart basic information to pupils. There are quite a few such programs on the market today. Several of these are particularly well suited for use with younger pupils. Some of the better programs teach skills and information that have relevance not just for the social studies but also for the other areas of the elementary curriculum. Let us look at several examples of programs of this type.

Title: Kids on Keys
Source: Spinnaker Software
215 First Street
Cambridge, MA 02142

Kids on Keys is a program that is designed for very young children (ages 3 to 7). The program helps them learn numbers, letters, and simple words as they become familiar with using a computer keyboard. It is an excellent program for introducing very young pupils to working with the computer.

Title: Letters and Words
Source: Learning Well
200 South Service Road
Roslyn Heights, NY 11577

As the title implies, the focus of this program is on simple reading skills. Letters and Words, helps youngsters master alphabetization skills, among other things. It is directed toward younger pupils. These learning outcomes can be of great help in other social studies activities that require youngsters to look up and organize information.

Title: Big Bird's Special Delivery
Source: Tandy-Radio Shack
Fort Worth, TX 76102

Big Bird's Special Delivery is just one example of a series of programs made available by the Children's Computer Workshop (CCW). The Children's Computer Workshop is an offshoot of the Children's Television Workshop (CTW), the group that produces the very popular PBS series, "Sesame Street." The CCW programs are based on the "Sesame Street" characters and are directed toward very young pupils.

In Big Bird's Special Delivery, youngsters are asked to help deliver packages to the correct store. The program helps to teach the concept of "direction" and the idea that certain objects always have the same names or labels.

Retrieving and Analyzing Information. Computer programs are especially well suited to helping youngsters develop proficiency in working with numerical and graphical data. The computer can display such information quickly. Computations can be accomplished almost instantaneously by making a few key strokes. Since much social studies content involves the analysis of isolated pieces of information, the computer has proved to be a useful instructional tool for helping youngsters engage in this important social learning skill.

A number of computer programs are available that are designed to enhance youngsters' ability to work with quantitative data sources. Most are suitable only for youngsters in the upper grades. An example of such a program is Interpreting Graphs and Tables.

Title: Interpreting Graphs and Tables
Source: Social Studies School Service
10,000 Culver Boulevard,
P.O. Box 802
Culver City, CA, 90232-0802

Developing Thinking Skills. Increasingly, computer programs that are designed to give youngsters opportunities to analyze information and draw conclusions are becoming available. They seek to improve pupils thinking skills.

Many such programs in the social studies are *simulations*. These sophisticated games are ordinarily based on historical or social events. The better ones are capable of transmitting basic information as well as encouraging youngsters to think and to make decisions.

Some authorities believe that the ability to deliver exciting simulated experiences is one of the unchallenged strengths of computer-based instruction. Geography Search is an example of one of the elementary social studies simulations that are available today.

Title: Geography Search
Source: McGraw-Hill Book Company
1221 Avenue of the Americas
New York, NY 10020

This simulation engages youngsters in making decisions about how a sailing vessel from the age of discovery should be navigated. The decisions about the various matters are fed into the computer, which then provides feedback about issues such as the position of the ship and the state of the provisions. Once the ship lands in the New World, youngsters are faced with the difficult choice of either returning home the same way they sailed or taking a risk by continuing to sail west. The simulation provides excellent insights into the dilemmas faced by the early explorers (see Table 8–2).

TABLE 8–2 Do Computer Simulations Teach What They Purport to Teach?

The following comments were made by a concerned parent at a PTA meeting.

My youngster has been coming home really charged up about the social studies computer games. At first I was ecstatic about this very positive reaction. It was a most welcome change from the usual grumbling about having to deal with "all this boring stuff." I thought to myself that at last some clever educator had figured out a way to "sell" content to kids in a way they would find interesting and even exciting. My enthusiasm began to fade quickly though when I asked him what he was learning.

Though the simulation was supposed to be teaching something about the problems the early settlers found when they arrived in the new world, I found my child had little to say about these difficulties. Rather, he was full of talk about which buttons to push to make the cursor race quickly around the screen. He said that the "really neat" thing about the game was that it was sharpening his general computer game–playing skills. He hopes to add at least 15,000 points to his "best ever" score the next time I break down and let him have a few quarters to throw away in the computer game parlor in the mall.

I am sure that the makers of the simulation intended to focus youngsters' attention on the academic content. But this hasn't worked out for my child. I find the simulations to be diverting attention from sound academics. Are we investing money to produce facile game players instead of scholars? We need to give this some real thought.

Think About This

1. To what extent do you feel that there *is* a possibility that computer simulations will divert focus away from academic content to game playing?
2. Is it possible for instructional activities focusing on "serious" content to be enjoyable for pupils? Why, or why not?
3. Would it be possible for a simulation both to transmit academic content and to produce other nonacademic kinds of learning?
4. If you were the teacher of this parent's child, how would you respond to these concerns?

Studying Computers as a Technological Phenomenon. The presence of computers in the classroom can provide a stimulus for lessons focusing on the impact of the computer on our society. Depending on the ages of youngsters, issues such as computer crime, computers and privacy, computers and economic life, and computers and ethics might be considered.

For example, with regard to the last issue, the nature of "private property," as it pertains to software, might be explored. There is a great deal of evidence that many Americans have difficulty accepting that computer software programs are private property. The developers of software despair when programs that have required hundreds of work hours are copied illegally and distributed to users who do not remunerate the programs' authors. The whole issue of computer technology and the question of honesty can provide a framework for productive social studies lessons.

A number of materials that focus on the computer as a technological phenomenon are available from commercial sources. The following set of filmstrips and cassette tapes is an example:

Title: Our Computer Society
Source: Social Studies School Service
10000 Culver Boulevard, Room 1
P.O. Box 802
Culver City, CA 90232-0802

Managing Classroom Tasks. Many of teachers' noninstructional routines can be simplified through the use of computers. Grades can be maintained, attendance can be recorded, materials for pupil use can be prepared, tests can be developed, course objectives can be laid out, and a host of other chores can be accomplished. The computer can dramatically reduce the volume of paperwork with which teachers have traditionally had to contend.

A number of new computer programs that are designed to assist teachers with classroom management and organization have come on the market. One of these is a program called Grade Averaging.

Title: Grade Averaging
Source: Educational Record Sales
157 Chambers Street
New York, NY 10007

Planning for Computer Use in Social Studies Classes

When planning for computer use, centering attention on the following basic principles can make the programs more successful.

1. Integrate computer-based social studies instruction with the other subjects and with the other parts of the social studies program.
2. Take into account youngsters' individual differences.
3. Make certain that there is adequate hardware and software.

Integrating Computer-Based Instruction. Computer-based instruction works best when it is not presented as a stand-alone experience. Experiences should be integrated both with the learning in the other subject areas and with the other elements of the social studies program. This integration allows for a cumulative impact of experience and, hence, more learning.

The ties with other subjects make especially good sense because—compared, for example, to science and mathematics—the supply of good software in the social studies is rather thin. Some excellent programs with a primary focus on science and mathematics teach skills and concepts that also have a relevance for pupils when they study social studies content. For example, a large number of mathematics programs focus on developing proficiency in working with the numbers presented on graphs. It is clear that the ability to learn from graphical displays of information is also critically important in the social studies.

The integration within the social studies program itself must also be a priority. Under no circumstances should the experience of working with computers be perceived as a diversionary exercise that is not important. Youngsters must understand that the computer is a serious learning tool.

Tying the use of the computer to content being studied helps assure its credibility as an instructional tool. Introducing a simulation that focuses on the American Revolution when the class is studying this period makes sense. Using such a simulation out of context cannot be defended and doing so might cause youngsters' to treat the exercise as a nonacademic diversion.

Planning for Individual Differences. Teachers know that there are enormous differences among youngsters in their classes. The publishers of textbooks and other commercially prepared prose materials also recognize these differences, and they publish a wide array of items targeted for youngsters whose reading proficiencies vary a great deal. Regrettably, relatively little of the attention of the people who develop educational software has been given to the issue of pupil diversity. While this situation is improving, teachers still need to be wary of software that claims to do all things for all youngsters.

An implication of what we know about pupil diversity is that a single piece of social studies software is unlikely to be suitable for use with every youngster in the classroom. In planning to use computer programs, it makes sense to look for a variety of programs that vary in terms of their difficulty levels. There should be an attempt to find a selection of programs that will allow all youngsters to experience success.

Given the limited selection of social studies software available today and the high costs of some of the programs, obtaining large numbers of programs at different levels of difficulty is not easy. Even though the objective cannot always be met in the short run, the effort to provide experiences that respond to the many, many needs of students should be continued (see Table 8–3).

Assuring Adequate Supplies of Hardware and Software. Successful computer-based instruction depends on whether youngsters have access to computers and software. Unless this access can be assured, little learning will take place. This point seems almost embarrassingly obvious, yet distressingly large numbers of schools have attempted to initiate computer-based experiences when the necessary equipment and software have been lacking.

The costs of computer hardware and software are unquestionably high. The pressures from parents on schools to introduce youngsters to computers so that they will not be "left behind" are considerable. School people in some communities have been compelled to expose youngsters to computer-based learning without having the funds to buy the necessary hardware and software.

Responsible educators work hard to resist the pressure to install computer-based programs too soon. Without the proper equipment and programs, youngsters cannot be expected to learn much from their exposure to the computer. Most of them would probably be better off having instruction delivered through more traditional means.

TABLE 8–3 Are Computers Cost Effective?

A teacher recently made these comments to a local school board:

"I am as much in favor of progress as the next person. I *know* the computer revolution is here. I accept the point that we must provide for some measure of computer literacy in our schools. But I wonder whether we are pushing this thing too fast?

I have 28 fifth graders in my class. To make really effective use of the computer, each one of them needs to have a machine to work on. Then, there have to be programs for the machines. These are high priced. The computers also break down occasionally, and repair is expensive.

When I think that we can buy a new textbook for each student at about twenty dollars a book and when I recognize that computers may cost us several thousand dollars a student, I wonder whether our priorities are proper. Wouldn't it be better to have a very limited number of computers and invest a great deal of money in the most recent and best books available?"

Think About This

1. Do commitments of scarce educational dollars to purchase computer hardware, software, and maintenance represent an irresponsible expenditure? Why, or why not?
2. How do you think the school board responded to this teacher? Why do you think so?
3. Are there political pressures forcing schools to purchase expensive computer equipment? If so, what is the source of these pressures?
4. Do you think a school board would be inclined to spend savings on new texts if it decided to reduce the number of computers it had originally decided to purchase? Why do you think so?

Evaluating Software

Social studies software packages vary tremendously in quality. When considering a software purchase, the entire array of materials needs to be evaluated. This array will include the instructional program itself, the general instructions for use, and the accompanying materials designed for pupil use. Allen Glenn and Don Rawitsch have developed a criteria checklist for assessing the quality of social studies software (see Table 8–4).

The Sources of Information About Computers in Education

A few years ago, the sources of information for teachers interested in using computers in their instructional programs were scarce. This situation has changed dramatically. Elementary teachers interested in using computer programs to support social studies instruction have a number of places to which they can turn for help and ideas. The sources indicated in the following subsections provide a sampling of what now is available.

Organizations. An organization with a specific mission to assist teachers who use computers in the classroom is the International Council for Computers in Education. The Council has chapters in many states, Canadian provinces, and foreign countries. It publishes an excellent journal called *The Computing Teacher*. In addition, the organization has published a number of outstanding monographs on issues of interest to educators who wish to make more effective use of the

TABLE 8–4   A Software-Quality Checklist*

_____ *Relevance.* Subject matter must fit the teacher's instructional objectives and learning plan.

_____ *Accuracy.* Subject matter must be accurate.

_____ *Reading level.* Reading level of the material (both in the written student materials and on the computer screen) must be appropriate for students in the class.

_____ *Length.* Learning activities must be an appropriate length, so that students have enough time to meet an objective without becoming tired of the work.

_____ *Sequence.* Learning activities must be sequenced in such a way that students can follow them clearly and are effectively guided toward the intended outcomes.

_____ *Instructions.* Both teacher and student instructions must be clear and concise.

_____ *Grammar.* Correct grammar, spelling and punctuation must be used.

_____ *Motivation.* Activities must be motivating to students. The design of the materials, including computer screen displays, should be attractive to students.

_____ *Reinforcement.* Appropriate methods must be used to reinforce both correct and incorrect responses during the activity. Correct responses should periodically receive a compliment. If motivating screen displays are used as reinforcement, they must be saved exclusively for correct reponses so that no reward results from incorrect ones.

_____ *Acceptability.* The materials must be socially acceptable and avoid stereotypes and other forms of bias.

_____ *Completeness.* The product, particularly the teacher support materials, must contain all the information and materials necessary for effective use.

_____ *Cost.* Although cost is important, it should be considered after other instructional criteria have been assessed. A superlative instructional product that costs too much is unfortunate; however, an inexpensive product with serious instructional shortcomings is no bargain in the end and should not be purchased.

*Reprinted with permission from Allen Glenn and Don Rawitsch. *Computing in the Social Studies Classroom.* Eugene, OR: International Council for Computers in Education, 1984, p. 37.

computer in the classroom. For additional information about its activities, you may wish to write to:

International Council for Computers in Education
University of Oregon
1787 Agate Street
Eugene, OR 97403-1923

The National Council for the Social Studies is the largest national organization of educators interested in social studies education. The excellent journal of the NCSS, *Social Education*, often publishes articles that are designed to respond to the needs of teachers using computers in their classrooms.

National Council for the Social Studies
3501 Newark Street, NW
Washington, D.C. 20016

Journals. In addition to *Social Education*, there are a number of other journals that publish articles on issues of interest to elementary social studies teachers. One of these is *The Social Studies.*

The Social Studies
Heldref Publications
4000 Albemarle Street, NW
Washington, D.C. 20016

Other journals seek to serve a broader audience of educators, but they often publish materials that could be used in an elementary social studies program. The following are two examples of such periodicals.

Electronic Education
1311 Executive Center Drive, Suite 220
Tallahassee, FL 32301

Classroom Computer Learning
5615 West Cermak Road
Cicero, IL 60650

Information About Software. There are several national groups dedicated to publishing evaluations of educational software. For information, write to the listed organization at the address indicated.

Conduit
P.O. Box 388
Iowa City, IA 52244

Educational Products Information Exchange
P.O. Box 620
Stony Brook, NY 11790

Microcomputer and Software Information for Teachers
Northwest Regional Educational Laboratory
300 SW Sixth Avenue
Portland, OR 97204

There are also a number of software directories that are published from time to time. Among these are the following:

Swift's Directory of Educational Software
Sterling Swift Publishing Company
1600 Fortview Drive
Austin, TX 78704

Educational Software Preview Guide
ICCE—Preview Guide
University of Oregon
1787 Agate Street
Eugene, OR 97403-1923

Educator's Handbook and Software Directory
Vital Information, Inc.
7899 Mastin Drive
Overland Park, KS 66204

A number of other sources for information about software are provided in the excellent International Council for Computers in Education booklet, *Computing in the Social Studies Classroom.*

Computing in the Social Studies Classroom
International Council for Computers in Education
University of Oregon
1787 Agate Street
Eugene, OR 97403-1923

Books. There are many fine books available for teachers interested in learning about computers and instruction. The following two have a focus on computers and the social studies.

1. Robert B. Abelson (ed.). *Using Microcomputers in the Social Studies Classroom.*
2. David H. Ahl (ed.). *Computers in Science and Social Studies.*

Both available from: Social Studies School Service
10,000 Culver Boulevard, Room 1
P.O. Box 802
Culver City, CA 90230-0802

Newspapers and School Programs _____

Newspapers are not new to the elementary social studies classroom; many teachers have used them for years. In the years past, it was a common practice for teachers in the upper grades to set aside one day of the week for the study of current events. Often, newspapers served as the basic information source for such sessions.

While such current-event days were commendable in their intent, they failed to take full advantage of the newspaper as an important learning resource. First, current events do not happen on just a single day of the week. Second, this sequence seemed to suggest that current topics stood apart from the regular and important content of the social studies. By compartmentalizing the work with the newspaper, there was a tendency to make this important part of the social studies program seem trivial.

The more contemporary approaches integrate newspaper use into the ongoing social studies program. The newspaper becomes another source of data that youngsters can use to find information on the topics they are studying. Teachers often find that newspapers present information in ways that pupils find much more interesting than the more conventional treatments in textbooks. (See Table 8–5 for a different point of view.)

The use of newspapers in classrooms is limited only by the imagination of the teacher. Several examples of the approaches that use newspapers follow.

Newspaper clippings help pupils keep up with current events.
(*Source:* © Juliann Barbato.)

Map Skills

The datelines in newspaper articles reference locations around the globe. Assign youngsters to find the datelines of locations outside of the United States. The datelines and the accompanying articles can be cut out. These can be posted on a bulletin board, around the perimeter of a large world map. Using an atlas, the coordinates of longitude and latitude, or other information provided by the teacher, youngsters can be asked to locate each city mentioned in the datelines. Colored strings can be used to physically tie the articles to the appropriate map locations.

A number of follow-up activities might be devised. For example, the students might be asked to compare and contrast the locations of dateline cities with their own towns and cities in terms of variables such as global location, elevation, and proximity to the sea. Some youngsters might be assigned to provide additional information about these locations. If available, photographs depicting life in these places might be put on the bulletin board beside each clipping.

TABLE 8–5   Should Children Stick to the Textbook?

At a recent social gathering, a number of parents were discussing the elementary school program. One parent made the following comments:

> My daughter tells me they're starting to use newspapers in her classroom as part of the social studies program. I'm not too sure about this for third graders. It seems to me that we're introducing a lot of extraneous material too soon. I mean, a teacher's got to watch a whole room full of kids. What's to prevent some of them from reading the comics when they're supposed to be reading some news article?
>
> It seems to me with these younger kids we would do better to restrict them to textbooks. The texts don't have any irrelevant information. They can build up a youngster's store of basic information. And they can prepare the child to really appreciate what's in the newspaper in later years. I think newspapers make sense for use with high school kids, but I have some real problems with them in elementary school classrooms.

Think About This

1. What do you see as this parent's major concerns about using newspapers with elementary school youngsters?
2. How valid are these concerns? Why do you think so?
3. Are there some classrooms in which newspapers probably should not be used? If so, what kinds of classrooms would these be?
4. If you had been in a discussion group with the parent who made these comments, how would you respond?

Career Education

Newspapers can be used to teach youngsters about different kinds of career opportunities. In addition to the articles about what people in different occupations do, the classified sections of the newspaper provide a great deal of useful information. Youngsters need to learn that jobs differ in terms of the wages or salaries, the required experience, and the needed training or education.

Individual pupils can be assigned to do newspaper research about different occupations. Each can be assigned a portion of a large bulletin board or a wall. (If space is severely limited, youngsters can be organized into teams of two, three, or four individuals each. Each team is assigned to one occupation). The name of the occupation can be written in large letters at the top of the wall or bulletin-board space assigned to each youngster.

Then youngsters can be taught how to scan the news and features sections of the newspaper for articles about their assigned occupation. Further information can be gained from the classified section. Ask youngsters to clip out relevant articles and put them up in their assigned bulletin-board or wall space. Conduct a debriefing discussion that focuses on the roles, the levels of remuneration, the required education and training, and other selected aspects of each occupation studied.

Consumer Education

Newspapers can be used as a source of data for many activities designed to help youngsters become more cautious buyers. Some elementary social studies teachers have found it useful to focus on grocery prices as reported in the newspaper. Large newspapers typically publish weekly grocery specials from a number of stores on one day of the week, often on Thursday.

By scanning these ads, a teacher can identify a number of items being advertised at different prices by different stores. A hypothetical "shopping list" can be prepared. For example, a teacher might decide upon a shopping list consisting of (1) two gallons of milk, (2) one dozen eggs, (3) six apples, (4) two loaves of whole-wheat bread, and (5) two rolls of paper towels.

The shopping list is provided to the youngsters. They are asked to read the newspaper to find stores selling these items. Their task is to buy the items on the list at the lowest total price. Some teachers find it interesting to organize youngsters into teams for this exercise. At the end of the exercise, the dollar totals can be compared. A debriefing discussion might focus on the similarities and differences between the prices at different stores and the reasons for these similarities and differences.

Area Studies

Youngsters study local, national, and international areas throughout much of the elementary social studies program. Newspapers can be used to supplement the area-study units. Youngsters can keep scrapbooks consisting of newspaper clippings about the various places they are studying. These scrapbooks work best if pupils are provided with some general categories that they can use to organize the clippings. For example, the teacher might suggest that clippings be organized under categories such as "political happenings," "young people," "business and farming," "military events," and "family life and social customs."

Youngsters should be invited to invent additional categories for interesting items that do not fit into any of the categories provided by the teacher. As a debriefing exercise, the teacher and the class might make a list of some entries under these same headings for the United States, the home state, or the home community. Then, using the clippings in the student scrapbooks, there can be a follow-up discussion that focuses on comparing and contrasting the events and lives in the other areas with those in the United States, the home state, or the home community.

Recognizing and Stating Opinions

Decision making is an important outcome of social studies programs. The editorial page of the newspaper can be used to help youngsters develop decision-making skills. Both the editorials and the letters to the editor can be used. With help from the teacher, pupils can identify the issues being addressed and list the arguments made for and against each issue.

This activity can culminate in youngsters making decisions about the issues. The teacher can help them to identify the "facts" that they considered before making their decision and the values that are implied by the decision they made (see Table 8–6).

Local Affairs

Newspapers do an excellent job of informing citizens about issues of interest to the local community. They are also a premier source of this kind of information for elementary social studies classes.

TABLE 8–6 Schools Should _Not_ Force Youngsters to Make Decisions.

Recently, a very unhappy telephone caller made the following comments to a host of a popular late-evening talk show.

My boy is a sixth grader. His teacher has been having the class read editorials and letters to the editor on this proposed law to take away a person's driver's license for two years after the second arrest for drunk driving.

The kids are being exposed to all this tripe from what I see to be an organized letter writing campaign. If you looked at the newspaper, you'd have to conclude that _everybody_ was for the new law. Yet, the opinion polls tell us that the vast majority of people are undecided.

Well, my point is this. Our kids are being exposed to this highly one-sided outpouring of feeling on the editorial page. Then they are going to be asked to make an opinion of their own. With so much exposure to bias, this is a real travesty. I think we're doing our kids a real disservice to expose them to this one-sided ranting and pretend that we are carefully allowing them to consider all sides of an issue.

What business does the school have in getting into the political process anyway? These people are supposed to be public servants. They shouldn't be propagandizing our kids and using them to promote a one-sided view of a controversial issue. People's opinions ought to be private. They have no place in a public school classroom.

Think About This

1. Why is this caller so upset? Is the concern justified? Why, or why not?
2. Is it possible to introduce controversial subject matter into the social studies classroom and also provide for fair treatment of each side's position? Why, or why not?
3. How can a teacher keep his or her personal values from intruding irresponsibly into a discussion of a controversial issue?
4. Should learning materials, such as newspaper editorial pages, that feature information about unresolved public issues be banned from elementary classrooms? Why, or why not?
5. How would you have responded to this caller?

One approach that some teachers have found successful asks youngsters to survey the local newspaper for about a month. They are required to list the local issues that are mentioned in the paper over this period of time and to note how many days the issues are mentioned. Then the class as a whole identifies the four or five most-frequently discussed issues.

Two follow-up activities are possible. There can be a simple discussion on each issue, including questions such as: Why is the issue important? What are the positions that have been taken? When is it likely to be resolved? Another possibility can involve pupils in writing a few short paragraphs about each issue, explaining its importance to someone in another community.

Political Cartoons

Older elementary youngsters can learn a good deal from political cartoons. Initially, many pupils find these to be very baffling. Teachers must take the time to explain the frequently appearing symbols. For example, it may be necessary to point out what Uncle Sam looks like and that he is used to symbolize the United States. If a cartoon contains John Bull, a traditional symbol of Great Britain, or other stock symbols, they must be explained to youngsters. Unless pupils know what these figures mean, they will have difficulty grasping the point of the cartoon.

After these basics have been covered, it sometimes works well to organize youngsters into teams. Several cartoons can be placed around the room, and the teams of youngsters can be invited to look at each. The teams should identify the issue that prompted the cartoon, the "message" that the cartoonist is attempting to get across, and some personal reactions to this message. A general class discussion can follow.

Main Ideas

Many social studies lessons seek to help youngsters arrive at conclusions. Newspapers lend themselves well to helping pupils master this skill. One approach requires the teacher to separate the newspaper headlines from the articles. The articles alone are given to the youngsters first. Pupils are asked to read the articles and create their own headlines. They should be told that a good headline tries to summarize the content of an article as completely and succinctly as possible. These headlines should be collected and saved by the teacher.

Next, the youngsters are given the headlines. They are asked to write an article from which they think this headline might have come. As a concluding activity, pupils are given the article for which they wrote their headline. There is a follow-up discussion focusing on the similarities and differences between the headlines and the articles written by the youngsters and the real articles.

Holidays

Holidays tell us a great deal about the cultures of different people. Newspapers can be used to build pupils' store of understanding about holidays and holiday practices in this country and around the world. The names of a number of major holidays can be placed across the top of a large bulletin board. These should be holidays occurring between September and June, when school is in session.

As each holiday approaches, youngsters can be assigned to look for newspaper articles describing celebrations, activities, and other holiday-associated events. Photographs, which can be placed on the bulletin board, may be included. This material can be used as the basis for a discussion about the purposes of each holiday, whether people in different places celebrate the holiday in the same way, and other information contained in the display of clippings.

The Sources of Information About the Classroom Use of Newspapers

Newspapers in large cities and even in medium-size cities and communities have education departments. These departments are dedicated to helping youngsters use newspapers as a regular part of the elementary program. Many of them make consultants from the newspapers available to work with teachers who would like to develop newspaper-oriented lessons. Some have very elaborate curriculum guides that include long lists of suggested activities and lesson plans. Many of these activities are well suited for use in social studies classes.

A national organization with an interest in promoting the classroom use of newspapers is the American Newspaper Publishers Association Foundation. For information about the available materials relating to the use of newspapers in the classroom, write to:

American Newspaper Publishers Association Foundation
The Newspaper Center
Box 17407
Dulles International Airport
Washington, D.C. 20041

Local-Community Studies _____

Local communities are excellent laboratories for social studies instruction. Here, many universal social studies concepts can be experienced directly. Local-community studies can help teachers establish the relevancy of social studies concepts for pupils' own lives. When properly planned, lessons based on the community can stimulate high interest in the social studies program.

Successful local-community lessons avoid a focus that is too narrow. Because youngsters today are involved in a world extending far beyond the limits of their home community, teachers must be careful that local-area studies allow opportunities for youngsters to compare and contrast the patterns that they find locally with the patterns of life elsewhere. This kind of analysis can produce powerful insights that allow youngsters to learn much about their home community.

There are many ways to organize successful local-community studies programs. One approach is to plan for experiences related to (1) the community's history, (2) the community's present status, and (3) the community's future prospects. Lessons under each category should be organized so that youngsters have opportunities to develop their decision-making skills.

Studying Community History: Some Examples

To begin a study of the history of the local community, some teachers find it productive to develop focus questions. Questions such as the following might be developed.

- What physical evidence remains in the community from times long past?
- What does this evidence suggest about how life here used to be lived?
- How representative is this evidence?
- What does the remaining physical evidence suggest about the values of the people who lived here in the past?
- What events in the past set desirable precedents? undesirable precedents?

Lessons in which youngsters gather evidence that can be used to respond to the focus questions should be planned. (Please note that the suggested questions are simply examples of what a teacher might develop. Each teacher should prepare questions that are appropriate for use in his or her community.) Old newspapers, interviews with long-time residents, invited speakers who are experts on the local area, and other similar data sources might be tapped.

The options available vary from place to place and from teacher to teacher. Teachers who are willing to do the ground work are often able to identify very interesting sources of information for youngsters. One teacher, for example, found

These booklets about the local community were prepared as a social studies activity by the members of one elementary class.
(*Source:* © Juliann Barbato.)

an old jailer's log hidden on a dusty shelf in the county courthouse. The log's entries from the 1890s spoke volumes about the attitudes of people toward certain minority groups at that time in the community's history. Another activity that has proved popular in a number of communities is the history fair.

The History Fair. A *history fair* is a public event presented by one or more elementary teachers and their classes. Typically, the fair focuses on a theme; for example, The Lives of the Early Settlers in Johnson Center. In preparation for the event, teachers and youngsters work hard to learn as much as they can about the theme. Based on their study, they identify a number of activities that might be displayed at the history fair to help the visitors better appreciate what life was like in earlier times.

There might be a decision to (1) demonstrate how eggs can be dyed by using onion skins for pigment, (2) make root beer from a traditional recipe, (3) find an Edison phonograph and play some "hits" from the turn of the century, (4) provide a "wishbook" center with reproductions of old catalogues that are open to the children's toy section, (5) set up an old school desk along with turn-of-the-century textbooks, and (6) prepare a photo gallery consisting of pictures of local buildings and citizens take in the past.

Each of these six activities or items are assigned a place on the night of the history fair. Several youngsters are assigned to work at each location, they become the "experts" on their display. With the help of a teacher or an interested parent, they help explain to visitors what is going on. Other youngsters serve as the general guides to the exhibit. The exhibit guides and general guides should be prepared to explain what is going on at each exhibit and the changes that have occurred in the community since its early days.

Some teachers follow up the history fair by having youngsters write short essays or make short oral presentations about what they have learned. They seek to probe pupils' understandings of the nature of changes and why the changes have occurred, and of the relevance of past local history for their own lives.

Oral History. Sometimes it is convenient to gather information about life in the early days of a community by interviewing long-time residents. Older elementary youngsters can be given tape recorders and instructed in the procedures for gathering and organizing the information. It is a good idea to invite the older people to the school, because they enjoy the experience, and it makes it much easier for youngsters to get the information. A successful exercise of this type requires careful planning.

First of all, a focus topic must be selected. For example, Life in Johnson Center During World War II might be selected. Then the individuals to be interviewed must be identified and invited to participate.

Next, a list of common questions should be prepared. This helps assure that all youngsters will gather similar kinds of information. They may ask other questions as well, but a common core makes sense.

After the interviews, youngsters need help to organize the information. Some teachers find it useful to write the focus questions on the chalkboard and to ask youngsters what they learned about each question during the interview. The relevant information can be written underneath each focus question. When all the information has been gathered, a culminating discussion focusing on all of the questions and all of the responses can be held. As a capstone activity, some teachers take time to make printed copies of the questions and the answers. These can be distributed to the youngsters and to the people who were interviewed.

History fairs and oral history approaches are just examples of what might be done to expose youngsters to the historical roots of their home communities. Museum trips, old newspapers, old photographs, diaries of early citizens, and many other sources of information can be used by elementary teachers interested in local-community studies.

Studying Life in the Community Today: Some Examples

Many youngsters, even in the upper elementary grades, know very little about their home community. Lessons focusing on the present status of the local community help youngsters to acquire two kinds of information.

First, they give pupils a general understanding of the nature of their home community and how it may be similar to and different from other communities. Second, they try to help youngsters grasp the point that communities are not randomly organized. Communities are physically arranged according to predictable patterns. Furthermore, the functions of the individual parts of the community differ from one another. The parts of communities are both independent and interrelated. These local-community lessons help youngsters to recognize both individual parts of the community and how these parts are tied into a unified whole.

Elementary teachers use many approaches to introduce youngsters to the nature of the local community (see Table 8–7). Two examples of what can be done are the community-use log exercise and the Yellow Pages activity.

The Community-Use Logs Exercise. The *community-use log exercise* helps students to grasp the point that life in a community involves the interactions among people and the functions and services offered by the community. It also helps pupils to recognize that these functions and services are not uniformly placed throughout the community, but tend to be clustered in certain areas. This exercise helps pupils to recognize some community-functions-and-services patterns.

The following steps are included in a community-use log exercise:

1. Youngsters are asked to interview family members every day for one week. They make a list of every community location visited by family members (including the pupil). If several visits were made during one day, then this information should be noted.
2. The teacher provides each pupil with an outline map of the city. With help from the teacher in class, each pupil places a dot (a red pencil works well)

TABLE 8–7 Planning a Home-Community Study.

One of this century's most eminent social studies educators was Herbert Gross. Dr. Gross was especially concerned about geographic education, and he had a particular interest in helping youngsters learn about their home communities. He felt that pupils should know something about the physical elements, the spatial elements, the human elements, the cultural elements, and the social thought of their local communities (Gross, 1959).

Think About This

Suppose you decided to plan some learning experiences for youngsters under each of the major headings identified by Gross. For each category, indicate how you would respond to each question.
1. The Physical Elements (natural phenomena)
    (a) What would be the objective of your lesson(s)?
    (b) What steps would you follow in implementing your plan?
    (c) How would you assess its effectiveness?
2. The Spatial Elements (locational issues)
    (a) What would be the objective of your lesson(s)?
    (b) What steps would you follow in implementing your plan?
    (c) How would you assess its effectiveness?
3. The Human Elements (nature of the population)
    (a) What would be the objective of your lesson(s)?
    (b) What steps would you follow in implementing your plan?
    (c) How would you assess its effectiveness?
4. The Cultural Elements (life ways, local institutions)
    (a) What would be the objective of your lesson(s)?
    (b) What steps would you follow in implementing your plan?
    (c) How would you assess its effectiveness?
5. The Social Thought (values of people in the community)
    (a) What would be the objective of your lesson(s)?
    (b) What steps would you follow in implementing your plan?
    (c) How would you assess its effectiveness?

at each location for each time it was visited by a family member during the week. (If someone went to a bank six times, then there would be six dots at the approximate location of the bank.)

3. When these pupil maps have been completed, each youngster will have a map with concentrations of dots in some parts of the community and a total absence of dots in other parts. Sometimes teachers pause at this point to ask individual youngsters about what parts of the community their families seemed to be using most.

4. Next, the teacher invites individual youngsters to place dots from their personal maps onto a large community map on the classroom wall. When completed, this map will show the community-use pattern for the whole class.

5. The exercise culminates in a discussion.
   (a) What places in the community were visited most?
   (b) What happens at those places?
   (c) What places were visited by only a few people?
   (d) What happens at those places?
   (e) Some parts of the map are empty. What goes on in those parts of the community?

The community-use log exercise helps students understand the functional differences of the parts of their local community. They should be able to see, for example, that the recreation areas tend to draw more people than the industrial-warehouse districts.

Another exercise that works well in moderate- to large-sized communities focuses on the distributional patterns of different economic activities in the community. This is the Yellow Pages activity.

The Yellow Pages Activity. The *Yellow Pages activity*, as the title suggests, requires the use of the Yellow Pages. It works best with youngsters in the intermediate and upper elementary grades. These are the procedures to be followed:

1. Divide the class into groups of about five pupils each.

2. Provide each group with an outline map of the local community and with several telephone books (or, if the community is large enough, with several Yellow Pages sections). Be sure that the maps you provide have the street names listed clearly and that there is a system that allows for the easy identification of locations (A-1 and so forth).

3. Assign each group to look up the addresses of all the examples of one service or function provided in the local community. For example, one group might focus on jewelry stores, another might concentrate on physicians, another might on used-car dealers, another on beauty salons, and still another on drug stores.

4. The members of each group will be asked to place a dot (a red pencil works well) at each location where they find an example of their assigned service or function.

5. When the groups have completed their task, ask a representative from each group to transfer the information from the group map to a larger map on the classroom wall. Give each group a different colored marker to make

its entries (for example, jewelry stores might be red, auto dealers purple, and so forth).

6. The result will be a map with the distributional patterns of various economic activities plotted. This can be followed up with a discussion.
   (a) What is the general distributional pattern of jewelry stores?
   (b) Are drug stores located near physicians' offices?
   (c) Are auto dealers more clustered together or more arranged along long streets than jewelry stores?
   (d) How do you explain the differences in these patterns?

This exercise can help youngsters perceive that there is an order, a regularity, to the distribution of the services in the community. For example, jewelry stores almost always are clustered in areas characterized by very heavy volumes of pedestrian traffic. Rents in such areas are high. Businesses such as jewelry stores can thrive because they can display a huge dollar value of merchandise in a small area. Auto dealers, on the other hand, require more space. They cannot afford the high rents demanded in areas where jewelry stores thrive. Therefore, their distributional patterns are different. Many other inferences can be made by studying the patterns that will be evident on the maps youngsters prepare.

The community-use logs exercise and the Yellow Pages exercise are provided as examples of learning activities focusing on the study of local communities as they are today. Field trips, in-school speakers, newspaper-associated lessons, and many other kinds of experiences can be utilized to develop youngsters' understandings of their home community.

Considering the Future of the Local Community

There are many possibilities for teachers who are interested in prompting youngsters to think about the possible future of their community. Some teachers use old photographs of the central business district along with more-recent photographs. Youngsters are encouraged to comment on the changes and to speculate about the future changes as well. Old maps and present-day maps of the communities can be used for the same purpose.

A more-elaborate activity that some teachers have used often is referred to as the community-futures day exercise. It involves many people from the community and demands a good deal of teacher planning.

The Community-Futures Day Exercise. The *community-futures day exercise* is an attempt to gather a number of people from the community in one place to think about what their community should be like in the future. This activity is best suited to the upper elementary school grades. These are the commonly used planning steps:

1. The teacher and the members of the class must identify who should be invited to attend: people from the local government, from the legal profession, from the business community, from organized labor, from churches, and from other groups in the community.
2. A speaker from each group should be identified. He or she should be asked to prepare a very short talk, from five to seven minutes, summariz-

ing what his or her group expects life in the community to be like in the future. The teacher needs to help these people to organize their remarks in a way that will communicate to elementary pupils.

3. A member of the class, helped by the teacher, will serve as moderator. He or she will introduce the speakers.

4. There will be an opportunity for the members of the class to ask questions after each speaker has finished.

5. On the following day, the teacher can lead a debriefing discussion with youngsters in the class.
   (a) What changes in government (in labor, in how the churches operate, and so forth) are anticipated?
   (b) Which suggestions surprised you the most? Why?
   (c) Which of these changes are you most happy about? least happy about?
   (d) What could you do to help bring about those things you would like to see?
   (e) Do you think the future here will be about the same as the future everywhere else? If not, how will it be different?

6. Some teachers might wish youngsters to use blank maps to suggest the extent of the business district, the community boundary lines, and the residential areas in the future.

Other approaches to encouraging youngsters to think about how their community might function in the future can also be productive learning experiences. For example, pupils might benefit from visits to planning-and-zoning commissions. Often, there are discussions of future community-development issues at their sessions. Newspapers often print candidates' opinions about future community development during political campaigns. The alert teacher will find many other sources of information relevant for the lessons focusing on the future direction of the local community.

Organizing Field Trips

Field trips to museums, historic buildings, government offices, and other locations are a feature of local-community–oriented lessons. Good field trips require careful planning. This is particularly true because school districts are vulnerable to negligence suits. Teachers who do not show evidence of careful prior planning are rarely granted permission to take youngsters on a field trip.

The following steps are among those that must be considered when planning a community-learning–oriented field trip.

1. Work with administrators well in advance of the trip to take care of the legal requirements, obtain the necessary clearances, and make the transportation arrangements.

2. Make arrangements with people at the sites to be visited well in advance of the trip. Make it as clear as possible to them what you and your class would like to see and what you would expect youngsters to learn from the experience.

3. Provide students in advance of the trip with some questions or other focus materials related to the trip. Make it clear to them that they should use

These attentive youngsters are participating in a field-trip lesson.
(*Source:* © Juliann Barbato.)

the trip to find out the answers to the questions or to do the assigned activity. Every effort should be made to reinforce the idea that the field trip is not a holiday, but rather a serious part of the school program.

4. At the conclusion of the trip, require pupils to use the information they have gathered on the trip. They might use the information as data to refer to during a discussion, in a short paper, or a project of some sort. Pupils must be required to put the new information to use in a meaningful way.

5. The teacher should prepare a personal report on the experience for administrators. This report should focus on the adequacy of the preplanning, the evidence that learning took place, and the suggestions for planning a future trip with a different group of youngsters.

This kind of attention to detail can make a field trip a highly productive learning experience. Without careful planning, the field trip may degenerate into a frivolous activity that, in the end, does little for youngsters' intellectual attainment and still less for the teacher's emotional well being.

Key Ideas in Summary _____

Computer programs, newspapers, and the resources of the local community are among the information sources that elementary teachers use in preparing lessons. Each of these sources can support the information delivered by the text and by the teacher-prepared materials. Some ideas related to using computers, newspapers, and local-community resources include the following:

1. In the past, much available software for elementary teachers did not focus on the social studies. This situation has begun to improve. Teachers are particularly interested in some of the new programs that actively engage youngsters in analytical thinking.

2. Much existing software in the social studies area has not provided specific information about how lessons fit into the larger social studies curriculum. Efforts are now underway to produce programs that can easily be integrated into the overall social studies curriculum.

3. Existing programs of interest to elementary teachers who wish to include computer-based instruction are designed for five basic purposes. Respectively, these purposes are (1) delivering content, (2) retrieving and analyzing information, (3) developing thinking skills, (4) studying computers as a technological phenomenon, and (5) managing classroom tasks.

4. When planning for the use of computers in the classroom, teachers are advised to (1) integrate computer-based social studies instruction with the other subjects and with the other parts of the social studies program, (2) take into account youngsters' individual differences, and (3) make certain that there is adequate hardware and software.

5. Today, a number of organizations and publications disseminate information about computer programs that are designed for use in the elementary school. Teachers are urged to refer to these sources for guidance as they prepare to incorporate computer-based instruction in the elementary social studies program.

6. Newspapers can be used for many purposes in the elementary social studies program. Most major newspapers have education offices or divisions. These offices provide suggestions and materials to teachers who are interested in using newspapers in their instructional programs.

7. Newspapers can be used to support learning directed toward a number of outcomes. There are applications in areas such as (1) map skills, (2) career education, (3) consumer education, (4) area studies, (5) local affairs, (6) political cartoons, (7) main ideas, and (8) holidays.

8. When they are used properly, newspaper-based lessons are integrated into the overall social studies program. This kind of use eliminates the kind of fragmentation that often occurred when teachers used newspapers only on special current events days.

9. The history fair is an approach to local-community studies that brings together parents, pupils, and other interested school patrons. The fair features exhibits designed to explain the selected aspects of a given place during a specific historic time. Pupils act as guides who explain the exhibits to visitors.

10. The community-use log exercise and the Yellow Pages activity are used to help pupils understand that communities provide many different kinds of functions and services. Furthermore, the exercises point out that these functions and services are not distributed evenly throughout the community but are, instead, arrayed in predictable patterns.

Questions

Review Questions

1. How much software is there available in the area of elementary social studies as compared to the areas of elementary science and mathematics?
2. What are the five ways computer-supported instruction can be used to support elementary social studies programs?
3. What are six criteria that can be used to assess the quality of computer software designed for use in elementary social studies classes?
4. What are some sources of information for elementary school teachers interested in using computers in their social studies program?
5. What objections have been made to using newspapers only one day a week for a current events period?
6. What are five examples of how newspapers can be used to support instruction in elementary school social studies classes?
7. What are some examples of learning activities that can be used to teach youngsters important information about their local communities?

Thought Questions

1. Why has the total supply of computer programs for elementary social studies programs lagged behind the software of other subject areas? Will this situation continue in the future? Why, or why not?
2. Is computer-based instruction simply a passing fad? Will there be more or less emphasis on computers in social studies classrooms in the future? Why do you think so?
3. Computers and computer software are so expensive that rich schools will have them and poor schools will not. If we allow computers into the schools, we are going to increase the gap between youngsters in rich school districts and those in poor school districts. How do you react to this statement? On what do you base your views?
4. Can newspapers be introduced into the elementary social studies program without taking valuable time away from the textbook and the other important learning resources? Why do you think so?
5. In local-community studies lessons, is it responsible for teachers to introduce topics that are subjects of heated political debate? Why, or why not?

Extending Understanding and Skill

Activities

1. Survey a number of local elementary schools about the extent of the use of computers for classroom instruction. Furthermore, determine the extent to which computers are being used to teach social studies lessons. Write a short paper summarizing your findings.
2. Use Table 8–4 to assess the quality of one social studies software program. If feasible,

make a presentation to the class in which you run the program on a computer and discuss your findings.

3. Prepare a folder containing reprints of at least ten journal articles featuring the uses of computers in elementary social studies classes. On one or two pages, prepare short abstracts of each article. Make enough copies to share with all the members of your elementary social studies methods class.

4. Survey the major newspapers in your area and determine how many have programs of support for teachers interested in newspaper-in-the-classroom programs. Develop a list of the newspapers, including the names and addresses of the contact persons, and make enough copies for all the members of your elementary social studies methods class.

5. Prepare a sample review-and-recommendations form that you will fill out and give to a principal following a field trip. Be sure that your form mentions the features of the trip that went well as well as ideas for changes and improvements. Provide the form to your instructor for critiquing.

Supplemental Reading

Armstrong, J. A. "The Microcomputer in Elementary Education: Learning Can Be Enjoyable," *Educational Computing Magazine* (September 1983), p. 18.

Fuller, M. J., et al. "Using State and Local Studies to Teach Geographic Concepts," *Journal of Geography* (November/December 1982), pp. 242–245.

Geisert, G. "Guide to Software Previewing," *Early Years* (January 1984), pp. 16–17.

Hart, Thomas L. "Microcomputer Software and Hardware—An Annotated Source List: How to Obtain, How to Evaluate, How to Catalog, How to Standardize," *School Library Media Quarterly* (Winter 1984), pp. 107–119.

Kreidler, William J. "Teaching Computer Ethics," *Electronic Learning* (January 1984), pp. 54–57.

Skovar, L. and Abeles, J. "Extra! Extra! Newspapers in Education," *Media and Methods* (February 1983), pp. 25; 27.

Staples, Betsy. "Growing Up Literate: Learning to Read and Write by Computer," *Creative Computing* (October 1984), pp. 66–70.

Truett, Carol. "The Search for Quality Micro Programs: Software and Review Sources," *School Library Journal* (January 1984), pp. 35–37.

References _____

Armstrong, David G., and Savage, Tom V. "A Framework for Utilizing the Local Community for Social Learning in Grades 4 to 6," *Social Education* (March 1976), pp. 164–167.

Glenn, Allen, and Rawitsch, Don. *Computing in the Social Studies Classroom.* Eugene, OR: International Council for Computers in Education, 1984.

Gross, Herbert H. *The Home Community.* Normal, IL: National Council for Geographic Education, 1959.

Maples, M. D. "The Social and Ethical Implications of Integrating Computers into Education," *Educational Computing Magazine* (September 1983), p. 24.

Morse, J. C. "Newspaper in the Classroom: An Important Social Studies Tool," *Curriculum Review* (September 1981), pp. 405–406.

Reque, B. "Making Choices: Studying Your Community's Economic History," *Social Education* (January 1983), pp. 32–35.

White, Charles S., and Glenn, Allen D. "Computers in the Curriculum: Social Studies," *Electronic Learning* (September 1984), pp. 54–64.

Chapter 9

Character Education

(*Source:* © Juliann Barbato.)

This chapter provides information to help the reader:

1. Describe the importance of teaching values and the patterns of moral conduct.
2. Identify the sensitive issues related to teaching values and morality.
3. Describe the components of a four-level framework that can be used to organize learning that is associated with values and morality.
4. Point out the basic parts of the moral dilemma approach to moral reasoning.
5. Prepare role-playing experiences for use in the elementary classroom.
6. Differentiate among the approaches to working with values and morality issues that are suitable for use with the primary grades, intermediate grades, and upper grades.

Overview

Every society wishes its young members to grow to maturity while embracing the broadly accepted values and the patterns of moral behavior. Collectively, school experiences that focus on values and morality are referred to as *character education*.

In the mid- and late 1980s, there has been a renewed interest in this part of the school curriculum. One well-known national survey revealed that 68 percent of public-school parents felt that a major goal of education should be to help children develop a sense of right and wrong. The poll revealed that this concern ranked second only to an interest that schools should teach children how to read and write properly (Gallup, 1984; p. 37).

Children's values are particularly important in the social studies. One of the primary missions of social studies instruction is the development of an ability to analyze and develop solutions to problems. Decisions about problems are not made based on the evidence alone. If they were, everybody who had the same kinds of analytic-thinking skills would arrive at the same conclusions. It is clear that this does not happen.

The reality is that judgments are made as a result of an interplay between evidence and personal values. Since this is true, there is a need for pupils to learn how to recognize their own values, as well as the values of others. This kind of understanding provides them with more-mature insights into the decision-making process.

Though a majority of parents favor the general idea of character education and the recognition of the role values play in decision making is a hallmark of mature problem solvers, the school's responsibilities in character education are often challenged. These challenges usually occur because of the differences in opinion about what kinds of content the character education lessons should include. Some parents, for example, are concerned that the values and patterns of morality that are emphasized in the school will conflict with those that are prized at home. Character education lessons must be carefully prepared so that they deal meaningfully with the important issues of right and wrong but do not intrude on parents' prerogatives in this area. The material presented in this chapter offers some suggestions as to how this might be done.

Defining Values and Morality _____

Values are those bedrock beliefs that give direction to a person's life. They are convictions so deeply rooted that they prompt individuals to prize them, cherish them, and act consistently in ways that are congruent with them. Values help people make decisions about how to choose among the competing demands for their time, talents, and money (see Table 9–1).

Suppose that a person is confronted with two things that are "good." He or she might have enough money either to buy an expensive new car or to pay for a college education. The final decision will be made based on that person's own sense of priorities, on his or her values.

Morality focuses on the questions of "right" and "wrong." Moral behavior concerns ideas such as justice, equality, fairness, compassion, responsibility, and truth. Individuals' values play a role in their perceptions of the kinds of behaviors that are deemed to be moral. Some values are so widely held throughout the world that they have become the bases for universally accepted views of moral behavior. For example, all world cultures hold human life sacred. The murder of a member of the culture is everywhere considered to be an immoral act. Other values, and, consequently, the conceptions of morality, vary from culture to culture.

James Rest (1983) has developed a four-level framework that identifies the elements that might be included in lessons that focus on values and morality. These components are discussed in the following subsections.

Moral Sensitivity. At the moral sensitivity level, people must understand that they are faced by a situation calling for the application of values and moral thinking. In the elementary social studies program, this stage would require pupils to appreciate that the making of a decision demands more than the simple consideration of evidence. Pupils need to understand that a value or moral judgment must precede the final act of deciding.

TABLE 9–1   Should Young Children Learn About Values?

A State Board of Education recently held public hearings on a proposed new elementary social studies program. The members of the public were invited to testify. The following comments were made by one person who spoke at the hearing.

> The proposed new social studies program asks children to inquire into the personal values of some of the historical people they're reading about. These children will even be asked to comment about whether they personally approve of the values of these people.
>
> It seems to me that this sort of thing is going to lead to boys and girls asking parents about their attitudes and values. I don't think this is appropriate for children this young. It may be all right when they are older. But their job now is to accept their parents as they are. I think the social studies program should just stick to teaching youngsters the facts.

Think About This

1. Why do you think the designers of the program included lessons focusing on values?
2. The person giving this testimony felt that such instruction might cause problems for parents. Do you agree?
3. What is your personal reaction to this testimony?
4. How does your reaction reveal some of your own deeply held values?

I'm All For Having Them Act on Their Personal Values, But . . .
(*Source:* Ford Button.)

Moral Judgment. At the moral judgment level, there is analysis of previous decisions that have the implications of "right" and "wrong" embedded within them. In the social studies classroom, lessons focusing on this level engage pupils in considering decisions they or others have made and analyzing the guiding principles or values that led to these decisions. Pupils are taught that people who have different basic values will have different conceptions of moral behavior. Hence, it is possible for very different decisions to be defended on moral grounds.

Moral Decision Making The moral decision-making level requires individuals to move beyond the analysis of decisions based on the values of the decision maker. Individuals are confronted with problems that are not yet solved. They are introduced to the evidence related to the problem. Next, they are challenged to consider a number of different value positions with respect to the issues suggested by the problem. They are asked to describe the decisions that would be consistent with the different value positions. Typically, they also are required to comment on the possible consequences of these decisions. Finally, individuals are asked to make personal decisions about the problem and to defend their positions.

Moral Action. At the moral action level, an individual is asked to move beyond a statement about what he or she would do about a given problem. He or she must go beyond "talking" to "doing." Some sort of action that supports the decision is required. For example, in an elementary classroom, if a pupil (or

Social studies lessons should help youngsters develop an interest in involvement in public issues.
(*Source:* © Juliann Barbato.)

several students) decided that the best way to "improve the school" was to clean up the trash on the playground, the moral action level would require them to remove the trash. Merely indicating that trash removal is their decision would not suffice. The level of moral action reflects a higher value commitment than the moral decision-making level.

Working with Values in the Primary and Intermediate Grades _____

Much of the work done by social studies specialists in the area of attitudes and values was originally designed for use with older elementary pupils and with secondary students. While some of these activities can be adapted for use in the primary and intermediate grades, many of them depend on extended discussions and sophisticated content that are too difficult for these younger pupils. A frequent difficulty is that the presented situations are too remote from the experiences of these young pupils. The key is the utilization of situations that tie closely to the problems faced by young people similar to the pupils in the class.

Furthermore, lengthy discussions are not practical with these youngsters. These pupils relate much better to learning activities that allow them more personal involvement. Among the best lessons are those that permit them to move out of their seats and actively engage the content in some kind of meaningful way. An instructional response to this need that has worked very well with younger elementary pupils is a very involving activity called *values-situation role-playing*.

Values-Situation Role-Playing

Values-situation role-playing can take a number of forms. A basic characteristic is that pupils are provided with a situation in which several alternative actions are possible. Each action will represent a different value choice. Pupils are invited to act out their responses. Then, in a short debriefing discussion, the teacher and the class discuss each response. In summary, these are the necessary steps:

1. Introduce pupils to a situation.
2. Select individuals to role-play their responses and discuss each response with the class as a whole.
3. Debrief after the entire exercise, drawing attention to the pros and cons of each response and to the other alternatives that pupils might not have thought about.

There are several possibilities for introducing pupils to a situation to be used as a focus for a values-situation role-playing exercise. The teacher might pose a simple situation. A situation might be suggested by the pupils themselves in response to a teacher question such as, Can you think of some time when you had a hard time deciding what was the right thing to do? An approach that many teachers have found useful is providing the class members with an unfinished short story. Typically, a character will be faced with making a difficult choice. The pupils role-play this character and select the choice that makes sense to them. The short-story approach works well because, when well written, the stories themselves capture pupils' interest and prompt enthusiasm for the follow-up role-playing activity.

Values-situation role-playing activities can focus on the issues related to the development of pupil's self-understanding, understanding of others, and ability to analyze the value decisions made by others. In the lower grades, most of these activities will focus on self-understanding and the understanding of others. In the middle grades, as pupils are exposed to more content from history and the social sciences, role-playing exercises can increasingly assist them in understanding the value dilemmas faced by people in other places and at other times.

A Self-understanding Example

Recall that the purpose of self-understanding in value-situation role-playing is to assist youngsters think through personal problems they may be having. These problems relate to issues such as self-doubt, worries about the future, concern about grades, fears of the dark, and a host of other issues. They do not focus on problems associated with interpersonal relationships. Problems of this type are addressed in role-playing exercises that focus specifically on how individuals and groups get along.

A self-understanding role-playing exercise might develop along these lines:

1. *Focus story.*

Joel *hates* the dark. When his mother tucks him in at night and turns off the light, he waits quietly until she leaves the room. Then he leaps out of bed and silently runs to turn on the light switch. When he hops back in bed, he feels good and goes right to sleep.

Joel's parents have told him that there is nothing scary about the dark. His father has offered to take Joel fishing this weekend if Joel can go a whole week without turning the light on in his room after his mother has tucked him in and left. Joel really wants to go fishing. His father has never taken him along before. But he *knows* something terrible will happen to him and that he'll never sleep if he's alone all night in a darkened room.

On Monday night, Joel's mother puts him to bed, reminds him about the possible fishing trip, turns off the light, and leaves the room. Joel is nervous. What should he *do?*

2. *Role-playing and discussion.*

TEACHER: John, you go first. Pretend that you're Joel. Come up to the center of the room. You're in the bedroom trying to decide what to do. Tell us your ideas.

JOHN: I really want to go fishing, but there's no way I can go to sleep in the dark. I'm going to stuff a pillowcase along the bottom of the door and turn the light on. That way, my mom and dad won't know I've turned it back on.

TEACHER: All right, class, we've heard John's ideas. How do we feel about that?

ROSA: I don't think Joel will be able to sleep. He'll worry about whether his father or mother will look in the room to see if the light's out.

JAMES: Maybe Joel won't feel good inside. I mean, he may fool his mom and dad, but he'll know he's done something wrong.

(Other comments follow.)

TEACHER: Sarah, why don't you play Joel this time.

SARAH: I really want to go fishing, but I am so scared of the dark I just can't stand it. I'd tell my mom and dad that I just can't go to sleep with the light off.

TEACHER: How about some ideas about Sarah's approach to the problem?

RODNEY: That idea is going to make Joel unhappy (he's not going to go fishing) and his parents unhappy (Joel still won't go to sleep in the dark). I don't think it's much of an answer.

JILL: Maybe Joel's mom and dad should make a new plan. If Joel is this afraid of the dark, a whole week is going to be tough. Maybe they should expect only one or two nights of sleeping in the dark at first.

(Other comments follow.)

3. *Debriefing.*

TEACHER: Let me list some of the ideas we have identified:
   (a) Joel should give up on the fishing trip because he's too afraid of the dark to sleep without a light.

(b) Joel should pretend he's sleeping in the dark by putting a pillow-case at the bottom of the door so that his parents won't know the light is back on.

(c) Joel's parents should be asked to set a more reasonable number of nights with no light. This will give Joel a better chance of succeeding.

(d) Joel should have a dog sleep with him to keep him company in the dark.

(e) Joel should convince his father to let him do something easier to qualify for the fishing trip.

(Other pupil responses are listed in the same way.)

Are there some other ideas that we need to think about?

PAULA: Maybe Joel's parents should talk to him more about why he's so afraid of the dark.

JOYCE: It might help if his mom and dad said they used to be afraid of the dark, too. Maybe they could tell him what helped them.

LUIS: I think Joel's parents should buy him one of those small night lights. You know, the kind that uses a Christmas-tree light bulb. Maybe they'd let him keep this small light on when they turned off the main light.

TEACHER: These are interesting ideas. Any others?

(Discussion continues.)

TEACHER: Have any of you faced a situation similar to Joel's? How did you cope with it? Why did you respond in this way?

(Discussion continues.)

(The idea here is to help pupils realize that many personal problems are complex. There are no absolutely "right" or "wrong" solutions. Solutions depend on many factors, including personal values.)

An Abbreviated Social-understanding Example

Role-playing also works very well when the purpose is to have pupils examine the relationships between individuals and groups. Striking a reasonable balance between individual interests and group or societal interests is a problem pupils will face all of their lives. The proper nature of this relationship has been long debated. There is no "right" or "wrong" answer (see Table 9–2). Rather, people work out responses based on their own value priorities. Because the nature of individual and group relationships is an issue that today's young people will face all of their lives, exercises designed to help youngsters focus on this issue are especially appropriate for the elementary social studies classroom.

Such an exercise might develop along these lines:

1. *Focus story.*

Jane had waited all year for this. All year. At last the invitation had come. She really *was* going to be a member of the Stephens Elementary Secret Society. Everybody knew it was *the* club. Everybody, that is, except the teachers, principals, and parents. They didn't even know it existed.

"You've been accepted for membership," Ruth was explaining to an eagerly nodding Jane, "but you have to do one thing before you're officially in."

"What's that?" Jane asked.

TABLE 9–2 Should Pupils Be Taught that Some Things Are Absolutely Right or Wrong?

The following editorial appeared in a local newspaper.

> We applaud the efforts of local school authorities to put some important new substance in the elementary social studies program. The new curriculum provides these youngsters with specific training in making complex decisions.
>
> The program works like this. Pupils are given unfinished stories. At the end of each story episode, a major character faces a very difficult situation. There is no clear-cut "right" answer. The elementary youngsters are asked what they would do in this situation. They role-play responses. Then the teacher follows up with a discussion focusing on the values implicit in the decision they have made.
>
> This kind of activity is outstanding, as far as it goes. Clearly, it can help young people understand that many of life's issues are complex. For many of them, there are no simple solutions.
>
> On the other hand, there _are_ some issues that our society refuses to acknowledge are debatable. For example, we do not countenance a discussion that murder might be right. As a society, we have decided this is an issue beyond dispute.
>
> We at _The Journal_ would be pleased if the present elementary social studies program would supplement what it is doing now with a few lessons pointing out to youngsters that there are positions we do not debate. All truths are not relative. Youngsters should learn this as part of their elementary school experience.

Think About This

1. What dangers does the editorial writer see associated with the existing elementary social studies program?
2. What kinds of things might be taught as being "beyond debate"?
3. What would you say in a letter to the editor commenting on this editorial?

"We believe in ruling the Society by majority rule. And every new member has to believe in that, too," explained Ruth.

"That'll be _no_ problem for me," Jane quickly assured Ruth.

Ruth smiled. "That's terrific, Jane. Here's what the group has decided you must do. Over the next month, we want you to take fifty dollars from your father's wallet or your mother's purse and give it to us. You might want to just take a few dollars at a time. But that's up to you. One month from today, we want that fifty dollars. And we'll expect you to swear that you took it from your mother or father."

"But that's stealing!" protested Jane.

"No, Jane, that's majority rule. If you want to join, you'll have to do it. You have one month. If you've got the stuff to become one of us, you'll get the job done," Ruth concluded.

2. _Role-playing and discussion._

TEACHER: Let me have a volunteer to role-play Jane. Pretend that you are meeting Ruth about a month later. Explain what you have done.

Several pupils role-play Jane and explain what they would have done in this situation. After each performance, the class reacts to the response of the role-player.

3. _Debriefing._ During this phase, the teacher helps pupils recall all the ideas that have been presented. Additional responses might be introduced at this time. The teacher draws attention to the potential value conflicts and explains how each suggested response reflects a particular value priority.

An Abbreviated Example of Recognizing Historical Value Dilemmas

Exercises with a historical focus are most suitable for use with pupils in the late-intermediate grades and the upper grades. The idea is to help them understand some of the very real value dilemmas that people have faced in the past. These lessons help pupils understand that value conflicts have always been a part of human existence.

A role-playing exercise centering on a historical situation might develop something like this:

1. *Focus story.*

Joseph Fender was 17 years old. In the year of 1862, he lived with his mother and father in central Kentucky. For months, talk had been of little else other than the Civil War. Joseph looked forward to June when he would join up. But which side should choose?

Joseph's mother's family, the Gibsons, came from central Ohio. All of his Gibson cousins were fighting in the Union army. His father's family came from Tennessee. His uncles and cousins on his father's side were fighting in the gray uniforms of the South.

"Joseph," his mother called, "here's a letter for you from Grandfather Fender." Grandfather Fender lived in Memphis in western Tennessee. Joseph read his grandfather's letter:

Dear Joseph,

Your father writes that you will be going off to join the war in June. In my heart, I know you will remember your southern roots. All of the Fenders are fighting for the South. Your Kentucky tobacco lands are really a part of the South. Your speech is like that of your family here in Tennessee. You belong in a gray uniform.

May God give you the light to make the right decision.

Your grandfather,

(signed)   Erasmus Fender

Grandfather Fender's letter certainly didn't make matters easier. Just yesterday, Cousin Norman, mother's nephew, had written him from Cincinnati. Joseph recalled again the words of Cousin Norman's letter . . .

Dear Joseph,

I am home on leave from the Union forces. Believe me, I'm proud to be in a blue uniform. With all of our factories, we have excellent equipment and supplies. There is little doubt that we will win. But even more important, we have "right" on our side.

All of the Gibson people have joined up. We expect so see you in a blue uniform soon, too. The Ohio River joins Ohio and Kentucky. Kentucky really has many more interests with Ohio and the North than with Tennessee and the South. Remember that even our brave President, Abe Lincoln, was born in Kentucky.

When you join up, let me know what outfit you are with. Maybe we can get together on leave some time.

Your cousin,

(signed)   Norman Gibson

Joseph thought about the letter from his grandfather and about the letter from his cousin. He talked to everyone he met. He read a lot, too. Finally, in the middle of May, he called his family together.

"I must leave next month to join up. This is what I have decided to do."

These teachers have made costumes as part of a historical role-playing lesson.
(*Source:* © Juliann Barbato.)

2. *Role-Playing and Discussion.*

TEACHER: I am going to ask several of you to pretend that you are Joseph. I want you to explain what you would have done and why. Who wants to be first?

(Several pupils play Joseph. After each portrayal, there is a follow-up discussion.)

3. *Debriefing.* (During this phase of the exercise, the teacher and the members of the class discuss all of the positions mentioned by the several role-players. The teacher steers the discussion so that there is a thorough understanding of the value conflicts inherent in the focus situation.)

These role-playing exercises actively involve youngsters in making choices that involve conflicts of values. They help pupils recognize that choices have consequences. Often, even the "best" choice has accompanying results that are not desirable. These exercises help pupils think seriously about the relative pluses and minuses of the alternative consequences associated with several courses of action. They help them, too, to realize that difficult problems rarely lend themselves to simplistic solutions. Role-playing develops an appreciation for the difficulties people face in making decisions about complex issues (see Table 9–3).

One key to success in values-situation role-playing is using good focus stories. Many teachers write these themselves. Several other sources of these stories are available. One that is particularly good is *Role Playing in the Curriculum*, by Fannie R. Shaftel and George Shaftel.

TABLE 9–3   Do Lessons Focusing on Values Help or Hinder Young Children?

Two teachers recently exchanged the following views.

Teacher A	Teacher B
Our first and second graders are going to have to make tough decisions all of their lives. I think we need to provide lots of opportunities for them to think about complex issues and practice making decisions now. It is not too early for them to learn that not all questions have easy answers.	I think we push our younger elementary pupils too fast. I know that exercises designed to help them deal with value-laden complex issues are well meaning, but are these youngsters really capable of thinking about sophisticated values' conflicts at such an early age? I think many go away from these experiences very confused. I think we should leave the job of dealing with values to the parents, at least when young children are involved.

Think About This

1. Are first and second graders too young for lessons focusing on values?
2. What personal experiences can you draw upon to support your position?
3. Suppose that you were to join Teacher A and Teacher B in this discussion. What would you say?

Working with Values in the Upper Grades _____

The values-situation role-playing approach recommended for use in the primary and intermediate grades is also appropriate for use with pupils in the upper grades. These more-mature young people can also profit from a number of other value-related instructional techniques that introduce relevant content in ways other than role-playing. Two techniques used successfully by many upper-grades teachers are introduced here. These are (1) moral reasoning discussions and (2) issues, values, and consequences analysis.

Moral Reasoning Discussions

Moral reasoning discussions are approaches derived from the work of Lawrence Kohlberg (1975). Kohlberg contends that people's responses to a given complex issue vary in terms of their individual stages of moral development. Six stages of moral development are discussed in the following subsections.

Punishment and Obedience Orientation. A person at the punishment and obedience orientation stage makes his or her decision based on the respect for raw power. He or she feels that if a different decision is made the "authorities" will see that something terrible happens. An elementary child at this stage might say something like this: "I made my bed this morning because my father would have spanked me if I hadn't made it."

Instrumental Relativism. People who are at the instrumental relativism stage make their decisions based on a feeling that they might receive a personal advantage. It is a logic of the you-scratch-my-back-and-I'll-scratch-your-back variety. "If you help me with my arithmetic, I'll help you write your theme."

Interpersonal Concordance. People at the interpersonal concordance stage make decisions that they feel are consistent with the feelings of a group with which they identify. "If you give to the charity drive, then our class will have 100 percent participation and can display the special door banner."

Law and Order Orientation. People at the law and order orientation stage decide issues based on respect for established rules, regulations, and traditional social practices. They prize duty and formal authority. "I may not like the 55 mile-an-hour speed limit, but it that's the law, I'll drive no faster."

Social-Contract Legalistic Orientation. The decision at social-contract legalistic orientation level is not based on law alone. Rather, it involves a consideration of the formal rules and guidelines of the entire society along with personal values and opinions. When no guidelines to action have been provided, people at this stage rely on personal insights. Moral reasoning is characterized by a willingness to take action to influence and change the formal rules and guidelines. "I'm going to challenge the way the district has drawn these school-attendance boundary lines. They are unfair to some people."

Universal Ethical Principle Orientation. At the universal ethical principle orientation level, the decision is based on individual conscience. The person making the decision takes into consideration universal principles such as the respect for human life, love, and dignity. He or she does not rely heavily on formalized rules, traditions, or other guidelines. The universal principles that guide the decision are chosen by the person making the decision; they are not suggested by others. "I know what I will say will not be popular, but my words are not my real message. I want to take a stand on behalf of the idea of freedom of speech. In the long run, respect for this principle will make people happy, even though, in the short run, my words may anger them."

According to Kohlberg's theory, people sequentially progress through these stages. For example, no one can be a third-stage decision maker who has not previously passed through the first and second stages. Individuals' moral development stops at different stages. A few people never go beyond the first stage. Relatively few people attain the highest levels of moral development.

Much of Kohlberg's research in recent years has been devoted to testing the existence of these theoretical stages in the "real world." Kohlberg has not been able to confirm the existence of sixth-stage moral reasoners in recent years (Kohlberg, 1980). This does not mean there are none. Kohlberg's work suggests, though, that their numbers are extremely small.

Kohlberg has also found very few people who are the fifth stage.

There is a suggestion in Kohlberg's more recent work that schools, as a realistic goal, should strive to develop pupils through the fourth moral stage (Kohlberg, 1980; p. 463). With this moral-reasoning foundation, there is a possibility that, in time, some of these young people will to move to higher stages of moral reasoning.

According to Kohlberg's theory, a person at a given stage is thought to be capable of making decisions based on the logic of that given stage and the lower stages. A high percentage of decisions will reflect the given stage. People cannot make decisions based on a logic of a stage higher than that which they have personally attained.

There is a feeling that movement from one moral stage to another is made easier when people are exposed to higher-stage moral reasoning. Not just any higher stage will do. People are thought to be capable of understanding the logic of moral reasoning at one stage higher than their own. If logic reflecting a moral stage two or more higher than that of a person is addressed, it is not likely to be understood.

Because there is generally more concern for others reflected at each higher moral stage, the followers of Kohlberg are interested in strategies that will help people move to the higher stages. One approach that has been used in the social studies classroom is the moral dilemma discussion (see Table 9–4).

A *moral dilemma discussion* involves these four steps:

1. Introducing the moral dilemma.
2. Asking pupils to suggest tentative responses.
3. Dividing pupils into groups to discuss their reasoning.
4. Discussing the reasoning and formulating a conclusion.

Introducing the Moral Dilemma. The dilemma selected should be an issue that has meaning for the pupils. It should also have some of the complexity of

TABLE 9–4   Moral Reasoning and Individual Pupil Counseling.

Moral reasoning can be used to counsel individual pupils as well as to consider more dilemmas as a class. In listening to pupil's explanations of misbehaviors, the teacher notes the logic and tries to identify the moral-reasoning stage it represents. The teacher attempts to respond with logic that is a single stage higher than that of the pupil. Consider the following examples.

Episode 1	Episode 2
TERESA: Yes, I did look at Anne's paper. I mean I did it just a little.	TERESA: Yes, I did look at Anne's paper. I mean I did it just a little.
TEACHER: Tell me exactly what happened.	TEACHER: Tell me exactly what happened.
TERESA: Anne's terrible in math, and I'm pretty good. I said I'd let her peek at a few of my math answers if I could see a few of her social studies quiz answers.	TERESA: Anne's terrible in math, and I'm pretty good. I said I'd let her peek at a few of my math answers if I could see a few of her social studies quiz answers.
TEACHER: Teresa, I'm concerned about your reputation. Do you want all of your friends thinking you're a cheater?	TEACHER: Teresa, I want to read you a section from our school hand-book. It says that 'any pupil who cheats may be subject to appropriate punishment as designated by the principal and the district policy.' We simply must follow the rules.

Think About This

1. What moral stage is suggested by Teresa's response?
2. What moral stages are reflected in the teacher's response in each episode?
3. Which teacher response is the more appropriate? Why do you think so?

the issues with which they will be faced as adults. The material introducing the dilemmas should be short and tightly focused on the situation. Dilemmas can be introduced in prose form, on film, on cassette tapes, or in some other manner. The following is an example of a moral dilemma that might serve as a focus for a moral reasoning discussion.

> Kim Kamatsu is in the sixth grade. She has an older brother in junior high school. Her twin sisters are in the third grade.
>
> Kim's father, Henry Kamatsu, used to make a good living as a steelworker. The plant where he worked closed down six months ago. He has taken an odd job here and there, but he has had no luck in finding something permanent. The family has had a very difficult financial time as a result. The savings are gone. Kim's mother, Katherine Kamatsu, works at a low-paying job. She worries about how she will feed and clothe her family.
>
> Today, Kim is shopping with her mother in a large grocery store. As she walks down an aisle, Kim notices $75 worth of food stamps that have fallen out of the purse of a careless shopper. She stoops to pick them up. She looks at them and thinks about what they will buy. Should she keep them, or should she return them to the person who lost them?

Asking Pupils to Suggest Tentative Responses. After the class has been introduced to the dilemma, each pupil is asked to write on a piece of paper what he or she would do, along with a brief explanation of his or her decision. Next, the teacher asks for a show of hands of those pupils who think Kim should keep the food stamps and of those pupils who think she should return them. This information provides the teacher with an idea about the division of opinion in the class, which will be needed in preparation for the next step.

Dividing Pupils into Groups to Discuss Their Reasoning. The teacher divides the class into five or six groups. Care is taken to assure that some pupils favoring the idea of Kim keeping the food stamps and some pupils favoring the idea of Kim returning the food stamps are in each group. Pupils are instructed to take turns in their groups explaining _why_ they chose the course of action they selected for Kim. The teacher emphasizes that the discussion is to focus not on what each person decided, but on why he or she made the decision. The teacher circulates quickly from group to group to keep youngsters on the task.

In a group setting, there is an excellent chance that there will be pupils who are at different moral reasoning levels. Pupils may be exposed to logic that is one moral reasoning stage above their own. This can help them grow to a higher moral reasoning stage.

These discussions should be kept brief. With upper-elementary pupils, five or ten minutes is plenty. The idea is to maintain a high intensity of interaction. When the teacher senses the discussions have gone on long enough, he or she should ask each group to select a spokesperson.

Discussing the Reasoning and Formulating a Discussion. During the concluding phase of the exercise, the teacher provides either a large chalkboard area or large strips of butcher paper with marking pens. A section is designated for the spokespersons to write the reasons supporting the idea that Kim should keep the foodstamps. A second section is designated for the spokespersons to write the reasons supporting the idea that Kim should return the foodstamps.

The teacher leads a discussion focusing on all reasons that have been noted. The idea is for the teacher to be nonjudgmental and accepting and to listen carefully to what each pupil says. The teacher should try to elicit comments reflecting a mixture of the stages of moral reasoning.

After all pupils have had a chance to share their ideas, the teacher asks each pupil to take a piece of paper and write down the three or four best reasons supporting the position he or she does _not_ support personally. This requires pupils to think carefully about logic other than their own. Finally, each pupil is asked to write down the three or four most compelling reasons supporting the positions that he or she has taken. The teacher does not collect these papers. However, if some youngsters would like to share this information with the teacher during a private conference, that is all right.

In summary, moral reasoning discussions help youngsters think about other people's logic as well as their own. They expose them to levels of moral reasoning different from their own. This exposure may help some youngsters move to higher moral reasoning levels.

The expectations of moral reasoning discussions should not be set too high. There are many variables over which the teacher has little control. For example, there may be little disagreement on the course of action to be taken regarding a presented dilemma. There may be a very limited range or moral reasoning represented within a given classroom. Some pupils may not be able to articulate the reasons they have selected a given response to a moral dilemma.

When teachers accept these limitations, moral reasoning discussions can play a useful role. They have the potential to sensitize pupils to the perspectives of others. And for some there may be growth toward higher stages of moral reasoning.

Issues, Values, and Consequences Analysis

Issues, values, and consequences analysis is an instructional technique designed to do two things. First, it helps pupils recognize that the decisions made by individuals reflect their values. Second, it gives pupils personal experience in making decisions of their own.

This technique is applicable in a variety of situations. It can be used in lessons designed on promoting learners' self-understanding, social understanding, and appreciation of decisions made by others. For this latter purpose, teachers often draw on subject matter content from history or the social sciences.

When the objective is to work with content focusing on self-understanding or on social understanding, these steps are followed:

1. Identifying the issue.
2. Gathering evidence from appropriate sources.
3. Considering the values that are relevant to the issue.
4. Identifying the possible solutions.
5. Pointing out the consequences of the possible solutions.
6. Making a decision and providing a rationale.

A diagram illustrating these steps and indicating the general flow of this activity is provided in Figure 9–1.

Let us look at examples of how this procedure might be applied to lessons focusing on self-understanding and social understanding, respectively.

A Self-understanding Example

1. *Identifying the Issue: Worry about the future.*

   Evidence suggests that many young people in the upper-elementary grades worry a great deal about the future. They wonder whether they will be able to "make it" in junior high school and high school. Older brothers, sisters, and friends tell them how difficult the work there is. Some pupils in the fifth and sixth grades even worry about their future social lives. Will they have good personalities? Will they be popular? Will they find a job? Many other concerns bother young people in this age group.

   Some authorities suggest that these anxieties will resolve themselves as these young people grow older. They contend that these worries will just naturally disappear as these fifth and sixth graders mature and increase in their confidence to cope.

   Other authorities point out that these worries will not just go away. At least, they suggest, some of these young people will continue to be plagued by very serious worries about the future even into their late senior high

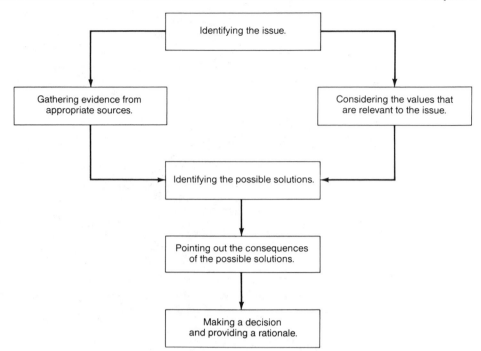

Figure 9–1 Lessons Focusing on Self-understanding or Social Understanding: A Framework for Issues, Values, and Consequences Analysis.

school years. These authorities believe strongly that fifth- and sixth-grade pupils should receive systematic help to relieve them of anxiety brought on by excessive worry.

The bottom line issue, then, is simply this: Should there be specific programs for fifth- and sixth-grade pupils to help them deal with their worries?

2. *Gathering evidence from appropriate sources.*

Information introduced at this point is directed toward shedding light on both sides of the issue. In looking for information to present to pupils, some teachers find it useful to develop some guiding questions. These questions suggest the kinds of information that might be needed. The following are some examples.

What is worry? Is all worry bad?

Do adults worry, too?

What conditions bring on worry?

What ways are there to reduce worry?

3. *Considering the values that are relevant to the issue.*

Teacher questions at this point can help pupils identify the values relevant to the discussion. The following are some examples.

If a person says people should not have worries, what does this tell us about what this person considers to be important in life?

Some people say worries will go away in time. Others say they won't and that we need to help people with worries right now. What differences are there in what each of these two groups thinks is really important in life?

4. *Identifying the possible solutions.*

   A number of possibilities might be suggested in a discussion. The following possibilities might occur after the teacher asks, What should be done about the worries of fifth and sixth graders?

   The school should have special "worry" counselors.

   Parents should take these problems seriously and make time to listen to their children as they talk about their worries.

   The school should introduce a course on dealing with worries about the future.

   Nothing should be done. Worrying will go away in time.

5. *Pointing out the consequences of the possible solutions.*

   At this point, the teacher asks pupils to think about the consequences of the possible solutions to the problem they have suggested. The following are teacher questions and a few illustrations of potential pupil responses.

   What might happen if we established special "worry counselors" in each school?

   Possible responses:

   (a) More people might have worries because now there is somebody to talk to about them.

   (b) Worries would not bother people so much because the "worry counselor" could help.

   (c) Counselors maybe couldn't do some of the things they do now because they would be so busy dealing with worry problems.

   (d) People might worry just as much but not be so concerned about these worries. This would be true because they would know that the counselors could help.

   What would happen if we did nothing at all about this problem?

   Possible responses:

   (a) Some would continue to worry so much that it would interfere with their ability to do well in school. That's what happens now.

   (b) When they get to high school, most people will have outgrown the worries they had in the fifth and sixth grade.

   (c) Some people will always worry no matter what is done. So if we do nothing, it really won't make much difference.

6. *Making a decision and providing a rationale.*

   At this point, the teacher asks some questions designed to force pupils to make a personal decision about the problem. Further, pupils are asked to suggest their rationale for making this decision. The teacher might ask the following questions.

   What should we do about the "worrying" issue?

   Why do you make this choice?

   What convinced you this choice was better than any other?

   What would your choice tell others about the things in life you consider to be really important.

This same general pattern is followed in lessons focusing on social understanding. Learning that focuses on social understanding helps pupils understand the operation of groups, because group action affects individual behavior. With elementary pupils, it makes sense to concentrate on the groups known to the experience of the pupils.

A Social Understanding Example

1. *Identifying the issue.*

   Madison Elementary School has an upper-grades student council. The student council advises the principal and takes on special projects. Recently, the group decided to raise money in the name of the school to send to Ethiopia to buy food for people starving because of the drought.

   George Eliot, a sixth grader, is a member of the student council. His parents own a business that specializes in making political campaign buttons as well as buttons and badges for other organizations. George told his parents about the Ethiopia project, and they gave him a suggestion.

   The Eliots have offered to prepare a large number of buttons that will say "Go Bucks!" The name of the school team is the Buccaneers. George has presented this proposal to the student council. The Eliots will provide buttons in two sizes. The two-inch size will cost the school 20 cents each and can be sold for 50 cents, for a profit of 30 cents a button. The four-inch size will cost the school 25 cents each and can be sold for $1 each, for a profit of 75 cents a button.

   After some discussion, the student council decides to sell the buttons to raise money. Members of the student council will do the selling. They decide something must be done to encourage people to buy the $1 buttons. The student council makes much more on these than they do on the 50-cents buttons. They decide that they will encourage people to buy the $1 buttons by announcing that the first two rows of seats for the big basketball game with Johnson Elementary School will be reserved for people wearing the $1 buttons. No one without a $1 button will be allowed to sit there.

   This decision is announced to the others in the school. It creates an uproar. Some say it is a very unfair idea.

   The issue reduces to this question: Is it fair to reserve the best seats at an important basketball game for people who are able to pay $1 for a booster button?

2. *Gathering evidence from appropriate sources.*

   The teacher will ask questions here designed to shed light on information related to the issue. The following questions might be asked.

   Is it customary for schools to raise money for worthy causes?

   Are people who are able to pay more expected to give more to charity work than people less able to pay?

   Are there examples where people are rewarded for giving to a good cause. (The teacher might point out the "gifts" frequently offered to people who make large pledges to support public television stations.)

3. *Considering the values that are relevant to the issue.*

   The teacher asks a series of questions to help pupils understand the value priorities associated with the differing positions on the issue.

What things are most important to people who favor giving favored seating to those who buy the $1 buttons?

What things are most important to people who are opposed to giving favored seating to those who buy the $1 buttons?

Is either group opposed to helping the Ethiopians?

4. *Identifying the possible solutions.*

The teacher asks students to suggest possible solutions. Pupils might provide the following answers.

The student council should stick to its plan of requiring people in rows one and two to have purchased the $1 buttons.

The principal should identify the people from homes where there is not much money and give a discount price on the $1 buttons to these people.

Basketball and Ethiopia should have nothing to do with one another. There should be no requirement to have a $1 button to get a good seat at the game.

5. *Pointing out the consequences of the possible solutions.*

The teacher introduces each suggested solution one at a time and asks students to think about the possible consequences of its adoption. The following are sample teacher questions and possible pupil responses.

What would happen if the student council decided to stick with the decision to require all people in the first two rows at the game to have purchased the $1 buttons?

Possible responses:

(a) Only the rich kids would have a good seat.

(b) People would be so mad that not many buttons would be sold. This would hurt the people in Ethiopia.

(c) One dollar is not that much. Most people who want a good seat could afford to pay that much.

What would happen if the student council completely abandoned the idea of connecting the purchase of a $1 button to getting a good seat at the basketball game?

Possible responses:

(a) The Ethiopians would be the real losers. Fewer buttons would be sold.

(b) It would be more fair. Everybody would have an equal chance to get a good seat. People wouldn't be as mad at the student council as they are now.

(c) More of the 50 cent buttons would be sold.

6. *Making a decision and providing a rationale.*

The teacher prompts students to make a decision about this issue and to provide a rationale for this decision. The teacher might ask the following questions.

What do you think the student council should do?

What leads you to this conclusion?

What does your decision tell you about your own priorities?

Lessons that focus on helping pupils appreciate the decisions made by others often draw on material from history and the social sciences. They help pupils understand that many of these choices required agonizing choices among competing values. An issue that is suitable for a lesson of this type must be one for which at least two opposing viewpoints can be found. The steps to be followed are slightly more complex than for lessons that focus on personal or social understanding. These steps are listed here:

1. Identifying the general issue.
2. Describing Faction A.
3. Identifying the Information perceived as relevant by Faction A.
4. Describing the relevant alternatives open to Faction A.
5. Pointing out the possible consequences of each Faction A alternative.
6. Describing Faction B.
7. Identifying the information perceived as relevant by Faction B.
8. Describing the relevant alternatives open to Faction B.
9. Pointing out the possible consequences of each Faction B alternative.
10. Relating and comparing the alternatives open to each Faction; relating and comparing the probable consequences of each alternative; making decisions.
11. Applying to another setting.

A diagram graphically depicting the flow of a lesson of this type is provided in Figure 9-2.

A lesson that focuses on helping pupils appreciate the decisions made by others might develop along the following lines.

An Appreciation of the Decisions Made by Others Example

1. *Identifying the general issue.*

Pupils are provided with the following information:

In 1710, when today's United States was still a colony of Great Britain, John Peter Zenger came to New York from Germany. He started a newspaper called *The New York Weekly Journal.* All went well until 1732.

In that year, a new governor, William Cosby, came to the New York colony from England. When he arrived, he found that the man who had been acting as temporary leader in New York had been drawing his salary. Cosby wanted the man to pay him the money, even though, in truth, the man had been doing Cosby's job. By using some shady tricks, Cosby succeeded in having a court decide in his favor, and there was a decision that Cosby should get the money.

After this had happened, John Peter Zenger reported in his newspaper about all of the questionable things Cosby had done. Cosby was furious. He accused Zenger of libel. Libel means damaging a person's reputation by circulating information about him in something like a newspaper. Zenger denied that he was guilty of libel because the things he printed were true.

Should John Peter Zenger have been found guilty of libel?

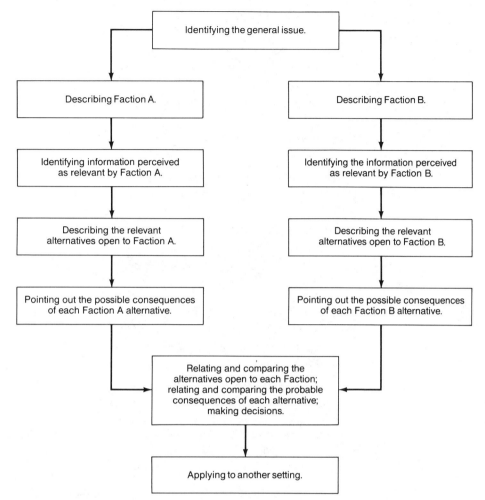

Figure 9–2 Appreciating the Decisions Made by Others: A Framework for Issues, Values, and Consequences Analysis.

2. *Describing Faction A: Cosby and his judges.*

Pupils are provided with the following information.

Cosby was the Governor of New York, the king's own representative. He had responsibility for the overall administration of the colony. He was concerned about letting the colonists develop the idea that they had any real powers of their own. He felt that any attack against him was also an attack against the king.

3. *Identifying the information perceived as relevant by Faction A.*

The teacher asks questions and provides information to assure pupils are familiar with the following facts.

The judges selected by Cosby felt that Zenger had committed libel. English law at this time did not allow a jury to make this decision. The judges decided whether a given act was libelous. For example, it was up to the judges to decide whether something written in a newspaper was libelous. The only job of the jury was to decide whether the person accused of writing the article had actually written it.

4. *Describing the relevant alternatives open to Faction A.*

The teacher asks pupils some questions about these alternatives. They might generate answers similar to the following.

They could do nothing. This might just be an episode that would "blow over" in time.

They could bring Zenger to trial.

They could banish Zenger from the colony.

5. *Pointing out the possible consequences of each Faction A alternative.*

The teacher asks questions. Pupils might identify the following consequences.

If they did nothing, these attacks on the governor might escalate. They could lead to real problems.

If they took Zenger to trial, it was always possible some unexpected outcome might result. But Cosby had had a good record of managing judges and juries.

If they sent Zenger out of the colony, he could make trouble elsewhere in America. If he went to England, he might make trouble for Cosby by planting vicious rumors among his enemies there.

6. *Describing Faction B.*

The teacher provides pupils with the following information.

John Peter Zenger was a journalist. He was anxious to increase his paper's circulation over that of the rival *New York Gazette.* He was interested in appealing to those interested in extending the rights of the colonists.

7. *Identifying the information perceived as relevant by Faction B.*

The teacher helps pupils grasp the following information.

Zenger and his attorneys felt that the old English idea that judges should decide whether something was libelous should be changed. Judges were too easy for the English to control. Juries, on the other hand, were something else. They tended to be made up of colonists. Zenger and his lawyers felt that juries, not judges, should decide whether the crime of libel had been committed.

Zenger's people also felt that someone should not be able to claim he had been libeled if the information printed in a newspaper could be shown to be true. Thus, they were very interested in demonstrating the truth of what Zenger had written.

8. *Describing the relevant alternatives open to Faction B.*

The teacher asks questions about alternatives. Pupils provide responses such as the following.

Zenger could have retracted what he had originally printed and published an apology to the Governor in the hope the libel suit would be dropped.

Zenger could have agreed to stand trial in the hope that he might win his case.

Zenger could have fled the colony.

9. *Pointing out the possible consequences of each Faction B alternative.*

The teacher asks questions about the consequences of each alternative. Pupils might respond in the following way.

If Zenger had retracted what he had said, he would have weakened the case the colonists were trying to make to extend their authority.

If Zenger had agreed to stand trial, he stood a chance to be found guilty. On the other hand, a trial would provide an opportunity for him to share his views with a larger audience. Also, he might win the case.

If Zenger fled, he would lose any immediate influence he might have in New York in support of increasing the authority of the colonists. On the other hand, he might be able to make life uncomfortable for Cosby if he could get to England and talk to some of Cosby's enemies.

10. *Relating and comparing the alternatives open to each Faction; Relating and comparing the probable consequences of each alternative making decisions.*

The teacher asks questions to help pupils contrast the positions of the two factions. The following are questions and possible responses.

What similarities and differences do you see between the alternatives open to each side?
Possible responses:
(a) both sides consider having Zenger leave.
(b) Both sides seriously consider the merits of a trial. Both ultimately decide to choose this alternative.

What differences in viewpoint are represented on each side?
Possible reponses:
(a) Cosby and his people feel that a libel had already been committed. The trial would be simply to see whether Zenger had written the libelous article. Zenger and his people deny that a libel has been committed. They claim there was no libel since the material printed in the newspaper was true.
(b) Cosby and his people are afraid of extending the power of the colonists.
(c) Zenger favors extending the colonists' power.

What is most important to each side?
Possible responses:
(a) Cosby sees preserving his authority as most important. He sees Zenger as a threat to his authority and that of the king.
(b) Zenger wants to extend the rights of the colonists. He wants to do this by establishing the idea that anything can be printed about a person so long as its truth can be proved.

Did Zenger have a right to print articles critical of the Governor?
Possible responses:
(a) I don't think so. The governor was the king's representative. Zenger was a threat against law and order.
(b) Yes. If he couldn't be critical, then very bad governors could have done all kinds of terrible things and few people would know about them.

(c) He might have had this right, but not in New York. If he wanted to print critical articles, he should have gone to England.

What do you think really happened in this case?

The teacher conducts a discussion on this issue. To conclude the discussion, information about what happened is shared with the class.

(The outcome of the Zenger case was shocking to Governor Cosby. First, the jury was convinced by the arguments of Zenger's attorney that judges should not decide when something is libelous or not. This should be left to juries. Second, the jury decided that there was no libel in a case where the person writing the article could prove the truth of what he or she had written. John Peter Zenger, as a result, was found innocent.

The Zenger case established the principle that juries, not judges, decide when a libel has occurred. Furthermore, the case established the important freedom-of-the-press principle that there is no libel when material printed can be shown to be true.)

11. *Applying to another setting.*

This last phase is an attempt to tie an episode from another time or place to something more familiar to pupils' own experiences. Teachers might ask questions such as the following.

The Zenger case changed some rules that courts had followed for a long time. Can you think of any new rules that have changed how we have done things? (If pupils have trouble, provide some examples—the 55-mph speed limit, the integration in the schools, the changes in local school rules, and so forth.)

How do people react to changes? Do some people like them and some people oppose them? Why might there be differences?

Are newspapers today free to criticize public officials? Is this right a result of the famous Zenger case?

How do you feel personally about what can be printed in the press? What does your answer tell us about what things in life you believe to be really important?

Issues, values, and consequences analyses have diverse applications. They actively involve pupils in thinking about values as well as the evidence associated with alternative positions. They deserve a place in the elementary social studies program.

Key Ideas in Summary _____

People do not make decisions based on only the evidence they have to consider. They also consider their personal values. These values act as filters that they use to identify evidence they consider relevant. Because values play such an important role in decision making of adults, it is important that learners begin dealing with them even as early as the elementary school years. Some ideas about values in the social studies program introduced in this chapter include the following:

1. Character education embraces the general issues of values and morality. There is increasing evidence today that parents are supporting the efforts of schools to teach young people what is "right" and "wrong." On the other hand, parents are also interested in preserving some value training for the home. Teachers must strike a reasonable balance between teaching the broadly accepted patterns of "correct" behavior and maintaining the parental rights to teach certain value patterns to their children at home.

2. Values refer to deeply held personal convictions that form the bases for personal decisions and actions. Morality is concerned with the issue of behavior that is consistent with broadly held values. Because some values are held by many different cultures, some standards of morality are nearly universal. Other values are unique to individual cultures. Hence, some behaviors that are regarded as immoral in one place may not necessarily be regarded as immoral somewhere else.

3. Values-situation role-playing is an instructional technique that is often used to help pupils in the primary and intermediate grades deal with values. The technique involves the presentation of a complex situation, assigning pupils to role-play their responses to it, and debriefing the class at the conclusion to help them think about the choices taken, the choices that might have been taken, and the reasons supporting the choices.

4. Values-situation role-playing can be used for lessons of three basic types. The first type attempts to promote pupils' self-understanding. The second type focuses on the issue of social understanding. Social understanding lessons are designed to help youngsters appreciate the conflicts between personal and group values. A third type of lesson exposes pupils to value conflicts experienced by people throughout history.

5. In general, values lessons for younger elementary children, particularly those in the primary grades, are best directed toward promoting self-understanding and social understanding. These immature pupils know too little history and social science for lessons focusing on more abstract content to have as much meaning for them as they do for older pupils.

6. Lawrence Kohlberg has identified a series of six stages of moral development. People must progress through these stages in sequential order. Because people at the higher stages are thought to be more sensitive to the needs of others than are people at lower stages, it is considered desirable to help pupils move toward higher stages of moral development.

7. Moral reasoning discussions are based on the work of Kohlberg. They begin with a teacher presenting a moral dilemma to the class. Then pupils are asked to provide tentative responses to the dilemma. Next, the teacher divides pupils into groups. The members of each group share the reasoning they used in arriving at their decision about the dilemma. In a concluding discussion, the teacher assists the class members to formulate individual final conclusions. Moral reasoning discussions ordinarily work best with upper-grade pupils.

8. Issues, values, and consequences analysis is a technique that helps pupils recognize the values others rely on in making decisions. The technique can be used for lessons focusing on the development of pupils self-understanding and social understanding. They can also be used in lessons that

help pupils appreciate the value dilemmas others have faced in making decisions. Issues, values, and consequences analysis is a technique that works best with upper-grade pupils.

Questions

Review Questions

1. What does the recent evidence tell us about parents' attitudes about teaching the concepts of "right" and "wrong" in school?
2. What are the four levels in Rest's (1983) framework for studying values and morality?
3. What are the steps in a values-situation role-playing exercise?
4. Who is Lawrence Kohlberg, and what are his six stages of moral reasoning?
5. What steps are followed in a moral reasoning discussion?
6. What are the general characteristics of issues, values, and consequences analysis?
7. For what grade levels are each of the following recommended: (a) values-situation role-playing; (b) moral reasoning discussion; and (c) issues, values, and consequences analysis?

Thought Questions

1. Why might some people object to when dealing with values in the elementary classroom? How might you respond to these concerns?
2. Suppose a friend scheduled to do student teaching in the second grade told you that he or she was interested in doing a series of issues, values, and consequences analysis lessons for social studies. What advice would you provide?
3. Would it be wise to choose an issue that was being hotly debated in the local community as a focus for an issues, values, and consequences lesson? Why, or why not?
4. If you were to make a prediction about elementary social studies instruction ten years from now, would you be inclined to predict that there would be more or less emphasis on the issue of values? On what evidence do you base your decision?
5. Should the teacher always keep his or her personal values out of a values discussion, or should these values be made public? Why do you think so?

Extending Understanding and Skill

Activities

1. Interview a social studies curriculum director for a district (if that cannot be arranged, find an elementary teacher interested in the social studies) about the relative emphasis on lessons that focus on attitudes and values. Ask about the nature of the instruction provided, the problems with parents and other school district patrons, and the teachers' reactions to working with this kind of content. Prepare an oral report to share with your college or university class.
2. Survey a number of elementary social studies textbooks to find out how many of the suggested activities focus on attitudes or values. Prepare a chart displaying your findings for your course instructor.

3. Read ten articles in professional journals that suggest practical techniques for dealing with attitudes and values in the elementary social studies classroom. Identify the articles using the *Education Index* in your college or university library. Write a short description of each approach, and provide it to your instructor and to others in the class.

4. Prepare three role-playing situations, two moral reasoning dilemmas, and one situation for an issues, values and consequences analysis. Develop these for the grade level you would like to teach. Give them to your instructor for review and comments.

5. Start a newspaper-clipping file featuring the conflicts between people that reflect different value priorities. Try to include at least twelve items. Discuss some of the items you have found with your class, and suggest how they might provide the beginnings of elementary social studies lessons.

Supplemental Reading

BILLINGS, H. "We Can't Allow Children to Grow Up in a Moral Void," *Instructor* (November/December 1982), p. 16.

BUTTERFIELD, SHERRI. *Value Tales Teacher's Resource Guide.* San Diego, CA: Value Communications, Inc., 1981.

CASEMENT, W. "Moral Education: Form Without Content," *Educational Forum* (Winter 1984), pp. 177–189.

ENGEL, B., and SEYFORTH, L. "Teaching Values: Does It Make a Difference?" *Educational Forum* (Summer 1982), pp. 475–482.

KRACHT, JAMES B. "Values Clarification: Some Observations," *Lutheran Education* (May/June 1984), pp. 274–281.

McCLELLAND, DAVID. *Education for Values.* New York: Irvington Publications, 1982.

SCHUNCKE, GEORGE, and KROGH, SUZANNE. *Helping Children Choose: Resources, Strategies, and Activities for Teachers of Young Children.* Glenview, IL: Scott Foresman & Co., 1983.

SIMON, SIDNEY, HOWE, LELAND W., and KIRSCHENBAUM, HOWARD. *Values Clarification: A Handbook of Practical Strategies for Teachers and Students*, 3d ed. New York: Dodd, Mead & Co., 1985.

References

GALLUP, GEORGE H. "The 16th Gallup Poll of the Public's Attitudes Toward the Schools," *Phi Delta Kappan* (September 1984), pp. 23–38.

KOHLBERG, LAWRENCE. "The Cognitive-Developmental Approach to Moral Education," *Phi Delta Kappan* (June 1975), pp. 670–675.

———."Education for a Just Society: An Updated and Revised Statement," in Brenda Munsey (ed.), *Moral Development, Moral Education, and Kohlberg.* Birmingham, AL: Religious Education Press, 1980, pp. 455–470.

RATHS, LOUIS, HARMIN, MERRILL, and SIMON, SIDNEY B. *Values and Teaching*, 2d ed. Columbus, OH: Charles E. Merrill Publishing Co., 1978.

REST, JAMES. "Developmental Psychology as a Guide to Value Education: A Review of Kohlbergian Programs," *Review of Educational Research* (Spring 1974), pp. 241–259.

———."Morality," in P. Hussen (ed.), *Handbook of Child Psychology*, Volume 4. New York: John Wiley & Sons, Inc., 1983.

SALEND, S. J., and MOE, L. "Modifying Non-Handicapped Students' Attitudes Toward their Handicapped Peers Through Children's Literature," *Journal of Special Education* (Spring 1983), pp. 22–28.

SCHUNCKE, GEORGE M. "Valuing in the Elementary Classroom: Dealing with the Problems," *The Social Studies* (May/June 1981), pp. 37–41.

SHAFTEL, FANNIE R., and SHAFTEL, GEORGE. *Role Playing in the Curriculum*, 2d ed. Englewood Cliffs, NJ: Prentice-Hall, Inc., 1982.

STAHL, ROBERT J. "Achieving Values and Content Objectives Simultaneously within Subject Matter–Oriented Social Studies Classrooms," *Social Education* (November/December 1981), pp. 580–585.

Chapter 10

Understanding the Map and Globe Skills

(*Source:* Juliann Barbato.)

1. Recognize certain problems that are experienced by elementary youngsters when they work with maps and globes.

2. Identify several important map and globe skills.

3. Describe the kinds of map and globe skills that are appropriate for pupils in kindergarten to second grade, third to fourth grade, and fifth to sixth grade.

4. Point out the basic characteristics of maps and globes.

5. Suggest some specific approaches to helping pupils master certain map and globe skills.

6. Recognize the basic concepts pupils must understand in order to engage in application activities that are related to maps and globes.

Overview

Try to answer the following questions.

1. Reno, Nevada is west of Los Angeles, California.
2. The west coast of South America is in the same time zone as New York City (Eastern Time Zone).
3. If a person flew first from New York to San Francisco and then flew an equivalent distance west from San Francisco, he or she would be more than one third of the way across the Pacific Ocean.
4. Because Juneau, Alaska, is much farther north, it has colder average January weather than Philadelphia, Pennsylvania.

Here are the answers: Numbers 1 and 2 are true and numbers 3 and 4 are false. You do not need to feel bad if you missed some of these. Many adults find such questions difficult. They would be even more perplexing to elementary youngsters who have little experience in working with map and globe skills. On the other hand, children and adults who are solidly grounded in these skills should be able to respond confidently to questions such as these. Before going on, let us pause a moment to explain the answers.

The question about Los Angeles and Reno is confusing because most people look at flat maps of the United States rather than at globes. Many of these maps distort the shape of the west coast. They make it look like a relatively straight north-south line. Since Los Angeles is on the coast and Reno is inland, it is only natural for people to conclude that Los Angeles must be farther west. In reality, the southern part of the west coast lies in a generally southeasterly direction. This is why it is possible for Los Angeles to be east of Reno. The relationship is quite apparent on a globe.

Perhaps because of the names of the two continents—North America and South America—many people assume that South America lies directly south of North America. It does lie south, but it is also considerably east of most of North

America. This is why it is true that the west coast of South America lies in the same time zone as the eastern United States.

Youngsters and adults, too, often greatly underestimate the size of the Pacific Ocean. The Pacific Ocean covers about one third of the earth's surface. In very rough terms, it is about 10,000 miles (16,090 kilometer) from the west coast of the United States to the western boundaries of the Pacific. This is more than three times the distance from New York to San Francisco.

Many middle-grade children have some understanding of the parts of the globe, such as the equator and the poles. They also recognize that, on the average, the winter temperatures in the northern areas of the northern hemisphere are colder than in the southern areas. Many of these pupils, though, have not grasped that other local conditions, such as elevations, proximity to warm water, and wind patterns, also influence temperature. They need this kind of understanding to be able to answer the question about the January temperatures in Juneau and Philadelphia.

Though it is much closer to the equator than Juneau, Philadelphia sits at the eastern edge of a large continental land mass. Because the prevailing winds here blow off the cold continental interior in the winter, the January weather can be very cold. Juneau, by way of contrast, sits on the coast and enjoys moderate winter temperatures because the prevailing west winds blow in off the warm Alaska current.

Map and globe skills taught in elementary social studies classes aid youngsters in understanding the many important physical dimensions of the world. Technological advances draw the peoples of the earth closer together. Map and globe skills provide youngsters with the analytical tools they can use to "make sense" of the world beyond their local communities (see Table 10–1). These skills have long received heavy emphasis in social studies programs, and this emphasis will certainly continue.

TABLE 10–1 Youngsters' Misinformation About World Geography.

Not long ago, a group of middle-grade youngsters was surveyed about a number of geographic topics. The following are some of the "facts" about the world many of these young people believed to be true.
1. On any map, the Atlantic always lies to the right.
2. It is impossible for a river ever to flow in a northerly direction.
3. In the northern hemisphere, every place north of location A has colder winters than those at location A.
4. Africa is a country.
5. More Spanish-speaking people in the world live in Spain than in any other Spanish-speaking country.
6. The most northern part of the 48 connected states is the northern tip of the state of Maine.
7. It is about the same distance from New York to London as from Seattle to Tokyo.

Think About This

1. Which of the above misinformation do you believe to be most widespread? Why do you think so?
2. In general, what is (are) the source(s) of this misinformation?
3. As a teacher, what might you do to help youngsters correct these mistaken impressions?

This teacher is helping pupils with the globe's horizon ring.
(*Source:* © Juliann Barbato.)

Globes _____

   Globes deserve more attention than they receive in many social studies classrooms. Some of the misunderstandings youngsters have about the world might be eliminated if they were provided more experience in working with globes and relatively less in working with maps. Globes provide the best representation of our spherical planet. Maps, dealing in only two dimensions, distort the shapes and areas; this distortion can lead to serious misconceptions.

   For example, many flat world maps use a projection that makes Africa look smaller in area than North America. Surprisingly large numbers of middle-school youngsters believe that this is true. Such maps also make Greenland look as large as South America. In fact, South America is nine times larger. Globes avoid these distortions. The relative sizes of the world land masses appear on the globe as they actually exist.

   Though the increased use of globes can help students gain a better appreciation of size relationships. their use poses problems as well. Globes are bulky. Ideally, there should be enough globes so that no more than three or four youngsters at a time need to work with one. In a class of 25, this would mean six or more globes. Often, there is simply not sufficient space to accommodate such a large number.

   There are serious problems associated with using globes to teach certain kinds of content. Globes include the entire earth's surface. Consequently, the individual areas of the earth appear to be quite small. If there is an interest in studying only a small part of the earth's surface, a globe might not be as good a choice as a map.

Global Awareness is *Great* as an Idea, But . . .
(*Source:* Ford Button.)

Suppose that a teacher wanted to teach something about Romania. Romania is about 425 miles (684 kilometers) across from east to west. On a standard 16-inch globe, Romania occupies less than one inch of space from east to west. Very little detail can be included in such a small space. One solution might be to make a larger globe. But this, too, creates difficulties. A globe large enough for Romania to be 36 inches across would be 48 feet in diameter. Such a globe would need to be installed in a special building.

Though they do have limitations when the purpose is to study small parts of the earth's surface, globes are ideally suited to helping youngsters grasp other kinds of content. As noted previously, they are excellent vehicles for displaying the proper area and location arrangements. They can be used to help develop the locational skills that involve the use of latitude and longitude. The concept of the great circle route is much better taught by using a globe rather than a map. Earth-sun relationships—as they relate to issues such as day and night, the seasons of the year, the 24-hour day, and time zones—are best taught using globes.

The Kinds of Globes

There are a number of globe types found in elementary schools. Four common varieties are (1) readiness globes, (2) elementary globes, (3) intermediate globes, and (4) project globes.

Readiness Globes. *Readiness globes* are designed to introduce the very basic information about globes. They are used mostly in the primary grades. Bright colors are often used to depict the individual countries. The detail does not go much beyond labels for the major countries, the names of capital cities and other very large population centers, the names of major oceans and seas, and the labels for the Equator and, sometimes, for the Tropic of Cancer and the Tropic of Capricorn. Occasionally, a few additional details are found.

Even readiness globes sometimes contain a bewildering array of information for very young children. Some youngsters in the early primary grades experience great difficulty in distinguishing between the areas of land and water. One teacher reported having a readiness globe that used the color blue to depict certain political areas as well as water areas. One youngster in the class described Wyoming as a major lake!

Elementary Globes. *Elementary globes* are good for use in fourth, fifth, and sixth grades. They include much more detail than readiness globes. This detail may overwhelm youngsters in the primary grades. The additional information often includes the lines of latitude and longitude, the details regarding the scale of the globe, the indications of major world wind patterns, and the depictions of the directions of the major ocean currents. Often, the locations of many more cities and towns than on readiness globes will be included.

Intermediate Globes. *Intermediate globes* are best suited for use with older intermediate-grades youngsters. They include even more detail than elementary globes. Many of them, for example, will include the notations of world time zones. Many, too, will include an analemma. An *analemma* is the figure-eight–shaped figure that cuts through the Equator. It indicates the locations where the sun is directly overhead at noon on each day of the year.

Some intermediate globes also have a horizon ring. A *horizon ring* is a circular band that surrounds the globe. It has the degrees marked off on its inner surface. The globe can be rotated at will within the ring. By using the degree markers, youngsters can engage in relatively sophisticated calculations of degree differences and time differences between pairs of locations on the globe.

Project Globes. *Project globes* ordinarily are larger in diameter than the typical 12-inch or 16-inch readiness, elementary, or intermediate globes found in the classroom. This is true because the project globe is designed to be written on. The larger diameter provides more surface for this activity.

There are several types of project globes. One common variety has a surface that can be written on with chalk. These globes ordinarily feature little detail beyond the outlines of land areas and, perhaps, some basic information about latitude and longitude. They can be used to plot routes, to illustrate how time zones work, and to teach many other aspects of globe use. They are designed for pupil use as well as for teacher demonstration. Not many individual classrooms have project globes because of their size and cost. This is a pity. They are excellent devices for helping youngsters master the important globe skills.

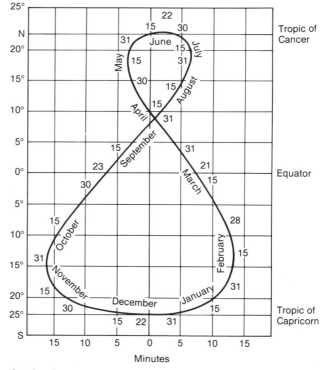

Figure 10–1   An Analemma.
An analemma is used to indicate the latitudes at which the noonday sun is directly overhead on each day of the year. The northern limit of the analemma is the Tropic of Cancer, where the sun is directly overhead on June 21–22. The southern limit is the Tropic of Capricorn, where the sun is directly overhead on December 21–22. The sun is directly overhead at noon at the equator twice each year: once on March 21–22 and again on September 21–22. The apparent movement of the sun is a result of the earth's annual movement around the sun. Because the earth's axis always points to the North Star, at some times of the year the sun's rays strike most directly at points south of the Equator, at the Equator, or north of the Equator. To receive a clearer picture of why this happens, see Table 10–8. Some teachers find that pupils enjoy pointing out where the sun will be overhead at noon on their birthdays.

The Parts of the Globe that Need To Be Emphasized

The information presented on globes is of no use until youngsters understand what it means. There are substantial differences in the types and amounts of information introduced on various kinds of globes. By the end of their elementary social studies experience, youngsters should recognize the functions of features of the globe such as the equator, the Tropic of Cancer, the Tropic of Capricorn, the North Pole, the South Pole, the International Date Line, the Prime Meridian, the horizon ring, the distance scale, the world time zones, and the analemma.

They should be able to apply the basic globe skills to solve problems such as finding locations using latitude and longitude, explaining the seasonal changes in terms of the alternating earth-sun relationships, pointing out the function of the international dateline, and explaining the time differences between selected pairs of world locations. Some examples of how proficiency in these skills might be built will be introduced in a subsequent section of the chapter.

Maps _____

Maps are used more frequently than globes in most elementary social studies classrooms. Properly used, maps can be very effective instructional tools. They can be designed to accomplish many purposes; they cost less than globes; and they do not consume much storage space, even in large numbers.

The strengths of the map as a teaching device need to be counterbalanced by an understanding that maps are an imperfect representation of the earth. A three-dimensional surface cannot be transformed to a two-dimensional surface without distortion. To illustrate how this might happen when explaining maps to youngsters, some teachers carefully remove half of the peel from an orange. By pushing down on the peel, the teacher can make a point that something must "give" before the spherical surface can be converted to a flat plane.

Many maps illustrate only a portion of the earth's surface. A survey of the wall maps permanently on display in elementary classrooms would probably reveal more United States maps than anything else. Pupils' continuous exposure to such maps has the potential to lead to false conclusions. The widespread notion among middle-grade youngsters that the "Atlantic is always found on the right-hand side of a map" may be a result of years of seeing it so positioned on the U.S. maps attached to classroom walls.

Constant exposure to the large wall map of the United States also has the potential to confuse pupils about the proper size relationships among world places. Elementary youngsters tend to overestimate the physical size of the United States. This tendency sometimes results in a failure to appreciate the magnitude and importance of the other places in the world.

During World War II, General MacArthur recognized this problem. He was concerned about the failure of many incoming officers to the Pacific Theater of the war to recognize the huge size of the Pacific area. To help the officers grasp this point, he had a special map prepared to illustrate the size of the United States relative to the area of the Western Pacific Ocean. This map is reproduced in Figure 10–2.

Elementary social studies programs have an obligation to help youngsters both to understand the information introduced on maps and to grasp the inherent limitations of maps. With regard to the limitations, some information about how cartographers have resolved the problem of displaying a round surface on a flat plane can contribute to their understanding. To provide such instruction, teachers need some basic information about the map projection techniques.

The Map Projections

Cylindrical Projections. To understand how a *cylindrical projection* is done, imagine a clear glass globe. The outlines of the land areas and the lines of latitudes are drawn in black ink. In the exact center of the globe there is a tiny

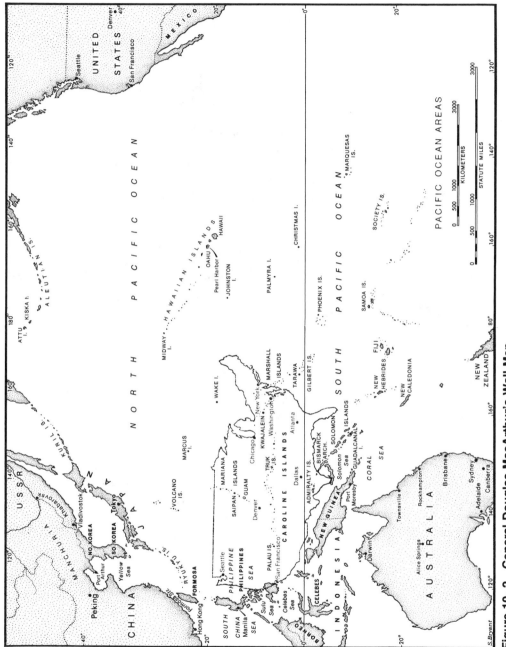

Figure 10–2 General Douglas MacArthur's Wall Map.

General MacArthur had this map in his headquarters during World War II, and he used it to illustrate the vast size of the Pacific Region to his incoming officers.

(*Source:* William Manchester, *American Caesar: Douglas MacArthur: 1880–1964.* New York: Dell Publishing Co., copyright © 1978 by William Manchester. Illustration section between pp. 320 and 321. Reprinted with permission.)

light. The cartographer arranges this globe so that a line through the North Pole and South Pole would make a perfect 90° angle with the table on which the globe is sitting. Then a cylinder of paper is carefully slipped over the globe.

Next, the cartographer switches on the tiny light in the center of the globe. When this is done, the black lines on the globe cast shadows onto the cylinder of paper. The cartographer traces these shadows in ink on the cylinder. When the cylinder is unwrapped, it becomes a world map. (In reality, this procedure is done using mathematics rather than a clear globe and a cylinder of paper, but the principles applied are as described.)

Now, how accurate a representation of the globe is this map? It is most accurate at the Equator because the cylinder of paper will actually touch the globe at this line. Hence, there is no distortion here on the flat map. The accuracy is not so great elsewhere on the map, however. For example, on the globe, the lines of longitude are converging lines that meet at the North Pole and the South Pole. On a cylindrical projection map, they are parallel lines. This means that the closer to the poles you get, the greater the distortion on a cylindrical projection.

There are also distortions involving the lines of latitude. On the globe, the lines of latitude are parallel lines spaced a similar distance apart. That is, the line of latitude measuring a distance 10° north of the Equator is the same distance from a line located 20° north of the Equator as that line is from a line 30° north of the Equator. On a cylindrical projection, these lines are unevenly spaced. As one goes farther from the Equator, the distances between the lines of latitude increase.

Putting all of the information together, you find that the places more distance from the Equator are less accurately depicted than the areas close to the Equator. The places in extreme northern locations tend to appear much larger in area than they appear on the globe. This can lead to great misunderstanding. Some youngsters believe that Greenland is larger than South America because of their exposure to maps made according to a cylindrical projection.

One of the most famous cylindrical projections is the *Mercator Projection*, which was developed centuries ago to serve the needs of navigators. Though the cylindrical projection distorts the relative size appearances, the projection does accurately depict the locations of places in terms of latitude and longitude. For this reason, these maps were highly prized by navigators.

Tangential Plane Projections. To understand how a *tangential plane projection* is made, again assume that a cartographer has a clear glass globe with the tiny light. This time, a flat sheet of paper is placed next to the globe. The sheet actually touches the globe at only one point. Then the cartographer turns on the light. The shadows on the paper are inked. This paper becomes the map. (Again, cartographers do not really use clear globes and lights. They use mathematics to gain the same information they could get in this more primitive way.)

There are two basic types of tangential plane maps. They differ in terms of the location of the imaginary light used to cast the shadows. In *gnomonic projection*, the light is assumed to be at the center of the globe. More frequently, in *stereographic projection*, the light is assumed to be at a point on the surface of the earth that is directly opposite the point where the paper surface touches the

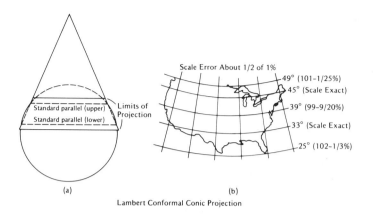

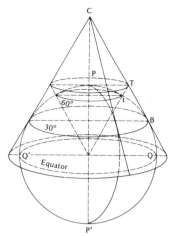

Scale Error About 1/2 of 1%

49° (101-1/25%)
45° (Scale Exact)
39° (99-9/20%)
33° (Scale Exact)
25° (102-1/3%)

Standard parallel (upper)
Standard parallel (lower)
Limits of Projection

(a)   (b)

Lambert Conformal Conic Projection

Cone tangent to the glove at Lat. 30°N.
An example of conical projection.*

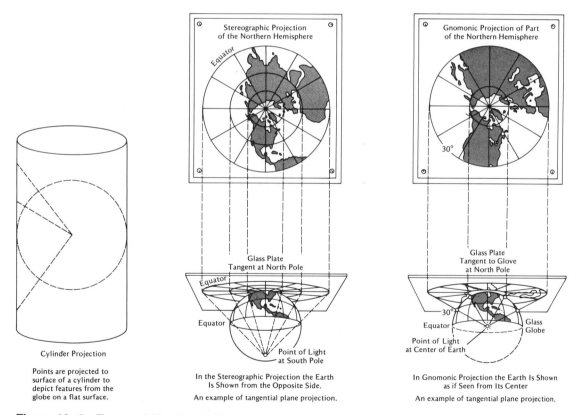

Cylinder Projection

Points are projected to surface of a cylinder to depict features from the globe on a flat surface.

Stereographic Projection of the Northern Hemisphere

Glass Plate Tangent at North Pole

Point of Light at South Pole

In the Stereographic Projection the Earth Is Shown from the Opposite Side.

An example of tangential plane projection.

Gnomonic Projection of Part of the Northern Hemisphere

Glass Plate Tangent to Glove at North Pole

Point of Light at Center of Earth

In Gnomonic Projection the Earth Is Shown as if Seen from Its Center

An example of tangential plane projection.

Figure 10–3 Types of Map Projections.

(*Sources:* [top] Samuel L. Greitzer, *Elementary Topography and Map Reading.* New York: McGraw-Hill Book Co., copyright © 1944 by Samuel L. Greitzer, pp. 45 and 42, respectively; [bottom] David G. Armstrong, *Social Studies in Secondary Education.* New York: Macmillan Publishing Co., copyright © 1980 by David G. Armstrong, pp. 182–183. All reprinted with permission.)

globe. For example, if a cartographer wanted to map the North Pole, he or she would assume the imaginary light to be at the South Pole.

A very common use of tangential plane projections is to map the polar regions. In such cases, the sheet of paper is placed at either the South Pole or the North Pole. The distortion on such maps increases with the distance away from the point that the flat sheet made contact with the globe (the North Pole in the case of maps of the north polar region, and the South Pole in the case of maps of the south polar region).

Conical Projections. Cartographers also rely on mathematical information to draw conical projection maps. In a simple *conical projection*, an imaginary cone of paper is wrapped around a globe so that it touches the earth's surface along a given line of latitude. There is an assumed light source at the earth's surface. This light source casts shadows on the paper cone. When the shadows are inked, the paper becomes a map.

In a basic conical projection, the most accurate representation of the earth's surface is along the latitude line where the cone of paper touched the globe. The distortion increases with the distance away from this line.

There are many modifications of this basic conical projection. One of these, the *Lambert conformal conic projection*, chooses two lines of latitude as the parallel standards. An imaginary cone that passes through these two latitudes is designed. To pass through the latitudes, the cone must pass through the globe's surface. The result of this procedure is a map that is accurate at two latitudes. There is some distortion between these lines of latitude. But where the areas are not overwhelmingly large, this error can be held to a very acceptable level. For example, a map of the United States can be constructed using this procedure, in which the distortion is so minimal that the accuracy varies no more than 2 percent from what one might find on a globe.

Sophisticated applications, *polyconic maps*, are sometimes used to map areas having large north-to-south extents. These are made by combining a number of conic projections to produce complex maps that are very accurate along a given line of longitude. The accuracy decreases with distances east and west of the line. This procedure is very useful for producing an accurate map of a country such as Chile. On the other hand, it would be a very poor choice to make a map of a place like Tennessee, which has a large east-to-west extent.

The Basic Map and Globe Skills _____

Eight basic map and globe skills are of interest to the elementary social studies teacher. These skills are the following:

1. Recognizing shapes.
2. Utilizing scale.
3. Recognizing symbols.
4. Utilizing direction.
5. Determining absolute location.
6. Pointing out relative location.

7. Describing the earth-sun relationships.
8. Interpreting the information on maps and globes.

Each of these skills can be understood at many levels of sophistication. In well-planned programs, they tend to be introduced so that youngsters in the early grades deal with only the very basic skills. In the middle and upper grades, youngsters are exposed to the more sophisticated skills.

Some specialists in geographic education have gone so far as to suggest that specific kinds of map and globe skills should be taught at each elementary grade level. This practice has often resulted in long lists of grade-level–specific learning activities. There is a danger of cutting the content into "bites" that may be too small. The learning outcomes may focus on trivial content.

Another argument against the practice of developing unique skills activities for each grade is that youngsters *within* a given grade level vary tremendously. Some second graders can handle fairly sophisticated content; on the other hand, some sixth graders experience difficulty with skills activities that are supposed to provide few serious challenges to second graders.

When thinking about sequencing skills, it makes more sense to think in terms of a general simple-to-complex pattern. It is useful to consider the sorts of skills activities that, *in general*, might be appropriate for youngsters in the early grades (Kindergarten to second grade), middle grades (third to fourth grade), and upper grades (fifth to sixth grade).

Even this kind of a three-stage sequence of skill development must be approached cautiously because of the individual differences among pupils. The most important point about skills development is that the more-basic information should be introduced before the more complex.

In the subsections that follow, some basic information about each basic skill is introduced. In addition, some ideas about sequencing instruction from the early grades, through the middle grades, and into the upper grades are provided.

Recognizing Shapes

Recognizing shapes is one of the most fundamental map and globe skills. Though the skill may appear to be simple or even simplistic, many sophisticated analyses in geography require a grasp of the importance of physical shapes, particularly those of land masses. For example, to appreciate that a narrow peninsula may have a climate that varies dramatically from the climate of a central location at the heart of a continent, a person must know what a peninsula is. The kinds of learning associated with recognizing shapes increase in complexity as youngsters move through the elementary program.

Utilizing Scale

Scale is an abstract and very difficult concept. Teachers find teaching the utilization of scale to be one of their most challenging assignments (see Table 10–2). Scale is difficult because it requires the concurrent understanding of two subordinate understandings. Each of these can frustrate students, especially those in the early elementary grades.

First, to appreciate scale, a person needs to know that "real" phenomena

This pupil is comparing the scales on two maps.
(*Source:* © Juliann Barbato.)

(mountains, rivers, oceans, and so forth) can be visually depicted in a convenient way. For example, it is possible to represent a mountain by taking a photograph of the mountain. Youngsters need to grasp that the mountain is real; they need to know the photograph is real; and, most importantly, they need to understand that there is a connection between the mountain as depicted in the photograph and the actual mountain itself.

Second, a youngster looking at a photograph of a mountain needs to recognize that there is a knowable physical size relationship between the size of the mountain as it exists on the earth's surface and the size as it is depicted in the photograph. A sound understanding of the principle of using small, convenient representations as reliable indicators of the size of large phenomena is fundamental to an appreciation of scale. Pupils who lack this basic knowledge have a very difficult time grasping the idea that the scales on maps and globes can be used

TABLE 10–2 Helping Young Children Learn About Scale.

Scale is a challenging concept for youngsters in the early grades. Some teachers have found it useful to take pictures of familiar objects in the classroom using a camera that produces instant prints. Then youngsters are asked to measure the object as it exists in "real life" and the object as it is depicted in the photograph. They can be asked how many heights of the object in the photograph would be required to reach the same height as the real object.

This exercise can help youngsters grasp the idea that multiples of units on a scale can be used to determine how large something is in reality. It is often useful to take pictures of similar objects at different distances. This helps develop the idea that scales can change.

Think About This

1. What major misconceptions do you think youngsters in the early grades might have at the beginning of this exercise? Why do you think so?
2. What kinds of objects in the classroom might be best suited as subjects for a photograph to be used to introduce the idea of scale?
3. What difficulties might you expect youngsters to have in understanding the scale differences revealed by photographs of the same object taken at different distances? How might these difficulties be overcome?

to make accurate statements about the actual sizes of the physical features of the earth.

Recognizing Symbols

Both maps and globes feature many symbols. These symbols represent a convenient shorthand for the kinds of phenomena that exist in the "real world." For people who understand them, they communicate a tremendous amount of information in a very space-efficient way. But for individuals who do not know what they mean, they are confusing marks that can lead to serious misunderstandings. Because symbols are so basic to an understanding of maps and globes, recognizing symbols has been long recognized as one of the most important map and globe skills (see Table 10–3).

Pupils must recognize that symbols represent real objects. Maps and globes in their entireties are symbols. They are representations of part of or all of the earth's surface. It is important that pupils understand that even the colors on maps and globes function as symbols. Younger pupils are sometimes confused about this. When they see Kansas depicted in orange, they may receive the impression that everything in Kansas literally *is* orange. Teachers, then, need to be careful to explain the symbolic nature of maps as a whole as well as the meaning of the more specific symbols indicating things such as airports, highways, boundary lines, and large cities (see Table 10–4).

Utilizing Direction

The proper use of globes and maps depends on an ability to become properly oriented to direction. A sound understanding of the major and intermediate

TABLE 10–3   Six ideas for Helping Beginners Learn About Symbols.

1. Cut out well-known symbols for businesses and other organizations from newspapers and magazines. For example, symbols representing the Olympics, the United Nations, Volkswagen, Texaco, and many other organizations, firms, and groups might be selected. Ask how many youngsters recognize each symbol. Explain why symbols are used (to save time, to provide for ready recognition, and so forth). Does the school have a mascot? Is there a symbol that represents this team? Lead into the idea that map makers and globe makers use many symbols.

2. Let youngsters decide on five new clubs that should be started in the school. Once they have identified these groups, set them to work developing a symbol for each club. Sometimes it works well to organize youngsters into teams for this activity. Follow up with a discussion about what goes into a good symbol. (It is easy to remember, and quickly communicates a great deal of information about the group or thing for which it stands.)

3. To prepare youngsters to work comfortably with the symbols that will appear on the maps or globe they will use, develop sets of flashcards. On one side will be the symbol. On the other side will be the thing for which the symbol stands. These cards can help youngsters grasp the meaning of symbols.

4. Another technique to help youngsters learn the meanings of symbols used on maps involves the use of simple two-part puzzles. These can be made from construction paper. From sources such as the *National Geographic,* pictures of things that are depicted by symbols on maps can be found. A picture can be pasted on the top half of a sheet of construction paper. On the bottom half, the symbol used for the thing depicted will be drawn. Then the sheet is cut into two parts. Youngsters are given a mixed group of top and bottom sheets. They try to fit the sheets together by using their knowledge of symbols. When the sheets fit properly, they know they have matched the symbol to the thing it depicts. See the example below.

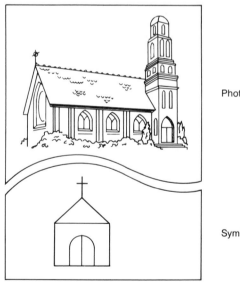

Photo of church

Symbol of church

5. Ask pupils to develop symbols for the school desks or tables, for the teacher's desk, for the doors, and for the chalkboards. Then give them a blank outline map of the classroom. Ask them to use their symbols to indicate the locations of the school desks or tables, the teacher's desk, the doors, and the chalkboards. Display the finished products, and ask several volunteers to explain their maps.

6. Provide pupils with a simple map featuring a key that explains the symbols. Ask them to explain what they might see if they took a trip along a specified route depicted on the map. Remind them to refer to the meanings of the symbols provided in the key. An example of such an exercise is provided here.

TABLE 10–3 (cont.)

Directions

Describe a trip a person might make along this route, starting at point *A* and finishing at point *B*. Use the key below to interpret the symbols on the map.

Map

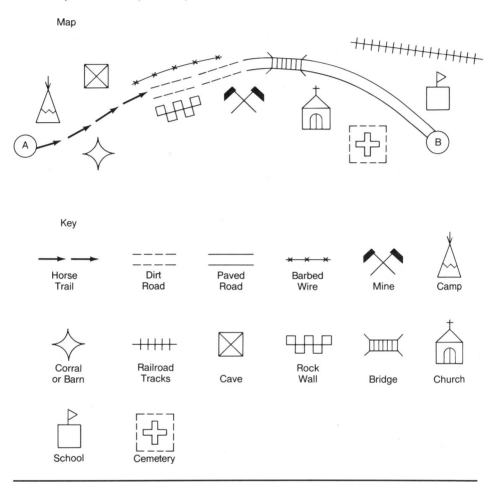

Key

Horse Trail   Dirt Road   Paved Road   Barbed Wire   Mine   Camp

Corral or Barn   Railroad Tracks   Cave   Rock Wall   Bridge   Church

School   Cemetery

The authors wish to thank Judy Harber for help with some of these exercises.

compass directions is basic to pinpointing locations. It is particularly important that youngsters master and use the concepts of directions before working with wall maps (Table 10–5). Otherwise, they tend to use terms such as "up" and "down" when referring to "north" and "south," and "right" and "left" when referring to "east" and "west." These inappropriate terms can contribute to the development of inaccurate information (The Pacific Ocean always lies to the left.).

Determining Absolute Location

Determining absolute location requires pupils to locate any point on the earth's surface. To adequately perform the skill, youngsters must be very familiar with

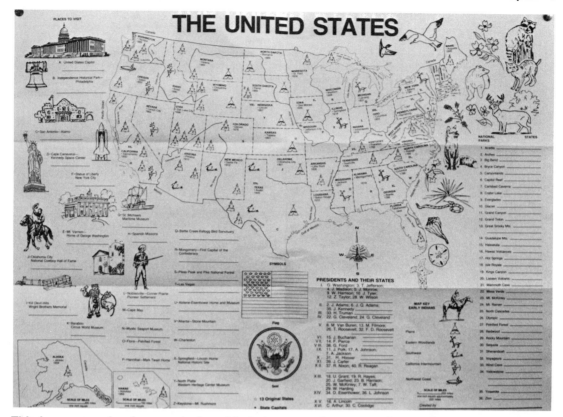

This is an example of a map designed to help youngsters recognize symbols.
(*Source:* © Juliann Barbato.)

the lines of latitude and longitude. Specifically, they must understand how a longitude-latitude grid system can be used to identify the "address" of every location on earth (see Table 10–6). Generally, teachers have pupils work with very simple grids before they introduce the global system of latitude and longitude.

Pointing Out Relative Location

Relative location refers to the location of one place in terms of one or more other places. When Chicago is described as being north of Houston, east of Omaha, and west of New York, the description is making reference to Chicago's relative location.

Many elementary social studies programs begin building the skill of pointing out relative location by helping youngsters to first recognize their relative location with regard to familiar places. The school's relative location might be described by pointing out its position in terms of the nearby parks and homes. Often, the local community is pinpointed first by reference to places in the state, later by reference to places in the nation, and still later by reference to other locations around the globe (see Table 10–7).

The compass is a useful tool for helping pupils learn about direction.
(*Source:* © Juliann Barbato.)

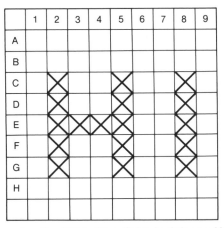

Figure 10–4 An Example of a Fill-In-The-Grid Activity to Help Pupils Learn How to Find Places When Given the Coordinates of Latitude and Longitude.
Directions: Find the secret word by placing an X in each of these squares: C2, C5, C8; D2, D5, D8; E2, E3, E4, E5, E8; F2, F5, F8; G2, G5, G8.

TABLE 10–4 The Grade Level Emphases for (1) Recognizing Shapes, (2) Utilizing Scale, and (3) Recognizing Symbols.

	Kindergarten to Second Grade Emphases	Third to Fourth Grade Emphases	Fifth to Sixth Grade Emphases
Recognizing Shapes	• Introduction to the very basic information about shape. • Recognition that the earth is basically round. • Recognition of the basic shapes of the contents and oceans (near end of second grade).	• Recognition of the shapes of smaller land masses, such as islands, peninsulas, and isthmuses. • Recognition of the shapes of smaller bodies of water, such as lakes, bays, and sounds.	• Recognition of certain kinds of map distortion. • Identification of the patterns of flow of the major rivers. • Identification of the shapes of the major physical regions.
Utilizing Scale	• Introduction of the basic concepts such as "larger" and "smaller." • Recognition of the simple increments of measure (city blocks, for example). • Identification of the objects of different sizes in pictures.	• Utilization of the scale on simple maps. • Solution of simple distance problems using scale. • Recognition that scale may vary from map to map and globe to globe.	• Utilization of the many kinds of scales. • Recognition that the amount of detail on a map varies with its scale.
Recognizing Symbols	• Recognition of the meanings of common signs (stop signs, for example). • Recognition that some colors on maps are regularly used to represent land and water. • Recognition that symbols stand for things in the "real world."	• Utilization of symbols for the major landscape features on maps and globes. • Recognition of the traditional symbols for cities, railroads, rivers, and highways.	• Utilization of the symbols on special-purpose maps. • Recognition that the same symbol may mean different things on different maps and globes.

Describing the Earth-Sun Relationships

The proper understanding of earth-sun relationships is an essential ingredient of knowledge regarding diverse topics such as global time, the seasons, and the changing annual wind patterns. Many elementary youngsters find content related to earth-sun relationships to be difficult.

Part of the problem is our language. We speak of the sun "rising" and "setting." This terminology is based on an illusion that makes sense. As residents of the earth's surface, we are not physically aware that the globe is spinning on its axis. Hence, the "rising" and "setting" terminology does accurately describe what we see, but this language does not properly describe what is going on. Adults (most of them, at least) know that the sun does not move, but rather that the earth's spinning only makes it appear to do so. Younger elementary children lack this understanding. Many of them really believe that it is the sun that does the moving.

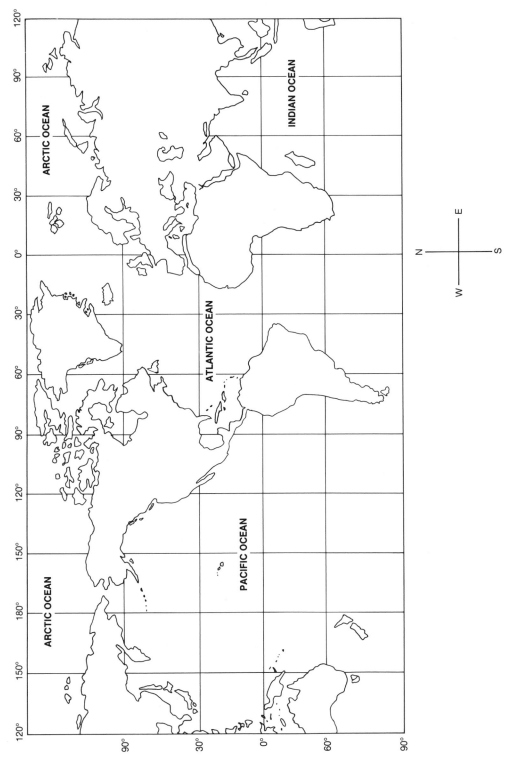

Figure 10—5   A Simple Outline Map of the World.

TABLE 10–5   Six Ideas for Helping Beginners Learn About Direction.

1. Draw 12 dots on the chalkboard. Arrange them and label them as follows (include a simple compass rose):

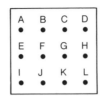

   Call on youngsters to respond orally to questions about relative locations of individual points. "John, if you went from *F* to *G,* what direction would you travel?" Start with simple cardinal directions. Build toward more complicated solutions involving intermediate directions. "Sue, what direction would a person be going if he or she went from *A* to *F?*

2. Position a large wall map of the world at the front of the class where all youngsters can easily see it. Point to individual countries. Ask youngsters whether each country is north or south of the Equator. Consider using these countries: Cuba, India, Mexico, South Africa, New Zealand, Nigeria, The Philippines, Saudi Arabia, Spain, China, and Venezuela.

3. Prepare a board game for pupils to play. Use sturdy cardboard as a surface to use for marking off horizontal and vertical lines. The result will be a matrix, something that looks roughly like a piece of graph paper. Make the squares one inch by one inch. Provide youngsters with bottle caps to use as playing pieces. Prepare a stack of playing cards. One fourth of the cards are marked, respectively, North, South, East, and West. The cards are shuffled and placed face down next to the playing board.

   To begin, the players (up to four per board) place their pieces on the four most central squares on the board. One at a time, the players draw a card. He or she moves his or her playing piece one square in the direction indicated on the card. The first player to reach the edge of the board is declared the winner.

   A more difficult version of the game involves the preparation of game cards that also include these directions: Northwest, Northeast, Southwest, and Southeast.

4. Prepare a huge map of the United States by using multiple pieces of butcher paper. The map should be simple. Just an outline of the United States, a compass rose, and a few really large cities will suffice. Ideally, the map should be large enough to cover at least a quarter of the floor of the classroom.

   Ask youngsters to take off their shoes. Have them look closely at the compass rose. Then ask a volunteer to "walk" from Chicago to New York City. Ask youngsters the direction of travel the volunteer took.

5. The teacher describes the compass directions that a person would need to follow to get from the classroom to another room in the school. (Go out the door, go west for twenty paces, then go north. When you have gone as far north as you can go, go east for ten paces. Then stop. If you turn south, you will be looking at the door that you would use to enter this room. What room am I talking about?)

6. Give each youngster a sheet of blank graph paper. The graph paper should have a clearly marked starting point (an *X* will do). Each paper should also have a compass rose for youngsters to refer to during the exercise. The teacher has a similar piece of graph paper on which he or she has drawn a simple figure, perhaps a line drawing of a fish. The idea is to have the youngsters reproduce this drawing by giving them drawing clues in terms of direction. (Put your pencils on the *X*. First move directly north two spaces and make another *X*. Then move east ten spaces and make another *X*. Draw a heavy line connecting the first *X* at the beginning point and this new *X*. Now go ten spaces east and draw a new *X*. . . . This same procedure is followed until all the *X*'s have been drawn. At this point, youngsters should have the same figure as the teacher on their papers, provided, of course, they have been able to follow the directions properly.

The authors would like to thank Judy Harber, who contributed several of these ideas.

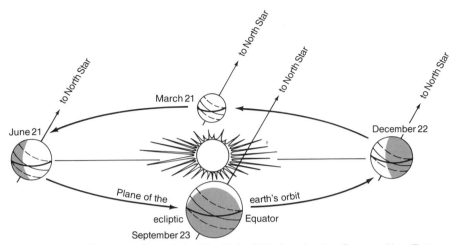

Figure 10–6   The Location of the Earth in Relation to the Sun on Key Dates.
Many elementary pupils have difficulty accepting the idea that the earth does not swing
back and forth or wobble on its axis. A figure such as this can help to explain what
actually happens. The earth's axis always points toward the North Star. Note that the
sun directly strikes its surface at different points at different times of the year.

As they progress through the elementary program, youngsters are exposed to
the concepts of the "seasons." They are taught that the seasons change because
the angle of the sun's rays strikes some parts of the earth's surface more directly
at certain times of the year than at others. Many youngsters who grasp this basic
idea have trouble understanding exactly how this happens. Some conclude er-

**Simple maps help young children learn the relative locations of places in their
community.**
(*Source:* Juliann Barbato.)

TABLE 10–6   The Grade Level Emphases for (1) Utilizing Direction, (2) Determining Absolute Location, and (3) Pointing Out Relative Location.

	Kindergarten to Second Grade Emphases	Third to Fourth Grade Emphases	Fifth to Sixth Grade Emphases
Utilizing Direction	• Introduction to the four cardinal compass direction. • Introduction, very basic, to latitude and longitude (referred to at this level as north-to-south lines and east-to-west lines).	• Description of the locations of continents in terms of their directional locations from one another. • Location of the Prime Meridian. • Utilization of a compass to orient a map, and of the compass rose on a map. • Introduction to the intermediate directions.	• Recognition of the difference between True and Magnetic North • Utilization of intermediate direction to provide precise information about locations and paths of travel.
Determining Absolute Location	• Utilization of relative terms such as "right," "left," "near," "far," "up," "down," "back," "front." • Location of the places on a globe as being north or south of the Equator.	• Introduction to the use of grid systems. • Location of the places on maps and globes using simple grid systems.	• Location of places using the coordinates of latitude and longitude. • Identification of the degree position of important lines of latitude including the Equator, the Arctic and Antarctic circles, and the Tropics of Cancer and Capricorn.
Pointing Out Relative Location	• Description of one place in a room in terms of the other places in the room. • Identification of the location of the school in terms of the other parts of the community.	• Description of the location of the state within the nation. • Identification of the local community in terms of its location in the state and nation.	• Location of the local community relative to any other place on the globe. • Description of the relative location of any two points on the globe.

roneously that the earth wobbles back and forth on its axis, thus causing a change in where the sun's rays strike most directly. Teachers find they must work very hard if youngsters are to grasp exactly how the seasonal change can occur without "global wobble."

Interpreting the Information on Maps and Globes

The skill of interpreting the information of maps and globes is the broadest of them all. It is perhaps the most important for elementary social studies programs because it establishes a purpose for many of the other map and globe skills. Unless programs involve pupils in using the other skills, they may perceive the instruction that focuses on these skills as boring and directed toward no useful end. But when these skills are applied to generate new information, pupils may

TABLE 10–7   Five Ideas for Helping Beginners Learn About Relative Location.

1. Prepare a simple grid with squares along the top identified by numbers and squares along the side identified by letters. In advance, determine which squares, when colored in, will spell a word. Give youngsters the directions to shade in squares that are identified by coordinates. (Shade in these squares: A-1, A-3, B-2, B-3, B-4, B-5, C-1, C-5, C-6 . . . and so forth.) When youngsters have completed the exercise, they should be able to see the secret word. See the sample provided in Figure 10–4.

2. Provide youngsters with a simple outline map of the world. The map should include the lines of latitude and longitude. Play a Find the Continent game with the members of the class. Give map coordinates. Then ask youngsters to name the nearest continent. (What is the nearest continent to 30° south latitude and 150° east longitude? [Australia]) Please see Figure 10–5 for a sample outline map that might be used in such an exercise. (Please note: The map should include a simple compass rose.)

3. In a learning center, provide several short books about various countries of the world. Inside each book neatly print a coordinate of latitude and longitude that would fall within the boundaries of the country about which the book is written. Provide students with an outline map of the world featuring the political boundaries of the nations. Ask students to use the coordinate of latitude and longitude to identify the location of the country the book describes. Then he or she shades in or colors this country on the outline map.

4. In a learning center, place several newspaper articles with datelines from a number of cities around the world. Attach each article to a sturdy piece of paper. Above the article, write the latitude and longitude of the dateline city. Then youngsters can use a globe or an atlas to locate the city.

5. Write an itinerary about a journey to various cities in the world. But instead of naming the cities, identify them only by referring to the coordinates of latitude and longitude. Give these to pupils. Ask them to name the cities and plot the route the traveler took on a world outline map. Here are some possibilities:

Latitude 22° 53′ 43″ S, Longitude 43° 13′ 22″ W. (Rio de Janeiro, Brazil)
Latitude 62° 28′ 15″ N, Longitude 114° 22′ 00″ W. (Yellowknife, Northwest Territories, Canada)
Latitude 48° 50′ 14″ N, Longitude 2° 20′ 14″ E. (Paris, France)

well appreciate their importance (see Table 10–8). They can increase youngsters' sense of personal power to understand and interpret their world.

Teaching All the Skills at Each Grade Level _____

Recall that the discussion in the previous section suggested activities for each of the eight map and globe skills. This arrangement of activities underscores the importance of providing youngsters with some exposure to all of these skills at each elementary grade level.

Sometimes, new teachers make an assumption that the more-basic skills (perhaps the recognition of symbols) should be taught to the younger children and that the more-advanced skills should not be. There are two difficulties with this approach.

First, there is nothing inherently "easy" or "difficult" about any of these skills. Each can be taught at varying levels of complexity. A teacher would not expect kindergarten youngsters and sixth graders to engage in similar learning activities or to develop similar depths of understanding about a given skill. Yet each group

TABLE 10–8   The Grade Level Emphases for (1) Describing the Earth-Sun Relationships and (2) Interpreting the Information on Maps and Globes

	Kindergarten to Second Grade Emphases	Third to Fourth Grade Emphases	Fifth to Six Grade Emphases
Describing the Earth-Sun Relationships	• Recognition of the terms "summer," "fall," "winter," "spring," "day," and "night." • Identification of the direction of sunrise and sunset. • Description of how the turning of the earth causes night and day.	• Description of how the earth moves around the sun. • Description of the inclination of the earth on its axis.	• Description of the relationship of the sun to the Equator, Tropic of Cancer, Tropic of Capricorn, Arctic Circle, and Antarctic Circle. • Recognition that the globe is divided into 360 degrees. • Recognition that the earth has 24 time zones that are 15 degrees wide. • Utilization of the analemma to determine where the sun's rays strike the earth most directly on each day of the year.
Interpreting the Information on Maps and Globes	• Interpretation of the information from pictures and simple maps. • Recognition that no one, not even an astronaut in space, can see the whole earth at one time. • Construction and interpretation of simple local-neighborhood and community maps.	• Preparation of more complex local-community maps and the interpretation of information contained on these maps. • Description of the population distributions and terrain features on maps. • Explanation of the basic causes of climate by referring to the information on maps.	• Prediction about the probable climate of a place by viewing maps to determine its elevation, proximity to ocean current, latitude, and continental or coastal position. • Explanation of the geographical constraints on historical or current events through reference to maps. • Prediction of elevation change by examining river-flow direction on maps.

should be exposed to the skill, and appropriate learning experiences should be devised.

Second, when teachers of younger children decide to omit the teaching of a "difficult" skill, they often eliminate the interpreting-information skill. This is a serious mistake. This skill allows youngsters to put the other skills they have learned to work as they seek to solve problems.

Interpreting-information exercises help pupils see the purpose for mastering map and globe skills. These activities extend pupils' abilities to make sense out of their world. If such activities are eliminated in the early grades, many youngsters will see little use in learning the other basic map and globe skills. Teachers, as a result, may face serious motivational problems, which can seriously inhibit learning.

Key Ideas in Summary _____

Map and globe skills have long been an important component of instruction in elementary social studies. These skills have the potential to greatly extend pupils' abilities to understand their world. Some of the key ideas introduced that are related to this general topic include the following:

1. Many adults have very confused ideas about the locations of places on the globe. Elementary youngsters are even more likely to have an inadequate grasp of the map and globe skills needed for the proper understanding of geographical location. Some misunderstandings result from a lack of any information at all. Others come about because of inadequate information. For example, large wall maps sometimes distort the east-to-west and north-to-south relationships as well as the relative sizes of places.

2. Globes should receive more attention in elementary social studies class-rooms. Only the globe shows places on the earth with a minimum of shape and size distortion and with an accurate relative placement of water and land areas. To be useful as teaching tools, there should be at least one globe available for every three or four pupils.

3. Globes do have some disadvantages as well. They are bulky. They are rather expensive. They do not lend themselves well to teaching certain kinds of content. For example, if a teacher wanted to teach about a relatively small area, perhaps the state of South Carolina, the area of interest would be too small on a globe to be of any practical value. A globe large enough to display South Carolina at a size sufficient for youngsters to see easily might well be too large to fit in the classroom.

4. There are four common types of globes. These are (1) readiness globes, (2) elementary globes, (3) intermediate globes, and (4) project globes. Readiness globes include only very basic information. Elementary globes include information about latitude and longitude and other details not included on readiness globes. Intermediate globes include even more information than elementary globes. Project globes are special globes that have a surface pupils can write on. They are used for globe skills activities of various kinds.

5. Maps are very useful for teaching certain kinds of content; for example, the study of relatively small areas. All maps are imperfect representations of the globe. In going from a three-dimensional to a two-dimensional surface there are distortions. For example, some maps make Greenland appear larger than South America (Greenland is much smaller). Teachers have an obligation to teach youngsters about the limitations of maps as representations of the globe.

6. There are a number of kinds of map projections. A projection is a technique that is used to produce a two-dimensional map from a three-dimensional globe. The three basic projection types are (1) cylindrical projections, (2) tangential plane projections, and (3) conical projections. Each has advantages and disadvantages; each is better for some purposes than for others.

7. There are eight basic map and globe skills. They are (1) recognizing shapes,

(2) utilizing scale, (3) recognizing symbols, (4) utilizing direction, (5) determining absolute location, (6) pointing out relative location, (7) describing the earth-sun relationships, and (8) interpreting the information on maps and globes.

8. The basic map and globe skills are properly introduced collectively at each level of the elementary program. The skills remain common throughout the program, but the activities used to introduce them and the depth of the understanding required will change with grade levels. The simplest activities are introduced in kindergarten to second grade, and the most complex are introduced in fifth to sixth grade.

9. It is especially important in teaching youngsters to work with map and globe skills that pupils have opportunities to use these skills to solve problems. This experience helps establish the usefulness of map and globe information. It can extend youngsters' sense of understanding of the world around them and can build interest in the social studies program.

Questions _____

Review Questions

1. What factors may contribute to the misunderstandings many pupils have about the relative locations of places on the earth's surface?
2. What are some advantages of using globes when trying to provide youngsters with some basic understandings about the nature of the earth?
3. What are the characteristics of (1) readiness globes, (2) elementary globes, (3) intermediate globes, and (4) project globes?
4. In principle, how are (1) cylindrical projections, (2) tangential plane projections, and (3) conical projections made?
5. What are the eight basic map skills?

Thought Questions

1. Suppose someone challenged you to defend the inclusion of instruction about map and globe skills in the elementary social studies program. How would you respond?
2. In the past, some people have suggested that the skill of interpreting information on maps and globes is too sophisticated for pupils in kindergarten to second grade. How do you feel about the suggestion that these skills be reserved for older youngsters? Why do you take this position?
3. Many pupils have a difficult time understanding that the earth does not wobble back in forth on its axis. The axis always points to the North Star, regardless of the time of year. What might you do to help youngsters grasp this point?
4. Suppose you were going to be assigned to teach map and globe skills to a group of third graders. What would you use maps for? What would you use globes for?
5. Youngsters in the elementary grades often greatly underestimate the size of the continent of Africa. What might you do to help them understand the size of this continent relative to North America and the United States?

Extending Understanding and Skill _____

Activities

1. Interview a group of four or five youngsters who are at a grade level you would like to teach. Ask questions to determine the accuracy of their information about subjects such as (1) the relative locations of U.S. cities, (2) the directions of flow of major U.S. rivers, and (3) the relative sizes of continents. Share your findings with the class.
2. For each of the eight basic map and globe skills, prepare a lesson directed at the age group you would like to teach. Discuss your suggestions with the others in the class or the instructor.
3. Look at a sample of elementary social studies textbooks. Do a content analysis to determine how much attention is paid to developing youngsters' grasp of each of the eight basic map and globe skills. Prepare a short paper in which you comment on those skills that receive a good deal of attention, those that receive a moderate amount of attention, and those that receive little or no attention.
4. Develop a series of five or six activities focusing on the skill of interpreting information on maps and globes for use by youngsters in kindergarten to second grade. Make copies of this material to share with the others in the class.
5. Prepare a complete plan for a field trip that will be used to strengthen youngsters' grasp of basic map and globe skills. Identify the preplanning procedures, learning objectives, teacher activities, pupil activities, and evaluation procedures. Turn your plan into your instructor for his or her reactions.

Supplemental Reading

ATKINS, CAMMIE L. "Introducing Basic Map and Globe Skills to Young Children," *Journal of Geography* (March 1984), pp. 228–233.

FRAZEE, BRUCE M. "Foundations for an Elementary Map Skills Program," *The Social Studies* (March/April 1984), pp. 79–82.

GILMARTIN, PATRICIA. "The Instructional Efficacy of Maps in Geographic Text," *Journal of Geography* (July/August 1982), pp. 145–150.

HATCHER, B. "Putting Young Cartographers on the Map," *Childhood Education* (May/June 1983), pp. 311–315.

HENNINGS, GEORGE. "Understanding Time-Space Relationships Through Map Construction in the Elementary Grades," *Journal of Geography* (April/May 1981), pp. 129–131.

LARKINS, A. GUY. "Selected NCGE Material for the Elementary Teacher: A Critique," *Journal of Geography* (September/October 1982), pp. 191–192.

MILLER, WILLARD. "Planning the Geographic Field Trip," *Journal of Geography* (November 1981), pp. 234–235.

PAINE C., and ELLEMAN, B. "The Stories Maps Tell," *Learning* (March 1984), p. 46.

References _____

ANDERSON, R. C. "Geography's Role in Promoting Global Citizenship," *NASSP Bulletin* (September 1983), pp. 80–83.

DEBLIJ, HARM J. *Geography: Regions and Concepts*, 3d ed. New York: John Wiley & Sons, 1981.

GREENHOOD, DAVID. *Mapping.* Chicago: The University of Chicago Press, 1971.

JAMES, PRESTON E. *A Geography of Man,* 3d ed. Waltham, MA: Blaisdell Publishing Company, 1966.

MILLER, J. W. "Development of an Audio-Tutorial System for Teaching Basic Geographic Concepts," *Education of the Visually Handicapped* (Winter 1982), pp. 109–115.

MOODY, W. G. *A Dictionary of Geography.* New York: Frederick A. Praeger Publishers, 1967.

PRESSOR, C. C. "Development of Map Reading Skills," *Child Development* (February 1982), pp. 196–199.

Chapter 11

Using Textbooks Effectively

(*Source:* © Juliann Barbato.)

1. Develop proficiency in teaching pupils to use a multipass approach to reading.

2. Recognize the components that should be included in a reading study guide.

3. Describe the use of visual frameworks in helping pupils learn content contained in prose materials.

4. Determine the approximate grade-level reading difficulty of individual prose selections using the Fry Readability Graph.

5. Recognize the characteristics that contribute to the difficulty level of an individual prose selection.

6. Describe the particular kinds of vocabulary problems that may interfere with youngsters' abilities to learn from prose materials.

7. Point out how pupils may be helped to work with the different parts of a textbook.

Overview

Debates about reading generate interest among both professional educators and the public at large. Perhaps more has been written and spoken about this issue than any other education-related topic. The discussions often focus on two basic issues.

First, there are broad disagreements about how the teaching of reading should be approached. Reading experts are by no means in total agreement on this issue. Many members of the public at large who are interested in reading hold strong views regarding how reading should be taught. They often make their positions known at school-board meetings and in other forums.

The arguments made by the partisans of individual approaches to reading instruction lie beyond the scope of concern of this text. These differing viewpoints do suggest a very deep professional and public interest in reading. The elementary social studies teacher must recognize that there is a broad concern for developing youngsters' capacities to learn from prose materials. Schools are increasingly being held accountable for producing youngsters who have adequate reading skills. In the social studies classroom, as elsewhere in the elementary program, teachers have an obligation to work on developing reading proficiency, particularly as such proficiency relates to subject-matter content.

Individual teachers, not surprisingly, have varying views on the kinds of reading instruction that ought to occur in social studies classrooms. A few place very heavy reliance on the adopted textbooks. Others rarely use textbooks in their program. Whether the textbook is a primary information source or not, prose materials tend to be heavily used to convey content to youngsters, particularly to pupils in the middle and upper grades.

Some people suggest that, in the future, there will be much more reliance on computer-based information in social studies classrooms. This may be true. For the present, however, prose materials tend to deliver a high percentage of the subject-matter content introduced in social studies programs. Hence, it makes sense for prospective elementary social studies teachers to develop expertise in

TABLE 11–1   Changing Patterns in Reading Achievement.

The following are the reading achievement scores of nine year olds reported by the National Assessment of Educational Progress.*

Year	Average Percent Correct
1971	64.0
1975	65.3
1980	67.9

Think About This

1. Do the figures suggest that reading proficiency of nine year olds increased or decreased from 1971 to 1980?
2. How would you explain this pattern?
3. Do you think this pattern indicates a change that is consistent with what most Americans think has been happening to youngsters' reading skills? Why, or why not?

*Source: The Condition of Education, 1983 ed. Washington, D.C.: National Center for Education Statistics, 1983, p. 54.

approaches that can help their pupils profit from these materials (see Table 11–1).

Developing Reading Study Skills _____

In recent years, reading specialists have suggested new approaches that help pupils monitor their own approaches to reading and use specific kinds of study strategies. These approaches are based on an understanding of how individuals take in and make sense of new information.

The human brain does not operate as a camera that passively records its exposure to reality. The brain actively organizes and transforms information as it is gathered. The way an individual's brain organizes data has an important bearing on his or her ability to retrieve information and use it at a later date. Prose learning can be much more effective when youngsters are taught to monitor their own learning processes in a way that helps them organize and store information efficiently. Pupils need help in each of three stages. These are (1) the prereading stage, (2) the reading stage, and (3) the postreading stage.

Instruction during the *prereading stage* should help pupils find a personal purpose for reading. At this time, pupils need to establish a scheme that will help them organize the material they will be reading. Teachers can assist in this process by relating the contents of a new reading assignment to the material that has been mastered earlier and by telling pupils what they will be expected to do to demonstrate content mastery after they have read the material.

During the *reading stage*, pupils read the assigned material. The teacher needs to monitor youngsters carefully to determine whether any class members are having difficulty understanding the material. This monitoring may involve questioning youngsters about what they are reading and encouraging them to think about the content. Pupils may be asked to create questions that can be answered from the content. They sometimes may be asked to think about the kinds of test questions that might focus on the content. On other occasions, teachers may encourage pupils to use reading-study aids such as outlining the main points or taking general reading notes.

During the *postreading phase,* pupils are encouraged to reflect upon and evaluate what they have read. They may be asked to discuss some of the important ideas that have been generated by the reading assignments.

There are a number of approaches teachers have found useful in helping pupils during the three stages of reading. Several of these techniques are described in subsections that follow.

Multipass Reading

Multipass reading is a technique that encourages a reader to go over the same material several times. Each time the material is read, the pupil approaches the content with a different purpose in mind. The purpose of the first reading, or first pass, is to help pupils develop a framework for the content and to relate it to what they already know. During the first pass, pupils are encouraged to skim the material quickly. They might be asked only to look at the major chapter divisions and to study any pictures. The first pass should be accomplished quickly.

Once youngsters have completed the first pass, the teacher asks some general kinds of questions. The following are examples of what might be asked.

These pupils are scanning the material to get a general feel for the pattern of content organization.

(*Source:* © Juliann Barbato.)

- What is this chapter or section about?
- What do we already know about these events?
- How is the chapter organized? What comes first, second, third, and so forth?

The second pass through the material is designed to help pupils identify some of the major ideas. At this time, the pupil should have a framework that can be used to organize the new information. During this second pass through the material, pupils are asked to read the major headings, the subsection headings, and the first sentences of paragraphs.

Most writers include the major ideas of their paragraphs in the first one or two sentences. When readers read only the first sentence of each paragraph, they are able to pick up a surprising amount of key information. Furthermore, they are able to do this relatively quickly because these first sentences are all they are asked to read. Even slow readers find that they can pick up a good deal of information in this way. After this second pass, the teacher again prompts students with some questions. The following are some examples of what might be asked.

- What are the main ideas covered in this material?
- How do these ideas relate to the information you already know?
- What information do you need to determine whether these ideas are true or false?

During their third pass through the material, pupils are asked to look for specific details. Since the readers at this point have a good idea about how the content is organized, they usually can get relatively quickly to the detailed information. Often, teachers will pose some questions at the conclusion of this phase as well. For example, a teacher might ask the following:

- What do people in Ethiopia eat?
- How are their houses different from ours?
- At what time did the bandit chief leave the station?

The purpose of the final pass through the material is review. Pupils are asked to quickly read the entire assigned material from beginning to end. This final pass can help those individuals who may have failed to acquire some of the important details.

Individuals who have not used multipass reading are sometimes concerned about the issue of time when they are first introduced to the technique. Surprisingly, the technique does not take as much time as one might suppose. Some of the passes through the material can be accomplished swiftly. Even the reading-for-details pass often takes very little time once pupils have developed, during the earlier passes, a feel for how the content is organized. Furthermore, the higher rates of comprehension that result from the technique save time later. Less time is needed for reteaching and review.

Visual Frameworks

Visual frameworks represent another way of helping pupils to organize content from the materials they read. Many teachers have traditionally responded

It's Called a "Book." If It's Easier, Think of it as Low-tech TV.
(*Source:* Ford Button.)

to the need to help youngsters organize material by teaching them to outline what they have read. Some pupils find outlining to be very tedious and fail to appreciate its value in helping them grasp new content. Younger elementary pupils often lack outlining skills. The visual-frameworks approach overcomes some of the difficulties with content outlining.

The numbers of reading purposes that might be established for a prose selection only two or three paragraphs in length are enormous. Assignments that require youngsters to focus on a specific category of fact might be made. Others might require them to identify certain cause and effect relationships. Still others might ask pupils to make predictions of future trends based on the information introduced in the reading assignment.

It is clear that an assignment asking youngsters to focus on certain kinds of facts requires them to look differently at the reading content than when they are asked to identify some cause and effect relationships. To assist pupils in developing an appropriate approach to their reading assignments, it makes sense for teachers to explain the nature of the task clearly. Then additional assistance can be provided through the use of visual frameworks. These are devices that will help youngsters "see" what on which elements of content they should focus. They also provide a means for taking good notes on the reading.

To see how a visual-frameworks approach might work, suppose that two teachers had very different purposes in mind when they assigned youngsters in their classes to read the very same short selection. Following the selection itself, there will be a brief description of the "purpose" established by each teacher and a related visual framework. Here is the selection:

Spanish Colonizers and the Caribbean

Christopher Columbus first landed on San Salvador Island. This happened in 1492. San Salvador is part of those islands that today we call the Bahamas. Later, Columbus went on to discover many Caribbean islands. He set up a fort on one of the biggest islands. This island is called Hispaniola.

Another famous Spanish sailor was Nicolas de Ovando. In 1502, he was sent to become the governor of Hispaniola. He brought many colonists with him. The colonists tried to make money in two ways. Some of them tried farming. Some of them tried mining. One of their big problems was finding people to do the hard work.

One thing the early Spanish colonists tried to do was to make slaves of the Indians. This did not work. The Indians died when they were forced into slavery. At first, the Spanish tried to solve the problem by capturing the Indians from other Islands. But many of these Indians died, too. Later, slaves were brought from Africa.

Even after all of these things were tried, there were still not enough people to do the work. Many of the original colonists from Spain gave up on Hispaniola. They moved to other islands in the Caribbean. Some of these colonists were led to island of Puerto Rico. This happened in 1508. The Spanish leader who led them there was Ponce de Leon. Another leader, Juan de Esquivel, took another group to Jamaica in 1509. The largest Caribbean island, Cuba, was reached by Spanish settlers in 1514.

The Purpose of Teacher 1

What islands were discovered by Spain between 1492 and 1509, and who were the four famous Spanish explorers who took part in these discoveries?

To help youngsters draw this information out of their reading, a visual framework something like the following might be developed.

The Islands and Leaders

Islands	Leaders
_____	_____
_____	_____
_____	_____
_____	_____

This framework could help a youngster read the material to find the information the teacher has established as a priority. Some pupils might choose to write the information they find on the appropriate line.

The Purpose of Teacher 2

How did the early Spanish settlers try to meet their need for workers, and what happened as a result?

To help youngsters draw this information out of their reading, a teacher might develop a visual framework something like the following for them to use.

Why Workers Were Needed

_____

_____

_____

_____

This Was Tried First   **This Was Tried Second**

_____   _____

_____   _____

_____   _____

Results   **Results**

_____   _____

_____   _____

Final Outcome

_____

_____

_____

Recall that both Teacher 1 and Teacher 2 are having their pupils read exactly the same material. But their purposes are very different. For this reason, the visual framework developed by Teacher 2 looks quite different from the one developed by Teacher 1. Teacher 2's framework helps youngsters focus on content they will need to respond to the cause-and-effect kind of question that this teacher sees as the major purpose of the reading assignment. The framework of Teacher 1, while very appropriate for that teacher's purpose, would not be appropriate at all for Teacher 2's purpose.

Visual frameworks can take a number of shapes. Some teachers help their pupils to work out their own frameworks. Whether developed by the teacher alone or with some active pupil participation, visual frameworks help youngsters to learn content assigned in required reading.

Reading Study Guides

Reading study guides are designed to help pupils monitor their own comprehension of what they are reading. A teacher who wishes to prepare a reading guide begins by scanning the material pupils will read to identify the appropriate pausing points. _Pausing points_ are places where readers might logically be asked to stop and check on their own understanding of what they have read. The reading guide takes the form of sheets of paper with printed questions or points for pupils to consider. The guide tells them how far to read before pausing to think about the questions or to consider the points. Reading guides are particularly helpful to pupils who have trouble recalling the specific details introduced in reading assignments.

Portions of reading guides can concentrate on each of the three major phases of reading. The following is an example of a reading guide that includes focus questions for (1) the prereading phase, (2) the reading phase, and (3) the postreading phase.

The categories and questions suggested in this example are simply samples of what might be included. Many guides will include fewer questions than have been provided here. It is important that the questions should not be so numerous or so difficult that they seriously interrupt the reading activity itself.

The Prereading Phase. The purpose of the prereading section of the study guide is to provide pupils with a framework for organizing the material they will be reading. This section should prompt pupils to think about what they already know about content to be introduced in the reading assignment. Pupils are often asked to think about the kinds of things that they might be required to demonstrate as evidence that they know the content after they have finished reading the assigned material. Questions such as the following might be included in the prereading section of a reading guide.

1. *Establishing familiarity with the content.*
    (a) How does the material relate to what I already know? (Pupils are encouraged to quickly skim the content as they prepare to respond to this question.)
    (b) How interesting does the material appear to be?
    (c) What are some of the new ideas I will learn?
    (d) How is the material organized?
    (e) What would be the best way for me to read this material?
2. *Establishing a purpose for reading.*
    (a) What will I be expected to know and do after I have finished reading?
    (b) Why is this material importance?

The Reading Phase. The reading section of the guide provides questions designed to help pupils monitor their own understanding as they read the material. The guide tells them when to stop and respond to the questions. The following are questions that might be included. Note the different purposes of the questions in this example.

1. *Monitoring understanding.*
    (a) Do I understand what I just read?
    (b) What are the really important ideas in what I just read?
    (c) How does what I read relate to what I already know and believe?
    (d) What kinds of pictures came to mind as I read this material?
2. *Predicting and hypothesizing.*
    (a) What do I expect to read about next?
    (b) Were the earlier ideas I had about what was going to happen correct?
    (c) What would be on a test that covers this material?
3. *Expanding and integrating.*
    (a) How do all of the ideas I read about fit together?
    (b) If I could talk to the author about some of the things I read, what would I ask?

(c) If I were to tell someone else about what I read, what would I say?
4. *Dealing with comprehension failures.* (This section of the guide is directed toward pupils who had difficulty grasping some of the content.)
   (a) Will it help if I reread the material?
   (b) Can I ignore the problem and hope I will understand the content better once I read on?
   (c) Is there something else I can read that would help me understand?
   (d) Who might I ask about content I do not understand?

The Postreading Phase. The postreading section of the guide is designed to help pupils evaluate the quality of their understanding of the content and to help them decide whether they need additional help with the new content. Questions such as the following might be included.

1. *Reflecting on what was read.*
   (a) How interesting was the material?
   (b) How difficult did I find it?
   (c) As I think about what I read, what pictures come to mind?
2. *Evaluating my learning.*
   (a) Am I able to write or state a summary of what I read?
   (b) Does my summary include all of the major ideas?
   (c) How do the ideas I read about compare to what I thought the material would be about before I started to read?
   (d) What parts did I find the most difficult?
3. *Anticipating the test.*
   (a) What questions are likely to be on the test?
   (b) How can I review for the test?
   (c) How can I remember the information I will need to know for the test?
4. *Recording the products of reading.*
   (a) What key words and ideas did I learn? (Pupils are asked to write these on their own paper.)
   (b) What questions did I have about the material? (Pupils are asked to write these on their own paper.)
   (c) How could I summarize the material? (Pupils are asked to write a brief summary.)
   (d) What kind of a visual framework could I design to help organize the key points? (Pupils are asked to develop their own visual framework.)

Readability Issues _____

Youngsters may face two general problems when they try to read the assigned materials in their social studies classes. First, the reading difficulty of the materials may be too high. Sentences may be long and complex. Second, the vocabulary used may contain many unfamiliar or difficult terms. The material that follows suggests several approaches to the general issue of reading comprehension focusing on these two general problems.

The Kinds of Vocabulary Difficulties

As we might expect in the elementary school, there are tremendous differences from grade level to grade level in the kinds of words that the mythical "average pupil" might be expected to know. Certainly it comes as no surprise that the vocabularies of average first graders are much more limited than those of average sixth graders. These differences are to be expected given the differences in physical maturity and in the extent of the life experiences of these youngsters. Even with these grade-to-grade differences, there are some common patterns of difficulty (see Table 11–2).

TABLE 11–2   Is School Reading Being Made Too Easy?

Recently, a concerned parent made the following comments at a meeting of a local school board.

> This past week, I had a chance to visit my son's third-grade classroom. While I was there, I looked over the textbooks that are being used. I am absolutely appalled by the extremely limited vocabularies used in these books. It appears to me that the publishers are pandering to the lowest common denominator. They have simplified these materials to the point that average and bright youngsters are not being challenged. In fact, I am very much concerned that my son will become terribly bored with this kind of material. It could affect his attitude toward school and toward learning. That concerns me.
>
> I would urge members of the board to look at some of the textbooks that were in the schools in Abe Lincoln's day. There was nothing simple or insulting about the vocabulary in those books. Of course, many youngsters didn't know all of the words when they had to begin reading them. But these books challenged the children. They made them stretch. They sought to *educate*. Can we say the same about the pap-filled textbooks we use now? I don't think so.

Think About This

---

1. Do educators today worry too much about the levels of difficulty of textbooks?
2. Do you think that textbooks are too easy, about right, or too difficult? Why do you think so?
3. If this parent is right in asserting that textbooks in Lincoln's day were more difficult to read, why might this have been true?
4. If this parent came to speak to you about this issue, how would you respond?
5. What do you think the members of the school board would say to this parent? Why do you think so?

Unfamiliar Vocabulary. From time to time, nearly every youngster will encounter words he or she does not recognize. Since this very same thing happens to adult readers who have much larger vocabularies, it is not surprising at all that it is a problem for youngsters in the elementary grades.

Teachers, particularly beginners, sometimes are not prepared for the very limited vocabularies of many of the pupils in their classrooms. Sometimes these problems are difficult for teachers to spot as the causes of youngsters' reading difficulties. Teachers' eyes tend to skim over "simple" explanatory vocabulary to look for new, specialized terms that they do not expect youngsters to know. For example, when looking over material on election trends, an inexperienced teacher might fail to recognize that some youngsters in the class might not know what a "trend" is. Without an adequate grasp of this term, pupils would have a high probability of experiencing difficulty with the content.

Out-of-date Words or Phrases. Out-of-date expressions are really a category of unfamiliar terms; but they are words or phrases of a particular kind: words or phrases that are no longer in common use. Such words pose a particular problem for youngsters when the prose material was written many years ago. Vocabulary changes over time. Some words that were in very common use years ago are used rarely today. For example, at the turn of the century, children often wore arctics to school on rainy days. "Arctic," a word meaning a high rubber overshoe, is almost never used today. Similarly, the word "lizzy" (sometimes "tin lizzie") was applied endearingly by the Americans of the 1920s to their Model-T Fords. Few youngsters in the schools today know this term.

Outdated words and phrases are somewhat easier than the general unfamiliar vocabulary for teachers to deal with. These words tend to strike teachers as unusual when they encounter them in materials they look over in preparation for providing them as reading assignments. When teachers spot such terms, they can explain their meanings to pupils at the time the reading assignments are made.

Specialized Vocabulary. Specialized vocabulary terms are those that closely tied to an academic subject area. For example, in geography, terms such as "latitude" and "longitude" might be regarded as words closely tied to the content of this subject. Most teachers do not expect youngsters to be familiar with the specialized vocabulary when they begin their study of a subject. For this reason, teachers often do a good job of explaining the meaning of these specialized terms before pupils are asked to read content in which they appear.

Vocabulary difficulties pose a very real problem for elementary youngsters in their social studies classrooms. In attempting to respond to these difficulties, teachers have tried a number of approaches. For example, some teachers have youngsters read short selections aloud and then ask questions about the meanings of words. Sometimes, they ask youngsters to stop reading every time they encounter a word they do not know and take the time to look it up in a dictionary.

Asking youngsters to look up unfamiliar vocabulary in the dictionary poses several problems. The first of these has to do with the nature of dictionary definitions. Some definitions themselves contain words that are unfamiliar. Suppose, for example, that a given youngster did not know the meaning of the word "measles." He or she might find something like this in a dictionary:

- *measles:* An acute contagious viral disease characterized by eruptive red blotching of the skin.

Would a youngster who did not know the word "measles" be likely to know such words as "acute," "contagious," "viral," or "blotching"? Probably not.

It is true that some school dictionaries do a marvelous job of defining words in language youngsters can understand. But there continue to be many classroom dictionaries that do not do this. In response to the problems their students have experienced when working with such dictionaries, some teachers take the time to construct glossaries of their own. These glossaries contain the definitions of words that, over time, the teachers have found to pose problems for students.

Words are defined in very simple terms. For example, a teacher-made glossary might define measles like this:

- *measles:* A common disease in children. It is a contagious disease. This means that someone who has it can pass it on to someone else. People with measles have skin that is covered with lots of red spots.

Most youngsters find it much easier to work with this kind of a definition than with a formal dictionary definition.

Some reading authorities express concern that many attempts to broaden youngsters' vocabularies by having them look up words interrupt the reading process. That is, the child must stop the reading activity and take time to look up the word. This delays the completion of the assigned reading. It has the potential to make even a relatively short reading assignment appear to be along and tedious undertaking.

An approach to helping youngsters broaden their vocabularies that does not interrupt the completion of the entire reading task is the *Language-Based Vocabulary and Reading Strategy* (Stansell, 1984) (see Tables 11–3 and 11–4). This procedure is designed to help youngsters identify the problem words while they are engaged in reading the text. It does not require them to stop reading. The Language-Based Vocabulary and Reading Strategy assumes that many problem words may "make sense" if pupils continue to read and come to understand how the problem words are used. Youngsters may infer the meanings of many initially troubling terms from the contexts in which they appear throughout the assigned selection.

The Fry Readability Graph

The general grade-level difficulty of a given prose selection is an item of interest to elementary social studies teachers. This is particularly true when new materials are being examined. It makes sense for teachers to have some way of determining how difficult, on average, a given prose selection might be. The Fry Readability Graph, developed by Edgar Fry, is a tool that many teachers have found very useful. It provides estimates of reading difficulty by grade level. That is, it suggests whether a given item might be approximately at a first-, second-, third-, fourth-, or some other grade level in terms of its general "readability."

It should be understood that the Fry Readability Graph provides information about average grade-level readability. It does not provide information about how an individual youngster might fare when asked to read a particular prose selection. For example, if the Fry procedure indicates that a story is at a fourth-grade level of readability, this by no means suggests that Joey Stone, a fourth grader, will be able to read this material with no difficulty.

Recall that the term "average" suggests a middle score. Even in a hypothetical classroom where pupils have all of the intellectual characteristics of the total national population of fourth graders, about half of the youngsters would have reading skills below the average and about half would have reading skills above the average. Thus, simply because a teacher might know that a given story is at the fourth-grade reading level does not assure that all youngsters in a particular fourth-grade classroom will be able to read and learn from the material.

TABLE 11–3   The Language-Based Vocabulary and Reading Strategy: The Instructions for Pupils*

1. If you find a new word or expression you do not know, mark it and *keep reading.* ("Marks" might be very light pencil checks, bookmarks indicating the page in the text with the problem word, a written list of words jotted down by the pupil, or some other means acceptable to the teacher.)
2. At the end of the reading time, look back over the list of words or expressions you have marked. List each one in the appropriate column of the handout sheet (see Table 11–4).
3. For the words you are not sure of, write your "best-guess" meaning in the appropriate column. Next, check your guess. Look in your glossary first. (This assumes that a glossary is available. If not, skip this step.) If you do not find the word, look in a dictionary.
4. If your guess was correct, place an *X* in the *Glossary/Dictionary* column of the handout. If your guess was not correct, then write the definition in this same column.
5. Choose one of the words you learned without the help of the glossary or the dictionary. This will be one of the words for which you provided an *X* in step 4. Be prepared to tell others how you learned the meaning of the word from your reading.
6. Turn in the completed handout to your teacher.

*The instructions are adapted from those developed by John C. Stansell, Department of Educational Curriculum and Instruction, Texas A&M University, College Station, TX (Stansell, 1984).

Note the directions for using the Fry Readability Graph that are included in Figure 11–1.

The Fry Readability Graph presumes that reading difficulty is associated with two major factors: the sentence length and the number of syllables in the individual words. In general, material is less difficult to read when the sentences are shorter and when the numbers of words with many syllables are small. This information is useful to elementary social studies teachers when they prepare prose materials of their own for youngsters. Also, Fry's information can be helpful to teachers when they decide to rewrite some material from a textbook or another source so that the reading difficulty is reduced.

Consider this situation. Suppose that a sixth-grade teacher is about to assign youngsters to read some material about the patterns of living in the cities of Brazil. This teacher knows that the textbook authors did a reasonably good job of keeping the material at about the sixth-grade level of reading difficulty. But, in this class, a few students have reading skills that are far below the grade level. This teacher might decide to rewrite some of the material to reduce its grade-level difficulty.

This is the version of the material as it appeared in the textbook. It is at about a sixth-grade level of reading difficulty.

In our country, the neighborhoods with expensive houses most often are not found close to the downtown areas of big cities. They tend to be located at some distance away. Frequently, these neighborhoods are in the suburbs, areas outside of the city itself, where people live in houses. People who live in these houses have cars. They drive to work and to stores. When they drive to work, they are usually gone from the house all day.

In Brazil, the high-priced neighborhoods are often very close to the downtown areas. Here, many people do not own cars. They like to live close to their work.

This is how the material looked after the teacher reworked it:

TABLE 11–4 Learning Words Through Reading Worksheet

Name: _____

Words I Learned from Reading the Material (ones I did not have to look up)	Words I am Still Not Sure About	My Best Guess	Glossary/Dictionary Meaning

In our country, the neighborhoods with costly homes are not usually close to the downtown part of big cities. They tend to be some distance away. Often, they are in suburbs. Suburbs are areas outside of the city itself where people live in houses. People living in these houses have cars. They drive to work. Once at work, they stay all day.

In Brazil, the costly homes are often close to the downtown areas. Many people don't own cars. They like to live close to their work. Even car owners like to live close to downtown. They like to go home for lunch. They think that's nice.

The teacher might decide to give the second version to the less-able readers in the class. Note that much of the information has remained intact from the original. But the sentences are shorter, and some of the words have been simplified. In general, it is easier to reduce the grade-level reading difficulty by writing shorter sentences than by finding shorter vocabulary words.

GRAPH FOR ESTIMATING READABILITY—EXTENDED* _____

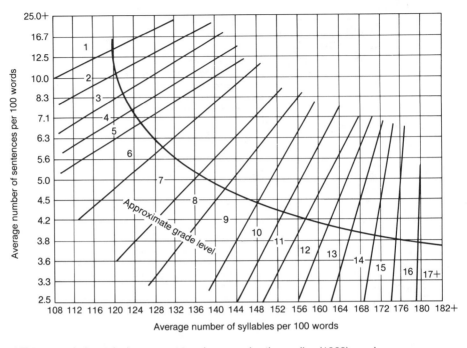

*This extended graph does not outmode or render the earlier (1968) version inoperative or inaccurate; it is an extension.

Figure 11–1   The Fry Readability Graph.
(*Source:* Edward Fry, "Fry's Readability Graph: Clarifications, Validity, and Extension to Level 17," *Journal of Reading* [December 1977], p. 249. Reprinted with permission.)

The second version has a measured level of reading difficulty of about the third grade. This represents a significant reduction in reading difficulty. It suggests that, when time permits, teachers can convey information in a simpler-to-read form by rewriting selected passages from more-difficult prose materials. The Fry Readability Graph can be used to determine the approximate grade-level reading difficulty of the rewritten material.

The Cloze Procedure

While the Fry Readability Graph can provide very useful information about the general level of reading difficulty of a given prose selection, it cannot predict how a given youngster will fare with this material. To get this kind of information, many elementary social studies teachers have found the Cloze Procedure (Taylor, 1953) to be a useful tool.

The *Cloze Procedure* can provide some indication of the appropriateness of a particular prose item for an individual youngster. The Cloze Procedure consists of a simple teacher-made test constructed from a part of the textbook (or other prose selection) that youngsters will be asked to read. The teacher should select a passage that is at least 250 words long. Somewhat longer passages are even

Expanded directions for working Readability Graph

1. Randomly select three sample passages and count out exactly 100 words each, beginning with the beginning of a sentence. Count proper nouns, initializations, and numerals.
2. Count the number of sentences in 100 words, estimating length of the fraction of the last sentence to the nearest one tenth.
3. Count the total number of syllables in the 100-word passage. If you do not have a hand counter available, simply put a mark above every syllable over one in each word; then when you get to the end of the passage, count the number of marks and add 100. Small calculators can also be used as counters by pushing numeral 1, then push the + sign for each word or syllable when counting.
4. Enter graph with _average_ sentence length and _average_ number of syllables; plot dot where the two lines intersect. The area where dot is plotted will give you the approximate grade level.
5. If a great deal of variability is found in syllable count or sentence count, putting more samples into the average is desirable.
6. A word is defined as a group of symbols with a space on either side; thus, _Joe, IRA, 1945,_ and _&_ are each one word.
7. A syllable is defined as a phonetic syllable. Generally, there are as many syllables as vowel sounds. For example, _stopped_ is one syllable and _wanted_ is two sylalbles. When counting syllables for numerals and initializations, count one syllable for each symbol. For example, _1945_ is four syllables, _IRA_ is three syllables, and _&_ is one syllable.

better. They represent a broader sample of the content. Hence, the resulting pupil scores will be more reliable.

The following directions should be followed in preparing, administering, and scoring a Cloze Procedure.

1. Identify a sample from some reading material to be assigned to the class.
2. Type this passage, using _triple_ spacing, so that every _fifth_ word is omitted. Leave a blank long enough for youngsters to write on wherever a word is omitted.
3. Follow the pattern of deleting every fifth word, except when the fifth word falls at the beginning of a sentence. When this happens, retain the first word, delete the second, and resume the practice of omitting every fifth word from this point.
4. Place numbers under each blank. Begin with "1" and continue on with consecutive numbers until the last blank has been numbered. (For example, in a 250-word passage, there would be 50 blanks.)
5. Prepare a teacher key. This will consist of a list of the words deleted and the numbers of the blanks indicating the location in the passage from which each word was taken.

6. Provide youngsters with these tests once copies have been made. Ask them to look at the test as a puzzle. Challenge them to fill in the blanks with words that will result in a passage that reads well and makes good logical sense. Tell them to look for clues that might help identify the missing words throughout the entire passage.
7. In scoring the tests, count as correct only words that are *identical* to those in the original passage. Accept misspellings. Do not accept synonyms.
8. Compute the percentage of the correct words. For example, if there were 50 blanks in the test and a given pupil had 38 correct responses, the score would be 76 percent (38/50 = 0.76).

For an example of a Cloze Procedure test, see Table 11–5.

The following guidelines should be used to interpreting pupil Cloze Procedure test scores.

1. A pupil who receives a score of 58 percent or higher is said to be operating at the *independent level* with regard to this reading material. This means that the youngster should be able to read and learn the material with minimal teacher assistance.
2. A pupil with a score falling between 44 and 57 percent correct is said to be operating at the *instructional level*. This means that the person should be able to read and learn from this material if teacher help is available.
3. A pupil who receives a score of 43 percent or lower correct is said to be operating at the *frustrational level*. Such a youngster might be expected to experience great difficulty in reading and learning from the material on which the test was based.

The percentage-correct figures that define each of the levels are those recommended by a leader in reading research, John Bormuth (Bormuth, 1968). The message to the teacher when youngsters score at the instructional or frustrational levels is simple. Considerable help must be provided if they are to profit from reading the material on which the test was based. Those youngsters scoring at the frustrational level are particularly probable to experience great difficulty.

When working with pupils who score at the frustrational level, two alternatives are to find another source of information that is written at a less-challenging level of difficulty or to rewrite some of the material so that it demands less-sophisticated reading skills. A teacher who took the latter option might check his or her work by comparing the grade-level reading difficulty of the original to the rewritten version using the Fry Readability Graph. Still another alternative might be to abandon the prose material entirely as an information source for some individuals. It might be possible to find cassette recordings, films, photographs, or other means of conveying the information that will not require the youngster to read.

The Fry Readability Graph and the Cloze Procedure can be used in tandem. If a teacher has used the Fry Readability Graph to determine the approximate grade-level reading difficulties of the prose materials that he or she has available, then he or she may have a good feel for some alternative prose materials that might be more suitable for a youngster who gets a low score on a Cloze Procedure test.

Suppose that the Cloze test had been built on material on Latin America from

TABLE 11–5   A Sample Cloze Procedure Test.

People have come to _____1_____ from many parts of _____2_____ world. Many European settlers _____3_____ from Portugal. Portuguese, Portugal's _____4_____, is Brazil's official language. Settlers _____5_____ from other parts of _____6_____, from Africa, from Asia, _____7_____, from other parts of _____8_____. Today, there are _____9_____ from many racial _____10_____ backgrounds in Brazil.

Brazil's _____11_____ is not evenly distributed. Most _____12_____ the people live close _____13_____ the Atlantic Ocean. Inland _____14_____ from the Atlantic, the population _____15_____ to be much less _____16_____. In some parts of _____17_____ country, there are almost _____18_____ people at all.

Brazil _____19_____ second to the United _____20_____ in population among the _____21_____ of the Western Hemisphere. Brazil's _____22_____ is growing much faster _____23_____ that of the United _____24_____. Some people believe that _____25_____ in the future may _____26_____ a larger population than _____27_____ United States.

Brazil's largest _____28_____ are located in the _____29_____ part of the country _____30_____ too far from the _____31_____ coast. São Paulo is the _____32_____ largest city. Rio de Janeiro is _____33_____ so large, but it _____34_____ be Brazil's best known _____35_____. Its famous carnival and _____36_____ beaches are known throughout _____37_____ world. Brasilia, the capital _____38_____ of Brazil, is located _____39_____ miles inland. It was _____40_____ planned city built in _____41_____ empty interior of the _____42_____. The capital of the _____43_____ States, Washington, was also _____44_____ planned city. Manaus is _____45_____ unusual city. It is _____46_____ miles up the famous _____47_____ River. It was originally _____48_____ by people hoping to _____49_____ a fortune in Amazon _____50_____.

Key			
1. Brazil	15. tends	29. eastern	43. United
2. the	16. dense	30. not	44. a
3. came	17. the	31. Atlantic	45. an
4. language	18. no	32. nation's	46. located
5. came	19. ranks	33. not	47. Amazon
6. Europe	20. States	34. may	48. settled
7. and	21. countries	35. city	49. make
8. the	22. population	36. splendid	50. rubber
9. people	23. than	37. the	
10. cultural	24. States	38. city	
11. population	25. Brazil	39. many	
12. of	26. have	40. a	
13. to	27. the	41. the	
14. from	28. cities	42. nation	

a textbook that the teacher had identified as being at about the sixth-grade level of reading difficulty by using the Fry Readability Graph. If the teacher also had on hand some other material dealing with Latin America that had been identified as being at a third- or fourth-grade level of reading difficulty, then it would make sense to provide some of these materials to youngsters who received low Cloze test scores on the sixth-grade level material. Using the Fry Graph and the Cloze Procedure together can help the teacher achieve a good "fit" between individual youngsters and the materials they are assigned to read.

Working with the Parts of the Textbook _____

Youngsters in elementary social studies classes work with many different kinds of prose materials. Most spend at least some of the time reading the material in social studies textbooks. Particularly at the middle- and upper-grade levels, there is a tendency for some of these books to be quite large and intimidating. The problem is not that they do not contain useful information, but rather that they contain so much material that youngsters often cannot find what they need. Time spent preparing youngsters to work with textbooks can result in much more effective use of this important information tool.

Textbooks have predictable organizational patterns. This statement is hardly startling news to adults, but many youngsters in the elementary grades have never thought about how textbook content is arranged. Lessons designed to help them recognize the organizational patterns can remedy this situation.

The Table of Contents

Simple lessons can be built around the table of contents. These can help youngsters grasp the nature of the content covered, the organization of the content, and the relative importance assigned to the various content elements. Figure 11–2 illustrates a typical table of contents. It is taken from *Follett Social Studies: Our Communities* (1983) by Janet E. Alleman-Brooks and James B. Kracht.

Questions such as the following might help youngsters come to understand something about the organization and the emphasis of this book.

1. How many units are there in the book? How many chapters? Why are there more chapters than units?
2. Some units seem to have more chapters than others. Why do you think this is so?
3. If you were to tell a friend about the subjects in this book, what would you say?
4. Is there more information in this book about cities or about farms? How can you tell? Why do you think the writers did this?
5. Do you think these authors are interested in maps? How can you tell?
6. Are these things in this book: an atlas, a glossary, and an index? If so, where are they? Can you tell your teacher what each of these things is?
7. If you wanted to learn about how cities began, what would you turn to? How did you decide?

8. Is information about the cities today and the cities of the future in the same chapter? How do you know?

In practice, the level of difficulty must be geared to the nature of youngsters in a given class. Properly constructed questions can provide youngsters with a good mental picture of the contents of their textbook.

The Individual Chapter Characteristics

Social studies textbooks tend to have chapters organized according to a repetitive format that remains quite consistent throughout the book. These basic chapter-design characteristics have been included to help youngsters master the content. Time spent familiarizing pupils with the particular chapter structure of their own text can assist them as they begin working with this material.

A questioning sequence somewhat similar to that used to familiarize youngsters with the table of contents is often appropriate. *Our Communities,* mentioned previously, is a fairly typical social studies text designed for pupils in the lower elementary grades. The chapters are short, and each tends to have three basic characteristics. First, there are a series of questions called "As You Read" that are designed to focus pupils' attention on certain topics discussed in the chapter. Second, at the end of each chapter there is a series of questions called "Checking Up." These are designed to help youngsters recall the information introduced in the chapter. Finally, throughout the body of the chapter, certain key words and terms are printed in the boldface type to draw pupils' attention to them.

A teacher using this text might develop questions such as the following to acquaint youngsters with the typical chapter-organization pattern.

1. What kinds of questions are asked at the beginning of the chapter in the "As You Read" section? Why do you think these questions are at the beginning of the chapter?
2. What kinds of questions are at the end of the chapter in the "Checking Up" section? Do you think you can find answers to these questions in the chapter?
3. Did you notice that some words in the chapter are printed much darker than the others? What kinds of words are these? Why do you think they were made to look different from the other words?

The Index

Exercises that focus on the index of a text can reinforce important alphabetizing skills. More important, they can help youngsters recognize some decisions that have been made about which content to recognize. Finally, they familiarize youngsters with the process of going to the index to find the locations of specific kinds of information in the textbook.

As a preface to having pupils work with the index, some teachers find simple alphabetizing exercises useful. These can be graduated in difficulty. For exam-

Table of Contents

Page

Figure 11–2 A Typical Table of Contents from a Social Studies Textbook.

(*Source:* From *Follett Social Studies: Our Communities* by Janet E. Alleman-Brooks and James B. Kracht. Copyright © 1983 by Allyn and Bacon, Inc. Reprinted with permission.)

ple, note the differences in the three lists of words on the following sample exercise.

Placing Words in Alphabetical Order*

Least Difficult	More Difficult	Most Difficult
_____ cat	_____ gill	_____ hood
_____ tent	_____ gaze	_____ hook
_____ wasp	_____ greet	_____ hoe
_____ log	_____ gun	_____ honey
_____ ant	_____ gob	_____ hoot

*Direction: Tell the class members to put a "1" in front of the word that comes first, a "2" in front of the word that comes second, a "3" in front of the word that comes third, a "4" in front of the word that comes fourth, and a "5" in front of the word that comes fifth.

Note that words in the "least difficult" list all begin with a different letter. Those in the "more difficult" list begin with the same letter, but the second letter in each word is different. The words in the "most difficult" list have identical first and second letters. In fact, some words in this list also have identical third letters.

Exposure to simple alphabetizing exercises such as this one can help the teacher identify youngsters who need help in this area. Even youngsters who are reasonably proficient can benefit from this review.

After youngsters are provided with review experiences on alphabetizing, their attention can be directed to the textbook index. Table 11–6 illustrates a page from a third-grade social studies textbook, *Follett Social Studies: Our Communities* (Alleman-Brooks and Kracht, 1983).

To help pupils learn something about the index, many teachers find it useful to have youngsters respond to a number of questions. Questions such as the following, based on the index page depicted in Table 11–6, might be appropriate.

1. Why is "Texas" listed in the index ahead of "Tiber River"?
2. To what page would you turn to find information about tea farming?
3. Where would you find information about the towns in Colorado? in North Carolina?
4. How many pages are devoted to Texas? How many are devoted to the United States?
5. Why would do you think that more pages deal with the United States than with Texas?

A teacher's personal list of questions would vary depending on grade level and the nature of individual pupils in the class. If skillfully constructed, the discussions centering on the index can help youngsters make much better use of this important part of their textbook.

**TABLE 11–6 A Page from a Typical Elementary
Social Studies Textbook Index.***

*Source: From *Follett Social Studies: Our Communities* by Janet E. Alleman-Brooks and James B. Kracht.
Copyright © 1983 by Allyn and Bacon, Inc., p. 255. Reprinted with permission.

Key Ideas in Summary _____

    Elementary social studies teachers rely heavily on textbooks and other printed materials as information sources for their youngsters. They need to be familiar with a number of approaches designed to help pupils learn from required reading assignments. Some of the key ideas related to this general topic include the following:

1. Much of the content in the elementary program continues to be contained in prose materials. While other sources—for example, computer software—are important, today's youngsters still do a good deal of reading for their social studies classes. Since this is true, it makes sense for elementary social studies teachers to become acquainted with methods for enabling youngsters to derive as much benefit as possible from their reading experiences.

2. Specific plans for assisting youngsters to learn from prose materials need to be made at three different times. These are during (1) the prereading phase, (2) the reading phase, and (3) the postreading phase.

3. Multipass reading is a technique that encourages pupils to read material several times. During each time, or pass, they read for a different purpose.

4. Reading guides are designed to teach pupils to monitor their own understanding as they read the assigned materials. Reading guides consist of prompt questions designed to stimulate pupils to think about what they are reading, what they already know about the content, what kinds of questions might be asked about the content, and how the content might be summarized and transmitted to others.

5. Two youngsters can receive very different information from the same content. This is true because selections often contain a tremendous amount of content. To help youngsters focus on content elements that the teachers believes are important, visual frameworks can be provided. These cue youngsters to look for specific things in their reading. Furthermore, they provide a scheme that allows for focused note taking.

6. The term readability refers to the general level of difficulty associated with a specific prose selection. In general, levels of reading difficulty increase (1) as sentences become longer and more complex and (2) as individual words become longer and more complex.

7. Many youngsters from time to time experience difficulty with some of the words contained in reading assignments. Teachers need to be prepared to assist youngsters when they encounter unfamiliar vocabulary, out-of-date vocabulary, and specialized vocabulary.

8. Many teachers have found it useful to prepare their own glossaries and to give these to their pupils. These teacher-made glossaries define unfamiliar words in terms pupils can understand.

9. The Language-Based Vocabulary and Reading Strategy is a procedure that youngsters can use to identify unfamiliar words they encounter in reading assignments. The approach helps them to learn words in context. Furthermore, it builds pupils' vocabularies without interrupting the reading process.

10. The Fry Readability Graph is a tool that can be used to determine the average grade-level readability of a given prose selection. It can provide information to teachers about the general appropriateness of some given material for youngsters at a particular grade level.

11. The Cloze Procedure provides a measure of an individual pupil's likelihood of experiencing difficulty when reading a given prose selection. Some teachers find it useful to work with both the Fry Readability Graph and the Cloze Procedure in preparing materials suitable for a particular student.

Questions _____

Review Questions

1. What kinds of vocabulary may present problems to pupils when they read social studies assignments?
2. What is multipass reading?
3. Describe the operation of the Language-Based Vocabulary and Reading Strategy.
4. What is the Fry Readability Graph used for?
5. What is the Cloze Procedure?
6. What are the components of a reading guide?
7. What is a visual framework, and how can it help pupils master content contained in reading material?

Thought Questions

1. Some people have suggested that in the future pupils will do a good deal less reading in their social studies classes than they do now. Why might some people have this view? Do you agree with it?
2. Reading problems should be taken care of during the *reading* period. During our *social studies* time, we should just do social studies. Do you agree with this statement? Why, or why not?
3. A good teacher of fourth-grade youngsters will see to it that every child is reading at the fourth-grade level. How do you react to this statement?
4. When teaching elementary social studies, should the teacher attempt to "stretch" every child by making sure that he or she is asked to read at least some material containing very difficult terminology? Why do you think so?
5. Does the use of visual frameworks make the job of the pupil too easy? Why, or why not?

Extending Understanding and Skill _____

Activities

1. Survey elementary school teachers regarding the reading problems their pupils typically experience with social studies materials. Share the results with the class, or prepare a short paper based on this information.
2. Look through a social studies textbook at a grade level you would like to teach. Then do the following:
   (a) Prepare a list of outdated terms contained in the text.
   (b) Prepare a list of specialized terms contained in the text.
   (c) Prepare a list of other terms from the text that may be unfamiliar to pupils.
   (d) Using a total of ten terms from lists prepared in (a), (b), and (c) above, prepare a teacher glossary. Be sure your glossary defines these terms in language youngsters at this grade level might be expected to understand.
3. Select a social studies textbook designed for a grade level you might like to teach. Then do the following:
   (a) Use a Fry Readability Graph to determine its approximate grade-level readability.
   (b) Select a 500-word passage from the book and prepare a Cloze Procedure test that you could give to pupils.
4. From a university-level text in history or the social sciences, find a passage dealing

with a topic that might be of interest to an elementary school child in the third or fourth grade. Using information you have learned about the factors that make reading difficult, rewrite the material to a third- or fourth-grade level of reading difficulty. Use the Fry Readability Graph to check on the grade-level difficulty of your rewritten material.

5. Look at a page of material in an elementary social studies textbook that might be assigned to a class as required reading. Prepare three different sets of purposes or focus questions. For each, develop a visual framework that might help youngsters to focus their attention on the specific elements of content.

Supplemental Reading

BLANKENSHIP, GLEN. "How to Test a Textbook for Sexism," *Social Education* (April 1984), pp. 282–283.

FITZGERALD, JILL. "Helping Readers Gain Self-Control over Reading Comprehension." *The Reading Teacher* (December 1983), pp. 249–253.

GARCIA, JESUS, and LOGAN, JOHN W. "Teaching Social Studies Using Basal Readers," *Social Education* (November/December 1983), pp. 533–535.

HANSEN, JANE. "Poor Readers Can Draw Inferences," *The Reading Teacher* (March 1984), pp. 586–589.

PATTON, WILLIAM E. (ed.). *Improving the Use of Social Studies Textbooks*, Bulletin 63. Washington, D.C.: National Council for the Social Studies, 1980.

POOSTAY, EDWARD J. "Show Me Your Underlines: A Strategy to Teach Comprehension," *The Reading Teacher* (May 1984), pp. 828–830.

VALMONT, WILLIAM J. "Cloze Deletion Patterns: How Deletions are Made Makes a Big Difference," *The Reading Teacher* (November 1983), pp. 172–175.

References _____

ALLEMAN-BROOKS, JANET E., and KRACHT, JAMES B. *Follett Social Studies: Our Communities*. Boston: Allyn and Bacon, Inc., 1983.

BAMBERGER, RICHARD, and RABIN, ANNETTE T. "New Approaches to Readability: Austrian Research," *The Reading Teacher* (February 1984), pp. 512–519.

BORMUTH, JOHN R. "The Cloze Readability Procedure," *Elementary English* (April 1968), pp. 429–436.

FRY, EDWARD. "Fry's Readability Graph: Clarifications, Validity, and Extension to Level 17," *Journal of Reading* (December 1977), pp. 242–252.

National Center for Education Statistics. *The Condition of Education, 1983*. Washington, D.C.: U.S. Government Printing Office, 1983.

ROBINSON, H. ALAN. *Teaching Reading and Study Strategies: The Content Areas*, 2d ed. Boston: Allyn and Bacon, Inc., 1978.

STANSELL, JOHN C. "Getting More Mileage from Sustained Silent Reading." Unpublished paper presented at the Sam Houston Area Reading Conference, College Station, TX. February 1984.

TAYLOR, WILSON L. "Cloze Procedure: A New Tool for Measuring Readability," *Journalism Quarterly* (Fall 1953), pp. 415–433.

Chapter 12

Evaluating Learning

(*Source:* © Juliann Barbato.)

This chapter provides information to help the reader:

1. Distinguish between formal and informal evaluation procedures.

2. Recognize the strengths and limitations of selected formal evaluation procedures, including true/false tests, multiple-choice tests, matching tests, completion tests, and essay tests.

3. Describe the procedures for gathering information using a selection of informal evaluation procedures.

4. Point out the relationship between the complexity of learning to be measured and the kind of test used to assess the learning.

5. Describe several ways of measuring the attitudes of pupils.

6. Explain how the results of evaluation can be used to critique the instructional program as well as to assess the progress of individual youngsters.

Overview

The assessment of pupils' progress has always been an important obligation of teachers. In recent years, teachers' responsibilities in this area have been increasing. Because of public suspicions that some school programs are not as sound as they might be, legislatures and local school authorities have become more insistent that teachers provide evidence that youngsters are learning.

In some states, new laws specify exactly what content must be taught in each part of the elementary curriculum. Often, these laws require teachers to regularly test youngsters' mastery of this "basic" required material.

All of these changes have dramatically increased the total amount of pupil testing that occurs in the elementary social studies program. Familiarity with assessment techniques is a must for teachers going into elementary education today. The evaluation of learning is a two-part process. First, measurements of some kind must be taken of pupils' individual performances. These measurements might involve the use of informal techniques (relatively open-ended exercises that can be completed successfully by youngsters who have mastered the relevant content) or formal techniques (ordinarily structured examinations such as those involving multiple-choice, true/false, matching, completion, and essay items). Once the measurements are in hand, then a judgment has to be made about the adequacy of the performance.

In general, teachers tend to use one of two major approaches in determining how well a given youngster has done. These approaches are norm-referenced assessment and criterion-referenced assessment.

In *norm-referenced assessment*, a given youngster's performance is compared to the average performances of other similar youngsters. In this scheme, low grades or ratings are given to youngsters with scores falling below the group average. While widely used, norm-referenced assessment has certain limitations. For example, suppose that a teacher computed a group average for scores made by his or her class of third graders. Suppose, too, that these youngsters were, as a group, very academically talented. It would be possible to award a low grade or rating to a youngster who scored below the group average but who, when compared to the total United States' population of third graders, would be one of the best. When norm-referenced assessment is used, it is essential that the group upon which the "average" is based is truly a representative one.

In *criterion-referenced assessment*, the grade or rating is given based on a comparison of a youngster's performance with a predetermined standard. For example, if letter grades are being used, a teacher would make a determination of what levels of performance would qualify pupils respectively for each letter grade. Once a commitment to the standard has been made, the letter grades are awarded according to the guidelines contained in the standard. This could result (at least theoretically) in every pupil in the class receiving exactly the same grade. (This would happen if every youngster performed, for example, at a level consistent with what had been decided as a standard for the grade of 'B.")

A difficulty with criterion-referenced assessment is identifying the appropriate standards of achievement. If these are set too low, then youngsters will do less than they are capable of doing. If they are set too high, youngsters will become frustrated and some may give up. Though there are difficulties with criterion-referenced assessment, the approach is widely used. If the standards are set with care, criterion-referenced assessment can provide a very reasonable basis for making judgments about youngsters' performances (see Table 12–1).

Both norm-referenced assessment systems and criterion-referenced assessment systems require the teacher to gather information about a youngster before any determination of the adequacy of the performance can be made. In the sections that follow, the procedures for gathering this kind of information through the use of both informal and formal evaluation techniques are introduced.

TABLE 12–1   Kids Should Be Measured Only Against Themselves!

Recently, two teachers engaged in an argument about the grading of pupils. The following is part of what each had to say.

Teacher A	Teacher B
Kids should not be graded against a standard. Kids should not be graded against a class average. They should just be graded against themselves. I like to know where a youngster is when he or she comes to my class. Then I can figure out how much progress he or she has made. That's how I award grades. If a youngster shows lots of improvement, then I give an "A."	It is a terrible mistake to grade a youngster against himself or herself. This makes it almost impossible for a bright child to show progress. Suppose that on a pretest a bright student received a grade of 90. He or she would be limited to an improvement of only 10 points on a posttest. A much less-able youngster might improve by 50 or 60 points. Does this mean we should give the less-able child the better grade and "punish" the other youngster for "knowing too much too soon"?

Think About This

1. How "fair" is grading based on individual improvement?
2. How do you feel about the logic of Teacher A?
3. How do you feel about the logic of Teacher B?
4. What is your own position on grading based on individual improvement? How would you respond to others who might criticize your view?

Informal Evaluation _____

Informal evaluation techniques depend on teacher observations of a variety of pupil performances. Sometimes these responses cannot easily be graded "right" or "wrong." The results of informal evaluation indicate the patterns of behavior that suggest an individual youngster either has or has not mastered a given skill or a given item of academic content. Often, informal evaluation requires the teacher to make professional inferences about what youngsters can and cannot do (see Table 12–2).

TABLE 12–2 *All* Evaluation of Elementary Youngsters Should be Formal Evaluation.

A parent made the following comments at a recent meeting of a parent-teachers' association.

> Our elementary youngsters are getting too little experience with formal tests. When they get to middle school or junior high school, teachers are going to expect them to be familiar with multiple-choice tests, true/false tests, essay tests, and other kinds of formal tests. If youngsters don't get exposed to these tests in elementary school, they will be very nervous when they are given these kinds of tests in the upper grades. I believe we need extensive formal testing at every grade level. In fact, I think informal testing should be all but abandoned.

Think About This

1. How serious a problem is it for youngsters to switch from informal testing to formal testing?
2. How would teachers at different grade levels react to these comments? Why do you think so?
3. Is there too much informal testing in the elementary schools today? Why do you think so?
4. What would happen if an elementary school did decide to give only formal tests to youngsters?

There are several important advantages of informal evaluation. First, informal evaluation procedures can often be accomplished quickly. For example, if a teacher is interested in whether a youngster can get along with others, an important human-relations skill, casual observation in class and on the playground can provide the answer. It is not necessary to commit time to prepare a formal test. A simple, dated notation in a notebook can record the information (Johnny played well at recess and got along well with others in class today. 1/25/87).

Informal evaluation raises few anxieties in youngsters. This is true because much informal evaluation takes place without pupils being aware that it is happening. This is a far different situation than a youngster faces when he or she is confronted by a formal test. Informal evaluation tries to make inferences about what youngsters know and can do as they perform more or less "naturally."

Informal evaluation is used throughout the elementary social studies program, but it is used more frequently by teachers of younger elementary school pupils than by teachers of fourth, fifth, and sixth graders. There are several reasons for this.

First, very young pupils lack the reading and writing skills needed to take formal tests. Realistically, teachers must rely very heavily on informal procedures when assessing these youngsters. Furthermore, the social studies program in the early grades is heavily oriented toward developing the basic skills and fostering the development of positive interpersonal-relations behaviors. These skills and behaviors are often easier to assess as youngsters demonstrate them spontaneously than on any kind of a formal test or examination.

There are some cautions that must be observed when using informal-evaluation techniques. Because these techniques require the teacher to make some inferences about a youngster from the observations of his or her "natural" behavior, it is essential that sufficient observations occur to make these judgments reliable. Multiple observations are a must. Furthermore, there needs to be a systematic scheme for recording the information. Because classes contain too many youngsters and too many things happen each day, elementary teachers find it difficult to recall the important behaviors of individual pupils. Some kind of record-keeping scheme is essential. When multiple observations are taken and careful records are kept, informal evaluation can result in a great deal of useful information about how pupils are progressing (see Table 12–3).

TABLE 12–3 I Don't Think _Good_ Kindergarten Teachers Need Records.

Recently, a prospective kindergarten teacher made the following comments.

All the Kindergarten teachers I've talked to say they spend too much time keeping records. They say they feel they must write down "everything" about every youngster. It seems to me that this is a big waste of time. It _has_ to take valuable time away from working with children. Also, I think a really _good_ Kindergarten teacher should know the children so well as individuals that he or she ought not to need a formal written record. I mean, if a youngster is slow to learn colors or something else, the teacher should know that. I can't understand why so many Kindergarten teachers waste so much time on record keeping.

Think About This

1. If many Kindergarten teachers do spend a great deal of time on record keeping, why do they do so?
2. Is time spent on record keeping "wasted"? Explain your position.
3. How might a Kindergarten teacher react to this person's comments?
4. If you were to argue with this person, what points would you want to make?
5. What is your personal reaction to this statement?

In the subsections that follow, a number of informal evaluation procedures are introduced.

Headlines

One measure of learning is an ability to summarize accurately. If the summaries are appropriate, then the teacher can then infer that the pupil has some grasp of the material on which the summary is based. Asking youngsters to write or orally suggest descriptive headlines for proposed newspaper articles about the topics that have studied is one way to test their abilities to summarize. Headlines can be written on butcher paper, placed on a bulletin board, or written on the chalkboard.

The headlines provide the teacher with insight regarding the levels of understanding of individuals in the class. A record about each pupil's performance can be noted in a grade book, on a progress chart, or in some other appropriate place. The display of the headlines can also provide a vehicle for the teacher to diagnose any general misconceptions that the class might have. These misconceptions can be dealt with in a follow-up discussion.

Newspaper Articles

With middle- and upper-grade youngsters, the newspaper headline activity can be expanded to include the writing of a short newspaper article to accompany the headline activity. Youngsters can be familiarized with the general formats for newspaper articles. They will also need information about the suggested length and about the kinds of information that they should include. The best articles might be "published" by the teacher and copies distributed to the members of the class. The content of the articles can suggest to the teacher what individual youngsters know and what general errors need to be brought to the attention of the entire class.

Word Pairs

In a word-pairs assessment activity, youngsters are presented with a set of cards. Each card features one word. Pupils are asked to find the cards that go together. The teacher checks each youngster's work and asks each to explain why the cards in each pair "go together." Records are kept of each youngster's progress. A follow-up discussion can be used to reinforce learning and to correct any mistaken impressions some youngsters in the class might have.

A word-pairs activity focusing on the idea of naming leaders and what they lead might begin with a preparation of cards containing these words:

- PRESIDENT   STATE   CLASSROOM   TEACHER
- UNITED STATES   CITY   MAYOR   GOVERNOR

The pairs should look like this after youngsters have worked with the cards:

- PRESIDENT—UNITED STATES
- GOVERNOR—STATE
- MAYOR—CITY
- TEACHER—CLASSROOM

Anagrams

Anagrams are words that are created by rearranging the letters of other words. For example, the word "tier" can be made by using all the letters of the word "tire." Anagrams can be used as part of informal assessment. Youngsters enjoy puzzles, and many of them will not be aware that their performance is being checked.

Suppose that a teacher had been introducing youngsters to content dealing with bodies of water and marine life. An anagram exercise such as the one on the top of page 297 might be devised.

Alphabet Review Game

The alphabet review game can be used to assess either individual or groups of youngsters. The exercise provides students with a review of the basic alphabetizing skills and, at the same time, encourages the review of content that has

---

Oral Directions*

Look at the word in capital letters. Then look at the definition. The definition describes a different word from the one at the left, but this new word uses all the letters in the word to the left. Write this new word in the blanks provided at the end of the definition.

LEAK   1. A large body of fresh water completely surrounded by land. _ _ _ _ (lake)

MASTER   2. A body of running water, such as a river or a brook. _ _ _ _ _ _ (stream)

FURS   3. The name given to the waves of the sea as they crash on the shore. _ _ _ _ (surf)

DIET   4. The twice-a-day rising and falling of the level of the ocean. _ _ _ _ (tide)

SALE   5. A sea animal with flippers that lives along rocky coastlines. _ _ _ _ (seal)

LOOP   6. A small and rather deep body of water. _ _ _ _ (pool)

ALIENS   7. This refers to something, such as sea water, that contains salt. _ _ _ _ _ _ (saline)

---

*Note: Answers are provided in parentheses.

been studied. The procedure is very easy to use.

The teacher simply asks youngsters to find as many important terms (the teacher will need to help youngsters decide what these are) beginning with each letter of the alphabet. For example, pupils start with 'A," and go on to "B," and continue in the same manner for as much time as is allowed.

It is a good idea to decide upon a maximum limit for each letter, perhaps three or four minutes. This prevents youngsters from spending too much time thinking about words beginning with a single letter. Youngsters also need to be told that there may be no words for some letters.

This exercise may be done either by youngsters individually or by teams of pupils. The teacher may wish to make some notations in a record book about each youngster's success on this task. As a follow-up activity, the lists for each letter can be shared, and there can be a discussion that focuses on the meanings of some of the more important terms.

My Favorite Idea

A space on the chalkboard can be reserved, or a large sheet of butcher paper can be provided, for this exercise. Periodically, perhaps twice a week, youngsters can be invited to write their "favorite social studies idea" in the space provided. Youngsters need to be given some hints: I like the idea of living in wigwams made of buffalo skin. I would *hate* to have had my feet bound like they used to do to girls in China. I think men here should be forced to wear pigtails like they used to wear in China.

Each youngster should be asked to write something. (Some may need help.) To personalize the activity, youngsters should be invited to sign their names after their "ideas." This exercise provides the teacher with some insight into the kinds of information and attitudes youngsters receive from their social studies lessons. Some of this information may need to go into the records the teacher keeps on each youngster. In addition to providing the teacher with a source of assessment information, the activity may motivate youngsters to think more seriously about their social studies lessons, because they know that they will be asked to contribute a favorite "idea."

Mystery Word Scramble

The mystery word scramble takes advantage of youngsters' love of puzzles. Typically, the exercise focuses on the key terms that have been introduced. The letters in these terms are mixed up or scrambled. A definition of the "unscrambled" term is provided for pupils to write the term after they have reorganized the scrambled letters. As an added embellishment, one blank is circled in the spaces provided for youngsters to copy the correct, unscrambled term. When all the terms have been properly unscrambled, these letters will reveal a "mystery word." Ordinarily, the mystery word is also an important vocabulary term.

Suppose that a teacher had introduced some basic concepts about maps and globes. He or she might devise the following mystery word scramble.

The mystery word scramble is an exercise many youngsters enjoy. For the teacher, it provides a means of assessing pupils' grasp of terms in a way that minimizes anxiety. The results can be noted in the records kept on each pupil. The results can be noted in the records kept on each pupil. The general problems that are revealed can suggest areas that need to be reviewed with the whole class.

Directions*

The words at the left are real words, but the letters have been mixed up. Arrange the letters to form the correct word. Write the word in the spaces provided. The definition at the right of each mixed-up word will help you decide what the correct word should be.

Mixed-up Word	Definition	Correct Word
tedolingu	Imaginary lines on a globe used to measure distances east and west.	_ _ _○_ _ _ _ _ (longitude)
uteltaid	Imaginary lines on a globe used to measure distances north and south.	○_ _ _ _ _ _ (latitude)
reqtuoa	An imaginery line around the globe that separates the northern and southern hemisphere.	_ _ _ _ _○_ (Equator)
mabroteer	A device for measuring air pressure on the earth's surface.	○_ _ _ _ _ _ _ (barometer)
hehepsimer	A term that means "one half of the earth's surface."	_ _ _ _ _ _○_ _ (hemisphere)

Mystery Word Directions

Notice that one letter in each of the above words is circled. Together, these letters form the mystery word. Write the letters in the blanks provided below. The mystery word is defined just to the right of the blanks.

_ _ _ _ _: A term used to describe a model of the earth. (globe)

*Note: Answers are provided in parentheses.

Teacher Observation

Teacher observation of individual youngsters is an important informal evaluation tool. Some of the aims of the elementary social studies can be assessed in no other way. These include the outcomes related to general attitudes and to skills having to do with interpersonal relations. For example, "work cooperatively with others" is one objective for Kindergarten youngsters that is found in the adopted social studies curriculum in many school districts. Clearly, this objective cannot be measured through the use of a paper-and-pencil test. Direct observation by the teacher is really the only reasonable approach to determining how well an individual child is able to get along with other youngsters.

Teacher observation plays some role at every grade level, but it is especially important in the early years of the elementary school program. Youngsters lack the sufficient knowledge and skills to take formal examinations (especially in Kindergarten and first grade). Also, social studies objectives for these early years focus very heavily on the development of self-confidence. These kinds of outcomes lend themselves very well to informal teacher observation.

Good teacher observation looks for specific behaviors (being polite when others are speaking, sharing, and so forth). Observations are routinely saved so that some type of an available record will indicate how individual youngsters are doing and what areas each needs to work on. Good record keeping is a hallmark of elementary teachers who make effective use of informal teacher observation.

Other Informal Observation Techniques

The informal observations introduced here represent a tiny sample of the informal observation procedures used in the school today. Among the other techniques favored by many teachers are sorting activities of all kinds that help youngsters recognize the major category labels and the items that belong within each category. Some teachers ask groups of youngsters to debate issues. The positions presented in the debates reveal the depth of understanding of individual participants. Crossword puzzles, find-a-word puzzles (puzzles where words are "buried" in an array of alphabet letters), and other puzzles and games are widely used. "What I Learned" diaries are favored by some teachers. The list of possibilities goes on and on.

The criterion for the selection of an individual procedure is this question: Will the procedure provide the information I need to make an adequate judgment about this youngster's performance? Many approaches allow teachers to answer "Yes" to this question. When the selected techniques are implemented, it is essential that some system be used to save information for future reference. Good evaluation procedures allow the teacher and the parents to check on a youngster's development over time. Proper record keeping makes this possible.

Record Keeping and Informal Evaluation _____

Good informal evaluation procedures can generate a great deal of useful information. Good record keeping is essential for a teacher who wishes to take maximum advantage of this information. Teachers work with too many youngsters to

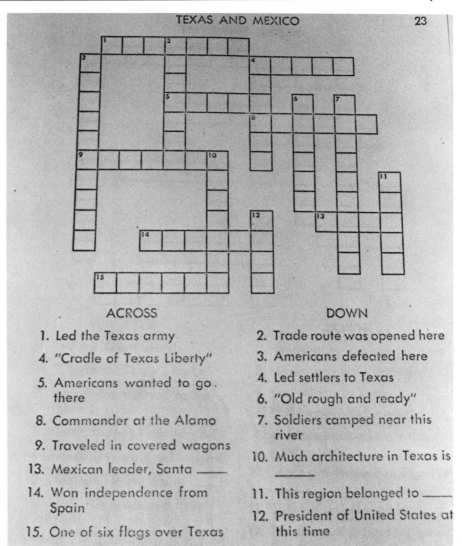

TEXAS AND MEXICO   23

ACROSS

1. Led the Texas army
4. "Cradle of Texas Liberty"
5. Americans wanted to go there
8. Commander at the Alamo
9. Traveled in covered wagons
13. Mexican leader, Santa _____
14. Won independence from Spain
15. One of six flags over Texas

DOWN

2. Trade route was opened here
3. Americans defeated here
4. Led settlers to Texas
6. "Old rough and ready"
7. Soldiers camped near this river
10. Much architecture in Texas is _____
11. This region belonged to _____
12. President of United States at this time

Crossword puzzles are sometimes used as an informal evaluation technique.
(*Source:* © Juliann Barbato.)

rely on their memories when asked to comment about how a child is faring on a given instructional task.

Secondary school teachers often rely only on a grade book to record the information about pupils' progress. This procedure does not work out as well in elementary classrooms, particularly in the earlier elementary grades. Older youngsters tend to pursue longer-term learning objectives. Progress is noted on formal examinations (true/false, multiple choice, essay, and so forth). The scores or grades from these tests comprise a reasonably good record of the progress of each pupil.

In the earlier elementary grades, the learning objectives tend to be much more limited in scope. Often, they are assessed by informal procedures that do not lend themselves well to a record reflecting either a numerical score or a letter grade. Many are of a "Can" or "Cannot" or a "Yes" or "No" nature. For example, one aim of many Kindergarten programs is for youngsters to know the name of their school and town. This is clearly an all-or-nothing kind of learning task. Either the child has the knowledge, or he or she does not. Given these circumstances, some kind of record keeping that allows for the frequent observation of rather small increments of learning is needed.

To keep track of youngsters' progress in elementary social studies classrooms, many teachers use *daily performance progress checklists*. (Despite the name, these are sometimes not used every day. Depending on the individual circumstances, several times a week may suffice.) These are easy-to-use sheets that allow the teacher to quickly note how each youngster is faring on a limited number of focus competencies. They can be tailored to fit content being emphasized, and specific notations can be altered to accommodate the teacher's needs. Some teachers find it convenient simply to note whether a youngster (1) has mastered the competency; (2) has partially mastered the competency, but still needs more work; or (3) has not mastered the competency. The following is an example of a checklist formatted in this manner.

Kindergarten—Mr. Bianca:
Daily Performance Progress Checklist

Today's Date: _____

Member of the Class	FOCUS SKILLS		
	Identifies Relative Location (near, far)	Cites the Pledge of Allegiance	Names the Days of the Week
Brenda	+	+	+
Erik	+	−	W
Gretchen	−	−	W
Howard	−	W	+
Juan	+	+	+
Karen	+	W	−
Lawrence	W	W	W
Adela	+	+	+
Paul	+	W	W
.			
.			
.	(This same pattern follows for the rest of the class.)		

Key: + = the pupil has mastered this competency; W = the pupil has partially mastered this competency, but more work is needed; − = the pupil has not even partially mastered this competency yet.

A daily performance record such as this one is easy to use. It can provide the teacher with a frequent measure of each youngster on every area being emphasized during a day's lesson. Collectively, this information can also be used to point out the overall strengths and weaknesses in a given class.

Periodically, the information from daily performance progress checklists can be entered on cumulative record forms. These forms include all of the grade-level competencies. They are a summary of what has been observed about an individual child over time. An example of a Social Studies Cumulative record form for Kindergarten is provided in Table 12–4.

TABLE 12–4 An Example of a Simple Social Studies Cumulative Record Form for Kindergarten.

Because youngsters in the early elementary grades do not take as many formal examinations (multiple choice, true/false, and so forth) as do older pupils, it is not practical to keep records in a grade book where little provision is made except for noting numerical scores and letter grades. Though grades will have to be given to youngsters (at least in most districts), the documentation of youngsters work is often accomplished more conveniently using a cumulative record form of some kind.

A separate cumulative record form is kept for each youngster. Often, these are kept in individual file folders. Periodically, the teacher will review the information taken from less-formal observations of daily performance. (See the daily performance record referenced in the material on "Record Keeping and Informal Evaluation.") The teacher typically notes on the cumulative record form those competencies a youngster has mastered. These forms provide data that can be used to compile information to share with parents during parent-teacher conferences and during formal pupil-progress reports from the school.

Cumulative record forms vary greatly from district to district. The following one is an example of what you might expect to find in a form designed to reflect the progress of a youngster in the social studies component of the Kindergarten program.

Cumulative Record: Social Studies—Kindergarten

Name of Pupil: _____

Directions

Place a checkmark in the blank before each competency the pupil has mastered. Also note the date the checkmark was entered.

Area I: History–Social Science—Knowledge, Skills, Values

_____ 1. Understands term "basic needs."
_____ 2. Tells how families meet basic needs.
_____ 3. Identifies property as his/hers/mine/ours/yours.
_____ 4. Defines work and play.
_____ 5. Names self, school, community.
_____ 6. Identifies basic time concepts (minute, hour, day).
_____ 7. Names days of the week.
_____ 8. Identifies relative locations (near, far).
_____ 9. Identifies relative size (large, small).
_____ 10. Identifies basic directions (right, left; up, down).
_____ 11. Identifies safety symbols.
_____ 12. Identifies simple road signs.
_____ 13. Explains what is meant by "change" and cites examples.
_____ 14. Identifies contents of photographs and paintings.
_____ 15. Makes inferences from pictures.
_____ 16. Notes sequences in multipart events (first, second, and so forth).
_____ 17. Accepts others' rights to their own opinions.
_____ 18. Identifies major national and state holidays.
_____ 19. Recognizes flags of the nation and state.
_____ 20. Describes alternative solutions to problems.

TABLE 12–4 (cont.)

Area II: Citizenship–Personal Education—Knowledge, Skills, Values

_____ 1. Identifies and states reasons for classroom and school rules.
_____ 2. Explains consequences of breaking rules.
_____ 3. Begins tasks promptly and stays on tasks until they are completed.
_____ 4. Volunteers to participate in discussions.
_____ 5. Behaves in a way reflecting an understanding of right and wrong behavior.
_____ 6. Recites Pledge of Allegiance.
_____ 7. Works cooperatively with others.
_____ 8. Participates in group decision making.
_____ 9. Helps others to learn.
_____ 10. Demonstrates courteous behavior.
_____ 11. Accepts leadership of others when asked to do so.
_____ 12. Accepts responsibility to assume leadership when asked.
_____ 13. Accepts basic idea of accepting decisions of the majority.
_____ 14. Listens when others are talking.
_____ 15. Takes turns willingly.

Formal Evaluation

Formal evaluation procedures include tests prepared by teachers and standardized tests prepared by commercial firms. Sometimes, when pupils are being assessed with informal assessment procedures, they do not know that they are being assessed. With formal evaluation, on the other hand, youngsters are almost always aware that they are being tested. As a result, the anxiety levels of children are often higher when formal evaluation is being used than they are when informal evaluation is being used.

As noted previously, there tends to be more formal evaluation with each succeeding year in the elementary social studies program. Many formal evaluation procedures require youngsters to have good reading and writing skills. These skills are better developed in older than in younger elementary children.

There are a large number of tests that qualify as formal assessment instruments. In the section that follows, a number of the most common kinds of teacher-prepared formal test types are introduced.

Rating Scales

Teachers are not only interested in those kinds of learning outcomes that can be assessed using a forced-choice test such as a multiple-choice or a true/false test. For example, some objectives may call on youngsters to give brief oral summaries of positions, to build models, or to increase their frequency of participating in class discussions. A *rating scale* is a tool that provides the teacher with information about youngsters' proficiencies in areas such as these.

Rating scale preparation begins with the identification of a specific set of focus characteristics. The rater makes judgments about a given youngster's relative

This Should Cure my Father of Thinking I'm a Know-it-all.
(*Source:* Ford Button.)

proficiency by circling or otherwise marking points arranged along the rating scale. The points on the rating scale must refer specifically to a range of pupil behaviors associated with the set of focus characteristics.

Many rating scales suffer because the rating points are not well defined. Suppose, for example, that a teacher were interested in a youngster's willingness to volunteer information during classroom discussions. One response to this interest might be the following rating scale.

Directions

Circle the appropriate number for each item. The numbers represent the following:
5 = Outstanding
4 = Above average
3 = Average
2 = Below average
1 = Unsatisfactory
How would you assess this youngster's willingness to volunteer to speak during classroom discussions?

5   4   3   2   1

This rating scale provides an illusion of specificity, but it fails to indicate exactly what each rating point means. This situation might result in different teachers assigning very different ratings to the same youngster.

A better rating scale would more specifically identify the meanings of rating points. Consider this example.

Directions

Circle the appropriate number for each item. The numbers represent the values indicated.
5 = volunteers on 80–100 percent of opportunities to do so.
4 = volunteers on 60–79 percent of opportunities to do so.
3 = volunteers on 40–59 percent of opportunities to do so.
2 = volunteers on 20–39 percent of opportunities to do so.
1 = volunteers on 0–19 percent of opportunities to do so.
How often does the youngster volunteer to participate in classroom discussions?

5   4   3   2   1

This rating scales allows for much more specificity than the first example. Specificity makes it more likely that different raters would rate similar behaviors in similar ways. Rating scales that are constructed with careful attention to providing clear definitions of rating points can contribute a great deal of information about certain important categories of pupil behavior.

Learning Checklists

Checklists share with rating scales the characteristic of measuring behaviors that are not easily assessed through the use of the paper-and-pencil tests taken by pupils. *Learning checklists* depend on the teacher's ability to see and record information about behaviors of interest.

Rating scales offer somewhat more flexibility than checklists. They allow teachers to scale ratings along a continuum that may have a number of ratings points. For instance, the examples introduced in the previous subsection allow a teacher to choose one of five possible rating points.

Most checklists, on the other hand, are designed only to indicate the presence or absence of a given behavior. This is not necessarily a limitation. Sometimes "Yes" or "No" or "Present" or "Absent" judgments are all a teacher needs to know. When this is the case, a teacher who has decided to use a checklist has made a wise choice.

A well-known measurement specialist, Norman Gronlund (1976; pp. 445–447), has suggested the following guidelines for developing a good checklist.

1. Identify and describe each desired pupil behavior as specifically as possible.
2. Add to these lists of desired pupil behaviors a number of the most common "incorrect," or "error," behaviors.
3. Arrange the list of desired behaviors and incorrect, or error, behaviors in the approximate order in which one might expect to see them.
4. Develop a simple procedure for checking each action as it occurs.

Suppose that a teacher were interested in how individual youngsters were grasping the distinctions among the terms "county," "country," and "continent." (Many pupils confuse these concepts.) By listening to youngsters present oral comments or by quickly interviewing individual children, the teacher could determine how individuals were faring with this learning task. The information could be recorded for each youngster on a checklist. The checklists, when completed, would not only provide information about each child but also suggest the general misunderstandings that were widespread throughout the class. The checklist might look something like the following.

Name of Pupil: _____

	Yes	No
Distinguishes between "county" and "country."		
Distinguishes between "county" and "continent."		
Distinguishes between "country" and "continent."		
Confuses "country" and "county," but not "country" and "continent."		
Confuses "country" and "continent," but not "country" and "county."		

To use this checklist, the teacher simply places a checkmark in the appropriate box or boxes.

Essay Tests

Essay tests are much more common in the upper grades than in the middle grades. Very few essay tests are used at all with primary-grade youngsters. The reason, of course, is that primary-grade youngsters lack the writing skills needed to provide the somewhat extensive responses needed for success on essay tests. These skills are still quite rudimentary even in middle-grade pupils.

Though they are not appropriate for all youngsters, essay tests do have their place in the social studies program. First, the essay provides pupils with an opportunity to practice writing skills on a real task. Aside from their function as a device to assess pupils' grasp of content, essays also contribute to developing students' fluency with the written language. In the realm of content, essay tests allow youngsters to put together bits and pieces of information into meaningful wholes (see Table 12–5).

Second, essay tests are well suited for purposes such as determining pupils' abilities to interpret, compare and contrast, and generalize about given information. In short, essays are useful when the teacher is interested in testing the more-sophisticated kinds of pupil thinking. On the other hand, when the purpose of assessment is to probe the less-sophisticated thinking skills (recall of specific names and places, for example), other kinds of tests—including true/false, multiple choice, and matching—are more appropriate.

TABLE 12–5 Needed: More Essay Tests In Schools.

The following comments appeared on the editorial page of a local newspaper.

Youngsters are poorer writers today than they were fifty years ago. Why has this happened? It surely cannot be that our children are not as smart. It surely *can* be said that something is terribly wrong with the school program. That "wrong" is simply this: Youngsters are no longer compelled to write essays.

Today, we have schools filled with mechanical grading machines that quickly score multiple-choice and true/false tests. These devices doubtless save time. However, they have also invited teacher irresponsibility. Because of easy mechanical grading, too few elementary teachers give essay tests. Since children are not asked to write, many of them never master the skill.

Mastery of the written word is a hallmark of the truly educated adult. We support the adoption of a school policy requiring elementary teachers to give only essay examinations after grade three. The step may be a radical one. However, given the lamentable decline in writing skills, a serious response is warranted.

Think About This

1. What problems for teachers would you see if this proposal were adopted by the school board?
2. What other "causes" for a decline in writing proficiency might you suggest, other than the increasing use of objective tests in the schools?
3. Would teachers at some grade levels find implementing this proposal more difficult than teachers at other grade levels?
4. Suppose that you were to respond to the writer of this editorial. What would you say?

These are some guidelines for the preparation of good essay items:

1. Write a question that focuses on a specific and somewhat limited content area. (Essays take time to compose. Not too much content can be covered in the time available for pupils to respond.)
2. Write questions so that youngsters are encouraged to include examples and specific details. Look at items (a) and (b). Item (b) is by far the better essay question.
   (a) What are differences between the northern and southern hemispheres?
   (b) Discuss the weather and the seasons in the northern and southern hemispheres. Tell me the differences in (1) the months of the year when summer occurs, (2) the months of the year when winter occurs. Also, (3) tell me why the relative position of the earth and the sun have something to do with these differences.
3. Give students specific instructions about how much they are expected to write. (Even upper-grade youngsters have trouble writing a full page on a given question. Usually the length expectations are better explained in terms of numbers of paragraphs.)

The correction of essay items poses problems. More is involved than a simple comparison of a pupil's response to the "correct" answers on the key, as can be done with multiple-choice or true/false tests. It is more difficult to reliably score essays, but there are some procedures that teachers can use to make the marking of essays consistent.

First, the teacher can prepare a sample response to each essay question. This helps point out the potential problems with the language used in the question itself. It also provides a source that can be used to identify the major points that the teacher will be looking for when he or she grades the responses. Some teachers make a separate listing of these points after they have written their sample responses. This listing is then used as individual pupil answers are read.

Usually, when they correct test papers, teachers look at all of the answers a given pupil has made before going on to another youngster's paper. When essays are used, particularly when there are several essay questions, it is better for the teacher to read every youngster's response to one question before going on to the other questions. This means, for example, that a teacher would read all of the pupil answers to essay question one before going on and reading the answers to question two. The procedure is desirable because different standards tend to be applied to different questions. If all of the answers to a given question are read before the answers to the other questions, there is a better chance that the same grading criteria will be applied to each child.

Sometimes, the order in which essays are read will make a difference in how a teacher grades them. For example, a teacher may become frustrated when the same mistake appears in paper after paper. Unconsciously, the teacher may grade the papers read later more harshly than the papers graded earlier. To guard against this possibility, it is a good idea to read the responses several times and to shuffle the papers so that the order is changed with each reading.

Finally, teachers sometimes find that they have expected too much. If a review of all the answers reveals that some youngsters have missed critical material, this may be an indication that the youngsters need more instructional time. The teacher may decide that it was unreasonable to expect youngsters to include some of the points he or she included in the sample response. The grading criteria can be adjusted so that pupils will not be punished for not knowing material that the whole class needs to work on.

Essays require a good deal of teacher time to prepare properly and to correct. But when they are well constructed, they yield a wealth of information about youngsters' sophisticated-thinking, organizational, and written-fluency skills.

True/False Tests

True/false tests are widely used in elementary schools. Individual questions can be prepared quickly. Pupils have little difficulty in learning how to take true/false tests. Because students can respond to a large number of questions in a limited time, a single true/false test can cover a good deal of content. The tests can be corrected quickly. (Many schools have machines that will electronically score these tests, provided that youngsters mark the responses on special answer sheets.)

True/false tests have certain limitations. Poorly constructed true/false tests can encourage youngsters to memorize content by rote rather than to seek to understand it. This is not really a problem with the true/false test as a test type. Rather, it is a fault of a test developer who uses true/false test to quiz only the recall of isolated facts. Good true/false tests that demand understanding, not just recall, can be prepared.

True/false tests do depend on absolute judgments. That is, the question posed must be something that is either "true" or "false," and not something in between. Sometimes, this feature results in the oversimplification of complex issues.

For example, suppose that a teacher asked a youngster to respond "true" or "false" to this statement: The sun set yesterday. The teacher was probably expecting youngsters to respond "true." However, the statement is not really a true/false issue, and it represents an irresponsible distortion of a more-complex issue. True, the sun did "appear" to set yesterday, but the sun did not really move at all. What happened was that the earth turned, and, to someone on the earth, the sun "seemed" to set.

True/false tests also have been accused of encouraging guessing rather than learning. It is argued that youngsters will sometimes get a higher score than they deserve as a result. Most measurement specialists doubt this is a terribly serious issue because youngsters are as probable to guess wrong as to guess right. Overall, guessing may not help a student who does not know the content.

The following are some basic guidelines used for preparing true/false tests. When these are followed, true/false tests are likely to provide reliable measures of learning.

1. Avoid giving unintentional clues. (These include use of words such as "all," "no," "never," and so forth, which tend to prompt an answer of "false.")
2. Approximately half of the questions should be false. ("True" statements are easier to construct. Youngsters who guess mark "true" more frequently than "false.")
3. Every statement should be clearly "true" or "false." ("The Yankees are the best baseball team" is a statement open to debate. It is not appropriate for a true/false test.)
4. Avoid double negatives in statements. ("It is never undesirable to drink milk for breakfast" is an example of a confusing double-negative statement. "Drinking milk for breakfast is recommended by a majority of health authorities" is a much less-confusing statement.)

When youngsters do not use electronic scoring sheets to record answers (these usually require them to use a pencil to fill in "bubbles" marked "true" or "false"), several options are available for the teacher. Some teachers provide blanks in front of each statement. When this is done, youngsters should not be allowed to enter a letter "T" indicating an answer of "true" or a letter "F" indicating an answer of "false." The printing of these letters sometimes results in marks that represent some hybrid form half-way between a "T" and an "F." Grading becomes a problem when the teacher is not clear as to whether a pupil really intended to indicate that the statement was "true" or "false."

Some teachers remedy this situation by requiring youngsters to write out the words "True" and "False" in their entirety. Others tell pupils to use a " + " sign for "true" and a "O" for "false." An even better solution is to print the words "true" and "false" to the left of the statement. Then youngsters can be simply asked to circle their choice. This practice allows a teacher to correct a paper with a good deal of confidence that he or she knows what the pupil's intended answer was.

Better true/false tests probe for understanding. Some of the best require youngsters to look at several pieces of information at the same time and to answer questions based on this information. For example, true/false tests can be used to assess pupils' abilities to grasp information presented in the forms of graphs, tables, and charts. An example of a true/false test that directs pupils' attention to a table of information is provided in Table 12–6.

TABLE 12–6   An Example of a True/False Test.

Name: _____

Ages at Which the Average American Man and Woman Married at Different Historical Times*

Year	Age of Average Man When He Married	Age of Average Woman When She Married
1890	26	24
1910	25	21
1930	24	21
1950	23	20
1970	23	21

*Data are adapted from the U.S. Bureau of the Census, *Historical Statistics of the United States, Colonial Times to 1970*, Bicentennial ed., Part I. Washington, D.C.: United States Government Printing Office, 1975, p. 19.

Directions

This is a true/false test. Each statement refers to the table above. Look at the table before you decide on your answer. Circle "true" for true statements; circle "false" for false statements.

true   false   1. In 1890, the average man was older than the average woman at the time of marriage.

true   false   2. The smallest difference between the age of the average man and the average woman at the time of marriage was in the year 1950.

true   false   3. In 1970, the average man was younger at the time of his marriage than the average man in 1910.

true   false   4. The greatest difference between the age of the average man and the average woman at the time of marriage occurred in the years 1930 and 1970.

true   false   5. This chart tells us that men married in 1890 at younger average ages than in 1970.

Multiple-Choice Tests

Multiple-choice tests have several advantages. Unlike true/false tests that give youngsters only two answer choices, multiple-choice tests provide three, four, or even five options. As a result, they can be used to test pupils' abilities to recognize the degrees of "correctness." Though the length of individual questions is typically longer than in true/false tests, multiple-choice questions still do not require a great deal of time. Pupils can complete a large number of items in a relatively short time, so these tests can be used to cover a fairly large body of content.

Multiple-choice tests reduce the chances that a youngster will get a high score as a result of guessing. This is true because there are many more answer options than in true/false tests. As with true/false tests, multiple-choice tests can be scored quickly. Schools with the necessary equipment have pupils provide the answers on forms that can be scored electronically.

There are some difficulties associated with preparation and use of multiple-choice tests. A good multiple-choice test takes time to prepare. It is not easy for teachers to think of good distractors (plausible incorrect choices). Also, older youngsters are inclined to argue that several options may be "correct." Most of the problems associated with the use of multiple-choice tests can be avoided if care is taken when the individual questions are prepared.

The part of the multiple-choice question that introduces the item is called the "stem." The alternative answers are called the "options." In a properly prepared multiple-choice item, the "stem" should provide youngsters with a context for answering. It should serve a focusing function. Consider these two examples:

1. Washington
   (a) is a common family name in France.
   (b) is the capital of the United States.
   (c) is a province of Canada.
   (d) is a state on the Mississippi River.
2. The capital city of the United States is called
   (a) Ottawa.
   (b) Washington.
   (c) New York.
   (d) Richmond.

The first example provides the pupil with no clues as to the category of the information the teacher is seeking. Is the purpose to identify a name, a capital, a province, or a state? The second example indicates clearly that the task is to identify a capital city. It is a much stronger item.

The options provided should be plausible. When some options make no logical sense, the student will respond to the correct answer as much because of the other nonsensical options as because of his or her content knowledge. For example, few youngsters would have difficulty responding correctly to this item:

Example 1. Which is the softest?

(a) cotton candy
(b) brick
(c) steel
(d) window glass

In good multiple-choice items, the stems and options are stated positively. The use of negatives can be very confusing. Note this example:

Example 2. Which is not a statement correctly describing the duties of a governor?

(a) The job of a governor cannot be said to include the supervision of his or her staff.

(b) The governor does not serve as a member of the state supreme court.

(c) The governor is not uninvolved in the affairs of a political party.

(d) The governor is not absent from ceremonial events.

When preparing multiple-choice items, care should be taken to assure that the item stems have a single correct answer. This means that the "correct" answer should not be a matter of opinion or judgment. Consider this example:

Example 3. The very best chili peppers are grown in the state of

(a) Arizona.

(b) Texas.

(c) New Mexico.

(d) California.

Obviously, the question of which state has the best chili peppers is a matter of debate and discussion rather than of "truth." It is not something that can be adequately tested by a forced-choice test such as multiple choice. Matters of opinion and debate are better handled in essays that allow youngsters to support their claims with logic and evidence.

Finally, when preparing multiple-choice questions, teachers need to exercise care in the placement of the correct answer. The placement should be varied. There is a tendency for some teachers to have either option (b) or (c) be the correct answer in a four option [(a), (b), (c), (d)] multiple-choice item. Some evidence suggests that youngsters who do not know the answer tend to answer (b) or (c). If too many correct answers are in those two places, some pupils may get scores higher than they deserve by guessing.

Matching Tests

Matching tests are especially useful when the teacher's purpose is to test pupil's understanding of new terms. These tests are easy to construct, and they can be graded quickly. Finally, they can focus youngsters' attention on the important vocabulary words that they will need to appreciate the lesson content.

Individually, matching tests are not as capable of assessing a broad range of content as true/false and multiple-choice tests. A properly constructed matching test focuses exclusively on the terms associated with a somewhat limited topic area. When terms are not related (for example, when the names of people, events, and places are all mixed up), youngsters often become confused because they have no focus for the activity. Consequently, they may not score well.

Matching tests consist of two columns of information. One column contains the definitions. The other column contains the terms. Pupils are asked to "match" the definition with the term it describes. Blanks are placed before each numbered definition, and letters of the alphabet are placed before each term. Pupils are instructed to place the letter of the term in the blank before its definition.

Measurement specialists prefer to set up matching tests so that the definitions are on the left and the terms are on the right. This practice encourages the youngster to read the definition first and then to look for the term. The definition provides specific clues and makes the search for an appropriate term a relatively focused activity. The alternative arrangement causes youngsters to look at single words and then to look through all of the wordy definitions. This is a less-efficient procedure than the preferred format.

It is essential for there to be at least 25 percent more terms in the right column than there are definitions in the left. If there are *exactly* the same number of items in each column, then a pupil who misses one item is forced to miss two. [If the answer for item 1 is (a) and item 2 is (b), and a youngster selects (b) for item 1, he or she has also missed item 2 where the (b) should have been placed.] Adding additional choices to the list of terms resolves this difficulty.

The entire matching test should be printed on a single page. Teachers sometimes prepare a matching test in which the right-hand column of terms is so much longer than the left-hand column of definitions that the right-hand column goes over on to a second page. When this happens, some youngsters invariably fail to notice the terms on the second page. Consequently, their scores suffer.

An example of a properly formatted matching test is provided in Table 12–7.

TABLE 12–7   An Example of a Matching Test.

Name: _____

Topic: Resources

Directions

This is a matching test. Look at the definitions on the left. Then look at the words on the right. Find the word on the right that matches each definition. Place the letter before the word in the blank before its definition. There is only one correct answer for each definition.

_____ 1. Materials people take from the earth to meet needs and wants.	a. human resources
_____ 2. Resources that cannot be replaced.	b. coal
_____ 3. The source of fuels such as gasoline and oil.	c. natural resources
_____ 4. Special skills, knowledge, and tools people use to create things to make life better.	d. technology
_____ 5. Resources that can be replaced.	e. petroleum
_____ 6. Known supplies of a resource that are available for use.	f. geology
	g. renewable resources
	h. nonrenewable resources
	i. reserves

Completion Tests

Completion tests are very easy to construct. They eliminate guessing, and they can sample a cross-section of content. In this latter regard, an individual completion test does not ordinarily cover quite as much material as either a true/false or a multiple-choice test. This is because pupils must write the responses in their own handwriting, which is a slower process than that involved in noting choices on true/false or multiple-choice tests.

The careful preparation of completion items is a must. One problem with this testing format has to do with correction. Unless an item is formatted properly, more than one answer may be logically defensible. Attention to the wording of the items can greatly diminish the importance of this problem. Consider these two versions of a completion item:

1. The navigator sailing for Spain who many consider to be the discoverer of America was _____.
2. The name by which we know the navigator who sometimes is called the discoverer of America is _____.

Many logical answers are possible to the first version. For example, pupils who answered "a man," "a native of Italy," "a Genoan," or even "a sailor" might make a case for the "correctness" of their answer. The second version provides a much better focus. It limits the range of probable answers. This is what a well-written completion item should do.

There are other correction problems associated with completion items. Paramount among these is the issue of spelling. If the major concern is mastery of content, then little attention should be logically paid to spelling. However, elementary teachers are charged with teaching spelling as well as social studies. They often find themselves in a quandary when dealing with completion-test responses. To take too much off for spelling tends to turn the exercise into an assessment of spelling ability rather than of social studies knowledge. To take nothing off for misspelled words seems to convey a message to pupils that spelling is only *really* important during the spelling period.

Another dilemma facing the teacher who corrects completion tests is what to do about synonyms. If the "correct" word for a blank is "hat," should the word "cap" be accepted? What about "chapeau" or "bandana"? Teachers agonize over how far they should go in accepting deviations from the word they had in their own correction key. The issue is an important one because doubts as to what constitutes a "correct" answer can undermine a test's reliability.

A number of teachers have found it useful to use a modified form of the completion test that deals with both the spelling and the synonym problem. This version of the completion test provides youngsters with the usual sentences and blanks to be filled in, but it goes one step further by providing a list of words at the bottom of the test page.

This list includes a mixture of words that are answers and other words that serve as distractors. Pupils are told to find the correct word at the bottom of the page and write it in the blank where it belongs. Since the words are there for youngsters to see, they can be held accountable for spelling (simply a matter of copying). No synonyms are accepted because pupils are directed to use only the words at the bottom of the page. (See Table 12–8 for an example of this format.)

The general guidelines for preparing completion tests include:

1. Use only *one* blank per item.
2. Put the blank at the end (or toward the end) of the item. This provides some context clues.
3. Avoid using "a" or "an" before the blank. (They will cue the pupil to look for either a word beginning with a vowel or a word beginning with a consonant.)
4. Avoid placing blanks in statements taken directly from the text.

TABLE 12–8   An Example of a Completion Test.

Name: _____

Test Topic: Climate

Directions

This is a completion test. You are to fill in each blank. Read the words at the bottom of the page, select the word that belongs in each blank, and write it there. You will not use all of the words at the bottom of the page. Every blank has a different correct word; no word at the bottom of the page will be used more than one time.

The four basic elements of climate are temperature, precipitation, air pressure, and

_____. The amount of direct sunlight a place receives depends on its
   1

_____. Little direct sunlight is received in _____ latitudes. Places in high
   2   3

latitudes are generally colder than places in _____ latitudes. Most of the United
                                               4

States is located in the _____ latitudes. Land surfaces cool more _____
                          5   6

than water surfaces. Air temperatures are _____ at high elevations than at low
                                           7

elevations. Temperatures are too low for the air to hold much _____ in high lati-
                                                               8

tudes.

Choose Answers from this List

wind	latitude	low	cooler	dusts
snow	longitude	hotter	slowly	rapidly
moisture	high	middle	clouds	

Using the Evaluation Results to Improve Instruction _____

The Evaluation results are not used only to assess the progress of individual pupils. They are also used by teachers to evaluate the quality of their own performances. To use evaluation results for this purpose, the scores of all youngsters need to be viewed collectively.

Suppose that a fifth-grade teacher gave pupils a test on the general topic of The Regions of the United States. The test included seven items focusing on each of these subtopics: (1) climates, (2) topography, (3) natural resources, and (4) population characteristics. After analyzing pupils' scores, the teacher found that the following percentages of youngsters had missed three or more questions related to each of these subtopic areas:

- climates - 10 percent
- topography - 12 percent
- natural resources - 25 percent
- population characteristics - 55 percent

These figures suggest that, as a group, the members of the class experienced the most difficulty with content related to "population characteristics." Large numbers of youngsters also missed items associated with "natural resources." This analysis might lead the teacher to provide additional instruction in these areas to clear up the misunderstandings. Furthermore, the next time this content is taught (perhaps the following year to a new class), this information might cue the teacher to reorganize his or her plan for delivering the instruction focusing on these two topics.

Teachers who make systematic use of the evaluation results are in a position to rationally refine their instructional plans. These results tell them what they are doing well and what areas might be presented more effectively another time. Over a period of several years, the weak spots in the program can be converted into real areas of instructional strength.

Key Ideas in Summary _____

The evaluation of pupils has always been an obligation of elementary teachers in social studies, as well as throughout the rest of the curriculum. Today, the demands by the public for evidence that schools are producing competent young people have resulted in an increased emphasis on evaluation. Today's teachers are expected to be familiar with a number of alternative evaluation procedures.

In elementary social studies classes, teachers use both informal and formal evaluation. Some key ideas related to the elementary social studies evaluation include the following:

1. Informal evaluation depends on teachers' observations of a number of different kinds of pupil performances. Often, youngsters do not even know they are being evaluated. Informal evaluation requires the teacher to make judgments about what a given youngster can and cannot do. Informal evaluation is used at all grade levels, but it is especially useful in the very early grades. Youngsters in the early grades lack the reading and writing skills they need to succeed with more formal evaluation procedures.

2. There are a large number of excellent informal evaluation techniques. Among these are headlines, newspaper articles, word pairs, anagrams, alphabet review games, My Favorite Idea displays, and mystery word scrambles. Much informal evaluation consists of teacher observations of youngsters as they complete projects and interact with others.

3. Good record keeping is essential if the maximum benefit is to be derived from informal evaluation procedures. Daily performance checklists can be used to keep track of youngsters' progress as it occurs. Relevant information later can be transferred to a social studies cumulative record form.

4. Formal evaluation includes tests prepared by teachers and standardized tests prepared by commercial firms. These are more common in the middle and upper elementary grades than in the primary grades. This is true because most formal evaluation procedures require youngsters to have mastered the basic reading and writing skills.

5. Rating scales and checklists can provide information about very specific

pupil behaviors. The rating scale allows judgments about several levels of performance quality. Most checklists allow for only an indication of whether a pupil can or cannot do something.

6. Essay tests are most common in the upper grades. They require quite highly developed writing skills and provide youngsters with opportunities to put together isolated pieces of information in a meaningful way. Essays require a long time to correct. The reliability of correction is a problem, but it can be overcome by careful attention to the design of the question and to the systematic correction procedures.

7. True/false tests can cover a broad range of content. Some critics say they encourage guessing. They are limited to content that can be described in terms of absolutes (something must be clearly "true" or clearly "false").

8. Matching tests are useful for testing pupils grasp of associations. Each matching test should focus on a single category of information. Also, all of the material for one test must be written on one sheet of paper. Care must be exercised to design the tests so that a pupil who misses one question does not automatically miss two.

9. Completion items pose dilemmas for the teacher when tests have to be corrected. To what extent should synonyms be accepted? To what extent should misspellings be tolerated? Some teachers prefer a completion-test type that provides youngsters with a list of words from which to draw answers. This reduces the correction problems.

10. The evaluation of learning has two important functions. First, it provides a basis for assessing the progress of an individual youngster. Second, analysis of score patterns of a class can suggest to the teacher areas where his or her instruction was not effective. This information can provide a basis for a productive discussion after the test to clear up misunderstandings. Also, it can provide a basis for instructional planning when the same content is taught again to another group of youngsters.

Questions _____

Review Questions

1. What differentiates formal evaluation from informal evaluation?
2. What are some examples of informal evaluation techniques?
3. What kind of record might a teacher keep of information derived through the use of informal evaluation?
4. What are some examples of formal evaluation techniques?
5. How can results of evaluation help the teacher evaluate and improve his or her instructional practices?

Thought Questions

1. Suppose that you were asked to defend the use of informal evaluation in the upper grades as part of a total evaluation scheme involving use of both informal and formal techniques. What would you say?

2. When they are taking a formal evaluation test, youngsters know they are being assessed. Often, they are not aware that their performances are being judged when the teacher uses informal techniques. Is this fair?

3. Suppose that you were asked to describe how evaluation procedures might differ in a Kindergarten class, a third-grade class, and a sixth-grade class. What would you say?

4. If someone were to argue against the use of essay tests on the grounds that teachers correct the quality of the handwriting rather than the quality of the content, how would you reply?

5. Suppose that you were asked to prepare a total evaluation program for a single grade level of your choice. What would be the mix of informal and formal evaluation techniques? How would you defend your selection?

Extending Understanding and Skill _____

Activities

1. Interview several teachers at the grade level you wish to teach about their record-keeping procedures. Be sure to find out how they keep track of information about pupils' performance when informal techniques have been used. If possible, make copies of some of their forms. Share these with your instructor and class members.

2. Read a textbook on the evaluation of learning. Prepare notecards on three of four formal evaluation techniques not mentioned in this chapter. Orally present these to the class.

3. Review several school social studies textbooks prepared for the grade level you would like to teach. Look at the end of the chapters. What kinds of tests are provided? Are there other suggestions relating to evaluation? Summarize your findings in a chart. Present it to your instructor for review.

4. Visit someone who teaches a grade level you would like to teach. Ask about the tests used in the social studies program. If possible, bring back some samples of formal tests. Present an oral report to the class, and share copies with other students who may have interest in the same grade level. Take care to point out the numbers of items on the tests and the tests' general levels of difficulty.

5. Begin a resource file of informal assessment techniques. Gather information from interviews of teachers and professors of education, from professional periodicals, from evaluation textbooks, and from other sources. Do not include any of the informal techniques mentioned in this chapter. Try to find at least twenty techniques appropriate for the grade level you would like to teach. Share this material with your instructor.

Supplemental Reading

ALLEN, W. H., and VAN SICKLE, R. L. "Learning Teams and Low Achievers," *Social Education* (January 1984), pp. 60–64.

ARMSTRONG, DAVID G. "Evaluation: Conscience of the Social Studies," *The Social Studies* (March/April 1977), pp. 62–64.

"A Nation at Risk." Final Report of the National Commission on Excellence in Education. Washington, D.C.: United States Department of Education, April 1983.

TORABI-PARIZI, ROSA, and CAMPBELL, NOMA JO. "Classroom Test Writing: Effects of Item Format on Test Quality," *The Elementary School Journal* (November 1982), pp. 155–160.

References ————————————————————————————————

GRONLUND, NORMAN E. *Measurement and Evaluation in Teaching*, 3d ed. New York: Macmillan Publishing Co., Inc., 1976.

MCKINNEY, C. W., et al. "Teach Social Studies Concepts to First Grade Students? Research on the Merrill and Tennnyson Model," *The Social Studies* (September/October 1982), pp. 235–238.

MOORE, D. W. "A Case for Naturalistic Assessment of Reading Comprehension," *Language Arts* (November/December 1982), pp. 957–969.

MUIR, SHARON, and WELLS, CANDACE. "Informal Evaluation," *The Social Studies* (May/June 1983), pp. 95–97.

SAX, GILBERT. *Principles of Educational Measurement and Evaluation*. Belmont, CA: Wadsworth Publishing Co., Inc., 1974.

United States Bureau of the Census. *Historical Statistics of the United States, Colonial Times to 1970*, Bicentennial ed., Part 1. Washington, D.C.: United States Government Printing Office, 1975.

WALBERG, HERBERT J. (ed.). *Evaluating Educational Performance*. Berkeley, CA: McCutchan Publishing Corp., 1974.

Chapter 13 _____

Managing the Social Studies Classroom

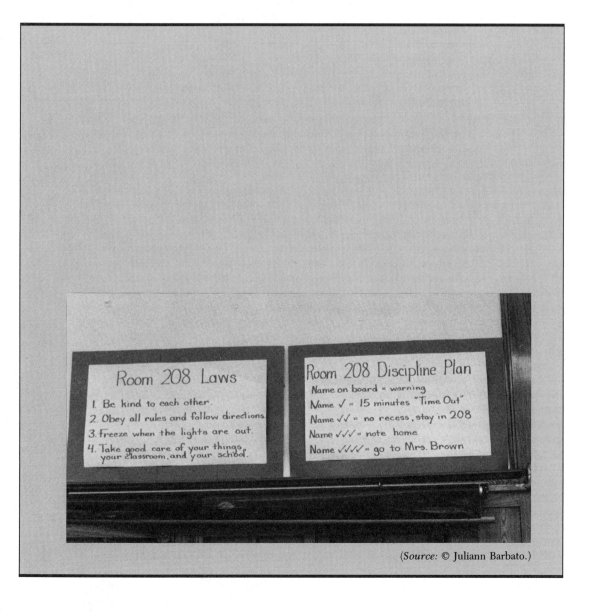

(*Source:* © Juliann Barbato.)

This chapter provides information to help the reader:

1. Identify the relationship between instruction and classroom management.
2. List the space-management principles that should be considered when arranging the classroom.
3. State how materials should be organized and managed.
4. Identify the routines that should be established to facilitate the smooth functioning of the elementary social studies classroom.
5. Point out the importance of planning for transitions.
6. Describe the basic goal of discipline.
7. List the characteristics of teachers who effectively manage the inappropriate behaviors of pupils.
8. Point out the basic principles that should be incorporated in a plan for discipline.
9. List a range of responses a teacher can use when responding to inappropriate behavior.

Overview

Instructing pupils and managing the classroom are two of teachers' most basic responsibilities. They are highly interrelated tasks. Success in one depends on success in the other. Good instructional practices can reduce the incidence of behavior problems. (They *never* disappear entirely; even the best teachers experience "difficult" days.) A teacher's ability to deliver "good" instruction ties closely to his or her classroom-management skills. If the class is not under control, little learning will take place. Failure in managing the classroom is synonymous with teaching failure. Hence, beginning teachers should consider the learning of classroom-management skills to be a very high professional priority.

Today, teacher-preparation programs are giving the issue of classroom management and control the attention it deserves. This represents a change from some practices in the past when prospective teachers received little advice in this area beyond tired bromides such as "be enthusiastic," "expect good behavior," "love the children," or "plan interesting lessons." Such statements represent good general advice, but they fall far short of providing the kind of specific information beginners need as they contemplate the realities of the elementary classroom.

Among these realities is that classroom management and control problems have been regularly found to be the number one concern of teachers for over a decade. Many teachers experience psychological stress. Of those who do, a very high percentage cite discipline problems as one of the major contributors to their anxieties.

Beginning teachers are well aware of the challenges they will face as classroom managers. One of their greatest fears is that they will be confronted with an incident that they just cannot handle. To a large measure, these concerns stem from a lack of understanding of the approaches to discipline prevention and to the proper responses when difficulties do occur. We hope to allay some of these fears by suggesting approaches to these very real challenges that face the elementary teacher.

To begin with, we want to point out that the vast majority of problems that elementary teachers confront relate to minor issues such as inattention, talking, youngsters who are out of their seats, and problems pupils have when the appropriate materials are not available. Certainly more serious problems do occasionally arise. However, these need to be kept in perspective. Few elementary social studies classrooms confront teachers with the kinds of terrible discipline and control situations that are sometimes depicted on television, in films, or in press exposés focusing on extremely poor teaching environments.

The social studies component of the elementary program is an area where teachers who lack good classroom management skills are likely to experience difficulty. In their college and university preparation for teaching social studies, prospective elementary teachers are told to develop lessons that keep pupils active and allow them to be grouped in different ways; include out-of-school experiences; and encourage independent, inquiry-oriented learning. Activity-oriented instruction of this kind provides many opportunities for youngsters to engage in appropriate behaviors. Teachers must have good management skills to make instruction of this kind work.

Sometimes, beginners have abandoned many productive teaching approaches because of their fear of discipline problems. Some have responded by returning to large-group, textbook-oriented instruction. In the short run, this kind of instruction may make control easier. A problem with this response, though, is that it can lead to pupil boredom. Boredom, itself, can contribute to classroom control problems. In our view, it makes better sense for new teachers to master the fundamental principles of classroom management. Teachers who have these principles well in hand are able to use a wide variety of instructional approaches with little fear that there will be a breakdown in their ability to manage the youngsters in the class.

Two basic dimensions of classroom management are introduced in this chapter. The first, the *prevention dimension*, provides the guidelines for averting problems through the application of sound management techniques. The second, the *response dimension*, details the approaches of reacting to inappropriate behavior in the classroom.

The Dimensions of Classroom Management _____

Classroom management focuses on what a teacher must do to organize and manage time, materials, and space efficiently and smoothly. It focuses on the prevention of potential problems. The focus on prevention has good support in the educational research literature. J. Kounin (1970), for example, found that the basic difference between effective and ineffective classroom managers was not in the way that they responded to inappropriate behavior but, rather, in the way that they organized and managed the classroom. Supporting this basic position, C. M. Evertson, E. T. Emmer, and L. Anderson (1980) found a smooth functioning classroom not to be an "accident" or something related to the characteristics of the pupils, but to be, instead, a result of the preparation and planning a teacher does even before the school year begins.

In general, studies have demonstrated that successful classroom managers "know" a systematic set of management procedures. They communicate their expectations clearly to youngsters. They plan in advance of their pupils' arrival how their rooms will be arranged, how the materials will be distributed and used, and many other issues that can influence a teacher's ability to control the class in a professional manner.

Space Management

Several parts of the classroom must be considered when decisions about space management are made. Among these are the floor space, wall space, equipment space, book-and-materials space, and pupils' work space.

The Floor Space. The floor space of the classroom needs to be arranged to accommodate the activities that are to take place. This kind of organization can communicate to pupils the types of behaviors that are expected (see Table 13–1).

In social studies classrooms, different activities clearly require different floor-space arrangements. If youngsters are to work in a single large group, the room must be arranged to facilitate large-group work. Chairs must be arranged so that the teacher can maintain good eye contact with pupils. Furthermore, individual pupil desks should be arranged so that opportunities for youngsters to interact with one another are minimized. If the teacher plans to make an assignment that will require the youngsters to do some seat work, enough space around the desks

TABLE 13–1 Let's Shape the Youngster to the Room, _Not_ the Room to the Youngster.

A parent recently made the following comments when the local elementary school parents' group was asked to raise money to buy screens so that groups of youngsters operating in different parts of the classroom would not interfere with one another's work.

> I think we're making a mistake. Aren't we making life too easy for our kids? Certainly they won't be able to talk to one another if we "cage" them in with visual screens. But is that our purpose? Shouldn't children learn how to be quiet regardless of their physical settings? Shouldn't the teachers teach this as part of the school program. I think they should. Our children will miss something valuable in their elementary school experience if we take the easy way out and make it physically impossible for them to behave in an irresponsible manner. In the "real world" they will be faced with many opportunities to misbehave. They need to learn how to deal with these temptations. A plan that will help them to avoid their responsibilities is a mistake.

Think About This

1. How do you think other parents at the meeting responded? Why do you think they responded in this way?
2. How much logic is there in the argument that schools should teach youngsters to deal with temptation by not making it impossibly difficult to misbehave?
3. If you were a teacher of a classroom in which these visual screens were to be installed, how would you respond to the concerns of this parent?

should be left to allow the teacher to move easily throughout the classroom to check on individual pupil progress.

If the chalkboard is to be used, the desks must be positioned so that youngsters can see it. Limitations such as the positions of windows and unique lighting patterns must be considered. Youngsters who cannot see what the teacher is doing may develop inappropriate patterns of behavior.

Many social studies teachers will find a need for at least one small-group meeting area. Small-group areas need to be arranged so that when the teacher works with one group he or she can maintain good visual contact with the other pupils in the class. There should be sufficient space between the members of a single group and the others in the class so that the activities of the group do not interfere with those of the others.

Some teachers may wish to use learning centers in their instructional programs. These centers need to be placed in areas of the classroom that are accessible to all the pupils in the class. They need to be designed so that the activities of youngsters working at a given center do not attract the attention of other pupils. If special equipment, such as filmstrip projectors or tape recorders, are to be used at a given center, arrangements must be made so that the sound does not interfere with the work of others. It may be necessary to provide earphones for pupils to use rather than to allow them to use the built-in speakers.

As we have briefly noted, the traffic patterns are an important consideration for teachers as they prepare floor plans of their classrooms. The areas of high traffic must be identified. Typical "high traffic" areas include the entrances to the classroom, the places where pupils store personal belongings, the drinking fountains, the book-storage areas, and the area around the teacher's desk.

Each of these areas needs to be kept free from obstructions. Part of the strategy here is to remove anything that might slow a youngster down or attract his or her attention. For example, no pupil desk should be too close to the main entrance of the classroom. A youngster seated at such a desk may well find his or her attention diverted every time someone enters or leaves. It is especially important to keep pupil desks well away from drinking fountains and pencil sharpeners.

The Teacher's Desk. The specific placement of the teacher's desk is an important issue. Many times the desk is situated at the front and center of the classroom. This may not be the best choice. A better option might be to place the desk in an unobtrusive place at the rear of the classroom. There are several advantages to this placement decision.

A teacher desk at the rear of the classroom cannot be used as a teaching station. This kind of placement assures that the teacher will not fall into the undesirable pattern of sitting down and attempting to teach from his or her desk chair. Teaching in that manner communicates a lack of enthusiasm, and it can result in control problems. Teachers who move about the classroom are perceived to be more interested in their youngsters and also to be "warmer" people.

The back-of-the-room placement of the teacher's desk allows the teacher to do a better monitoring of independent work. Youngsters tend to stay at their assigned tasks better because they are unable to see whether the teacher is looking at them. (Many will conclude, "I'd better get busy, because the teacher may be looking at me.")

A final consideration related to the teacher's desk has to do with its use as an instructional location. In general, it is better for teachers to go to the desk of a pupil who is having a problem than for the pupil to move to the teacher's desk. Pupils who must get out of their seats and walk to the teacher's desk may have to pass close to many others in the class. This may result in a disruption of the work patterns of several youngsters. When the teacher walks through the class to assist a given individual, there is a tendency for youngsters to increase their attention to the assigned task.

The Wall Space. The constructive use of wall space can contribute to a healthy classroom learning environment. Walls can be used for diverse purposes. For example, they might be used to display materials that are designed to spark pupils' interest in social studies materials, the pupils' work, the classroom rules and regulation, and the good models youngsters are to follow in completing certain assignments.

Planning for wall-space use should be done before the beginning of the school year. Attractive and interesting walls can motivate and excite youngsters when they come into the classroom for the first time. Basic "classroom rules" should also be displayed where youngsters can see them. These rules should be discussed with youngsters on the first day of school. As needed, the rules can be amended throughout the school year.

On the first day of school, there should be one bulletin board that features a display of materials that are designed to spark interest in the initial social studies unit. Some teachers attempt to prompt pupils' curiosity by posing a puzzling question that youngsters should be able to answer once the unit has been completed. As work on the unit progresses, the initial display can be modified to include materials developed by pupils as they study the unit content.

A place for the display of the daily schedule and for special assignments should be provided on one wall in the classroom. Elementary youngsters do better when they feel secure about what they are doing and about what is expected of them, so this kind of display can be very helpful. A daily schedule also communicates to youngsters that their teacher is well organized. Abundant research points out that large numbers of successful teachers operate in a very organized, business-like fashion.

The Equipment Storage. Good elementary social studies programs utilize many support materials. Among these are films, filmstrips, cassette tapes, videotapes, and computer software. The machines required to use these materials are bulky. Special arrangements must be made to store this equipment. The individual machines should be easily accessible, but they should be stored in places that do not subject them to a risk of being damaged. This kind of equipment is very expensive, and professional teachers work hard to keep it in good working order.

The Materials Storage. Social studies teachers use a wide variety of materials. These include textbooks, supplementary books, artifacts, pictures, recordings of all kinds, computer software, documents, charts, and many other items. The plans for storing these items must be included in the classroom-utilization scheme. Student projects, duplication masters, reams of duplication paper, and the other materials teachers use to support instructional activities will also re-

TABLE 13–2 A Space-Management Checklist.

	Yes	No
1. Traffic patterns are free from distractions.		
2. Seating is arranged so that the teacher can easily get to each pupil.		
3. All pupils have an unobstructed view of the main instructional area.		
4. Materials are stored in secure, yet accessible, places.		
5. Small-group areas and learning centers are arranged so that they will not interfere with other instructional activities.		
6. Rules are posted in a prominent place.		
7. The daily schedule is posted.		
8. The teacher's desk is placed in an unobtrusive place.		

Potential Problem Areas: _____

_____

_____

_____

Possible Solutions: _____

_____

_____

_____

quire space. These items need to be stored with a view both to safety and to accessibility.

The Personal-Belongings Storage. Many elementary teachers designate places in the classroom for youngsters to store personal items. Sometimes the individual desk tops have adequate storage space. Some teachers devise racks of empty plastic dish pans, stacked boxes, or other storage areas. There is a need for personal-belongings areas to be designated before pupils arrive. When this is done, they can be provided with very explicit instructions regarding what they are to do with their personal items.

See Table 13–2 for a checklist on space management.

Time Management

The responsible allocation of class time is a hallmark of the effective teacher. Time-management planning considers the ways to minimize time spent on noninstructional tasks, to keep pupils' attention engaged when formal instruction is being presented or when they are working on assignments, and, in general, to reduce the total amount of time spent on nonproductive sorts of activities.

Transitions. Smooth and efficient movement from one aspect of a lesson to another is one aspect of effective time management. Unless there is careful planning for transitions, a good deal of time can be wasted. Such "slack time" also presents youngsters with opportunities to behave inappropriately. Thus, transitions planning has the twin advantages of making lessons flow more smoothly and of reducing the probability that classroom-control problems will develop.

To deal with the issue of transitions, lesson planning has to go beyond the thought about what kinds of content and what kinds of activities will be featured. The "boundaries" between the activity types need to be identified clearly, and specific plans must be made to move youngsters quickly out of one phase of a lesson and into another phase.

This kind of planning does not need to be complex. For example, if papers will be returned, designated youngsters can be identified to distribute them quickly. The papers can be presorted so that each "teacher helper" gets only the papers for those few pupils for whom he or she is responsible. Such procedures can greatly speed up the process of returning papers and can save scarce classroom time for the important instructional tasks.

Activity changes that call for pupils to move from one place to another can cause difficulties. Youngsters should be provided with instructions that specify exactly how they should change seats, enter and leave the room, and move through the hallways to the library, gymnasium, or other designated areas.

Beginning Class. Every effort should be made to start promptly the instructional phase of the class period. Role-taking, materials-development, and announcement-making procedures should be planned with a view to time efficiency. Without good planning in these areas, many beginning teachers find themselves using a substantial part of the class period taking care of noninstructional matters. When this happens, there often is not sufficient time left for youngsters to derive as much from lessons as they might under circumstances where more instructional time was provided.

Distraction from the assigned tasks cuts into pupils' learning efficiency and may result in classroom-control problems. Before a lesson begins, the pupil-work areas should be cleared of all the items not specifically needed for the day's lesson. When the learning areas contain only the materials closely tied to the central focus of the lesson, pupils find it much easier to stay on the task.

Some teachers find it useful to teach pupils to look for a specific signal indicating that the administrative procedures have been completed and the instructional activities are about to commence. For example, pupils might be taught to look for a movement by the teacher to the front and center of the classroom, followed by a quiet gaze over the class. When this occurs, they might be told, they should understand that the instruction is about to begin, and that they should quiet down and look up at the teacher.

When the teacher gives the instruction-is-about-to-begin signal, he or she should refrain from beginning until _all_ youngsters in the class are quiet and paying attention. It may be necessary to have a word with one or two pupils before all are paying attention.

When the teacher refuses to begin until all are paying attention, he or she communicates to pupils that it is important for them to hear what will be said. A quiet, attentive class assures that all youngsters will be able to hear the teacher's instructions. This may not happen if some youngsters continue to talk. A failure to hear can lead to misunderstandings, and misunderstandings can lead to time-wasting confusion and potential control problems.

Pacing the Lesson. The lesson pacing, the rate at which a teacher helps youngsters move through their daily work, needs to be brisk enough to provide a sense of productive movement, but not so quick that youngsters become lost. Repetition of the key points is important, but the teacher needs to avoid over-dwelling on items that youngsters have already mastered. When this happens, boredom sets in. Boredom is a painful form of sensory deprivation. Some pupils may seek relief by engaging in unacceptable behaviors.

To determine an appropriate pace, some teachers consciously identify a few representative pupils to serve as a class-reference group. The teacher carefully monitors the understandings of these pupils to determine whether the pace is too slow, too fast, or about right.

Different pupils in the class will finish their work at different times. Activities must be designed for those youngsters who are early finishers. These need to be selected with care. It is important that these activities are not viewed as "punishment" for completing work quickly, accurately, and efficiently. If these activities are something to which youngsters look forward, they will act as stimuli to the others in the class to work quickly and productively on the assigned tasks.

Providing Assistance. Developing procedures for responding to pupils who need help is another important dimension of time management. Sometimes, a large number of youngsters will indicate a need for help. When the teacher spends too much time with a single pupil, the others in the class may become frustrated. Furthermore, because the teacher's attention may be concentrated on one youngster, the others in the class may be tempted to misbehave. Developing a system for responding to youngsters who need help can result in better assistance for the pupils and can reduce the possibility of classroom-control problems.

As noted in a previous section of this chapter, organizing pupils' seats so that the teacher has free and easy movement is an important consideration. Ease of access by the teacher to each youngster in the classroom saves time and makes it easier for the teacher to work with larger numbers of youngsters.

A basic consideration when responding to youngsters' appeals for help has to do with the issue of how much help ought to be provided. The teacher clearly has an obligation to assist youngsters who find themselves "blocked" because of some critical misunderstanding. On the other hand, the teacher does not want to do the work for youngsters who are perfectly capable of doing it themselves. We do not want to reinforce pupils who are not applying themselves to the assigned task.

F. Jones (1979) provides some suggestions to encourage pupils to do as much of their own work as possible. His research revealed that the average teacher spends much more time working with individual pupils than is really necessary. To remedy this, he proposes that the teacher, when working with a youngster seeking help, begin by finding something that the pupil has done well. The youngster should be complimented on what he or she has done. This helps build self-confidence.

Next, the teacher should give the youngster a very direct suggestion regarding what he or she should do next. For example, the teacher might say something about how the very next step in a process should be begun. It is important that the teacher should not actually do the pupil's work. Once the suggestion is

This teacher is assisting a pupil. Providing prompt help can prevent the behavior problems that may arise when youngsters are frustrated.
(*Source:* © Juliann Barbato.)

made, the teacher should move on to the next youngster. Jones (1979) suggests that the teacher should not spend more than about twenty seconds with each pupil. If this time schedule can be maintained, the teacher can get to each individual in the class. Once all pupils have been visited, then individuals can be rechecked to assure that they are back on track.

Some teachers have found that "peer helpers" can work effectively with youngsters in the class who experience difficulty. Peer helpers are other youngsters in the class who have a good grasp of the material. Some teachers provide peer helpers with special badges to provide them with some valuable recognition for their own good work.

Establishing Routines and Procedures

Routines need to be developed for managing recurring and predictable events. This general-management principle is very much applicable to elementary teaching. Teaching is a very people-intensive occupation. During a typical day, teachers have more numerous and more intensive interpersonal contacts than do many other professionals. Unless there is a system to manage these interactions, a severe emotional strain can result. To assure that the reservoirs of energy remain sufficiently high to deal with the many incidences of interpersonal interaction, teachers need systems that will impose some pattern on their work day (see Table 13–3).

Some routines should relate to administrative matters. For example, the teacher should think through how tasks such as taking attendance, collecting assignments, and returning corrected work can be best accomplished.

Other routines apply to pupils' behavior. For example, what should pupils do and how should they behave when entering and leaving the classroom? What

**TABLE 13–3 Questions to Consider When Planning
Needed Routines and Procedures.**

1. What should pupils do upon entering the classroom?
2. What procedures will be used to take attendance and to handle the other routine administrative matters?
3. What signal will be used to capture pupils' attention?
4. How will the materials be distributed?
5. How will the materials be collected?
6. Where will the books and supplies be stored?
7. How will assistance be provided to pupils who need help?
8. What will be the rules for the use of the pencil sharpener, the drinking fountain, and the restrooms?
9. What will be the policy regarding out-of-seat behavior?
10. How will youngsters' participation be managed during classroom discussions?
11. How will youngsters move from one part of the classroom to the other?
12. What will be the routine for bringing an activity to a close?
13. What procedure will be established to provide guidelines for youngsters who finish work early?
14. What procedures will govern dismissal and leaving the room?

are the expectations the teacher has for them when they are using the drinking fountains or the pencil sharpeners? How should they move from one part of the room to another?

The routines for pupils can also relate to the special information they will need when certain learning activities are taking place. Suppose, for example, that a teacher is interested in having youngsters do some work in small groups. Youngsters in the elementary school do not, as a matter of course, know how to function as members of small groups. They need directions that will help them to work productively in the small-group configuration. (You may wish to review the specific small-group techniques that were introduced in Chapter 7, "Involving Pupils: The Individualized Approaches.")

Once the teacher has decided upon his or her expectations for pupils in a variety of recurring classroom situations, these expectations need to be explained to youngsters. Such information should be treated with the same level of attention as content related more clearly to the academic subjects. The routines should be explained, demonstrated, and practiced until all the members of the class clearly understand the teacher's expectations.

When pupils master these routines, the teacher will be free to deal with situations that are exceptional or out-of-the-ordinary. Without the worries associated with routine matters, such as using the pencil sharpener, the teacher will have more time to devote to these serious matters that deserve his or her undivided attention. A result can be more the effective use of the teacher's time and a reduction in the teacher's level of stress.

Responding to Incidents of Misbehavior _____

Every teacher from time to time faces misbehavior problems. Almost every child at some time or other during his or her years in school will misbehave. The objective of classroom management is not to completely eliminate inappropriate behaviors but to reduce their frequency.

The avoidance of problems on field trips is a result of careful planning and management.
(*Source:* © Juliann Barbato.)

The purpose of good classroom discipline is not simply to make the job of the teacher easier. There are also important educational goals for pupils. Discipline programs should help pupils develop self-control and accept responsibility. These learnings are very socially useful patterns; they will have a broad application throughout the lives of youngsters presently in the schools (see Table 13–4).

The goals of discipline are very compatible with the academic goals of the elementary social studies program. A citizenry who are self-controlled and responsible is a keystone to the survival of a democracy. Given this reality, an episode of misbehavior does not need to be viewed as requiring a teacher response that has little to do with the academic program. Rather, it might be looked at as an opportunity to teach pupils the socially desirable patterns of behavior, an outcome clearly consistent with the aims of the social studies.

The methods used to confront discipline problems need to be evaluated in terms of how well they help promote the goals of self-control and personal responsibility. For example, coercion and fear may be used to get a pupil to refrain from an unacceptable-behavior pattern, but they may do little by way of advancing the youngster toward the goal of more self-controlled behavior. There need to be incentives for the pupil to change his or behavior in the desired direction. Skilled teachers vary these incentives in light of their understandings of the personal characteristics of the pupils in their classrooms.

The "Flow" of Discipline Problems Through the School Year

There should be a somewhat predictable pattern to the frequency of discipline problems a teacher faces throughout the school year. If the teacher is succeeding

TABLE 13–4   The Approaches to Promoting Pupil Growth in Self-control.

Approach 1: Punishment/Coercion

In general, coercion and punishment are not very effective means of moving individuals toward self-control. This is true because control remains external to the individual. Once the fear of punishment is removed, the individual may return to an unacceptable pattern of behavior.

Advantages

Punishment is better than no control at all. It might be an appropriate "last resort" response for pupils under certain sets of circumstances. Punishment is almost never a responsible "first-choice" response to a pupil's misbehavior.

Disadvantages

Punishment can lead to a breakdown of communication. Resentment often results. Many times pupils will not see the connection between their misbehavior and the punishment. Rather, they will view the punishment as a capricious act on the part of the person administering it. Finally, punishment, in and of itself, fails to teach the pupil an appropriate substitute behavior.

Approach 2: Affection/Praise

This approach depends for its effectiveness on the existence of a positive relationship between the pupil and his or her teacher. This approach does not foster growth in self-control. "Good" pupil behavior is a result not of self-control, but rather of a youngster's expectation that his or her behavior will be rewarded by praise from the teacher.

Advantages

This approach does tend to create warm working relationships between pupils and teachers. Thus, it can change pupil behaviors in a positive direction in a way that does not create an atmosphere of disharmony.

Disadvantages

This approach can cause a pupil to develop an overly dependent relationship with his or her teacher. This kind of a relationship is not conducive to helping pupils develop internal mechanisms to control their behaviors.

Approach 3: Tangible Reinforcers

The use of reinforcers to shape pupils' behaviors is a powerful tool. It has proved particularly effective in small-group settings. The approach is sometimes difficult to apply in large-group arrangements.

Advantages

This approach does have the potential to help youngsters internalize appropriate behavior patterns.

Disadvantages

The teacher must find out what a problem youngster considers to be reinforcing. This is a very difficult task. For example, those things that might reinforce a youngster may be unavailable to the teacher or inappropriate for use in the classroom. Also, the youngster may become too dependent on the expectation of a reward.

TABLE 13–4 (cont.)

Approach 4: Rules and Regulations

Children learn responsibility as they become familiar with the application of rules in many social settings. Effective rules must be reasonable. Youngsters need to understand the reasons for rules before they will accept them.

Advantages

Youngsters gain an initial security by learning what behaviors are expected of them. By learning that they personally choose the consequences that follow from either obeying or disobeying the rules, pupils are encouraged to develop personal responsibility for their actions.

Disadvantages

If for some reason pupils who have been used to operating where a set of formal rules is available find themselves in a situation where there are no formal rules, they may be at a loss as to how they should behave. If teachers do not enforce rules, then their presence will have little influence on youngsters' behaviors.

Approach 5: Behavior Based on Values or Self-chosen Principles

This is a goal toward which teachers should strive. At this point, youngsters "choose" good behavior on their own, not because of external pressures.

Advantages

Youngsters learn how to adjust to a variety of situations. They tend not to depend on others when they have to make values choices. Independent decision making improves self-concepts.

Disadvantages

A high degree of maturity is required of pupils who base personal decisions based on their own values or self-chosen principles. Much adult guidance is required before most youngsters can begin to operate at this level.

in his or her goal to have pupils develop more self-control and behave responsibly, there should be a general decline in the number of discipline problems as the year progresses.

This does not suggest, however, that there will not be flare-ups and problem spots during the year. For example, youngsters in elementary schools tend to get very excited before the major holidays or before the end of the school year. A break of warm sunny weather in early spring after weeks of snow or dreary rain will sometimes divert youngsters' attention from their school tasks and make them more difficult to work with.

Despite the inevitable "challenging days" that all teachers face, the general trend should be in the direction of fewer discipline problems as the year progresses. If this is not the observed pattern, the teacher needs to reassess his or her responses to discipline problems. It may be that changes in what is being done to promote self-controlled, responsible behavior need to be implemented.

The Characteristics of Teachers Who Are Good Discipline Managers

Teachers who have established effective discipline-management procedures share certain characteristics. First, they tend to be individuals who are willing to assume personal responsibility for dealing with discipline management. They accept discipline management as an integral part of their roles as teachers, and reject the idea that such problems result from factors beyond their control. Additionally, they tend, as much as possible, to deal with discipline problems themselves rather than referring them to the principal or other school authorities.

Second, these teachers favor long-term approaches to solving discipline problems. They are not interested in simply stopping an immediate undesirable be-

You Can Stop Worrying About Those Angry Phone Calls from my Teacher. I've Been Suspended from School Indefinitely.

(*Source:* Ford Button.)

havior. Their concern is for long-term strategies than can be used to diminish the likelihood that the undesirable behavior will occur again.

The third characteristic bears some relationship to the second. These teachers are very much interested in determining whether the observable misbehavior is a manifestation of a deeper, but unseen, cause. They recognize that youngsters' home lives, nutritional problems, and personal difficulties may play a part in unacceptable-behavior patterns that manifest themselves in the classroom. When feasible, these teachers attempt to deal with underlying causes of misbehavior, not just with the misbehavior itself (Brophy, 1983).

The Basic Principles of Discipline

1. *The dignity of the pupil must be preserved when the teacher responds to a behavior problem.* One of the basic purposes of the social studies is to help bolster youngsters' beliefs in their individual worth and importance. This purpose must be kept clearly in focus when teachers respond to misbehavior problems. Teacher responses that pupils see as undercutting their personal dignity are counterproductive. They can give rise to additional behavior problems as youngsters feel compelled to assert themselves. Teacher comments should be directed toward a specific behavior and never to the general character or worth of the individual child.

2. *Private correction is preferable to public correction.* This admonition is consistent with the intent of the first principle. When youngsters are corrected in private, they are not faced with the sometimes difficult task of "saving face" in front of their peers. Furthermore, a private conversation enables the teacher to deal with the problem on a much more-personal basis than is possible when a large audience of pupils is privy to the exchange between the teacher and the misbehaving pupil.

3. *The causes of the misbehavior, not just the misbehavior itself, need to be addressed.* If there is to be a long-term revision of behavior, the conditions causing the unacceptable behavior need to be identified and changed. Youngsters who misbehave often are seeking help through behavior that draws the teacher's attention (even the teacher's unfavorable attention). Professional social studies teachers work to determine the basic source of the difficulty.

Looking for the source of misbehavior problems calls for a strong and personally secure teacher. The teacher must be prepared to consider the possibility that his or her own behavior has contributed to the youngster's difficulty. For example, a teacher who yells at children who are misbehaving may be reinforcing misbehavior on the part of youngsters who crave attention. The teacher must be strong enough to consider a change in his or her own patterns in the classroom if an investigation reveals that the existing patterns are contributing to a youngster's problem.

4. *There is a need to distinguish between trivial and serious problems.* Many of the incidents that occur in elementary social studies classes reflect little more than childish irresponsibility. Teachers do need to respond to these problems, but they should not overreact to the point that these minor episodes take on a crisis-level dimensions. Teachers who react too harshly to relatively minor lapses in behavior may find that they have an increasingly difficult time establishing warm and productive working relationships with pupils in their classes.

5. *The responses to misbehavior must be consistent and fair.* A first "rule" associated with this principle is that all misbehavior should be responded to by the teacher. Few classroom problems disappear when the teacher pretends they do not exist. More commonly, these problems escalate to become more serious.

In the social studies, we are interested in helping youngsters to respect one another's rights to follow certain social rules. For example, many teachers in the early grades emphasize the importance of seeking recognition and taking turns during a class discussion. If this is an expectation, the teacher should think through how he or she will respond to youngsters who fail to behave in this way. Consequences of misbehaving in this way should be made clear to learners. If a learner misbehaves in this way on Monday, the consequences should be the same when a different learner misbehaves in this way at any other time. Clear behavior expectations, a planned set of responses, and consistent application of responses go together to reduce the incidence of behavior problems.

6. *Pupils should be taught to recognize the link between misbehavior and the consequences of misbehavior.* Citizenship education, a major theme in the elementary social studies program, places heavy emphasis on youngsters' developing responsibility for their own actions. In the area of discipline, this means that teachers should work to teach their pupils that the consequences for misbehaviors are not random or chance events. They do not fall on someone because he or she is "unlucky." Rather, they are the direct result of an unacceptable-behavior pattern. Furthermore, pupils must come to understand that they have chosen this unacceptable pattern and, having done so, must be prepared to bear the consequences.

Effective elementary social studies teachers incorporate these basic principles in many ways. There is not a single set of procedures that all teachers follow; there are many alternative choices available. More-experienced teachers tend to use a much broader variety of responses to discipline problems than do beginning teachers. One of the tasks of the newcomer to elementary social studies teaching is to expand the repertoire of responses to discipline problems and to think through how a decision to use a given response should be made. The next section introduces a number of categories of responses that experienced teachers have found to be effective.

Selecting the Responses to Misbehavior _____

A general guideline to follow in selecting a response to misbehavior is that the response should vary in terms of the seriousness and duration of the misbehavior. With regard to the question of duration, the teacher must consider whether this is a first-time misbehavior or whether it is one in a recurring series of misbehaviors. Some teachers have found it useful to think through a series of responses that they might make, given the various levels of seriousness of the problem behavior. Less-severe responses are planned for minor problems, and more-severe responses are planned for serious misbehavior difficulties (see Table 13–5).

The sections that follow suggest the three general categories of teacher re-

TABLE 13–5   A Discipline-Observation Form.

This form might be useful to note how teachers deal with problems of misbehavior. The responses might be compared to the principles of discipline and classified according to the range of responses.

Directions

In the first column, identify the time when the misbehavior occurred. Next, write the misbehavior and, in the third column, note the response of the teacher.

Time	Behavioral Incident	Teacher Response
1.		
2.		
3.		
4.		
5.		

Think About This

1. When do most problems seem to occur in classrooms?
2. What type of problems seems to be most common?
3. What conclusions could you draw about the type of responses generally used by the teachers who you observed?

sponses: (1) supporting self-control, (2) providing situational assistance, and (3) implementing punishment. The suggested responses for less-severe difficulties should be drawn from those described for the first two categories. The suggestions for more-severe misbehavior problems are found under the third category heading.

The suggestions under each category heading are scaled in terms of their severity. The scaling runs from least severe to most severe. These lists are not meant to be definitive guidelines. They are intended to suggest the wisdom of planning in advance to respond differently to different types of misbehavior problems in the classroom. Such advance planning, particularly for teachers new to the profession, can provide a much-needed sense of confidence in the important area of classroom management.

Category 1: Supporting Self-control

The responses in the first category, as its name suggests, focus on helping youngsters reassert personal control over their own behavior. Many of these techniques can be accomplished with minimum disruption of the other pupils in the class.

Reinforcing Productive Behavior. Pupils grow in self-control when teachers reinforce them for self-controlled behavior. When individual youngsters do a good job of following directions and obeying discussion rules during a social studies discussion, the teacher can single out individuals for praise. Sometimes, a whole class can be awarded if all pupils have done well. The prospect of seeing a good social studies film sometimes works well to reinforce good self-control behavior of an entire class.

Using Nonverbal Signals. Minor problems should be handled so that they do not interrupt the flow of a lesson. Nonverbal teacher responses communicate to misbehaving youngsters that their actions have been noted. Common nonverbal signals include eye contact (known in the trade as the "cold, hard stare"), hand movements, and facial expressions.

Nonverbal communication does not disrupt the ongoing lesson. At the same time, the teacher's actions do let youngsters who are misbehaving know that a change in their behavior is expected. In essence, the teacher is giving them time to adjust their behavior before imposing more-serious consequences.

Using Proximity Control. Experienced teachers have long known that minor behavior problems often disappear when they quietly move to the area of the classroom where the behavior is occurring. Many youngsters find it difficult to misbehave when the teacher is nearby. Alert teachers frequently manage to walk to a potential trouble spot in the classroom while maintaining the flow of the lesson. When this happens, they are able to influence youngsters' behavior in a way that is not disruptive to the learning process.

Using the Pupil's Name. Using the pupil's name is somewhat more obtrusive than the options discussed above. It simply involves the teacher mentioning the name of the misbehaving student as an integral part of the lesson. Suppose that a teacher and a class were discussing the exploration of the New World. The teacher might say something like this to alert a misbehaving pupil that his or her inappropriate actions had been noted: "Now, if John were a member of the crew sailing for the New World, he would have to . . ." This technique is guaranteed to attract John's attention. Often, this is all that is required to help a pupil change from an unacceptable to an acceptable pattern.

Redirecting Pupil Activity. Teachers who work with very young elementary youngsters especially like this technique. It simply involves focusing pupil attention away from an inappropriate activity. This is done by drawing their interest to an acceptable substitute activity. "Jill, have you seen the new state flags in this box? Would you like to look at them? Do you think you could tell me how many have the colors blue and red?"

Self-monitoring Study Behavior. This approach can take several forms. Some teachers specify a specific behavior youngsters are to engage in when they feel themselves losing their self-control. For example, pupils might be taught to put their heads on their desks or to clench their fists and count to ten before doing anything else. This substitute behavior, one that is not disruptive to the learning of the others in the class, provides some emotional release. It also gives youngsters time to think about the alternatives to behaving in a way that the teacher will find distressing (Brophy, 1983).

In another and quite different version of this general approach, the teacher asks the misbehaving youngster to move to another part of the classroom. The teacher quietly talks to the child and asks him or her to think out loud about the problem, to consider the possible causes, and to suggest the possible solutions. This version works especially well in social studies classes where the teacher has helped pupils learn the problem-solving techniques by thinking through the processes of problem solution with the whole class (Camp and Bash, 1981).

Category 2: Providing Situational Assistance

The second category suggests some approaches teachers can take to change environments or situations that might be supporting inappropriate behavior patterns. In general, these responses are somewhat more disruptive of the learning process than those introduced in the first category.

Giving a Quiet Word. To give a quiet word, the teacher simply moves close to the misbehaving pupil and quietly reminds him or her of what he or she needs to do to behave properly. This should be accomplished quickly. The idea is to communicate with the child without drawing the attention of the entire class to the situation. A gentle verbal reminder of this type will often suffice to prompt a positive change in a pupil's behavior.

Providing a Rule Reminder. The rule-reminder approach is used when one or more youngsters are behaving in a manner in violation of the adopted classroom rules. When this happens, the teacher acts quickly to remind the misbehaving students about what the rule says. Often, this is done in the form of a question. "Bill's group, what is rule number three?" Once an acceptable response is forthcoming and the undesirable behavior ceases, the work on the ongoing lesson continues.

Removing the Pupil from the Situation. The implementation of the removal approach might consist of a teacher's asking a misbehaving pupil to move temporarily to another area of the classroom and to resume his or her work in the new location. The directions to the youngster should not take the form of an angry confrontation. The idea is to politely and calmly direct the youngster to change his or her location. "Manuela, please take your material and move to the empty table. Continue working there."

Responding to Misbehavior with Clarity and Firmness. If the responses described in the first three approaches fail to bring about a change in behavior, the teacher will need to respond with stronger measures. A number of options are available to reinforce the teacher's displeasure with the present pattern of behavior.

The teacher might decide to use an oral response. This could involve a very firm and clear statement from the teacher that identifies the misbehaving pupil by name, describes exactly what behavior is unacceptable, and suggests an appropriate alternative behavior. "Joanne, you cannot talk when someone else has been recognized. You must wait your turn. Raise your hand, and I will give you a chance to speak."

Other options for the teacher include making strong eye contact with the misbehaving pupil, moving in his or her direction, and placing a hand on his or her shoulder. These physical actions are designed to underscore the teacher's displeasure with a pupil's present behavior. They will often result in a change to a pattern the teacher finds more acceptable.

Holding a Conference with the Pupil. If a youngster's misbehavior persists, a teacher-pupil conference is in order. The teacher might begin by identifying the problem, sharing his or her feelings about it, and asking the pupil to suggest how the problem might be remedied.

Some teachers find it useful to conclude a conference of this type with a *behavior contract*, which should specify some actions the pupil might take to improve the situation. The contract should suggest some benefits for the pupil when he or she is successful in changing the undesirable behavior pattern. It might also mention the consequences that might follow if unacceptable behavior patterns persist.

Soliciting Parental Assistance. Parents of youngsters with undesirable behavior patterns can be important allies of teachers. Telephone calls to parents need to be conducted in a professional manner. The emphasis should be a positive one, focusing on the nature of the problem and the possible approaches to solving it. If parents are approached in this manner, most are very willing to help. Sometimes, they are not even aware that their youngster(s) has (have) problems behaving in class. A call to parents affirms the teacher's sincere interest in their child's welfare. Parents will often eagerly join hands with the teacher to help resolve the difficulty (see Table 13–6). Most parents sincerely want their youngsters to do well in school.

Category 3: Implementing Punishment

Punishment is an option that should be used only after all of the alternatives discussed in the first two categories have been exhausted. Punishment that is administered capriciously for minor lapses from appropriate behavior patterns is counterproductive. If punishment is meted out frequently, it loses its potency. For example, if a teacher regularly punishes youngsters for unimportant incidents that reflect childish irresponsibility more than serious behavior problems, he or she has little left in his or her repertoire of responses when something truly serious occurs.

There are a number of punishment options. Those that are described in the following subsections are scaled from least-severe to most-severe.

Loss of a Privilege. The loss of a privilege is a very effective punishment for elementary pupils. Its effectiveness depends on each pupil having a privilege he or she is loathe to lose. Part of the citizenship training in elementary social studies classes often involves assigning each child some job or responsibility. These small duties give youngsters a sense of importance and help build a commitment to the idea that contributing adults in our society assume certain civic obligations. Youngsters often become quite personally committed to the duties to which they are assigned. Many of them will view the loss of the right to perform these assigned responsibilities as punishment.

TABLE 13–6 Working with Parents.

Parents can be the teacher's best allies. However, good parental relationships do not happen by chance. They result from good planning and hard work. Most parents want what is best for their children and are concerned about their progress. Many are uncertain as to how they might help. Some of the following ideas can be useful to teachers interested in building positive relationships with parents of youngsters in their classrooms.

I. Building a Foundation for Positive Parent-Teacher Relations

A. An introductory letter to parents the first week of school. The letter should be positive in tone, giving a time and a phone number for reaching the teacher. A brief overview of the class rules should also be included.
B. Regular communication to parents, informing them of the objectives and the future projects that will be required of the pupils.
C. Positive notes sent home when the youngster has done what is expected.
D. Sending home examples of pupil work.
E. Making homework clear, meaningful, and free from errors.
F. Telephoning parents about good things their children have done.

II. Expanding Parent-Teacher Contact

A. Inviting parents to visit school. These should be in addition to regular parent organization meetings.
B. Visiting parents at their homes.
C. Providing suggestions to parents concerning the activities that may help their children achieve.
D. Setting up parent-pupil-teacher conferences.

III. Parental Assistance

A. Involving parents as classroom aides.
B. Securing parental assistance on field trips.
C. Asking parents to share an interest with the class.
D. Involving parents in tutoring.

Many teachers introduce high-interest activities as rewards for doing well on assigned work. In one school, the fourth and fifth graders are allowed to play chess once or twice a week, provided that the class has done well on the assigned tasks. Many youngsters have become very interested in the game. The loss of the right to play chess certainly would be regarded as punishment by many of these pupils.

To be effective, punishment that involves the loss of a privilege should be arranged so that the privilege is not lost for too long a period of time. When the punishment is administered, the teacher must let the youngster know that if he or she improves the inappropriate behavior, the privilege will be reinstated.

In-Class Isolation. Some teachers have an isolation area in their classrooms. This is simply a part of the classroom where a pupil can be sent so that he or she will be unable to interact with the other children in the classroom. Because most youngsters enjoy being with their peers, this kind of isolation is often viewed as punishment.

Under some circumstances, the teacher may allow a misbehaving youngster to continue working on the assigned tasks while he or she is in the isolation area. Under others, the teacher may ask the youngster to reflect on what he or she has done and write down some ideas about how the behavior might be changed. The ideas produced by the pupil can be used as a basis for a teacher-pupil conference. Under still other conditions, the teacher may not allow the pupil to do anything in the isolation area. This latter option is often reserved for situations when the youngster's offense has been particularly serious. The boredom resulting from this situation is regarded by many pupils as an especially severe punishment.

Removal from Class. When very serious misbehavior persists, it is sometimes necessary to remove a pupil from the classroom. This might mean sending him or her to the principal's or to the counselor's office for a conference. The teacher should never send a youngster to an unsupervised area such as the hall. If something happened to the child while he or she was in this unsupervised setting, the teacher might be legally liable.

A decision to send a youngster to a principal or to another school official should be done only after this individual has been informed about the situation. If a teacher becomes convinced that a youngster's behavior over time is not improving, the appropriate school officials should be briefed about what the teacher has tried to do to resolve the problem. This information provides a context these professionals can use as they attempt to work with the misbehaving child.

Occasionally, disruptive children are sent to the room of another teacher. This option depends on previous communication with another teacher who agrees to cooperate. When this happens, the misbehaving child should not be allowed to participate in fun-type activities in the other teacher's room. Part of the punishment involves the denial of the right to participate in the ongoing instructional experiences of the other pupils.

Make-up of Time Wasted in Class. Some pupils waste a good deal of time when they are misbehaving. Consequently, they fail to complete their assigned work. One response to this situation is for the teacher to punish these youngsters by asking them to remain in the classroom at recess time or after the end of the regular school day. If this is done, the teacher must take care not to give these youngsters special attention or privileges. If this is done, the so-called "punishment" could be viewed as a reward. This might encourage rather than discourage the inappropriate patterns of behavior.

All attempts to implement punishment should go forward with the understanding that punishment is not an end in itself. It is something implemented as a step in a larger effort to teach pupils to behave in an acceptable manner. Every effort must be made to suggest appropriate patterns to pupils and to help them commit to these patterns.

In this section, no mention has been made of corporal punishment. This is not an accidental omission. Corporal punishment of any kind is illegal in some states. Even where it is legal, the authors believe that the other alternatives are much better. Corporal punishment may sometimes stop an undesirable behavior, but—in general—the physical, emotional, and even legal risks associated with the practice are too great to justify its use.

Category 4: Involving Others

The fourth category is of last resort. When all the other measures have failed, the teacher must seek outside assistance. Assistance can be sought from several sources.

A Face-to-Face Conference with Parents. With a problem this serious, there should already have been phone or letter contact with parents. The teacher needs to prepare for a face-to-face meeting by organizing all the available records relating to the pupil's misbehaviors. The teacher should have begun documenting the instances of misbehavior and his or her attempts to change it long before a decision is taken to call in the parents. These records should be dated, and they should describe the misbehavior and the teacher's responses in very specific terms. When this information is available, it is much easier to make a convincing case to parents.

The teacher should strive to maintain a positive tone throughout the conference. The idea is for the parents and the teacher to agree cooperatively on the steps to resolve the situation. When a spirit of cooperation rather than confrontation guides the meeting, there is a good chance that both the teacher and the parents will dedicate their best good-faith efforts to helping the misbehaving youngster.

Problem-Solving Conference with Other Professionals. In especially difficult cases, a team of professionals who have worked with a youngster may need to be brought together. This group might include the teacher, the school principal, the counselors, the psychologist, and other school and outside agency people who might have worked with the youngster. The purpose of a meeting of this kind is to decide upon a course of action.

A number of decisions might result. The possibilities include permanent placement in another classroom, assignment to another school, recommendations for additional counseling, suspension, and other options. Many of these decisions call for administrative concurrence. The decisions of the group need to be reported to the administrators who will be responsible for accepting and implementing recommendations.

See Table 13–7 for a personal discipline plan.

Concluding Comments _____

Teaching is a complex activity. It requires a masterful blending of knowledge and skill. The complexity of the activity extends beyond the issue of subject-matter instruction to include classroom-management obligations. These latter responsibilities sometimes unnecessarily intimidate beginners.

Part of this anxiety, we believe, stems from a tendency of many beginners to look at classroom management and discipline as something apart from their roles as subject-matter teachers. This is a mistake. There is a "content" for pupils that is associated with what the teacher does in the area of classroom management and discipline. One legitimate outcome of schooling in general and of the social

TABLE 13–7   A Teacher's Personal Discipline Plan.

A discipline plan prepared before the beginning of the school year can eliminate many problems associated with classroom control. This form identifies some areas that frequently are included in such a plan.

I. Positive Reinforcement

The following rewards will be given to individuals who follow class rules.

1. _____

2. _____

3. _____

The following group reinforcers will be given to the entire class when the group follows class standards.

1. _____

2. _____

3. _____

II. Class Rules

The following basic rules are needed in my classroom.

1. _____

2. _____

3. _____

4. _____

5. _____

III. Consequences

When the rules are not followed, the following range of consequences will be applied.

First violation: _____

Second violation: _____

Third violation: _____

Serious violation: _____

studies program in particular is the development of self-controlled, responsible citizens. It is precisely this end to which the teacher's activities in the areas of classroom management and discipline are directed. Therefore, teachers should embrace the challenges of teaching this important part of the curriculum with the same level of commitment they give to the more traditional subject-matter content of the school program.

Key Ideas in Summary _____

Class management and discipline are very important responsibilities for elementary teachers. Because of the need for much group work and for a diversity of instructional materials, good control skills are especially important in the area of social studies. These are some of the ideas related to management and discipline that were introduced in this chapter:

1. Instruction and classroom management are two teacher tasks that are interrelated. High-quality instruction lessens the likelihood that discipline problems will occur. Unless there is a good classroom management plan, the teacher will not be able to provide good instruction.

2. Planning for space management in the classroom involves planning for seating arrangements, equipment storage, small-group and large-group activity areas, learning centers, placement of the teacher's desk, and use of wall space.

3. Time management is an important dimension of classroom management. It is especially critical for teachers to plan carefully for the opening of each class period, for transitions from one part of a lesson to another, and for methods to be used to assist pupils who experience problems.

4. A brisk pace of instruction and a lesson that provides for a good deal of pupil success are ingredients that are important in the prevention of discipline problems. To assure that pupils are not being left behind, some teachers find it useful to identify a reference group. Pupils in this group can be checked periodically to assure that the pace of instruction is appropriate.

5. Teachers need to plan routines and procedures for handling the recurring events in the classroom. This kind of planning allows teachers to direct their energies to dealing effectively with unexpected occurrences.

6. The teacher needs to keep in mind that the goals of discipline are to teach youngsters self-control and responsibility. The methods used to respond to misbehavior need to be evaluated in terms of how well they respond to these goals.

7. Teachers who are regarded as effective discipline managers regard the responsibilities for maintaining classroom control as an integral part of their overall instructional responsibility. They plan their programs of classroom control much as they plan subject-matter content lessons. They seek long-term solutions to misbehavior problems by attempting to address their underlying causes.

8. Teachers need to attend to several basic principles as they consider the possible responses to behavior problems. They need to (1) respect their pupils, (2) deal with problems as quietly as possible, (3) distinguish between acts reflecting only childish irresponsibility and those that are truly serious, and (4) help pupils understand that their misbehavior represents a choice to suffer the consequences of making an inappropriate decision.

9. A teacher has a range of available alternatives from which to chose when deciding how to respond to misbehavior. The alternatives range from ways to support pupils' attempts to reassert control of their own behavior, to punishment, and to involving other professionals.

Questions _____

Review Questions

1. What kind of classroom-management planning should take place before the beginning of the school year?
2. What special kinds of needs should be considered when a teacher plans for seating arrangements and for traffic patterns in the classroom?
3. What arguments are there for placing the teacher's desk in an unobtrusive place in the rear of the classroom?
4. How should the teacher go about the task of providing help to youngsters who need assistance?
5. Why is planning for transitions such an important part of classroom-management planning?
6. How can a quiet word help to bring about a productive change in a misbehaving pupil?

Thought Questions

1. During which kinds of social studies lessons would control problems be most likely to occur? Why?
2. Describe your idea of the "ideal teaching space arrangement" for teaching social studies lessons at a grade level of your choice. Be prepared to defend your answer.
3. Should the teacher establish the classroom rules by himself or herself? Should they be established by the pupils themselves? Should they be jointly established by the teacher and the pupils? Explain your answer.
4. Describe ways in which you feel time might be wasted during elementary social studies lessons. What might a teacher do to make more efficient use of this time?
5. Which two basic principles of discipline do you think are most frequently overlooked by teachers? Why do you make these choices?
6. As you think about the possible alternatives to responding to discipline problems, with which aproach do you feel most comfortable? least comfortable? Explain your feelings.

Extending Understanding and Skill _____

Activities

1. Visit a classroom in a nearby school. Sketch the physical arrangement of the classroom. In a report to your instructor, comment on what you observed and suggest possible changes you might like to make.
2. Develop a master list of routines and procedures you think you might need for the first day of school. Share these with the others in the class, and ask for their comments.
3. Interview several teachers about the special rules they have for youngsters during social studies lessons. Put your list together with those of others in the course to form a master list. Ask your instructor to comment on this list and to consider sharing copies of an edited version with each person in the course.
4. With several other members of your class, participate in a role-playing exercise that features a parent conference about a misbehaving child.
5. Visit a classroom and observe how the teacher handles the discipline problems. Report on how the teacher's responses related to the basic principles of discipline.

6. Based on what you now know about discipline, prepare a written plan describing how you would approach misbehavior problems in your own classroom. Share your plan with your instructor, and ask for his or her comments.

Supplemental Reading

CHARLES, C. M. *Building Classroom Discipline: From Models To Practice*. New York: Longman, Inc., 1985.

————. *Elementary Classroom Management*. New York: Longman, Inc., 1983.

DUKE, D. L., and MECKEL, A. M. *Teacher's Guide to Classroom Management*. New York: Random House, 1984.

EVERSTON, C. M., EMMER, E. T. , CLEMENTS, B. S., SANFORD, J. P., and WORSHAM, M. E. *Classroom Management for Elementary Teachers*. Englewood Cliffs, NJ: Prentice-Hall, Inc., 1984.

O'LEARY, K., and DUBEY, D. "Application of Self-Control Procedures by Children," *Journal of Applied Behavior Analysis* (Fall, 1979), pp. 449–465.

PRESSLEY, M. "Increasing Children's Self-Control Through Cognitive Interventions," *Review of Educational Research* (Spring 1979), pp. 319–370.

RINNE, C. H. *Attention: The Fundamentals of Classroom Control*. Columbus, OH: Charles E. Merrill Publishing Co., 1984.

References _____

ARONSON, E., BLANEY, N., STEFAN, C., SIKES, J., and SNAPP, M. *The Jigsaw Classroom*. Beverly Hills, CA: Sage Publishing Co., 1978.

BROPHY, J. "Classroom Organization and Management," *The Elementary School Journal* (March 1983), pp. 265–285.

CAMP, B., and BASH, M. *Think Aloud: Increasing Social and Cognitive Skills—A Problem-Solving Program for Children, Primary Level*. Champaign, IL: Research Press, 1981.

EMMER, E. T., EVERSTON, C. M., and ANDERSON, L. "Effective Classroom Management at the Beginning of the School Year," *The Elementary School Journal* (May 1980), pp. 219–231.

JONES, F. "The Gentle Art of Classroom Discipline," *National Elementary Principal* (June 1979), pp. 26–32.

KOUNIN, J. *Discipline and Group Management in Classrooms*. New York: Holt, Rinehart & Winston, 1970.

Chapter 14

Meeting the Special Needs of Younger Pupils

(*Source:* © Juliann Barbato.)

1. Identify the characteristics of young children in Kindergarten and the first three grades of school.

2. Name the social studies topics usually included in the curriculum for young children.

3. State the importance of including social studies in the curriculum for young children.

4. Identify the basic principles to be considered when planning experiences for young children.

5. State the specific understandings that might be included in the curriculum for young children.

6. Provide examples of experiences that might be included in a social studies program.

7. Design a social studies lesson for a group of young children.

Overview

Observations in classrooms, conversations with teachers, reviews of journals, and surveys of national meeting programs reveal that the social studies curriculum receives relatively little emphasis in primary-level classrooms. Several views of the social studies contribute to this situation.

First, some teachers feel less pressure to teach social studies than they do to teach reading and mathematics. Parents are vitally concerned about their youngsters' progress in these two areas, and many standardized tests focus very heavily on them. As a result, a great deal of instructional time is devoted to reading and mathematics in the early-elementary grades.

Other teachers have concerns about the nature of social studies content and its appropriateness for young elementary students. Some feel that these children are too immature to profit from exposure to this content and that these pupils only need minimal exposure to the social studies until they reach the middle- and upper-elementary grades.

The authors do not subscribe to either of the above positions. We believe that the social studies is a "basic" component of the curriculum even in the primary school years. Furthermore, there *is* relevant social studies content to be taught to pupils in Kindergarten through third grade.

In fact, we believe the information introduced in this book has relevance for *all* elementary grades. However, because much that has been written about elementary social studies does appear to have more to say to middle- and upper-grades teachers, we felt it desirable to point out some specific approaches to dealing with social studies in the early grades. This chapter identifies the special characteristics of young elementary pupils and suggests how they might be profitably served by the social studies curriculum.

What Young Children Can Learn

The notions that young children are incapable of learning ideas that are normally taught in the social studies has been widely challenged. L. J. Buggey (1972) found that the achievement of second-grade youngsters was greatly enhanced through the use of the kinds of higher-level questions that are frequently featured in social studies lessons. Another study found that youngsters as young as three or four could solve problems that called for prediction and could even explain how they arrived at their solution (Blank, Rose, and Berlin, 1981). O. M. Stevens (1982) conducted a study of the social development of young children in Australia. She found that these youngsters were capable of handling more-sophisticated social studies content than they were typically encountering in their classrooms.

Young children have special problems in understanding their social world. If these problems are not addressed, they will develop theories of the world around them that will have to be unlearned in future years (Damon, 1977). Elementary teachers need to provide social studies lessons that enable them to listen to children and to understand how they are processing information about the world. The early identification and correction of mistaken interpretations will facilitate pupils' future development.

When teaching young children, the contents and contexts must be selected with care. The tasks presented and the problems to be solved need to be concrete, familiar, and related to youngsters' needs and interests. The lessons should deal with the here and now as opposed to the long ago and far away.

Children want to find out about themselves and about how others view them. Understanding their social world and themselves helps them develop a sense of self-esteem and a feeling of personal competence. Helping pupils develop a sense of personal worth is a very important goal for social studies instruction in the early elementary years (see Table 14–1).

TABLE 14–1   Helping Young Pupils Develop a Sense of Self-esteem.

Self-esteem is one of the most important outcomes for early childhood education. The social studies can provide many opportunities for enhancing the self-esteem of young children.

Brainstorm with others the ways you might use social studies instruction to develop the self-esteem of young children. Next, list the practices that might inhibit the development of positive self-esteem.

1. Ways of developing self-esteem through the social studies:

2. Practices detrimental to the development of positive self-esteem:

The Special Characteristics of the Young Child _____

Planning a program for these youngsters requires an understanding of their unique needs. Individuals at this age perceive and process information in ways that are different from older elementary pupils. They differ, too, in their physical characteristics and in their tolerance for nonactive kinds of learning experiences.

Younger elementary pupils are very active both physically and mentally. Their energy levels are very high, and they have difficulty sitting still for long periods of time. Their physical activity and concrete interactions with objects and people are the "raw material" for their mental processes.

These youngsters require learning experiences that allow them to engage new content in physically active ways. They need to manipulate objects and to exercise the physical senses of smell, taste, and touch. Their need for physical activity and their high curiosity level need to be channeled and challenged by the social studies program. These pupils lack the skill and patience to read extensively from a text. They will not sit still for prolonged periods of teacher talk. The lessons must be short and activity oriented. Teachers motivate these youngsters by building on their desire to know and explore and to engage in "grown-up" activities.

Young children do not see and understand the world in the same way adults do. Programs that are based on adult views of reality often make little sense to these youngsters. Teachers need to take into consideration the very special views of the world that characterize primary-grade pupils.

The work of Jean Piaget (1981) provides important insights into the thinking patterns of younger children. Piaget discovered that, as children grow, they progress through several intellectual stages. The "thinking style" of children varies with each stage. Three of these stages are especially pertinent for the teacher of young children. These are (1) the sensorimotor stage, (2) the preoperational stage, and (3) the concrete operations stage. Table 14–2 provides a summary of these stages.

Piaget's developmental theory was applied to how youngsters understand their social world by Hans Furth (1980). Furth discovered that young children are actively involved in constructing theories about their social world. This finding suggests a need for teachers to assist in this process to prevent misconceptions that could interfere with later social learning.

Young pupils lack an adequate historical or time perspective. They think things in the past were pretty much as they are now, and they do not look for much change in the future. They see themselves as growing older while everything else stays the same.

Related to this are poorly developed notions of change and of cause-and-effect relationships. Few younger children feel any need to question why things happen as they do. For example, Furth found that children viewed an ordinary daily event such as purchasing things in a store as a ritual. They observed the exchange of money but did not attach a cause-and-effect relationship to the exchange (Furth, 1980; p. 77).

Young children also have difficulty distinguishing between truth and fiction (see Tables 14–3 and 14–4). Furth (1980, p. 62) reports that children up to about the age of six live in a world that is about half-way between reality and fantasy.

TABLE 14–2   Piaget and the Developmental Stages of Young Children.

The Sensorimotor Stage (birth to two years of age)

The child gathers and processes data from the environment through his or her senses. The major intellectual activity is thought to be the interaction between the senses and the immediate environment. It is only with the development of language at about 18 to 24 months that the child seems to be able to mentally manipulate objects and events. This occurs when words come to be understood as standing for concrete objects.

The Preoperational Stage (two to seven years of age)

The most dramatic development during this stage is in the use of language. Increasingly, the growing child is able to use words to represent objects. The immediate presence of an object is no longer necessary for the youngster to think about the object. The mode of thought appears to be very imaginative and illogical to adults. Several factors contribute to this situation.

First, because they are just developing conceptual labels or words to characterize objects, the conceptual boundaries that define concepts are ill-defined. As a result, a youngster may include an item as a part of a set or concept group that appears quite creative or even humorous to adults. A young child, in an effort to please adults, may recite what an adult tells him or her, but he or she may have no understanding of the concept or concepts being verbalized. This often proves to be very frustrating for adults who spend a great deal of time explaining things to the young child only to observe the child persisting in his or her original pattern of behavior or understanding.

Children at this stage have difficulty dealing with abstract thought and logic. What they perceive is what they believe to be correct, even if their conclusion makes no sense to the adult mind. It is helpful to remember that adult logic appears as incomprehensible to young children as theirs is to adults.

The Concrete Operations Stage (seven to eleven years of age)

At the concrete operations stage, adult-style "logic" rather than "perception" begins to appear and to dominate children's thought processes. Increasingly, children begin to use logic to arrive at solutions when they are confronted by concrete problems. The emphasis here is on "concrete." Children at this stage have difficulty dealing with problems that require abstract logic.

Youngsters at this level tend to be very literal minded. They have trouble identifying irony, sarcasm, and other subtle forms of communication. When they adopt an opinion, they tend to hold to it tenaciously. They are often unmoved by conflicting evidence. In fact, they may go to great lengths to make conflicting evidence fit their conclusion. These youngsters exhibit a strong desire for definite answers to problems. Individuals at this stage are uncomfortable with ambiguity.

They are quite willing to believe that events happen for unexplainable, or even "magical," reasons.

Using the data he gathered from his observations, Furth described four developmental stages that young children go through as they grow toward an adequate understanding of their social world. These are the stages: (1) elaborating on personal experience, (2) simple linking of events, (3) constructing simple systems for interpreting events, and (4) developing a systematic framework for interpreting events.

Elaborating on Personal Experience. At the first stage, the child relies only on what he or she has personally experienced to interpret what is happening in

TABLE 14–3   The Strange and Wonderful World of Young Children.

Wouldn't it be wonderful if the world operated something like this?

> If you want something, you simply walk into the store and ask the clerk to take it off the shelf and give it to you. There is no thing such as price, but you must go through a polite ritual of asking before the clerk will give the object to you. Part of this ritual requires you to take a little money out of your pocket. A penny will do. You give the money to the clerk. The clerk hands over what you want with a smile. The same procedure works whether you are "purchasing" a piece of bubble gum, a fur coat, a one-carat diamond, or a solid-platinum brick.

To adults, this situation has a far-fetched ring. However, it represents a kind of "truth" that is quite representative of how many young pupils see the world as operating.

Think About This

1. Can you recall any mistaken ideas you held as a young child that you modified later as a result of gaining more experience?
2. Where do you think these faulty impressions came from in the first place?
3. Do you think that people today are more likely or less likely than youngsters ten or twenty years ago to come to school with misinformation? Why do you think so?
4. What do mistaken impressions tell us about the thinking styles of younger children?
5. What implications do these mistaken impressions have for the social studies program in the early elementary grades?

his or her social world. Children at this stage have no abstract or complex interpretive system. Some of their "insights" appear humorous to adults. However, these interpretations are rooted in their own limited experience.

For example, they may see individuals receiving change at the grocery store and conclude that the way one gets money is to go to the store and buy something. Because they have little understanding of the concept of abstract value, they may not recognize any difference in the worth of pennies, nickels, dimes, and quarters. The observation of one person giving a bill to a clerk and receiving several coins or bills in return leads them to conclude that store clerks dispense money to customers.

Simple Linking of Events. At the second stage, youngsters begin to establish simple relationships among phenomena. For example, they start to grasp the relationship between money and its function as a medium that can be exchanged for goods. However, they still have difficulty understanding that different items have different values and prices. They may believe that any item can be purchased with a few coins. In their minds, there is a linking between the exchange of money and a good; however, they may see the exchange as a game where the rules call for the merchant to give a product to a customer in return for whatever amount of money is tendered.

Constructing Simple Systems for Interpreting Events. At the third stage, young children begin to construct a simple system that they can use to interpret the events of their social world. For example, they may now understand that different coins have different values and that objects cost varying amounts of money. However, they do not understand *why* some objects cost more than others. They may now understand that people get money by working, but their understanding of wage and salary differences is not fully developed. When asked

TABLE 14-4 Reality, Fantasy, and Pupil Motivation.

Many young children believe the "real world" is just as arbitrary and capricious as the "fantasy worlds" they see on television or read about in books. Their beliefs present teachers with both problems and opportunities.

Think About This

1. With a group of others in your class, make a list of the potential *difficulties* that might result from youngsters' tendency to confuse fantasy and reality. Then suggest a number of things a teacher might do to respond to these difficulties.

2. With another group of students in your class, list some potential *opportunities* for learning that might result from youngsters' confusions about fantasy and reality. Suggest how a teacher might take advantage of these opportunities.

why some things cost more money than others or why some people make more money than others, they may simply answer "just because" or "that's how it is."

In short, youngsters at this age are beginning to develop what adults would understand as a logical framework, but their understandings are not very sophisticated. A danger here is that adults may overestimate children's sophistication at this stage and fail to provide concrete experiences that will help them fill in the gaps in their understanding so that they may move to the next stage.

Developing a Systematic Framework for Interpreting Events. A pupil at the fourth stage has a fairly complete grasp of connections between events and of cause-and-effect relationships. He or she also has an ability to separate reality and fantasy. However, the pupil is still very much dependent on concrete experiences as a basis for developing an understanding of events. The abstract framework used by adults is still missing.

These youngsters may now have a good understanding of the value of money. However, credit cards, checks, loans, and other more-complex financial transactions are still mysterious. Similarly, they may now have some grasp of the idea of government, but they may remain confused about how the system works. It is not unusual for pupils to ascribe power and authority to individuals in government that far exceeds what leaders in a democracy can do.

Furth (1980) pointed out that the movement from one stage to another is gradual (see Table 14-5). There are no absolute age ranges when a given young-

TABLE 14–5   The Stages of Thinking About the World.

Furth (1980) identified four stages that youngsters go through as they grow in their capacities to make more accurate interpretations of the events in the world about them. The names of these stages are provided below. For each stage, identify one example that illustrates how a youngster at this stage might interpret something in his or her environment. Then suggest something a teacher might do to help a pupil broaden his or her understanding and facilitate his or her movement to the next stage.

Stage 1: Elaborating on Personal Experience

Stage 2: Simple Linking of Events

Stage 3: Constructing Simple Systems for Interpreting Events

Stage 4: Developing a Systematic Framework for Interpreting Events

ster might be expected to be in one of the four stages, but, on the average, youngsters tend to be in the first stage until they are about six years of age. Many seven and eight year olds are in the second stage. The third and fourth stages are usually passed through by about the ages of eleven or twelve.

Furth (1980, p. 11) noted that the movement between the stages is facilitated when youngsters are provided with concrete experiences that help them observe and participate in the "real" nature of the world. This underscores the importance of a planned, concrete-experience–oriented social studies program for youngsters.

Children in the early elementary grades need lessons that stimulate them to discuss their observations and describe their understandings. Teachers must be open and accepting. If they are not, youngsters will hesitate to participate, and teachers will be unable to gain insights into the problems individual youngsters are experiencing as they try to make sense out of their world.

The Social Studies Curriculum for Young Children _____

The social studies content normally studied in the early grades begins with the concrete and familiar. Generally, the topics taught in the early grades follow the expanding horizons concept. This sequence begins with the self and gradually moves to the family and then to the community or city. For example, The National Council of the Social Studies Task Force on Scope and Sequence (Jarolimek, 1984) recommended the following sequence of studies.

Kindergarten: The Awareness of Self in a Social Setting

The emphasis here is on experiences that help youngsters learn about themselves and others through face-to-face encounters with others. They need to become aware that the world is composed of a variety of different people. The intent is to begin building a bridge between the home and the group life of the school.

First Grade: The Individual in Primary Social Groups: Understanding School and Family Life

At this level, it is suggested that children learn concepts such as the division of labor by learning the specialized role of family members and school personnel. The essential activities of the family in meeting the basic material and psychological needs are stressed. The dependency of family members on each other, and the need for rules and laws in order to have an orderly group life are emphasized. Families with different life styles as well as families living in different environments are included to avoid stereotyping.

Second Grade: Meeting the Basic Needs in Nearby Social Groups: The Neighborhood

Using the neighborhood as a context, the second grade introduces the study of education, production, consumption, communication, and transportation. Skills relating to functioning in a group continue to be emphasized, along with the importance of rules and laws. These are related to everyday life of the children. The study of how children and people meet their needs in a culture very different from that of the child is included. The neighborhood today can be contrasted to what it was like in the past. Geographic concepts relating to direction and to physical features in the environment are featured.

Third Grade: Sharing Earth-Space with Others: The Community

At this grade, the relationship of the community to other communities is stressed. The interdependence of the local community with other communities on a local, national, and international level provides a primary focus. The concepts of communication, education, transportation, production, begun in earlier grades, continue to be emphasized in this broader context. Major new concepts include government, distribution, and trade. Lessons focusing on geographic concepts and skills are expanded to include lessons on the interactions between human beings and their environments.

The general pattern reflected in this NCSS Task Force report is reflected in many local curriculum guides and in most textbook programs. Often, curriculum guides suggest certain approaches to teaching the focus concepts. The suggestions may also be provided in teachers' editions of textbooks. Many of these suggestions have merit. However, these should not be regarded as rigid guidelines. The emphasis should be on the concepts to be taught and not on a particular recommendation for planning a lesson.

Social studies lessons for younger children can help them learn about themselves, their families, their neighborhood, and their community.
(*Source:* © Juliann Barbato.)

The task required of the teacher of young children is to combine an understanding of the way young children think and view the world with the curriculum that is to be taught (see Table 14–6). For example, a teacher in Kindergarten might ask, What are the ideas that children have about themselves? Where do they have trouble separating reality from fantasy? What concrete experiences do they need to help them begin to understand simple cause-and-effect relationships and change? The answers to these and other related questions can provide the beginning points for planning a responsible social studies program for young children. Some basic principles and approaches for working with pupils in the early grades have been suggested by S. H. Leeper, R. L. Witherspoon, and B. Day (1984).

1. *Reinforcing, clarifying, explaining, and discussing the incidents that affect children during the school day.* The daily events of life provide much raw material for building social studies understanding.
2. *Cooperative planning.* Getting the children involved in making decisions about activities or coming events, such as field trips, helps them learn decision-making skills.

TABLE 14–6   Planning Learning Experiences for Young Children.

Curious and active young children need concrete experiences to help them develop a better understanding of their world. Some excellent examples of programs for very young pupils are those found in certain British Infant Schools. In these schools, the entire instructional program centers on concrete learning experiences.

For example, a class field trip, perhaps to a local museum, will provide a focus for many other instructional experiences. Writing skills can be developed as pupils prepare short accounts of the trip. Arithmetic skills can be honed as youngsters are given problems built around the experiences at the museum. (If there were three elephants in the big room when we were there, and the museum director decided to take two to another museum for a visit, how many would be left?) Reading can be developed as youngsters read about the kinds of things they saw.

Think About This

Think about a major concept you might like to teach young children. Then identify as many concrete activities as you can that might help make the concept "real" for early elementary youngsters. Identify your target grade level.
Grade Level:
Concept:
Activities:

3. *Using a variety of centers, such as block centers, listening centers, and housekeeping centers.* The use of centers can allow pupils to explore while remaining active. They can build things in the block center, play family roles in the housekeeping center, listen to stories and songs in the listening center, and learn how to work cooperatively with others as a member of a group.
4. *Cooking.* Cooking activities can be helpful for reinforcing problem-solving skills and group-work skills while at the same time acquaint them to the ways a variety of people go about meeting their need for food.

Political Understandings

Political understandings are among the most important outcomes of the social studies program (see Table 14–7). Some political understandings begin to develop early in life. Among the concepts related to this area that can be introduced to young children are "power," "authority," "rules," and "leadership."

In one key study that focuses on young people's development of political understanding, O. M. Stevens (1982) found that young children learn a great deal of political vocabulary from television. These new vocabulary terms often lack any practical utility for very young children. They are simply words that these youngsters have heard and can reproduce. The meanings they attach to the words often bear little relationship to the meanings attached to them by older children and adults. Stevens has implied that systematic efforts to teach the meanings of political vocabulary terms that youngsters have heard might be worthwhile.

TABLE 14–7   The Political Understandings and Younger Elementary Pupils.

Our national record of involvement in political decision making is appalling. We pride ourselves on being a "leading democracy," yet the percentage of people who vote in elections in the United States is much lower than in many other world nations with democratic forms of government.

Some of the blame for this situation must rest on our schools. Studies of pupil achievement have been made in many nations. These studies reveal that American youngsters rank very low in terms of their grasp of their own political system and their understanding of the nature of the political roles and responsibilities of adult citizens.

Think About This

1. To what extent do you feel the elementary social studies program (particularly in the early grades) bears responsibility for low levels of pupil understanding of their own political system?
2. How might youngsters' early views about the arbitrary and capricious nature of rules and laws be related to later attitudes they will hold as adults?
3. If you were to make specific recommendations to improve the ability of the social studies program in the early elementary years to promote an appreciation for the American political system, what would your recommendations be?

R. W. Connell (1971) found that, by about age seven, children have begun to differentiate between political affairs and other events and have begun to acquire a substantial number of "political facts." By about the age of ten, youngsters begin to reason about social events in quite a sophisticated way (Damon, 1977). Research, then, suggests that relatively young children can profit from appropriate instruction focusing on political and social events.

Current events are excellent vehicles for introducing youngsters to their political world. Local events can often be presented in ways that have meaning to young pupils. However, current events in the national and international arenas can also be included. Teachers who successfully use current-events instruction with young children are careful to diagnose their levels of interest, levels of knowledge, and possible misconceptions. When these are ascertained, it is easier to plan lessons that introduce content appropriate to youngster's needs.

Many teachers find that short newspaper and television accounts are good sources for current-events lessons. Large numbers of young children are attracted to stories dealing with animals, pets, and families. In the hands of a creative teacher, such topics can be a starting point for lessons that concentrate on concepts such as "fairness," "justice," and "authority."

Authority is an especially important concept for young students. W. Damon (1977) has noted that authority is an idea that is central to the lives of young children. They find their lives influenced daily by authority exercised by parents, family members, teachers, neighbors, church officials, and others. Sometimes, youngsters are unclear as to whom they should obey. Social studies lessons can help them develop insights that will be useful as they face decisions about what to do when others place demands on them.

In addition to dealing with authorities who try to exercise personal control over their lives, young children also need to understand the concept of authority as it applies to political figures. Because pupils in the early grades sometimes have difficulty separating reality from fantasy, political figures—such as presidents or prime ministers—may take on "super hero" status. Many youngsters

If Washington's Birthday is a Holiday, Why Isn't Philadelphia's?
(*Source:* Ford Button.)

see such leaders as people having almost unlimited personal power (Stevens, 1982). It is not uncommon for a child in the early grades to declare that the leader of a country is the person who makes all of the laws, owns all of the property, and controls all of the money. Some researchers have found that young children even sometimes feel that political leaders choose the occupations of all the citizens of a country (Furth, 1980).

Misconceptions about the nature of political authority can be addressed in social studies lessons. Youngsters need to learn that laws are developed according to strict rules and procedures and that they are not imposed at the discretion of the President. To illustrate how rules are made, teachers can develop lessons that call on youngsters to make rules governing classroom behavior. Such lessons can enrich the understanding of the concept of authority while giving pupils experience in democratic decision making.

Some teachers have used playground time to teach youngsters the function of rules. Pupils can be asked to play a game in which no one pays any attention to the rules. The ensuing chaos represents a good opportunity for a productive function on the value and purposes of rules.

Geographic Understanding

Geographic literacy can aid an individual as he or she tries to make sense out of a wide array of world problems. Contacts among the areas of the world are increasing. Because all of us are more and more affected by the events in other lands, there is a need to place special emphasis on geographic understandings in the elementary grades (see Table 14–8).

Geographic literacy involves much more than being able to read a road map, name capital cities, or identify the location of an isolated range of mountains.

TABLE 14–8 Preparing to Teach Information Related to Geography.

Successful lessons based on geography require a teacher who is sensitive to the differences in physical and man-made environments. To prepare for lessons with a geographic focus, you might consider taking a walk or drive around your community or neighborhood. Record the answers to the following questions.

1. How many types of stores did you see?
2. Are there businesses that send products elsewhere? Where do the products go? Where do the raw materials come from?
3. How many examples of symbols did you observe?
4. Where are the busiest intersections in the community? (Consider, also, the busiest intersections within shopping malls.) What types of businesses did you notice located close to these busiest intersections?
5. What types of physical features did you observe?
6. Do these physical features pose any special problems for members of the community? Do they offer special opportunities (recreation and so forth)?
7. Sketch a simple map of your neighborhood or community from memory. Are there any vacant spots on your map? What can you remember about these places? How might you increase your understanding about what goes on in these places?

Geography is the study of locations and the transactions among phenomena arranged across the surface of the earth. Basic geographic concepts that can be taught effectively in the early grades include "direction," "location," "accessibility," "spatial interaction," "earth-sun relationships," "symbol," "map," and "globe."

Maps and globes are tools geographers use to study specific phenomena and to identify patterns. Map and globe skills represent an important component of geographic literacy. In the past, some people have argued that map and globe skills are too abstract for early elementary youngsters to grasp. Most people, today, reject this argument, noting that teachers are not hesitant at all to teach reading in the early grades. Reading involves a symbol system that is, in many ways, much more abstract than that youngsters confront when they begin working with maps and globes. Researchers have demonstrated that even children in the first grade have few problems dealing with most map sills (Savage and Bacon, 1969).

Effective work with maps requires some understanding of concepts associated with direction. Teachers typically begin to build toward this understanding by introducing lessons calling upon youngsters to master the concepts "right," "left," "up," and "down." Next, the cardinal directions of "north," "south," "east," and "west" can be introduced. Some teachers have found it useful to label the walls of the classroom with the four cardinal directions. The concept of direction can be reinforced by relating objects in the environment to direction. For example, children can be introduced to the idea that the sun rises in the east and sets in the west. Once they are sure about the directions east and west, children can be taught to face so that their right hand points east and their left hand points west. When they are oriented in this way, they will be facing north. South will be behind them.

Lessons focusing on map-skill development should emphasize concrete and observable phenomena. These help youngsters understand the connection between map symbols and "reality." Some teachers have found it useful to work with children to construct a model of the school or the community on the floor of the classroom.

Before the actual construction begins, youngsters should be taken on a tour of the area to be mapped. This gives them first-hand experience with the streets, buildings, and other things in the area to be mapped. When the project is ready to begin, objects can be selected to represent things the youngsters have seen. Building blocks or cardboard boxes serve well as initial construction materials. With teacher guidance and questioning, children are encouraged to decide on the proper placement of objects on the classroom floor map.

Once the initial map is completed, the teacher can work with youngsters to substitute more-abstract symbols for the building blocks or cardboard boxes. For example, youngsters might substitute pictures of houses for the blocks or cardboard boxes that represent houses. After this new map has been completed and discussed, the teacher can ask youngsters to create special symbols for houses and other items on the map. These can be substituted for the pictures. When this map has been completed and discussed, a final map can be created using the conventional map symbols. This step-by-step process often works well to teach young pupils the relationship between symbols on the map and items in the "real" world.

The effective use of maps and globes requires individuals to view phenomena from different perspectives. A change in perspective challenges even adults. (If you doubt this is true, place an outline map on the wall upside down, stand back, and try to name the major countries of the world. It is difficult.) Perspective is an even more difficult matter for young children. To help pupils understand that one place's relationship to another depends, in part, on the position of the person looking at the places, some teachers find it convenient to have children move about a large map on the floor. Pupils can be asked to comment on the relative locations of different places as they are viewed from different angles. This kind of activity can help youngsters overcome the erroneous impressions that they sometimes get from their experience of looking only at large maps of the United States hung on the wall. A frequent mistaken assumption that results from this kind of exposure is that "the Atlantic Ocean always lies to the right." This conclusion makes sense given that many youngsters have had a history of seeing only flat wall maps of the United States. In reality, the Atlantic, as depicted on a map, can lie to the right, both to the right and to the left, or to the left. The impression depends upon the perspective of the viewer and the global location depicted at the center of the map.

Once children learn something about how map symbols work and about the issue of perspective, these skills need to be reinforced through the use of pupil-involving lessons. Some teachers have had great success with younger pupils by using a treasure-map activity. The teacher hides a few items in the room or on the playground. Individual youngsters or groups of youngsters are given simple maps using symbols for the hidden items. The maps typically indicate a point where youngsters are to begin the activity. This helps them put the locations on the map into a proper persepctive. Youngsters get very excited about finding "pirates' treasure." The activity is a highly motivational one and, at the same time, it helps teach important geographic content.

Map and globe activities for young children need to be heavily oriented toward physical activity and toward a focus on the child's immediate environment. The earth-sun relationships are sometimes difficult for even older elementary youngsters to grasp. However, even youngsters in the early elementary grades can

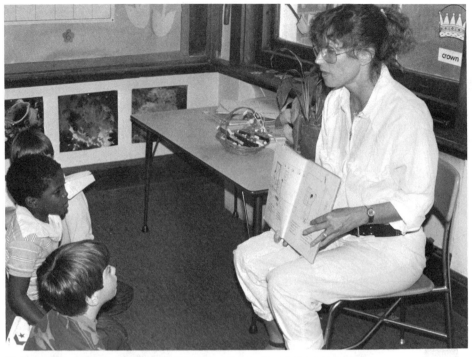

This teacher is introducing the basic ideas about map symbols.
(*Source:* © Juliann Barbato.)

profit from some introduction to this topic. The changes in vegetation and weather can stimulate an interest in the earth-sun relationships. Some teachers measure the length of each child's shadow at a particular time of the day over several months' time. The changes in shadow length can be used as a beginning point for a discussion of the earth-sun relationships.

The patterns of human activity and movement are very appropriate topics for early elementary grades' geography lessons. Almost daily, youngsters see cars, trucks, trains, and airplanes. Teachers can pose questions about where these vehicles have come from and where they might be going. Such questions appear simple. However, they can lead to discussions that can help youngsters develop better understandings. Large numbers of younger elementary pupils, for example, think that trucks simply buzz around the neighborhoods in the community. The idea of intercity and interstate transportation is quite foreign to them.

The understandings of transportation and interconnections within and among communities can be further developed through field-trip experiences. Trips to farms and supermarkets can expose children to trucks loading and unloading merchandise. Many early elementary youngsters do not realize that merchandise has to be assembled in stores from a wide variety of sources. It is not uncommon for some of these pupils to have the impression that all of the items sold in a supermarket are made in the back of the store.

Geography lessons can also be used to expand youngsters' decision-making and problem-solving abilities. A class might be asked about the best location for a new piece of playground equipment. The teacher can guide them to consider the ease of access, the freedom from interference with the other playground equipment, and other issues. Other lessons might focus on topics related to locational requirements, accessibility, and relative locations of stores, factories, schools, and individual family houses.

Historical Understanding

Sometimes, very little content associated with history is introduced in the early elementary grades. Though these young children do not have fully developed senses of time and chronology, they still can profit from history-oriented content. D. Elkind (1981) has pointed out that children have an intuitive interest in the past. This interest, however, tends to be of a very personal nature. They are interested in knowing about themselves and their families.

Historical understanding depends upon some appreciation of the ideas of time and chronology. These ideas can be introduced to pupils in the early elementary grades. As a minimum, pupils need to be introduced to (1) clock time and (2) calendar time.

Clock time requires an understanding of the concepts "hours" and "minutes" (and, perhaps, "seconds"). Lessons calling on youngsters to set the hands of the clock and to tell time can facilitate clock-time learning.

Calendar time refers to days, weeks, months, and years. The calendar-time concept poses more problems for pupils. As a beginning, lessons can focus on defining days and weeks. Teachers can draw attention to the changes that occur during the year as seasons change. As pupils begin to appreciate the idea of the passage of time, the teacher can work toward helping them develop a historical perspective.

To develop pupils' appreciation for the relationships among events over time, some teachers like to use time lines. These are simply lines drawn on the chalkboard or on butcher paper that begin and end with specific dates. For example, a time line might run from 1900 to 1988. For each listed date, the teacher writes information about an event that happened at that time. For example, the 1900-to-1988 time line might include these notations: "1918—World War I Ends" and "1945—World War II Ends." The idea is that youngsters, by visualizing time and events spread out on the line, will develop a better appreciation of their relationship over time.

Elkind (1981) has cautioned against using complex time lines with very young children. Too often, events on time lines are too abstract for young pupils to understand. If time lines are used, they should focus on relatively short spans of time, perhaps a week or a year. The events that are noted should be things close to the experience of the youngsters. When time lines are constructed in this way, they can help give youngsters a valuable historical perspective.

The admonition to use events that have personal meaning on time lines holds for other early elementary social studies as well. Lessons that require the memorization of dates or insist on youngsters' memorizing a strict order of chronological events are inappropriate. Among the historical concepts that are appropriate for youngsters in the early elementary years are "the past," "change," "time," and "continuity of life."

Family and personal histories are especially useful for introducing youngsters to the concept of "the past." Teachers can supply youngsters with a few common questions that they can use in interviews of parents, grandparents, and other relatives. Questions focusing on the interests of younger pupils should be used. ("What kinds of clothes did you wear in the first grade?" "What time did you have to go to bed?" "What were your favorite games?") Other questions, perhaps those that focus on issues such as changes of place of residence, birthplaces of family members, and problems during special historical periods (depressions, wars, and so forth), can also be asked.

The artifacts families have saved are especially good for introducing youngsters to the past. Photo albums, old toys, old clothing, old tools, and other objects can stimulate useful discussions about how life was "long ago." Discussions about the past should help youngsters grasp the idea that some things change over time, while other things remain the same.

Studies of the local community over time can help pupils develop a sense of history. The lessons might involve pupils in gathering and discussing old photographs. Pupils might look at older buildings in the community and comment on how they differ from newer buildings. Senior citizens might be invited to the classroom to talk about the life in the community in years gone by.

Studies of the past help youngsters to become acquainted with the concept of "change." Many youngsters in the early elementary grades are disturbed by change. Large numbers of them expect things to remain as they are now, and they may become somewhat concerned when they learn that many things change with the passing of the years.

Lessons focusing on change can begin with a study of changes that youngsters have experienced personally. Events such as losses of baby teeth can be recorded. Charts and graphs might be kept in the room to record the changes in youngsters' heights during the year. Attention might be drawn to the changes in families that occur when new children are born and older members die. Other lessons can focus on the changes in the natural environment. With the changes of the seasons, the vegetation grows and dies, the climate varies, and the lengths of day and night do not remain constant.

As children begin to grasp the idea of change, they can be introduced gradually to cause-and-effect relationships. Teacher questions can facilitate pupil learning in this area. C. Sunal (1981, p. 483) has suggested that teachers ask pupils questions such as these: Is something different? What is changing? What is causing the change? What do you think might happen because of the change?

The "continuity-of-life" concept can be approached through lessons focusing on holidays and other special days that occur at various times during the year. The "holiday curriculum" is popular with many elementary teachers. When properly constructed, holiday-curriculum lessons can focus on the origins of holidays, the ways holidays were celebrated in the past, and the traditional ways families celebrate holidays. Holiday-oriented lessons can help students develop an appreciation for the continuity between the past and the present.

Well-written stories about the past, oral histories, and stories about the past told by older adults can also develop pupils' grasp of the continuity-of-life concept (see Table 14–9). Parents and older members of the school community are often eager to assist teachers in this aspect of the elementary social studies program.

Economic Understandings

A grasp of certain economic principles helps youngsters to more fully appreciate their social world. Among concepts that can be introduced in the early

TABLE 14–9 Historical Perspectives.

Children's books are excellent resources for introducing pupils to information about the past and about change. Visit a library and go to the children's books section. Identify the specific books you could use to teach the following concepts. List the names of authors, titles, publishing company, and date of publication.

1. *Books About "Time".*

   (a)

   (b)

   (c)

2. *Books About "The Past".*

   (a)

   (b)

   (c)

3. *Books About "Holidays".*

   (a)

   (b)

   (c)

4. *Books About "Change".*

   (a)

   (b)

   (c)

elementary grades are "scarcity," "trade," "money," "consumer," "producer," "specialization," and "goods and services."

Young children have incomplete understandings of economics. Their concept of money is especially confused. As noted previously, many younger children view the exchange of money as some kind of ritual adults go through. Few have a good grasp of the connection between employment and salaries or wages. They think many people do what they do simply because it gives them pleasure. It is not unusual for them to express surprise when they learn that teachers are paid. Many think teachers teach because it is some kind of a hobby they enjoy. (In fact, some of them think teachers like their work so much that they actually live at the school at night after the members of their classes go home!)

The concept of "scarcity," a situation resulting from a world in which the wants are unlimited and the resources are limited, is central to the study of economics. Even very young children can master this important idea. Simulation activities are especially effective. Each child might be given a limited number of tokens or stickers. The teacher would allow them to "spend" these resources on one or more items that are listed "for sale." Each "for-sale" item would have a "price" (so many tokens or so many stickers). Youngsters quickly learn that their resources fall far short of their desires. They simply cannot afford everything they want. A guided discussion can help pupils grasp the idea that, because of scarcity, all people are forced to make very difficult choices.

Some teachers help pupils understand the relationship between work and money by providing youngsters with "salaries" in the form of tokens for tasks that they perform in the classroom. Jobs such as taking out waste baskets, watering the plants, and so forth are assigned a "wage" payable in tokens. When the jobs are performed properly, the teacher awards the tokens. When they are not, the youngsters receive no "salaries." The tokens can be exchanged for things pupils desire.

The "classroom store" is an activity elementary teachers frequently use to teach basic arithmetic concepts. The activity can easily be extended to include an emphasis on some important ideas from economics as well. For example, the concept of money and its use as a medium of exchange can be introduced.

Younger children can be introduced to the concepts "specialization" and "trade" during role-playing exercises. Pupils can be assigned to play the roles of various people included in the community. These roles might include peace officers, firefighters, mail carriers, retail clerks, and others.

With the teacher's help, each youngster can identify the special contribution each person makes to the community. The concepts "goods" and "services" might be introduced at this time. Once the teacher has explained the concepts, youngsters can attempt to categorize the various community members they have portrayed as providers either of goods or of services.

This role-playing activity can lead naturally into another one that stresses the concept of "trade." This can be done by structuring the role-playing exercise so that Pupil A provides one needed service, Pupil B another needed service, Pupil C another needed service, and Pupil D another needed service. Suppose that the four youngsters were "experts" in these areas:

- *Pupil A:* Cutting out wheels for a model car.
- *Pupil B:* Cutting out a body for a model car.
- *Pupil C:* Attaching wheels to a model car.
- *Pupil D:* Coloring a model car.

The teacher tells these youngsters that each will be allowed to do only his or her assigned task. However, the objective for each youngster is to get a completed car of his or her own Then, without providing any additional instruction, the teacher tells the youngsters to start. Typically, pupils are somewhat confused, but in a short time they usually figure out that the way to complete the cars is to trade services. They often start a Detroit-like production line. A debriefing discussion can help youngsters focus on the concept of trading services and how such trading tends to make everybody better off.

Cultural Understandings

Young children find other people fascinating. Because of this curiosity, H. M. Walsh (1980) has suggested that the early elementary years are a particularly good time to help young people develop an awareness of and an appreciation for cultural differences.

Today, young people derive many of their impressions of other people from television. Consequently, many youngsters come to school with distorted and stereotyped impressions of some cultural groups other than their own. There is a need for the social studies program to directly address this problem. There is evidence that studying others not only increases a person's appreciation of different people, but also increases the understanding of his or her own culture (Walsh, 1980).

The approaches to teaching about cultural diversity must be planned carefully. The lessons should go beyond stressing only the point that there are people in the world who are "different." Lessons that fail to emphasize the additional dimensions of cultural diversity may unwittingly leave youngsters with the idea that cultures that are "different" are, somehow, "inferior." The thrust of programs focusing on cultural diversity should be to develop an appreciation for and a tolerance of other cultures, not to develop a mistaken sense of cultural superiority.

The holiday curriculum that is a frequent feature of the elementary program provides an excellent opportunity to begin introducing younger elementary youngsters to other cultures. The similarities and differences in holidays and in holiday celebrations can be emphasized. Holiday costumes from other lands might be featured. The nature of family celebrations in different parts of the world can be stressed.

Many library resource books that focus on children in various world locations are available. Films, filmstrips, and other learning resources also frequently reflect the theme of "children around the world." When done well, such information sources can greatly contribute to pupils' appreciation of other cultures.

Guest speakers from other countries often find excited audiences when they talk to younger elementary children. The speakers need to be told to keep their remarks brief and concentrated on the issues of interest to young pupils. Some comments about a typical day in the life of a family might be appropriate. Plenty of time should be allowed for questions. The experience of talking directly to a person from another culture can be an important learning opportunity for children.

The music and foods of other lands can also be used to increase pupils' awareness of other cultures. Exchanges of simple letters with a primary-grade class in another country is another possibility. Teachers need to write the letters for very young children. Some second and third graders are capable of writing quite good letters of their own. The exchange of letters allows children an opportunity to speak directly to people in other lands. Even the differences in envelopes and stamps can provide bases for interesting class discussions.

Lessons that focus on the understanding of other cultures deserve an important place in the social studies program in the early elementary years. During these years, youngsters begin to develop attitudes toward others that may last a lifetime. In a world where the contacts across cultural boundaries are increasing, it is important that learners understand the perspectives of others (see Table 14–10).

Key Ideas in Summary _____

Social studies instruction has important roles to play in the early elementary years. Youngsters at this age are actively involved in creating personal theories about the world. Much of the information they use comes from television and

TABLE 14–10 Understanding Other Cultures.

Events are drawing peoples of the world closer together. People from greatly different cultural background are finding themselves called upon to interact with increasing frequency. Ours is a time either of great intercultural opportunity or of intercultural danger. With mutual understanding, people from diverse cultural background will work together for a better world for all. With a lack of understanding, conflict, war, famine, and other disasters may undermine the quality of life throughout the planet.

Think About This

1. What public experiences that focus on the development of an appreciation for other cultures have you had?
2. How effective were these experiences?
3. Which of these experiences do you remember most vividly? Why?
4. How do you respond to the view that teachers should spend their time developing pupils' understanding of the dominant culture rather than on developing their appreciation for other cultures?

other sources that may not always accurately portray reality. The early grade social studies program helps youngsters develop the foundations that are needed for sound social and civic understanding. Among the ideas introduced in this chapter regarding social studies programs for very young elementary pupils are the following:

1. Young children have patterns of thinking that differ from those of older children and adults. As a result, it is difficult for young children to understand the logic of adults. Special thinking patterns of pupils in the early elementary grades must be considered when social studies lessons are planned for them.

2. Children in the early elementary years do experience some difficulty with abstract ideas and concepts. This does not mean, however, that they cannot engage in higher-level thinking or in problem solving. It does mean that the information they use as they begin to think and solve problems should be of a concrete nature.

3. Furth (1980) found that children pass through a number of stages as they grow toward more-complete social understanding. Youngsters move from the first stage, a condition characterized by a confusion of reality and fantasy, to the fourth stage, a condition in which a systematic framework is used by pupils as they interpret and understand the connections among events in the social world. Furth has suggested that good instruction can facilitate pupils' growth from one stage to another.

4. Many social studies programs for the early elementary years are based on the expanding horizons principle. These programs begin with an emphasis on the self and move outward to include a study of the family, the neighborhood, and the community. More-modern versions also include the studies of children, families, neighborhoods, and communities in other cultural regions.

5. Experiences for young pupils should be designed so that pupils can experience high levels of success. Success is an excellent motivator. These experiences can help develop pupils' self-esteem. Furthermore, such programs should be activity-oriented and concrete-experience–oriented.

6. Even very young children bring some understanding of political events and vocabulary to school. The social studies program can help them make sense out of this limited store of knowledge. Among the concepts that can be emphasized are "power," "authority,' "rules," "democracy," and "leadership."

7. Geographic understandings can be developed as part of the early elementary social studies program. Among the concepts appropriate for this age level are "location," "direction," "interdependence," "spatial interaction," and "earth-sun relationships." Basic map skills can also be introduced.

8. Children in the early elementary grades have an interest in the past, especially as past events can be shown to relate directly to them. Concepts such as "continuity," "change," "time," and "the past" are among those that can be introduced to youngsters in this age group.

9. Many young children bring to school very confused ideas about economics. The social studies program can help clarify some of these misunderstandings. Concepts including "scarcity," "trade," "specialization," "producer," "consumer," "goods," and "services" are among those that can be introduced to these pupils.

10. An important purpose of the social studies is to develop youngsters' appreciation for the perspectives of other cultures. In the early elementary grades, cultural-understanding lessons help pupils abandon the stereotyped views of other people. These lessons can develop an appreciation for not only other cultures, but for their own as well.

Questions _____

Review Questions

1. What are basic characteristics of the thought of children in the early elementary grades?
2. What did the National Council for the Social Studies Task Force recommend for social studies programs in Kindergarten to third grade?
3. What are some basic principles associated with planning social studies programs for pupils in the early elementary grades?
4. What are some concepts from history, geography, and political science that can be taught to youngsters in kindergarten to third grade?
5. Why is it important to begin studies in cultural understanding in the early elementary grades?

Thought Questions

1. Some evidence suggests that young children learn a great deal of "information" from television regarding the nature of their social world. What kinds of perceptions do you think they are likely to get from watching television?
2. Teachers of young children are advised to "take their ideas seriously" and to avoid doing anything to undermine their self-concepts. How might a teacher communicate to youngsters that their contributions are being taken seriously?
3. Elkind (1981) has pointed out that not all activities have merit for young children. Activities that are worthwhile include those that have "meaning" for the child. How can a teacher determine whether an activity is likely to be "meaningful"?

4. Much research points out that the early elementary program should help each pupil develop a sense of self-esteem. How can self-esteem be developed as part of the early elementary social studies program?

5. Stevens (1982) has argued that the political understandings of the child must be developed if our democracy is to be preserved. They are too important to be left to haphazard development. Do you agree with this position? What problems with the local community might a teacher have to be alert for in planning instruction about political understandings?

6. This chapter mentioned a number of concepts that might be included in the elementary social studies program. Time constraints will not allow as much attention to be given to some of these concepts as to others. Which three concepts do you believe should receive the greatest attention? Why do you think so?

Extending Understanding and Skill _____

Activities

1. Visit a library and browse through the children's section. Prepare a list of books that you might use to stimulate early grades pupils' interests in history and in other cultures. Prepare copies of your list to share with the others in the class.

2. Build a file of clippings that illustrate people performing different kinds of jobs. Suggest ways that the pictures might be sorted into categories. If possible, use the pictures with a small group of children as you teach them to distinguish between the producers of goods and the consumers of goods.

3. Construct handpuppets illustrating various community helpers. Write some brief scenarios featuring the community helpers for which you have made puppets. Pupils could use these scenarios in role-playing situations using the handpuppets.

4. Read a number of folk tales from other countries. Prepare a list of those you have read along with your comments to share with your instructor and others in the class. Prepare, also, a list of questions that you might use after presenting each tale to youngsters to help them better understand the special cultural perspectives of the country from which the tale came.

5. Choose a holiday that is normally observed in the schools. Develop a plan indicating how you might use the holiday as a vehicle for teaching some important social studies content. Share the plan with your instructor.

6. Make a list to include no more than six people you know who come from cultural backgrounds different from your own. Prepare a list of questions designed to elicit information for early elementary pupils about topics such as daily-living patterns, foods, holidays, family life, recreation, and so forth. Interview one or more of your friends, using the list of questions. From the answers you receive, prepare a lesson for young elementary children.

Supplemental Reading

DAMON, W. *The Social World of the Child.* San Francisco: Jossey-Bass Publishing Co., 1977.

EARLE, D. "Current Events Should be Taught in Primary Classrooms," *Social Education* (January 1982), pp. 27–28.

LEEPER, S. H., WITHERSPOON, R. L., and DAY, B. *Good School for Young Children.* 5th ed. New York: Macmillan Publishing Co., Inc., 1984.

SEEFELDT, C. *Social Studies for the Preschool-Primary Child.* 2d ed. Columbus, OH: Charles E. Merrill Publishing Co., 1984.

SUNAL, C. "The Child and the Concept of Change," *Social Education* (October 1981), pp. 438–441.

WALSH, H. *Introducing the Young Child to the Social World.* New York: Macmillan Publishing Co., Inc., 1980.

References _____

BLANK, M., ROSE, S. A., and BERLIN, L. J. "Reasoning and Problem-Solving in Young Children," in M. P. Friedman, J. P. Das, and N. O'Connor, eds. *Intelligence and Learning.* New York: Plenum Press, 1981.

BUGGEY, L. J. "A Study of the Relationship of Classroom Questions and Social Studies Achievement of Second Grade Children," *Dissertation Abstracts International.* Ann Arbor, MI: Volume 32, 1972.

CONNELL, R. W. *The Child's Construction of Politics.* Carlton, Victoria, Australia: Melbourne University Press, 1971.

DAMON, W. *The Social World of the Child.* San Francisco: Jossey-Bass, 1977.

ELKIND, D. "Child Development and the Social Science Curriculum of the Social Studies," *Social Education* (October 1981), pp. 435–437.

ELKIND, D. *Children and Adolescents: Interpretive Essays on Jean Piaget.* New York: Oxford University Press, 1970.

FURTH, HANS. *The World of Grown Ups: Children's Conception of Society.* New York: Elsevier North Holland, Inc., 1980.

HUNT, M. *The Universe Within: A New Science Explores the Human Mind.* New York: Simon and Schuster, 1982.

JAROLIMEK, JOHN, Chairperson, National Council for the Social Studies Task Force on Scope and Sequence. "In Search of a Scope and Sequence for Social Studies," *Social Education* (April 1984), pp. 249–262.

LEEPER, S. H., WITHERSPOON, R. L., and DAY, B. *Good Schools for Young Children.* 5th ed. New York: Macmillan Publishing Co., Inc., 1984.

SAVAGE, T. V., and BACON, P. "Teaching Symbolic Map Skills with Primary Children," *Journal of Geography* (November 1969), pp. 491–497.

SEEFELDT, C. *Social Studies for the Preschool-Primary Child.* 2d ed. Columbus, OH: Charles E. Merrill Publishing Co., 1984.

SENN, M. J. (ed.). *Speaking Out for America's Children.* New Haven, CT: Yale University Press, 1977.

STEVENS, O. M. *Children Talking Politics: Political Learning in Childhood.* Oxford, UK: Martin Robertson and Co., Ltd., 1982.

SUNAL, C. "The Child and the Concept of Change," *Social Education* (October 1981), pp. 438–441.

WALSH, H. M. *Introducing the Young Child to the Social World.* New York: Macmillan Publishing Co., Inc., 1980.

Subject Index

Name Index